INDIA IN THE
SHADOWS OF EMPIRE

'This is a truly original and path-breaking book in more ways than one can list. It provides an innovative history of the construction of the idea of justice and its institutional locations in modern India. It has an original argument about the forms in which colonial power operates. It presents a refreshingly original reading of the relationship between discourses of law, justice, and sovereignty. In doing so it opens up a veritable new research agenda on the relationship between power and politics in Indian history. The book contains a wealth of new archival material. But it also brings freshness to familiar material. The book is unfailingly stimulating and will transform your thinking about how power is legitimized and contested.'

PRATAP BHANU MEHTA
President, Center for Policy Research, New Delhi

'This is an enormously ambitious book that makes good on its intention to offer a legal and political history of India over the past two centuries. In doing so, it connects some of the most contentious aspects of public policy in contemporary India with the history that precedes it. This book will offer rich and illuminating insights not only to those interested in India's imperial association, but also to those engaged with the vexations of public policy in independent India.'

UDAY S. MEHTA
Clarence Francis Professor in the Social Sciences,
Amherst College, Amherst

India in the Shadows of Empire

A Legal and Political History (1774–1950)

MITHI MUKHERJEE

OXFORD
UNIVERSITY PRESS

OXFORD
UNIVERSITY PRESS

Oxford University Press is a department of the University of Oxford.
It furthers the University's objective of excellence in research, scholarship,
and education by publishing worldwide. Oxford is a registered trademark of
Oxford University Press in the UK and in certain other countries

Published in India by
Oxford University Press
YMCA Library Building, 1 Jai Singh Road, New Delhi 110001, India

© Oxford University Press 2010

The moral rights of the author have been asserted

First published 2010
Second Impression 2011
Oxford India Paperbacks 2012

ISBN 13: 978-0-19-807943-9
ISBN 10: 0-19-807943-5

Typeset in Sabon 10/12 by Jojy Philip, New Delhi 110 015

To my father
Amalendu Mookerjee

CONTENTS

ACKNOWLEDGEMENTS

This book began in research that I undertook as a graduate student at the University of Chicago. It is with real pleasure that I acknowledge the great number of debts that I have accumulated in the years of researching and writing it.

I would first like to thank all the scholars and friends who have offered detailed comments on the entire draft of this book: Bernard Cohn, Sanjay Gautam, Ronald Inden, Carole McGranahan, Marjorie McIntosh, Clinton Seely, and Timothy Weston. I was fortunate to have been Bernard Cohn's last graduate student in the Department of History at the University of Chicago. I benefited enormously from his incisive questions and criticism, and his pioneering work in the study of British colonial discourse in India, particularly in the field of legal history. Ronald Inden has contributed in the most important ways to this project through his probing questions, his insightful suggestions, and his encouragement to draw out the implications of the project for the understanding of contemporary India. I owe a special debt of gratitude to Clinton Seely, not only for his comments on the draft but also for his exceptional kindness and generosity on innumerable occasions throughout my stay in Chicago. Tim Weston and Marjorie McIntosh gave invaluable comments and suggestions on the final draft that helped me to both identify and address specific shortcomings, and also to bring out the implications of the project for a broader international readership. Carole McGranahan took great care in reading the book's final draft, providing valuable suggestions, and alerting me to many errors.

I also acknowledge with pleasure all those who have read and commented on parts of the book: Lucy Chester, Carla Jones, Pratap

Bhanu Mehta, Uday Singh Mehta, Richard Reitan, and John Willis. I am indebted to William Novak of the University of Chicago from whom I learnt a great deal on many aspects of American legal history and theory. I would like to thank Sabyasachi Bhattacharyya, Majid Siddiqi, Satish Saberwal, Muzaffar Alam, Aditya Mukherjee, and Mridula Mukherjee for their encouragement and support during my years at Jawaharlal Nehru University in New Delhi. I also thank Partha Chatterjee and Gautam Bhadra for insightful conversations about legal history at the Center for Social Sciences in Calcutta. I am richly indebted to the late Dr Pratap Chandra Chunder who was extremely encouraging about this project and generously shared his deep knowledge of Indian legal history. At the Calcutta University I would like to thank Sanjukta Dasgupta, Sireen Maswood, and Amit Dey for providing me with the opportunity to present my work to the students and faculty of the Department of History. I am also deeply grateful to Tarapada Maity and Niranjan Haldar who helped me in innumerable ways not just with their knowledge of the history and politics of India, but also in tracking down important and rare archival resources in Calcutta.

Over the years I have benefited from the generous support of various institutions. My graduate research was made possible by fellowships from the University of Chicago, the American Institute of Indian Studies, the Mellon Foundation, the Indian Council of Historical Research, and the Committee on Southern Asian Studies at the University of Chicago. I received various research and travel grants from the University of Colorado at Boulder. I would like to acknowledge in particular the Junior Faculty Development Award, the IMPART grant programme, the Graduate Committee on the Arts and Humanities, and the Council on Research and Creative Work. The University of Colorado also provided me with valuable time off from teaching to complete the final version of this manuscript. For their many acts of assistance I thank the staff of the Regenstein Library at the University of Chicago (particularly James Nye), Norlin Library at the University of Colorado, the National Archives of India and the Nehru Memorial Library in New Delhi, the National Library in Calcutta (especially Shamim Akhtar), the Calcutta University Library, the West Bengal Secretariat Library, the Judges Library at the Calcutta High Court, the Calcutta University Law Library, the West Bengal State Archives, the Asiatic Society Library, Calcutta, and the British Library, London.

Material contained in chapter 1 appeared earlier in an article in the Fall 2005 issue of the journal *Law and History Review*. I thank the editor and publisher of the journal for permission to reproduce the material here.

I am grateful to the two outside readers of Oxford University Press, New Delhi for their suggestions for improving the manuscript. I owe a special debt of gratitude to my editors at Oxford University Press for their enthusiasm and willingness to accommodate all my concerns. I also thank them for their immense patience and care with the manuscript. Dan Forrest-Banks and Ted Rogers provided invaluable help in the final round of editing.

Finally, I would like to thank friends and family whose support and encouragement have been invaluable: Balasubramanian Krishnan, Sharmistha Bannerjee, Sangeeta Dasgupta, Sanjukta Dasgupta, Sharad Kumar, Seema Khanwalkar, Padmanabh Samarendra, Rupamanjari Sen, Poonam and Shankar Sharan, Amarjeet Singh, and Radha Sreenivasan in India, Steve Hughes, Sarah Hodges, Andy Rotman, Manju Rupani, and Sunil Sharma in Chicago, and Peter Boag, Jane Garrity, Donna Goldstein, Kira Hall, Carole McGranahan, Timothy Weston, John Willis, and Marcia Yonemoto in Boulder. I am deeply indebted to my family: I would like to acknowledge in particular Arka Mukherjee, Krishna Dutta, Kamalendu Dutta, Tamanash Dutta, Bharati, Arun Kumar, Amitabha Mookerjee, Manisha Mukherjee, the late Abhijit Mukherjee, and Radha Krishna Singh. My mother Sarbani Mookerjee's strength, unfailing curiosity, and abiding love of history were a constant source of inspiration. Without my father Amalendu Mookerjee's sacrifices, unwavering commitment, and constant encouragement this book would not have been possible. Finally, many of the ideas in this book have emerged out of conversations with Sanjay over the last eighteen years. I would like to thank him for his companionship, enthusiasm, and encouragement through the years, and for being my most critical reader. This book could not have been completed without the indulgence and patience of my twin toddlers, Avanti and Yosha. They have been a daily source of inspiration in all that I do.

INTRODUCTION

The nature and evolution of the postcolonial polity in India, most
scholars would acknowledge, has eluded any comprehensive
understanding. With countless political parties ever mutating and
metastasizing, the ferment of the postcolonial Indian polity often
appears like a veritable chaos that defies any attempt to logically
understand it. While many works have discussed specific aspects of
Indian politics in the postcolonial period, these studies—mostly by
political scientists—have, in general, not identified a unifying and
dominant discursive framework that structured and animated the
seemingly fragmented and chaotic Indian polity in the decades after
independence.[1] It should, therefore, not come as a surprise that
'functioning chaos', a phrase coined by John Kenneth Galbraith,
the famous economist and one-time American ambassador to India,
has become probably the most cited short descriptor of postcolonial
India. A contradiction in terms, the phrase 'functioning chaos' is a
paradox—a motif, once again, frequently encountered in studies
on postcolonial India—which is itself often described as a land of
paradoxes. The implied self-evident nature of Galbraith's phrase to
describe India is symptomatic of the widespread acknowledgement
that it is difficult to make sense of the postcolonial Indian polity.

My contention in this book is that the Indian polity is tied
together by a discursive structure with precise historical origins that
is every bit as coherent as that of any other modern polity. This
discursive structure is anchored in the concept of justice that has

[1] A. Kohli, *Democracy and Discontent: India's Growing Crisis of Governability*.
Also see his 'On Sources of Social and Political Conflicts in Follower Democracies'
and his edited work *The Success of India's Democracy*.

come to be the ground of independent India's democratic polity. It is reflected in the Indian state's social policy of reservation of jobs in government institutions on the basis of caste (social justice as compensatory discrimination), an economic policy of centralized state planning designed to control and regulate production and distribution of wealth (justice as fair distribution), and a foreign policy of non-alignment in opposition to the cold war discourse of balance of power (justice as neutrality and impartiality).

The primacy of the category of justice in determining the nature of the postcolonial Indian polity is often approached in terms of its utility for the country, as if it were entirely a matter of choice. My contention in this book is that the centrality of the discourse of justice in independent India was determined by a historical necessity, the nature and origin of which remains largely unproblematized. This book presents a new perspective on the specificity of the postcolonial Indian polity by way of an alternative historical narrative of the British Empire in India and India's struggle for independence under the Indian National Congress and Gandhi. It is an exploration of the historical process through which the notion of justice—imperial justice as equity and liberty, to be more precise—provided a discursive framework for the British Empire in India and subsequently also became the ground for anticolonial representational politics under the Indian National Congress. It was the discourse of justice as equity that ultimately came to be instituted as the sovereign legislative principle in the Constitution of independent India. National independence from British rule in 1947, therefore, did not mark a complete break from the colonial past. Rather, in so far as the Constitution came to be anchored in the discourse of justice as equity, the Indian polity in the wake of independence continued to evolve in the shadows of empire.[2]

This study focuses on a largely neglected area of research in modern Indian history: the role of judicial institutions and juridical

---

[2] Recent works by postcolonial authors on India have focused on the implications of colonial discourse for the postcolonial state. See, for example, Partha Chatterjee, *The Nation and its Fragments: Colonial and Postcolonial Histories*; Gyan Prakash, *After Colonialism: Imperial Histories and Postcolonial Displacements*. For these scholars postcolonial discourse is a legacy of colonial discourse in so far as both are bound up with the 'nation-state project'. In contrast, this book aims at tracing the specific discursive-institutional continuities between the colonial state and the postcolonial political formation as reflected in the Indian Constitution.

categories and practices in the framing of both the British Empire and the anticolonial movement under the Indian National Congress. It brings together four fields of enquiry in the history of modern India that have been approached so far largely in isolation: the nature and history of the British Empire in India, the history of law and legal institutions, the genealogy and modes of anticolonial resistance movements, and the origin and nature of the postcolonial polity as articulated in the Indian Constitution. The enquiry begins in 1774, the year in which a Supreme Court was established by the British Parliament in Calcutta, and ends in 1950, when the Indian Constitution was enacted.

In what follows, I will first briefly outline the central argument of the book, distinguishing it in its most important substantial aspects from existing historiography. I will then discuss my theoretical and methodological approach in its difference from other approaches.

THE CENTRAL ARGUMENT

This book presents a genealogy of the democratic polity in India by exploring the ways in which the twin discourses of imperial justice as equity and imperial justice as liberty came to determine the origin, nature, and evolution of representational politics in colonial India.[3] In contrast to much current historiography, this book argues that the British Empire in India for over two centuries was not a simple and homogenous phenomenon but rather a complex one, internally divided between what I identify as two competing but also collaborating political discourses: the discourse of the 'colonial', and the discourse of the 'imperial'.[4] The 'colonial' was a discourse of

---

[3] For classic works on the legal and constitutional history of modern India, see Keith, *A Constitutional History of India, 1600–1935*; Pylee, *Constitutional History of India, 1600–1950*; Banerjee, *The Constitutional History of India*; Jois, *Legal and Constitutional History of India*; Jain, *Outlines of Indian Legal History*; Austin, *The Indian Constitution: Cornerstone of a Nation*. The approach of this book is different from the above works in that it is a discursive history of categories in their alignment with institutions, not a narrative of institutional developments or ideas alone. Also see Saberwal 'Introduction: Civilization, Constitution, Democracy'.

[4] In earlier writings colonialism had been understood as an inevitable phase in the larger narrative of the development of world capitalism. Examples of works that have focused on the relation between capitalism and imperialism include Hobson, *Imperialism: A Study*; Dobb, *Studies in the Development of Capitalism*; Gallagher and Robinson, 'The Imperialism of Free Trade', pp. 1–15; Fieldhouse, *Economics of Empire, 1830–1914*; Cain and Hopkins, *British Imperialism*. For more specific

governance driven by ideas of territorial conquest, power, violence, domination, and subjugation of the colonized. The 'imperial', on the other hand, was based on a supranational deterritorialized discourse of justice under natural law, and was critical and censorial towards the arbitrary exercise of power by the colonial government even as it claimed to speak on behalf of the people of India. The British Indian polity unfolded as a complex dialectic of the colonial as a discourse of governance grounded in power and domination, and the imperial, as a critical–censorial discourse of justice.

The complex history of the discourse of imperial justice in the colonial period had its origins in three separate and crucial moments. The first moment was that of the impeachment trial of Warren Hastings, the first Governor-General in India (1772–85) for 'high crimes and misdemeanors' in the British House of Lords in 1788.[5] While Hastings defended his actions in India in this trial

---

works on India that see colonialism primarily in terms of its relation to capitalism, see Chandra, 'Colonialism, Stages of Colonialism, and the Colonial State', pp. 272–85 and *Nationalism and Colonialism in Modern India*; Habib, 'Colonization of the Indian Economy 1757–1900' and 'Studying a Colonial Economy—Without Perceiving Colonialism'. Also see Gough and Sharma (eds), *Imperialism and Revolution in South Asia*. In the process of privileging the economic over other domains, these works in general tended to dismiss most discourses of empire and even those of nationalism as either false consciousness or ideology that, as such, have no history. More recently, authors like Bernard Cohn, Edward Said, and Ranajit Guha argued that colonial rule could be understood not by looking at its economic logic or at its military power, but rather at the forms of knowledge it produced both about itself and it's other, the colonized. See Cohn, *An Anthropologist among the Historians and Other Essays* and *Colonialism and its Forms of Knowledge*; Ranajit Guha, *Dominance Without Hegemony: History and Power in Colonial India*. Also see Inden, *Imagining India* and Dirks, *Castes of Mind: Colonialism and the Making of Modern India*. This work seeks to contribute to this discussion on the relationship between colonial power and colonial discourse. One of the important works that has brought attention to the contradictions within empire in the recent past is Cooper and Stoler, (eds), *Tensions of Empire: Colonial Cultures in a Bourgeois World*.

[5] For a general account of the trial see Marshall, *The Impeachment of Warren Hastings*. Also see Carnall and Nicholson, (eds), *The Impeachment of Warren Hastings: Papers from a Bicentenary Commemoration*. Some works in the recent past that have emphasized the centrality of Burke's writings on India are Suleri, *The Rhetoric of English India*; Wheelan, *Edmund Burke and India: Political Morality and Empire* and Mehta, *Liberalism and Empire: A Study in Nineteenth Century Liberal Thought*; Dirks, *The Scandal of Empire: India and the Creation of Imperial Britain*. Also see Mukherjee, 'Justice, War and the Imperium: India and Britain in Edmund Burke's Prosecutorial Speeches in the Impeachment Trial of Warren Hastings', pp. 589–630.

in the language of what I have identified as the colonial discourse of power, it was in the prosecutorial speeches of Edmund Burke representing the case of the people of India that the imperial discourse of justice under natural law was constructed as a possible basis for British rule in India. Even as the East India Company's government found itself in the position of a defendant in the person of Hastings, India represented by Burke came to occupy the persona of a plaintiff for justice in the House of Lords—the highest court of appeal in the British Empire. Significantly, it was as a lawyer that Burke, otherwise a legislator in the House of Commons, came to speak in this trial on behalf of India. The meaning of the British Empire and the being and destiny of India came to be tied together in a single knot of justice in this judicial act of representation by Burke. For the next century and a half of colonial rule, it was in the persona of a plaintiff for imperial justice that India was to remain turned to the British Empire as the ultimate judge, until Gandhi brought the discourse of justice to an abrupt end in 1920.

The second moment of the origin of the discourse of justice was the establishment of the Supreme Court in India in 1774. What distinguished the nature and origin of the Indian polity from its European counterparts is that historically the idea and practice of representation—the very ground of a democratic polity—was not original to the space of legislative-political practice, but developed in and around the British law courts introduced into India in the late eighteenth century. [6] The British Supreme Court was established

[6] The past few decades have produced a substantial corpus of literature on the impact of colonial law on the domains of property, trade, religion, and law. Most recently, the important debates in this field have had to do with the extent to which colonial law was imposed on the colonized, or alternatively, the extent to which colonial law was either used by the colonized against the colonial state itself, or resisted by the colonized. This book's focus, in contrast, is on the sources of law-making and on the role that juridical categories, discourses, and institutions played in the construction of representational practice and the subjectivity of the colonized. For seminal essays on British colonialism and law in India see Cohn, 'From Indian Status to British Contract', pp. 613–28; 'Some Notes on Law and Change in North India', *An Anthropologist among the Historians and Other Essays*, pp. 554–74; and 'Anthropological Notes on Law and Disputes in North India', in ibid., 575–631. Cohn's most recent article on British colonialism and law was 'Law and the Colonial State', pp. 57–75. Also see Derrett, *Religion, Law and State in India*. For some of the most recent works on law and colonialism in this field see Hussain, *The Jurisprudence of Emergency: Colonialism and the Rule of Law*; Singha, *A Despotism of Law: Crime and Justice in Early Colonial India*; Chatterjee, *Gender, Slavery and Law in Colonial*

in 1774 under the authority of the British Parliament with the specific purpose of serving as an external check on the government of the East India Company, an English mercantile body that had come to acquire absolute political and executive power over parts of India and exercised this power without any internal or external restraint.[7] The Supreme Court had a unique role in India both as the sole legitimate space for the representation of grievances and complaints against the East India Company's administration and as the predominant lawmaking or legislative body in the absence of a formal legislature and clearly laid out laws. In its active efforts to restrain the arbitrary exercise of power by the Company's bureaucracy, the Supreme Court in colonial India turned into a site for a public critique of power in the name of justice under natural law. It was the Supreme Court, I contend, that opened up a whole new space of representation constituted by a complex and dynamic economy of discursive positions or personae: the lawyer and his client, the judge, the jury, and the observing public that were in a constant state of negotiation, manoeuvre, dialogue, and conflict.

The dialectic of colonial power and imperial justice often unfolded as a grand spectacle in the Supreme Court where colonial power was subjected to public scrutiny and was forced to answer to imperial justice in the language of law. The spectacle of high-ranking government officials being tried in public caught the popular imagination and gave the court, the notion of justice, and the very idea and practice of representation an immense political and ideological weight, disproportionate though it was to the rather limited real impact of the Supreme Court in curbing the arbitrary

---

India; Kolsky, 'Codification and the Rule of Colonial Difference: Criminal Procedure in British India'. Some recent works that have moved away from seeing law primarily as an 'instrument' in the hands of the colonial power or alternately the colonized and focused on important public trials in the nineteenth and twentieth century as sites around which discourses of colonialism and nationalism came to be articulated are Amin, *Event, Metaphor, Memory: Chauri Chaura, 1922–1992*; Bhadra, *Jaal Rajar Kotha: Bordhomaner Pratapchand* and Chatterjee, *A Princely Impostor? The Strange and Universal History of the Kumar of Bhawal*. For a recent work on the bourgeois legal subject in colonial Bengal, see Mukhopadhyay, *Behind the Mask: The Cultural Definition of the Legal Subject in Colonial Bengal (1715–1911)*. For an incisive critique of the Subaltern Studies Collective's approach to legal history before 1990, see Baxi, 'The State's Emissary: The Place of Law in Subaltern Studies'.

[7] Stokes, *The English Utilitarians and India*, p. 2. Also see Setalvad, *The Rise of the Common Law*, pp. 1–62.

rule of the Company government. It was the Supreme Court as the theatre of justice—and not the countless treatises on politics by the philosophers in the West—that emerged as the primary historical source of much of Indian thinking and imaginings about politics and the state. It was also under these precise historical circumstances that the figure of the lawyer emerged as the quintessential public representative. Given that the very idea and practice of representation in India had its origin in the law court, it is not surprising that the notion of justice came to determine the nature of representational politics in general in the decades to come.

The third moment in the origin of the discourse of justice came in the immediate aftermath of the 1857 Revolt. The Revolt of 1857 that started off as a mutiny but soon mutated into a popular uprising spreading across much of North India dramatically exposed the vulnerabilities of the East India Company's rule over India and the carefully maintained façade that the Company's government ruled on behalf of the Mughal emperor.[8] The Revolt also brought home the fact that significant parts of the Indian population, seemingly hostile to each other, were capable of uniting against the colonial government, and that force alone would not suffice to maintain the British Empire in India. For the rebels of 1857, Bahadur Shah Zafar, the last Mughal, was more a symbol of national sovereignty and identity against foreign rule than simply a monarch.

If the British Empire was to survive in India, it had to both find a way to overcome its foreignness as a source of provocation for new uprisings in the future and also to dismantle all sources of Indian national unity and identity—cultural, political, and historical—and thus render the very idea of India meaningless. The most visible source and symbol of this unity was, of course, the Mughal Empire itself that had over the last three hundred years come to be deeply embedded in Indian culture. Not surprisingly, in the wake of the suppression of the Revolt, even as the British monarchy took over

---

[8] For some of the most important recent works on 1857 see Mukherjee, *Awadh in Revolt, 1857–1858: A Study of Popular Resistance*; Stokes, *The Peasant Armed: The Indian Revolt of 1857*. Bhadra, 'Four Rebels of Eighteen-Fifty-Seven'; Dalrymple, *The Last Mughal: The Fall of a Dynasty, Delhi 1857*; Nayar, (ed.) *The Trial of Bahadur Shah Zafar*. For a general discussion of the implications of 1857 for British policy in India see Cohn, 'Representing Authority in Victorian India', pp. 632–82; Hutchins, *The Illusion of Permanence: British Imperialism in India*, pp. 79–100; Metcalf, *Aftermath of Revolt: India, 1857–1870* and *Ideologies of the Raj*.

the colonial state in India in 1858, the last Mughal Emperor Bahadur Shah Zafar was convicted of treason and exiled to Burma, marking the end of the Mughal Empire. With the transfer of power from the East India Company to the Crown, the British monarch was presented as a denationalized and deterritorialized figure who stood above the identity and interests of England as a nation as a way to mask the foreign origin of the colonial state. However, these acts were neither sufficient to fill the vacuum left at the political centre of India by the demise of the Mughal Empire, nor to overcome the alienness of the British Empire in India.

It was under these historical circumstances that the British Empire came to invent the twin discourses of justice as equity and justice as liberty as the pillars of the British Empire in India. These two distinct but related discourses were meant both to turn the foreign origin of the colonial state into a political advantage and also to deny India its national unity and identity. With the help of these two discourses, the colonial government in India sought to preempt any future claim that the state be grounded in 'native' society, even as it secured the necessary legitimacy from that very society. What is remarkable about the imperial deployment of the categories of justice and liberty is that, while these categories were the basis of the struggle for emancipation from both absolutist monarchies and foreign rule in the West, in India they became the foundation of colonial rule under a monarchy that was also foreign: they were made to serve a purpose exactly the opposite of their meaning. To get to the root of how these categories of emancipation were turned into categories of colonial rule, therefore, one needs to look at the nature and precise mode of their deployment rather than their philosophical meaning.

The precise mode in which the category of justice was deployed in post-1857 India was as equity—justice as equity. What is distinctive about the notion of equity as it historically developed in Britain is that, as opposed to the concept of justice under the law—natural or common (on which the Burkean discourse of imperial justice was based), the principle of justice as equity was grounded in the 'conscience' of the monarch, that is, in the person of the monarch. Unlike the common law courts in England based upon the notion of the universality and rationality of an impersonal law and upon rigorous formal procedures, the equity courts, based ultimately upon the notion that the monarch was the source of all justice, were grounded in moral principles like duty, trust, and conscience, and were addressed to the compassion and mercy of the king. Justice as equity thus assumed the sovereignty of the person of the monarch and of the courts that administered justice on the ruler's behalf and not of an impersonal system of common or natural laws.[9] As is evident, the rather subtle mutation of justice into equity in colonial India went hand-in-hand with the transfer of power from the East India Company to the British crown.

The other side of the discourse of justice as equity as deployed in India involved a discursive and political reconfiguration of India as a society of warring communities that needed an outside force to rule over it. In so far as equity by definition is directed to the particular— rather than the universal—the representation of India as a group of particular communities lacking unity and universality was entirely in keeping with it. Torn by internal conflict, it was claimed, India was in desperate need of a neutral and impartial power at the helm of the state to secure both justice and order—or justice as order.[10] Given that Indian society was divided into communities in conflict with each other, only an alien foreign power could be trusted to be neutral and impartial. In other words, for India to have any order and unity, the state would have to be exterior to the civil society or the nation. It was this invention of the discourse of imperial justice

[9] See Allen, *Law in the Making*, pp. 383–425; Lieberman, *The Province of Legislation Determined: Legal Theory in Eighteenth-century Britain*, pp. 71–87, 159–75; and Baker, *An Introduction to English Legal History*, pp. 97–116.

[10] It was in the context of this new discourse of imperial justice as equity as a dominant discourse of colonial governance that the construction and reification of new categories of rule in the post-1857 period such as caste, tribe, and community need to be understood. While recent historiography has emphasized the colonial construction of knowledge, the precise relationship between this knowledge and changes in the nature and imperatives of colonial and imperial power that made the construction of these categories necessary has not been the focus of attention. Metcalf, for example, while arguing that the ideas of India's 'difference' were dominant during the years from 1858 to 1918, sees these 'underlying assumptions' of 'similarity' and 'difference' as formed independently of power and demonstrating an 'enduring commitment' on the part of the British 'to the production of knowledge' in itself. These categories may have shaped different strategies of governance for the Raj, but did not derive from these strategies of power. See Metcalf, *Ideologies of the Raj*, p. x. Sudipto Kaviraj has called this process of the construction of knowledge in the post-1857 period 'an enormous discursive project' of the colonial state. See Kaviraj, 'Modernity and Politics in India', pp. 1, 144. My contention is that the construction of the categories of colonial rule needs to be seen as the outcome of a more foundational discourse of imperial justice as equity that became the ground of colonial rule and colonial legitimacy during the post-1857 rule.

coupled with the state representation and enforcement of India as a divided society that turned the exteriority, or foreign origin, of the colonial state into its greatest strength rather than a weakness.

In this new discourse of governance, India in itself was a society in chaos without a being or identity. The Empire alone with its foreign origin could confer unity and identity on it.[11] In other words, India could only receive its being as a gift from the Empire. The claim was thus in effect that a divided Indian society needed a foreign imperial government more than Britain itself needed a colony in India. India, in other words, could be a nation only as a colony; it was only as British India that India could be itself.

Justice as liberty, on the other hand, took the form of a teleology or imperial goal that was based on the assumption that whatever India may have been in the past or continued to be in the present, it could still move towards a future of liberty. It was this teleology

---

[11] Recently, some scholars have assumed the absence of India as a nation as their methodological premise and then gone on to focus on the historical processes under the British Empire that brought it into being. See for example, Goswami, *Producing India: From Colonial Economy to National Space.* Interestingly, Goswami uses the term 'methodological nationalism' to characterize what she sees as the unproblematized assumption of India as a nation in modern Indian historiography. At a philosophical level, historians like Goswami assume that only affirmative statements—'India was always there'—have a history, and negative ones—'there was no India before the British Empire'—do not; as if negative statements were an instance of pure and ahistorical thought. This assumption, however, is historically problematic: negative statements are as historical as positive ones. Even a casual look at the history of British Empire in India makes it evident that the assertion that 'there was no India nor could there be one without the Empire' was deployed as the main weapon of imperialist ideology only in the wake of the Revolt of 1857. The strategic deployment of this assertion by the Empire was meant to preempt the possibility of another national uprising like the Revolt of 1857 that could threaten again the very existence of the British Empire in India. It is ironic—though not surprising given her methodological premise—that Goswami's historical narrative of how India came into being begins after 1857, precisely the period in which the British Empire deployed its ideology based on the denial of India's existence as nation. If Goswami failed to notice the central plank of post-1857 imperialist ideology, then that was because she had already adopted this ideology as her methodological premise. This 'methodological imperialism' consists in repeating that there was no India before the advent of the British Empire as if it were a self-evident fact. What is characteristic about such assertions is that they are made without any real inquiry into the notions of India before the advent of the British Empire. Not surprisingly, Sheldon Pollock in his important book on premodern South Asia, *The Language of Gods in the World of Men,* finds such assumptions 'historically shallow' and 'conceptually naïve'. See Pollock, pp. 557, 560.

of justice as liberty that allowed the British Empire to present itself as a pedagogical mission whose ultimate goal was to take India in the direction of self-government. Even as justice as equity came to be deployed as the discourse of colonial governance in the present, justice as liberty held the promise of self-governance for Indians in the future. Paradoxical as it sounds, Indians were to receive liberty as a gift from the imperial monarch. This new dialectic of the twin discourses of justice as equity and justice as liberty replaced the earlier dialectic of the colonial and the imperial, even as they also incorporated much of the substance of the earlier discourses.

What needs to be noted about the precise mode in which the categories of justice, equity, and liberty were deployed in post-1857 India is that they were anchored in the figure of the Queen. The relationship of the British monarchy with its Indian subjects was mediated by these principles. It was as subjects to the principles of 'liberty, equity, and justice' that Indians became subjects to the British monarchy. The reverse, however, was as true; it was as subjects of the British imperial monarchy that Indians became subject to the principles of liberty, equity, and justice; this historical relationship came to be mediated through the figure of the Queen. Much of the British imperial political legacy in postcolonial India consists of the continuing relevance of this historical development. As I show in the last chapter on the Indian Constitution, even today in India, justice, equity, and liberty remain as embedded in the figure of the monarch as when they were first introduced into India in the wake of 1857. It is this imperial shadow that has stayed with India long after the Empire ended.

It was within this historical–discursive context that the Indian National Congress was born as the first representative organization for Indians. In contrast to dominant historiography that interprets the anti-colonial movement led by the early Indian National Congress as a 'nationalist' movement against colonialism, this book argues that it was on the basis of the imperial discourse of justice as equity and liberty grounded in the figure of the monarch that the Indian National Congress developed an anticolonial discourse and movement.[12] Indeed it was in the Congress' faith in the inherent

---

[12] All dominant schools of Indian historiography including the Nationalist, Subaltern, and Marxist schools assume that the Congress was driven by the ideology of nationalism. In nationalist historiography a homology is constructed between the Indian nation and the Indian National Congress as a party, so that

justice of the empire and its promise of liberty that its opposition to colonialism was grounded.[13]

The Congress' discourse of liberty, however, was anchored in the figure of the monarch, not in the sovereignty of the people. Not surprisingly, the discourse of the Congress was addressed not to the people of India but to the Queen as Empress of India. It was as

---

the accomplishments of the anticolonial struggle are represented largely as the achievements of the party. It is assumed that like nationalist parties in other parts of the world, the Indian National Congress based its movement against British colonialism on the discourse of freedom, modernity, and reason. See for example Nehru, *The Discovery of India*. Sitaramaya, *History of the Indian National Congress, vol.1, 1885–1935.* Some Marxist historians like Bipan Chandra share this view of the Indian National Congress. See Bipan Chandra, Aditya Mukherjee, Mridula Mukherjee, K.N. Panikkar, Sucheta Mahajan, *India's Struggle for Independence, 1857–1947;* also see Bipan Chandra, *The Rise and Growth of Economic Nationalism in India: Economic Policies of Indian National Leadership, 1880–1905.* In contrast to the Nationalist school, the Marxist and the Subaltern school collective in its early phase were both critical of the 'bourgeois nationalism' of the Indian National Congress and critiqued it for denying agency to subalterns in the anti-colonial movement. They emphasized the agency, often autonomous, of the lower classes—the peasantry and the proletariat—in the struggle for independence. The classic texts written from a Marxist perspective are Dutt, *India Today;* Desai, *Social Background of Indian Nationalism;* Sarkar, *Modern India, 1885–1947;* Habib, *Essays in Indian History: Towards a Marxist Perception.* Sarkar, *Swadeshi Movement in Bengal 1903–1908;* Siddiqi, *Agrarian Unrest in North India-United Provinces 1918–1922;* Pandey, *The Ascendency of the Congress in Uttar Pradesh 1936–34. A Study in Imperfect Mobilization.* For representative works from the Subaltern Studies in its early phase, see Guha (ed.), *Subaltern Studies,* vols I–VI, *Subaltern Studies,* vol. VII, Pandey and Chatterjee (eds), *Subaltern Studies,* vol. VIIII, Arnold and Hardiman (eds). Also see Prakash, 'Subaltern Studies as Postcolonial Criticism', pp. 1475–90. In its later phase this collective's critique has focused on the Congress' discourse of nationalism and its reproduction of orientalist thought. See Guha, *Dominance Without Hegemony: History and Power in Colonial India;* Chatterjee, *Nationalist Thought and the Colonial World; A Derivative Discourse;* Chatterjee, *The Nation and Its Fragments;* Chakrabarty, *Provincializing Europe: Postcolonial Thought and Historical Difference;* Chakrabarty, *Habitations of Modernity: Essays in the Wake of Subaltern Studies.*

[13] In my analysis of the Indian National Congress, I exclude the discourse and politics of the party that has been characterized in Indian historiography as 'Extremist,' and seen as part of the Congress. I contend that while there were temporary alliances between the dominant leadership of the Congress and the 'Extremists,' and at some points even adoption by the Congress of 'extremist' tactics of agitation, this group and the discourse on which their politics was grounded was fundamentally in conflict with, and, in the ultimate analysis, exterior to the dominant discourse of the Indian National Congress which remained grounded in a juridico-epistemological framework. For an elaboration of this argument see Chapter 3.

the subjects of the Queen that the Congress pleaded for freedom and hoped to receive it; it was as subjects of the British Empire that the Congress hoped Indians to become free, not as citizens of India. In contrast to other major polities in the world that had won freedom by either driving out a foreign colonial state or by putting an end to the institution of the monarchy, the Congress hoped to receive freedom as a gift from a monarchy that was also foreign. It is not surprising, therefore, that the Congress thought of freedom as a 'privilege'—not a right. It was this understanding of freedom as a privilege and a gift of the Empire that also determined the precise mode of its pursuit by the Congress in the form of pleading and petitioning.

I contend that it was because the Indian National Congress was firmly placed within an epistemologico-juridical paradigm determined by the telos and procedures of justice that its mode of politics took the form of pleading and petitioning by a small group of the educated elite led by lawyers, the quintessential political representatives at the time.[14] An overwhelming majority of the top political leaders of the anticolonial movement, including M.G. Ranade, B.G. Tilak, C.R. Das, M.K. Gandhi, M.A. Jinnah, Motilal Nehru, and J. Nehru were lawyers, a fact whose significance has been

[14] The rise, development, and significance of the legal profession have received surprisingly little attention from scholars of colonial legal history. The only article-length work on the legal profession is Schmitthenner, 'The Development of the Legal Profession in India,' presented at the Conference on the Comparative Study of the Legal Profession with Special Reference to India, August 1967. In so far as the connection of lawyers to politics is concerned, historians of the Cambridge School have alone emphasized their importance in the Indian National Congress. However, these historians attribute the importance of lawyers in the Congress to the nature of patron–client relationships, which, they argue, was vital to the growth of political associations in this period. In other words, in the view of these historians lawyers rose to prominence in the Congress precisely because their legal expertise connected with a broad spectrum of society. See Seal, *The Emergence of Indian Nationalism: Competition and Collaboration in the Later Nineteenth Century*, pp. 112–13; Johnson, *Provincial Politics and Indian Nationalism: Bombay and the Indian National Congress 1880 to 1915*; Bayly, *The Local Roots of Indian Politics: Allahabad 1880–1920*; Washbrook, *The Emergence of Provincial Politics, The Madras Presidency 1870–1920*. For a similar view on the lawyer's importance in linking the national and the local, see McLane, *Indian Nationalism and the Early Congress*, pp. 52–4. Also see Misra, *The Indian Middle Classes: Their Growth in Modern Times*. In contrast this book argues that it was because representational politics was itself grounded in a juridical framework that the lawyers became the quintessential political representatives.

missed in the historiography of modern India. The idea of armed struggle, or even unarmed resistance, was altogether incompatible with the understanding of freedom as a privilege. Not surprisingly, therefore, the very notion of resistance, let alone a violent one, was alien to the discourse and general ethos of the Congress.

It was because the Indian National Congress was grounded in the discourse of justice as equity and liberty that it was constrained to identify with the empire even as it opposed colonialism. This framework also explains why the discourse of justice as equity that had helped launch the Congress politics of anticolonialism also emerged as its ultimate limit, in that it was unable to envision complete national independence outside the Empire; the Congress failed to articulate a discourse of political freedom. The goal of home rule that the Congress articulated in its most radical phase before Gandhi took on political leadership was not the same as the demand for national freedom, because home rule, in so far as it sought legislative powers within the Empire, assumed the ultimate sovereignty of the British monarch.[15] Indeed, within this framework, freedom itself was hoped for as a gift of imperial justice; its source lay not in the strength of the people, but in the benevolence of the Emperor as an impartial judge. The Congress goal of home rule was in fact the culmination of the imperial teleology of justice as liberty. As far as the Congress was concerned, it was not as citizens of India that Indians were going to become free, but as citizens of the Empire.

Only with the emergence of Gandhi did a political breakthrough occur, both in the form of a demand for complete national independence rather than imperial justice, and in the launching of a mass movement as opposed to the politics of elite pleading and petitioning. In contrast to much of the current historiography that assumes an identity between Gandhi and the Indian National Congress, I propose a rigorous and nuanced distinction between them in terms of their separate historical lineages, the separate projects they pursued, and the separate legacies they left behind.[16]

---

[15] Owen, 'Towards Nation-Wide Agitation and Organization. The Home Rule Leagues, 1915–1918', pp. 159–95.

[16] For the most important works that have emphasized the distinctiveness of Gandhian thought in relation to other Indian Nationalists see Chatterjee, *Nationalist Thought and the Colonial World: A Derivative Discourse?*; Nandy, *The Intimate Enemy: Loss and Recovery of Self Under Colonialism*. Also see Suhrud, 'Emptied of all but love: Gandhiji's first public fast', pp. 66–79.

The nature and extent of the break Gandhi's entry marked was brought out dramatically in 1920 on the eve of the non-cooperation movement, the first nationwide mass movement led by Gandhi in India, with the announcement of a ban on practicing lawyers from taking leadership positions in the Congress and boycott of law courts. The law court as the structure of anticolonial politics, the figure of the lawyer as the quintessential leader, and pleading and petitioning as the favoured mode of politics were all abolished in one bold stroke. This gesture was symptomatic of the general rejection of the discourse of imperial justice as liberty, the very bedrock of both the Empire and the Congress. It was a signal that the anticolonial movement in India had come out of the labyrinth of justice in which it had been lost for almost a century and half. The figure of the lawyer was replaced by that of the renouncer as the leader of the anticolonial movement.

To put the Gandhian breakthrough in historical perspective it is important to recall the nature of crisis the anticolonial movement had run into. In post-1857 India, portrayed by the British Empire with its monopoly over the state apparatus of representation as a society deeply and permanently fragmented, each community found itself to be a minority, always afraid that in the event of national independence and the departure of the British Empire it would become vulnerable to domination by other more powerful communities. This development undercut the very possibility of a discourse of political freedom in India, because only a group that could hope to constitute a majority and govern a democratic polity in free India would have the incentive to fight for national independence under the discourse of political freedom. British policy was designed precisely to prevent such a majority from emerging. The colonial hope was that this fragmentation of Indian society into innumerable minorities would keep it trapped in the discourse of imperial justice with no access to the discourse of political freedom, thereby making the British Empire permanently indispensable to Indian society.

What was it about the Gandhian discourse and movement, then, that allowed it to break out of the discursive trap that the anticolonial movement had fallen into? I contend that what was distinctive about the Gandhian teleology of freedom was that it was grounded in the Indic discourses of renunciative freedom known as *moksha* and *nirvana*.[17] This was very different from western discourses of political legislative freedom grounded in the ideas of national identity, nation state, private property, and individual rights. While the western discourse of freedom had ideas of individual and collective self or identity as its very foundation, the Indic discourse of freedom as reflected in the Gandhian discourse and movement required renunciation of the self or identity itself as both its primary condition and ultimate goal.[18] Gandhian discourse continued to be anchored in renunciative freedom even as it was brought to bear upon the historical–political task of Indian independence. It was because the Gandhian discourse of renunciative freedom transcended the discourse of identity that the Gandhian movement was able to break out of the paralysing conflict of identities that formed the other side of imperial justice as a discourse of governance and call for national independence on the basis of mass movement. The legacy of renunciative freedom, often thought to have been rendered irrelevant and insignificant by modernity, became the unlikely historical agent to rescue India from its political labyrinth. The immense appeal of this new mode of politics compelled the Congress to suspend its own teleology of imperial justice along with the enunciative persona of the lawyer,

[17] While some works by political scientists, such as Bhikhu Parekh, have looked at the indigenous roots of Gandhian discourse, none of these works have focused exclusively on the Gandhian discourse of freedom in its difference from the Western discourse of freedom or the implications of this difference for the nature of anticolonial resistance. See Parekh, *Colonialism, Tradition, and Reform: An Analysis of Gandhi's Political Discourse*. Others who have emphasized the indigenous sources of Gandhi's thought are Pantham, 'Thinking with Mahatma Gandhi: Beyond Liberal Democracy', pp. 165–188 and Basham, 'Traditional Influences on the Thought of Mahatma Gandhi', pp. 17–42; Suhrud, 'Emptied of all but love: Gandhiji's first public fast', in *Rethinking Gandhi and Nonviolent Relationality*. For another important work on Gandhi, see Akeel Bilgrami, 'Gandhi's Integrity: The Philosophy Behind the Politics', in A. Raghuramaraju (ed.), *Debating Gandhi: A Reader*, pp. 248–66.

[18] For a comprehensive work on the development of ideas of freedom in the West, see Adler, *The Idea of Freedom*. Adler argued that what united the diverse reflections on freedom in the modern West through its history was the critical difference between the self and other. See *Idea of Freedom*, 2:15. There has been considerable work on the national specificities of ideas of freedom within Europe. See, for example, Krieger, *The German Idea of Freedom: History of a Political Tradition*; Kley (ed.), *The French Idea of Freedom: The Old Regime and the Declaration of Rights of 1789*; Baker, *Inventing the French Revolution: Essays on French Political Culture in the Eighteenth-Century*; Konig (ed.), *Devising Liberty: Preserving and Creating Freedom in the New American Republic*.

and affiliate itself as an organization to the Gandhian discourse and movement towards national independence.

This discourse of renunciative freedom, however, was not unique to Gandhi. In contrast to existing historiography that tends to see Gandhian ideas in personalized terms as if Gandhi was an isolated and unique, if not odd, figure in history, I argue that he was part of a legacy that developed in the wake of the encounter between Indic and Western discourses and traditions of freedom in the colonial period.[19] The Gandhian discourse of freedom was, in fact, the historical culmination of an intellectual conflict and competition between the two rival concepts and traditions that emerged as the central problematic for Indian political thinkers in the colonial period. It engaged the leading Indian thinkers of nineteenth and early twentieth centuries such as Rammohan Roy, Bankim Chandra Chatterjee, Vivekananda, and Rabindranath Tagore.[20] Gandhi's was one such experiment in resolving this conflict, even if, given the essential difference between the two traditions, it was bound to be limited and temporary.[21]

[19] Even those works that have explored Gandhian discourse in its specificity have not departed from the idea of Gandhi as subject. See Parekh, *Colonialism, Tradition, and Reform.*

[20] The only author who has explored the genealogy of this culturally specific discourse of freedom is Dennis Dalton. See his *Indian Idea of Freedom: Thought of Swami Vivekananda, Aurobindo Ghose, Mahatma Gandhi, and Rabindranath Tagore.* For an interesting article on the theme of freedom in India, see Kaviraj, 'Ideas of Freedom in Modern India', pp. 97–143. Unlike Dalton, Kaviraj does not take the Indian idea of renunciative freedom seriously, arguing that freedom makes sense only in the context of societies. Because Kaviraj's definition of freedom is inherently western, he misses the significance of the contest and confrontation between the western concept of political freedom and the Indian concept of renunciative freedom in modern India. He also overlooks the centrality of the discourse of renunciative freedom in the Gandhian movement of non-violent non-cooperation against British rule.

[21] All schools of Indian historiography see non-violence as a strategy or tool and divorce it from the discourse on which it was grounded. While Nationalist historians have interpreted the ethical practice of non-violence as an ingenious tool devised by Gandhi and the Indian National Congress for mobilizing a disarmed and passive population and forging it into a powerful anticolonial resistance movement, historians of the Cambridge School have interpreted non-violence as a strategy developed by a collaborationist elite for affecting a peaceful transition of power from the colonial state to the Indian state. For the Nationalist School see, for example, Sitaramaya, *History of the Indian National Congress, vol.1, 1885–1935* and Nehru, *The Discovery of India.* The Marxist historian Bipan Chandra also shares this view

The deployment of the discourse of renunciative freedom for national independence that allowed the Gandhian movement to rescue the anticolonial movement from the paralysing conflict of identities, however, also emerged as its greatest limit; being grounded in the discourse of renunciative freedom it was both unequipped and unwilling to offer a legislative discourse of governance to the new state of independent India. Gandhi, after all, had imagined his ideal society to be a state of 'enlightened anarchy'; a society without the state driven solely by each individual member's personal sense of ethics. Not surprisingly, with the departure of the British Empire, Gandhi publicly called upon the Indian National Congress to disband itself as a political party and turn into a '*Loka Sevak Samgha*' or a public service organization. That the call of Gandhi went unheeded by the Congress reveals its original and essential difference from Gandhi.

As soon as national independence was achieved, Gandhian discourse receded into the background. As the reins of the government fell into the hands of the Congress, it resurrected the temporarily suspended discourse of imperial justice as equity as a discourse of governance and made it the foundation of the Indian Constitution. The other element of the legacy of justice as equity, the imperial monarch, soon reproduced itself in the dynastic leadership of the Indian National Congress, represented by the Nehru–Gandhi family, which continues to be a powerful force in Indian politics even today.

of the Gandhian movement. See Chandra, *Indian National Movement: The Long-term Dynamics*, pp. 1–5. For the Cambridge perspective on Gandhi see Brown, *Gandhi's Rise to Power, Indian Politics 1915–1922*; Gallagher, Johnson and Seal, (eds), *Locality, Province and Nation: Essays in Indian Politics, 1870–1940*. Marxist historians, have, in the latter vein, interpreted Gandhi's ethical practices as a mask to lure the masses into politics on behalf of the Indian bourgeoisie and, therefore, as an aspect of his politics that need not be taken seriously. See Dutt, *India Today*, and Desai, *Social Background of Indian Nationalism*. Subaltern historians like Shahid Amin, Ranajit Guha, and Partha Chatterjee have interpreted the Gandhian use of popular Hindu concepts and idioms as clever strategies to involve the masses in the struggle against colonialism only to subsequently betray the values, interests, and culture of the lower classes in favour of the needs of the national bourgeoisie. Non-violence in this view was thus nothing more than an inventive bourgeois tactic devised to foreclose the possibility of violent political revolution in India. Shahid Amin, 'Gandhi as Mahatma: Gorakhpur District, Easter UP, 1921-2', in Guha (ed.), *Subaltern Studies*, pp. 1–61. Guha, *Dominance without Hegemony*; Chatterjee, *Nationalist Thought and the Colonial World*.

THEORETICAL AND METHODOLOGICAL APPROACH

This book has benefited from the theoretical and methodological insights of Foucault.[22] It explores the history of representational politics in terms of the history of contesting discursive formations with their respective teleologies, and networks of categories in their precise alignment with institutions. It looks also at the specific enunciative personae that function as the subjects of these discourses. Two of Foucault's insights are fundamental to this book. First, that power operates through discourses and not just through violence or force. Second, in so far as discourses constitute subjectivities, power operates in and through historically constructed subjects, and is not simply there to be captured by already existing subjects.

Since Foucault did not focus directly on the genealogy of political discourse, this book attempts to extend Foucauldian methodology to the domain of political history. One of the ways in which I depart methodologically from Foucault is in my use of the category of teleology together with discourse. I use the term teleology as a combination of the terms 'telos' or goal and 'logos' or discourse. In other words, teleology refers to a discourse organized around a specific goal or end to be realized—for example, the teleology of justice or legislative freedom. My aim in using this term is to emphasize and capture the temporal dimension or the future-oriented nature of discourse, in so far as the goal remains to be realized in the future. The term discourse is often deployed as a synonym for 'perception' or a reflection of historical actors' understanding of facts on the ground. In contrast, a teleology is not meant to register or reflect reality as it is on the ground, but rather to alter that reality, thereby assuming the difference between what it envisioned as the ideal or final goal, and the political conditions and facts on the ground. Moreover, teleologies are beyond perceptions and subjective intentions. Indeed subjectivities themselves are constructed in and through these teleologies.

 - Also, since a teleology is not just a discourse but also a goal that needs to be pursued through time, the use of this term allows me

---

[22] Foucault, *Power/Knowledge: Selected Interviews and Other Writings, 1972–77*; *Discipline and Punish: The Birth of the Prison*; *The Archaeology of Knowledge and the Discourse on Language*; and *The Order of Things: An Archeology of the Human Sciences.*

to capture the categories, institutions, and practices in their precise historical mode of deployment, which the notion of discourse does not allow.[23] In the absence of any specific goals to pursue, discourses tend to be reduced to systems of thought without much contact with practice.[24] The notion of teleology allows me to see discourses in their

[23] In Indian historiography, discourse analysis has been central to the work of later Subaltern historians in the wake of Edward Said's immensely influential book *Orientalism*. The most significant works of subaltern scholars that focus on discourse analysis are Guha, *Dominance without Hegemony*; Chatterjee, *Nationalist Thought and the Colonial World: A Derivative Discourse*; Chatterjee, *The Nation and Its Fragments*; Chakrabarty, *Provincializing Europe: Postcolonial Thought and Historical Difference*; Chakrabarty, *Habitations of Modernity: Essays in the Wake of Subaltern Studies*. Also see *Subaltern Studies*, vol. IX, Shahid Amin and Dipesh Chakrabarty (eds); vol. X, Bhadra, Prakash, and Tharu (eds); vol. XI, Chatterjee and Jeganathan (eds); no. XII, Mayaram, Pandian, and Skaria (eds). Also relevant for this discussion are the works of postcolonial scholars like Bhabha, *Nation and Narration*; and Spivak, *A Critique of Postcolonial Reason: Toward a History of the Vanishing Present*. What is common to the considerable scholarship built on the basis of this notion of orientalism it that it has privileged thought, and thus philosophy, over the actual mode of operation of the British Empire in India. Centered on the historical phenomenon of orientalism, these scholars have increasingly tended to see discourse in isolation from the colonial polity in its operational aspect. The history of colonialism has come to be reduced to the history of orientalism, which, in turn, appears to be primarily, if not entirely, an intellectual phenomenon. So for example, subaltern scholars like Partha Chatterjee and Dipesh Chakraborty have made little attempt to precisely locate the categories of colonial rule within the institutions of British colonial power. As Gyan Prakash has pointed out, 'Europe or West' in Subaltern scholarship 'refers to an imaginary though powerful entity created by a historical process that authorizes it as the home of Reason, Progress, and Modernity'. See Prakash, 'Subaltern Studies as Postcolonial Criticism', pp. 1475–90. Though some gesture is made in the direction of how Orientalism may have been grounded in a pursuit of power, it is rarely clear in such writings what exactly the nature of that power was and how it worked in practice. For a critique of Said's impact on Subaltern historiography, see Sarkar, 'Orientalism Revisited: Saidian Frameworks in the Writing of Modern Indian History'. Also see Sarkar, 'The Decline of the Subaltern in Subaltern Studies'.

[24] One of the most important scholars to rigorously relate the discourse of colonialism to the operation of colonial power in practice was Bernard Cohn. While subaltern scholars reduce colonialism to orientalism as I have argued above, Bernard Cohn's approach was grounded in a much more concrete historical and archival analysis of the imbeddedness of colonial categories of knowledge in the institutions of colonial power. Cohn's seminal articles have been collected in *An Anthropologist among the Historians* and *Colonialism and its Forms of Knowledge*. See these essays in *An Anthropologist among the Historians*, 'The Initial British Impact on India: A Case Study of the Benares Region', pp. 320–42; 'From Indian Status to British Contract', pp. 463–82; 'Representing Authority in Victorian England',

dynamic contact with practice.[25] Also, in contrast to discourse as a system of thought, a teleology, given that it has a goal as its driving force, is vulnerable to running into crises—even failure—in case those goals seem impossible in the face of insurmountable practical difficulties, or because other teleologies appear more attractive and also more possible. This vulnerability to crisis and failure help expose the historical nature of these discourses that may otherwise appear abstract. Though I make a distinction between dominant and subordinate teleologies, I do recognize multiple competing teleologies to be operating at any given historical juncture. For example, even as I focus mainly on the origin and evolution of the teleology of imperial justice, I set it off against two other powerful teleologies of legislative freedom and renunciative freedom.

Methodologically, I have also used the category of 'enunciative persona' to emphasize the position of enunciation from which statements constituting a specific discourse come to be made, rather than the personal intentions of the individual articulating

---

pp. 632–82. Also see *Colonialism and its Forms of Knowledge* for 'The Command of Language and the Language of Command', pp. 16–56 and 'Law and the Colonial State', pp. 57–75. While sharing the cultural critique of colonial discourse with Subaltern historiography, Cohn's approach was very different in that he studied not just Western representations of India, but also traced the construction of colonial categories through a careful archival analysis of colonial institutions and networks of colonial power. Indeed Cohn was one of the first to focus on the construction of colonial categories of village, caste, and tribe in the late nineteenth century within colonial administrative practices like the census and surveys that served to facilitate colonial rule. See Cohn, 'The Census, Social Structure and Objectification in South Asia', in *An Anthropologist among the Historians*, pp. 224–54. For Cohn, unlike Chatterjee and Chakrabarty, the object of analysis was not Western forms of knowledge per se or orientalism in general but rather what he called 'the investigative modalities of the British colonial state,' that is, the production of usable knowledge in the form of published reports, statistical returns, official proceedings, legal codes, and administrative histories. He also categorized these types of modalities, such as historiography, observation, travel, survey, enumeration, museology, and surveillance. See Cohn, 'Introduction' in *Colonialism and its Forms of Knowledge*, pp. 3–15.

[25] In contrast to the later Subaltern scholars, I argue that a more historical approach would be to see the history of orientalism as the history of colonialism and not the other way around. The real history and meaning of such notions as justice, freedom, or liberty lay more in their concrete deployment than in their philosophical meanings. After all, these categories of emancipation were turned into the very foundation of the British Empire in India. For example, the categories of justice, equity, and liberty as historically introduced into India by the British Empire were mediated through the figure of the monarch. An entirely philosophical approach to these categories would fail to capture their precise historical meaning.

the discourse.[26] The conception of enunciative persona serves three functions. First, such a category lets me approach discourses in terms of larger historical, institutional, and discursive genealogies rather than attribute them simply to substantive subjects, either individuals, social groups, or identities.[27] The emphasis on substantive subjects and their motivations in existing historiography is based on the assumption that the pre-given subject stands above history while determining its movement, thus forgetting that the subject itself is a historical construction and is shaped by larger historical forces. From my methodological perspective, the real persons of Burke or Gandhi are primarily the bearers of principal enunciative personae—the lawyer and the renouncer—as the real subjects of the discourse.[28] Second, the category of enunciative persona allows me

[26] For Foucault's thoughts on related issues see his *Archaeology of Knowledge*, pp. 88–105. A similar category of conceptual persona is used by Gilles Deleuze and Felix Guattari in *What Is Philosophy?*, pp. 61–83. For Deleuze the conceptual persona is a figure of thought, not one historically produced.

[27] In Indian historiography, the school that most clearly denies the role of discourse in the construction of subjects/subjectivity or, in their own words, agency, is the Cambridge school. Founded by Jack Gallagher in the 1960s, the important members of this school include Francis Robinson, Gordon Johnson, Christopher Baker, David Washbrook, and Christopher Bayly. See Seal, *The Emergence of Indian Nationalism: Competitition in the Late Nineteenth Century*; Gallagher, Johnson, and Seal (eds), *Locality, Province, and Nation: Essays on Indian Politics 1870–1940*. The works by these scholars are based on an ahistorical notion of the subject as always already there. They view subjects or identities only as agents of history, but not as constructs of history, as if subjects and subjectivity do not have any history. This is an extreme form of empiricism that denies the role of thought or categories. Under this methodological regime the only form of agency that is possible is at an individual or personal level—stripped of any discursive connection—the form of agency one is born with. History then becomes nothing more than a scramble for power, where power is seen as a piece of property to be possessed by pre-existing subjects. Agency, therefore, is most evident in individual pursuits of power and wealth—political ideology being nothing more than a cover. It is not surprising therefore that these historians deny the existence of nationalism in India; nationalism after all is a discursive phenomenon. The Cambridge school is bound by its methodology to deny nationalism. See Seal, 'Imperialism and Nationalism in India', p. 2. The other form in which the historians of this school recognize agency is as caste, religion, or ethnicity. This is not surprising, given that caste, ethnicity, even religion, often operate in everyday life as forms of identity one is born with, without any association with discourse. What is overlooked is that power operates in and through the creation of new subjects and subjectivity.

[28] In the case of Gandhi, the honorific 'Mahatma' has been used variously to refer to a saint, renouncer, or one who has dedicated himself to the service of mankind.

to bring the discursive and the institutional together and to study them in their interrelationship. For example, the enunciative persona of the lawyer brings the institutional modality of the law court with all its procedures and other characters together with jurisprudential categories. In short it helps to integrate the judicial-institutional and the juridical-discursive. This methodology helps me to avoid studying politics simply as a history of ideas or thought. Moreover, it allows me to circumvent a simple chronological, descriptive history of institutions as a series of administrative acts. Third, the term enunciative persona lets me account for cases of transference where one institution can be reconfigured in terms of another. For example, the Indian Legislative Council of 1853 was reconfigured in the image of a court of law with the enunciative personae of the lawyer and the judge playing the dominant roles in this institution.

It is quite clear that by making the law court and the legislature the central sites in the historical analysis of representational politics in India, this book departs in significant ways from Foucault's analysis of law and discipline.[29] His argument in *Discipline and Punish* that the juridico-political discourse of sovereignty is simply a mask hiding the 'real' operation of disciplinary power is ultimately not very different from the classic Marxist critique of law in the modern state as a mere 'superstructure' that simply reflects 'class relations'.[30] What that view overlooks is that even as law could be

---

For a discussion of how the title came to be fixed on Gandhi see Dieter Conrad, 'Gandhi as Mahatma: Political Semantics in an Age of Cultural Ambiguity'. Dalmia, Malinar and Christof (eds), *Charisma and Canon: Essays on the Religious History of the Indian Subcontinent.*

[29] For critiques of the place of law in Foucault's works see Hunt, 'Foucault's Expulsion of Law: Toward a Retrieval', pp. 1–38. Laura Engelstein, pointing in a similar vein to Foucault's indifference to the adjudicatory and arbitration aspects of law, has argued that it was Foucault's dismissal of law in favor of discipline and his stance that 'law actually abets the modern polity's violation of the promise of freedom' that rendered him incapable of seeing the essential difference between the rule of law societies of the West and states like Imperial and Soviet Russia that operated on discipline in the absence of rights.' Engelstein, 'Combined Underdevelopment: Discipline and the Law in Imperal and Soviet Russia', pp. 338–53. For another incisive discussion of Foucault's relation to the law, see Ewald, 'Norms, Discipline, and the Law', pp. 138–61.

[30] See Foucault, *Discipline and Punish*. Foucault argues that the history of domination could be written not by looking at legal discourse but rather at the operation of power at the microlevel, for which the emblematic institution was that of the prison. For similarities between Foucault's understanding of the law court

an instrument of class repression, it at the same time contains within itself the potential of being turned into a site for a public critique of power.[31] This is because the rules that govern the procedures of the law court make it essentially a public, contested, and performative space, not always amenable to subjective intentions.

The crucial importance of the law court and the concept of justice in the establishment of ideological hegemony of the state is particularly evident in colonial India where British military power by itself would have been inadequate for the establishment and maintenance of British Empire for two hundred years. Moreover, it explains why the anticolonial movement in India under the Indian National Congress continued to ground itself until 1920 in imperial justice, even as the repressive aspects of colonial power were more than evident.

In exploring these issues and formulating the argument summarized above I have drawn upon a wide variety of sources from India and Britain. These include British Parliamentary Debates and Parliamentary Papers of the House of Commons and the House of Lords, court records that include appeals to the Privy Council in Britain (Moore's Indian Appeals), reports of the Calcutta Supreme Court, the Calcutta High Court, the Sadar Diwani, and Sadar Nizamat Adalats. I have also looked at records of the legislative and judicial departments of the British Government in India located in the National Archives in Delhi, memoirs and biographies of British administrators, English-language newspapers from India, Proceedings of the Legislative Council of India from 1853 to 1947, Proceedings of the Indian National Congress, All India Congress Committee Papers, and Proceedings of the Constituent Assembly of

---

and that of Marxists, see Foucault, *Power/Knowledge,* pp. 1–36. This interview has generally been overlooked by scholars who have discussed Foucault's relation to law.

[31] E.P. Thompson famously demonstrated this in his work on law in eighteenth century England, *Whigs and Hunters: The Origin of the Black Act.* Thompson asserted in this work that 'the essential precondition for the effectiveness of law, in its function as ideology, is that it shall display an independence from gross manipulation and shall seem to be just.' Contesting the reductionist notion that law is simply a mask for class power, Thompson argued that 'The rhetoric and rules of society are something a great deal more than sham. In the same moment they may modify in profound ways, the behaviour of the powerful, and mystify the powerless. They may disguise the true realities of power, but at the same time, they may curb that power and check its intrusions', pp. 263–5.

India that drafted the Constitution from 1946 to 1949. At the India Office Library in London, I have looked at the Public and Judicial Department Records, the Home Miscellaneous Series, and the private collections of the different Viceroys of India, including their private papers and correspondence with the British monarch that are part of the European Manuscript collection, and the Political and Secret Correspondence with India. Since my book is centrally concerned with bringing out the perspectives of Indian political thinkers and people in colonial India, I have also used substantial vernacular sources in Indian languages. I have looked not only at vernacular newspapers from India but also at speeches, memoirs, novels, biographies, and autobiographies of Indian political thinkers in nineteenth- and twentieth-century India.

OVERVIEW OF THE BOOK

In the first chapter of the book I explore the dramatic clash of the competing visions of empire in late eighteenth-century England through a discussion of the impeachment trial of Warren Hastings, the former Governor-General of India for the British East India Company, who was tried for 'high crimes and misdemeanors' against the people of India in 1788. I show how a discourse of imperial justice, critical of colonial power, came to be constructed in the speeches of the prosecutor, the famous political thinker Edmund Burke.

In Chapter 2, I show how the difference between the colonial and the imperial played itself out in India in the enduring conflict that began in the late eighteenth century between the British East India Company's administration and the Supreme Court set up in Calcutta under the aegis of the British Parliament. I explore the process of the formation of the first Legislative Council of India in 1853 that modeled itself procedurally on a British court of equity.

In Chapter 3, I pursue the nature and profound implications of the discursive rupture caused by the political upheaval of the Revolt of 1857. I argue that the transfer of the government of India from the Company to the imperial monarch in the wake of the Revolt resulted in major discursive and institutional realignments to put the empire on a new foundation and remove any possibility of similar upheavals in the future. I show in this chapter how the old conflict of the colonial and the imperial became internal to the figure of the monarch in the post-1857 period giving rise to two new discourses of justice as equity and justice as liberty.

In Chapter 4, I argue that the discourse of the Indian National Congress, founded as a party in 1885, was firmly lodged within an epistemologico-juridical paradigm determined by the telos and procedures of justice as equity and liberty. This juridical paradigm explains, I contend, why the lawyer emerged in the late nineteenth and early twentieth centuries as the dominant enunciative persona for the articulation of political discourse. It also explains why the Indian National Congress, even as it opposed the colonial regime, continued to operate within an imperial juridical framework grounded in the figure of the monarch.

In Chapter 5, I explore the genealogy of the discourse of renunciative freedom under which Gandhi led the movement for independence. The emergence of this new discourse of freedom signified the rejection of the imperial discourse of justice on which Congress politics was grounded and its dominant mode of politics as elite pleading.

I contend in Chapter 6 that because the Gandhian movement did not construct a legislative discourse of governance and freedom, when independence came, the Congress immediately restored its original discourse of imperial justice. The critical category of imperial justice as equity (rather than freedom) was thus transformed in the Constitution of independent India into the dominant legislative category, unifying and structuring seemingly disparate domains in postcolonial India like the economy, society, and foreign policy in the decades after independence. The Indian Constitution marked the re-emergence in post-independence India of the two constitutive aspects of the British imperial–political formation in the form of an overdetermining discourse of justice as equity, and in the consolidation of dynastic leadership in the Congress party that ruled over India with only brief interruptions for the first fifty years of independence.

In Chapter 7, I conclude that the British imperial idea of justice embodied in the Indian National Congress and the Gandhian ethos of mass resistance as two competing and conflicting legacies have been the major driving forces determining the nature and evolution of the Indian polity after independence.

1

THE COLONIAL AND THE IMPERIAL[1]

India and Britain in the Impeachment Trial of
Warren Hastings

The impeachment trial of Warren Hastings has long been considered one of the key political trials in the history of the British Empire. It was the first major public discursive event of its kind in England, and arguably in Europe as a whole, in which the colonial ambitions and practices of European powers in the East stood exposed to a close and comprehensive critique, and the legal and moral legitimacy of colonialism itself as a phenomenon thrown into question before the highest judicial body in Britain, the House of Lords. The fact that the prosecution was led by Edmund Burke, one of the most articulate and prescient political statesman of modern Europe, has only added to the trial's enduring significance as a moment of critical reflection on colonial practices. Indeed, it could be argued that, it was on this occasion, and in this act of defending the rights of an alien population against coercive colonial rule that some of Burke's long held political and ethical convictions found their sharpest articulation.

Paradoxically, the historical contribution of the trial and Burke's intervention in India to the construction of a discourse of imperial sovereignty, have remained largely unexplored in existing

[1] A version of this chapter has been published as an article in *Law and History Review* 23, (3), Fall 2005, pp. 589–630. I thank the journal for the permission to reprint. For a general account of the trial see Marshall, *The Impeachment of Warren Hastings*. Also see Carnall and Nicholson, (ed.), *The Impeachment of Warren Hastings: Papers from a Bicentenary Commemoration*.

scholarship.[2] While historians have focused almost entirely on the question of the legality of the trial and the truth of Burke's allegations against Warren Hastings, political theorists have analysed the trial only to the extent that it throws light on what they believe to be Burke's political philosophy or core political beliefs.[3] In most of the interpretations by political theorists, India emerges either as an instance of, or as an exception to an otherwise coherent set of political beliefs, such as natural law, trusteeship, liberal utilitarianism, etc., that in being European in origin were manifested in their essences in the western context.[4] In general, almost all these interpretations

[2] Indeed, some historians of eighteenth-century England and India, most prominently Peter James Marshall, have argued that Burke's vision of an empire of justice had little significance for the British Empire as it evolved over the nineteenth century and, in fact, 'was already beginning to look irrelevant to the British empire of the 1790s.' See his Introduction in *The Writing and Speeches of Edmund Burke*, p. 36.

[3] In the course of the nineteenth century, liberal historians like Macaulay and Morley defended the truth of Burke's accusations against Warren Hastings. See Babington Macaulay, *Warren Hastings*, and John Morley, *Edmund Burke, a Historical Study*. On the other hand, in the late nineteenth and early twentieth centuries, a series of imperial historians like James Fitzjames Stephen, John Strachey, Sophia Weitzman, Lucy S. Sutherland, and Keith Feiling dismissed Burke's accusations that Hastings had been personally corrupt and argued that his arbitrariness was justified by the necessities of maintaining empire in the East, a view that Hastings himself articulated in the trial. See James Fitzjames Stephen, *The Story of Nuncomar and the Impeachment of Elijah Impey*; John Strachey, *Hastings and the Rohilla War*; Sophia Weitzman, *Warren Hastings and Philip Francis*; Lucy S. Sutherland, *The East India Company in Eighteenth-Century Politics*; Keith Feiling, *Warren Hastings*.

[4] For example, Peter Stanlis, whose work has been invaluable in bringing to attention the centrality of natural law doctrine in Burke's works, leaves the implications of the fact that the discourse of natural law and the law of nations found its sharpest articulation in Burke's speeches in the impeachment trial unexplored, concluding that Burke's understanding of international relations was limited to the European context, his intervention in India being merely an exception to his deep-seated convictions about European solidarity based on a common cultural inheritance. As a result, Burke emerges in his analysis primarily as a European conservative, and the radicality of his deployment of natural law and the law of nations for the defence of an alien, non-European people against colonial oppression passes unnoticed. See Stanlis, 'Edmund Burke and the Law of Nations', p. 400. Also see his *Edmund Burke and the Natural Law* and Canavan, *The Political Reason of Edmund Burke*. Again, scholars like Coniff have used the Indian case only to prove the inadequacy of Burke's political categories such as trusteeship, that, in his view, fail the test of universality when applied to a non-European people who lacked the political culture of the West. See Conniff, 'Burke and India: The Failure of the Theory of Trusteeship', pp. 291–309; and Dreyer, *Burke's Politics: A Study in Whig*

THE COLONIAL AND THE IMPERIAL 3

presuppose the boundaries between Europe and India, and the latter appears as a mere appendage to what is essentially the history of European political thought, as it found articulation in Edmund Burke, one of its most eloquent spokesmen.

The relative marginalization of Burke's intervention in Indian affairs in the historical scholarship on Burke has resulted in a neglect of what was arguably one of the more radical and innovative aspects of his thought—his effort in the historical context of the eighteenth century to go beyond the territorially bounded discourses of political sovereignty and institutional practices of nation-states, and to conceptualize a form of deterritorialized juridical–imperial sovereignty, that would be exercised not in the pursuit of the exclusive interest of the colonizing nation, but rather in ensuring that colonial administration in India remained firmly grounded in 'native' society and prevented from exercising absolute and arbitrary power over it. In this chapter, I will examine the construction of Burke's discourse of juridical-imperial sovereignty as it found articulation in his speeches for the prosecution in the impeachment trial of Warren Hastings, in opposition to a discourse of colonial sovereignty based on absolute power and national interests, articulated by Hastings' defence.

In recent years there has been a noticeable surge in interest in empires of the past and their continuities and discontinuities with the present global order.[5] While most earlier works on empire focused primarily on the essential links between imperialism as a political form and the economic phenomenon of capitalist expansion, lately

---

Orthodoxy. The most significant works that have attempted to establish Burke as a theorist of liberal utilitarianism are Morley, *Edmund Burke, a Historical Study* and Macpherson, *Burke*. Some excellent works in the recent past that have departed from this general tendency and have emphasized the centrality of Burke's writings on empire, particularly on India, for an understanding of his political theory are Wheelan, *Edmund Burke and India: Political Morality and Empire*; and Mehta, *Liberalism and Empire: A Study in Nineteenth Century Liberal Thought*. Also see Suleri, *The Rhetoric of English India*. For connections between Burke's writings on India and other parts of the British Empire like Ireland, see Janes, 'At Home Abroad: Edmund Burke in India', pp. 160–74, and O'Brien, *The Great Melody: A Thematic Biography and Commented Anthology of Edmund Burke*.

[5] Darby, *Three Faces of Imperialism: British and American Approaches to Asia and Africa 1870–1970*; Lieven, *Empire: The Russian and Its Rivals*; Ferguson, *How Britain Made the Modern World*; Hobsbawm, 'America's Imperial Delusion: The US drive for world domination has no historical precedent', *The Guardian*, 14 June 2003; Ignatieff, 'The Burden' in *New York Times Magazine*, 5 January 2003.

the realization that existing political institutions at an international level are proving inadequate to the task of meeting the challenges of globalization has prompted more work on questions of national and imperial sovereignty and their changing dynamics over time.[6] In one of the most significant works in this direction, that has gained a lot of attention worldwide as an ambitious attempt to theorize the emergent processes of globalization, authors Antonio Negri and Michael Hardt have proposed that one way to understand the complex dynamics of the new global order would be to see it as a new Empire, continuous in some aspects with older world empires but also fundamentally different.[7] Departing from other theorists, who have denied the novelty of the processes of globalization and argued that globalism is merely a continuation and perfection of imperialism, Negri and Hardt contend that globalization marks a fundamental rupture and a paradigmatic shift, not only in contemporary capitalist production and global relations of power, but also in the creation of a new supranational sovereign power that is decentered, indeterminate, continually shifting, discontinuous, and virtual. The authors contend that this new form of supranational, deterritorialized imperial sovereignty is radically different from the sovereignty that characterized earlier colonial empires, which were, in their opinion, centralized political formations that had extended national sovereignty over various subject peoples, while being firmly rooted in national institutions and metropolitan culture. The new Empire, in their view, marks a departure from past imperialism, which was nothing but the extension of the sovereignty of European nation-states beyond their own boundaries. One of the most important signs that the Empire has come into being, in the authors' opinion, is the existence of the United Nations as a global juridical institution, which, while predicated on the recognition and legitimation of the sovereignty of nation-states, has also emerged

---

[6] Works that have focused on the relation between capitalism and imperialism include Hobson, *Imperialism: A Study*; Lenin, *Imperialism, the Highest Stage of Capitalism: A Popular Outline*; Dobb, *Studies in the Development of Capitalism*; Gallagher and Robinson, 'The Imperialism of Free Trade', pp. 1–15; Fieldhouse, *Economics of Empire, 1830–1914*; Cain and Hopkins, *British Imperialism*. Recent works that has brought attention to the question of political sovereignty in a globalizing world are Sassen, *Losing Control? Sovereignty in an Age of Globalization*; Luard, *The Globalization of Politics*; Ohmae, *The End of the Nation State*; Albrow, *The Global Age*.

[7] Hardt and Negri, *Empire*.

as a real supranational institution whose legitimacy is grounded on the essential universal values of justice and morality, that transcend the national interests of its member states.

While agreeing with Negri and Hardt that a distinction needs to be made between the category of 'imperialism' and that of 'empire', I contend in this chapter that the two categories need to be seen not as characterizing two distinct chronological phases in the history of the contemporary world, but rather as contesting and contradictory historical forces that pointed to radically different directions that Empire could take even in the early years of European expansion in the eighteenth century. One of the problems with Negri and Hardt's analysis is that they make little attempt to rigorously trace the historical genealogy of the discourses and institutions that, in their view, characterize Empire. Therefore, they fail to recognize that what they describe as 'Empire' and its basic discourses and institutions emerged not after but contemporaneously with the advent of colonialism. Indeed, efforts to create both a discourse of deterritorialized, supranational sovereignty and institutions on which to ground it are evident even as early as the eighteenth century in the period of the American Revolution and the establishment of a second British Empire in the East.

The relationship between nation and empire was one of the most contentious issues in late eighteenth-century British political circles. The critical question at the heart of this debate over empire was whether conquest based on national interests was a legitimate foundation for the sovereignty of empire, which was no more than an extension of the sovereignty of the nation-state, or whether the sovereignty of empire was different from national sovereignty and had to be founded on juridical principles of universality and extraterritoriality, that transcended the discourse of national interests and the simple domination and subjugation of one nation by another. An equally important related question was, could empire be grounded on existing national institutions or did existing institutions have to be reconstituted to ground the new supranational discourse of imperial justice?

I will examine the articulation of this crucial debate in the speeches for the prosecution by Edmund Burke and defense in the impeachment trial of Warren Hastings. Hastings was impeached by the British House of Commons for 'high crimes and misdemeanours' as the Governor-General of the East India Company's Government in India (1772–85), and in 1788 proceedings began in the British House of Lords for a verdict. Along with charges of corruption, use of political power for extorting bribes from native rulers of India, abuse of judicial authority, despotism, and arbitrary rule, Hastings was being tried specifically for illegally occupying territory in India by launching aggressive offensive and criminal wars against native rulers, treaty violations, and for open violence against native rulers and the people of India.[8]

Through an analysis of the trial, I will argue that the British Empire was a complex political phenomenon that often carried conflicting and competing visions and agendas of rule.[9] Under the

[8] Some significant works on Warren Hastings' life and times include Macaulay, *Warren Hastings*; Lyall, *Warren Hastings*; Penderell Moon, *Warren Hastings and India*; Feiling, *Warren Hastings*; Trotter, *Warren Hastings*; Bernstein, *Dawning of the Raj: The Life and Trials of Warren Hastings*.

[9] The predominant tendency among historians of empire in general and of the empire in India in particular has been to arrive at a single essence of empire, thus reducing what was complex and contained within it differences, contradictions, and even conflicts to a homogenous phenomenon. While one of the oldest traditions of imperial historiography which I identify as the pedagogical school developed a seamless narrative of the spread of progress and enlightenment from the imperial center to the colonies, economic histories of empire have similarly constructed the development of empire in terms of homogenous narratives of the development of capitalism. Elphinstone's *The Rise of the British Power in the East*, Seely's *Expansion of England*, and more recently Low's *Eclipse of Empire* are representative of the first school, while Dobb, *Studies in the Development of Capitalism* and Fieldhouse's *Economics of Empire, 1830–1914* are good examples of the second. In fact, even Marx who constructed contradiction as a driving force of history described the process of colonization in India very much in pedagogical terms, as the spread of the capitalist mode of production and also the values and knowledge systems of the enlightenment to the colonies. For a general Marxist interpretation of the Empire, see Kiernan, *Marxism and Imperialism: Studies*. It was only later Marxists, like Lenin and other economic historians like Hobson who, in their studies of imperialism, focused on conflicts and the fact of economic exploitation rather than on pedagogical transfers of ideas, values, and institutions. See Hobson, *Imperialism: A Study*; Lenin, *Imperialism, the Highest Stage of Capitalism: A Popular Outline*. Cain and Hopkins' *British Imperialism*, a recent economic history of empire has also developed some of the arguments of Hobson. However, the problem with these studies is that they confined contradictions to the economic domain at the expense of potential and real contradictions in other institutional domains, such as the judicial, bureaucratic, military, intellectual, educational, etc. In the process of privileging the economic over other domains, they also tended to dismiss most discourses of empire and even those of nationalism as either false consciousness or ideology that, as such, have no history. It is only recently under the rubric of postcolonial studies that works on empire have focused on the study of discourse in the analysis of empire. See Said,

general phenomenon of empire, I delineate two converging but also often competing and conflicting aims and strategies of rule with respect to India, which I identify as the 'colonial' and the 'imperial'. While the phenomenon and discourse of the colonial as the discourse of governance articulated and operated in terms of conquest and domination of the colonized in the name of the national interests of the colonizing nation, and was institutionally grounded in the Governor-General's council in India, with the bureaucracy, the army and the police as its most important instruments, the imperial as a censorial discourse articulated and operated in supranational critical juridical terms of justice, equity, and impartiality, with the Crown-in-Parliament, the House of Lords, and the Supreme Court in India providing the institutional agency. It was in the trial under study that these two visions of the future of empire in India dramatically clashed. And, as the eighteenth century drew to a close, it was by no means clear whether the new empire in the East would unfold along one of these two visions or some form of a combination of the two.

In what follows, I locate the beginnings of the historical construction of a denationalized and deterritorialized discourse of empire in the impeachment trial of Warren Hastings. The primary question that I will be asking is, under what imperatives and through what discursive and strategic maneuvers was the discourse of empire constructed as a deterritorialized discourse of justice? How did a homology between the categories of justice and empire come about and how was it institutionally grounded?

THE TRIAL

The impeachment trial of Warren Hastings took place in the last two decades of the eighteenth century in the midst of a chaotic phase of political turmoil and party intrigues in the British Parliament following the loss of the American colonies. As Bowen has pointed out, the years between 1756 and 1783 had been years of particular imperial instability, when Britons vigorously sought to rework ideas of empire, governance, rule, and supremacy.[10] An integrated

---

Orientalism and Gyan Prakash, (ed.), *After Colonialism: Imperial Histories and Postcolonial Displacements*. One of the important works that has brought attention to the contradictions within empire in the recent past is Cooper and Stoler, (eds), *Tensions of Empire: Colonial Cultures in a Bourgeois World*.

[10] Bowen, 'British Conceptions of Global Empire', pp. 1–27.

concept of the British Empire, according to David Armitage, had already emerged throughout the British Atlantic world by the 1730s, and both imperial officials and provincial elites had come to share some basic conceptions of what distinguished the British Empire from both past empires and contemporary imperial formations. While Protestantism, commerce, and maritime supremacy had emerged as some of the British Empire's distinguishing attributes, what contemporary observers saw as crucial to British imperial identity was the idea of liberty, the notion that its inhabitants, unlike those of other empires in the past and in the present, were free, a freedom that was embedded in, and found expression in institutions like the law (particularly the common law), property, rights, and the Parliament, which were exported all over the British Atlantic World.[11]

The precise relation between empire and liberty, therefore, had become one of the central points of contention as the British Atlantic Empire grew in size and prosperity in the eighteenth century, and both metropolitan and provincial spokesmen on both sides of the Atlantic World debated vigorously both the nature of the constitutional relationship between the metropolis and the colonies, and the possibility of viable institutions that would balance the needs of empire and the requirements of liberty. The question that had emerged in these debates as fundamental was whether the colonies should be reduced to perpetual dependencies of Britain (as in the case of imperial Rome), which would make laws and appoint governors over them, a model that was advocated by metropolitan spokesmen like James Abercromby, Henry McCulloh, William Shirley, and others, or whether the relationship between the metropolis and the colonies was to be a more balanced partnership (advocated by provincial spokesmen like Benjamin Franklin) in which the colonies would be more in the position of self-governing confederates, as in ancient Greece.[12] Closely related was the other critical question—were colonists to share equal rights and liberties with all Englishmen, or did the necessities of empire require that they be reduced to a greater level of dependence than other Britons,

[11] Armitage, *Ideological Origins of the British Empire*, p. 8. Also see Greene, 'Empire and Identity from the Glorious Revolution to the American Revolution', pp. 208–30.

[12] Shannon, *Indians and Colonists at the Crossroads of Empire: The Albany Congress of 1754*, pp. 57–113.

and denied the liberties and privileges that were enjoyed by British subjects in the metropolis?

In the years preceding the impeachment trial, the reasons for the American Revolution were still being hotly debated in political circles in England, but there was little dispute about the fact that, at the center of the crisis had been the inability of the two sides, the colonists and the English Parliament, to come to an agreement on the Constitution of the British Empire and the distribution of power within it. As Jack P. Greene pointed out in his analysis of the American Revolution, for a century and a half preceding the Revolution, there had been no explicit articulation of the precise relationship between the metropolis in England and the American colonies within the larger structure of empire, and when the debates over the English Parliament's right to tax the colonies came to the fore during the Stamp Act Crisis in 1764–5 and the Townshend measures in 1767–72, there was little by way of precedent in the British Constitution that could point to a resolution of the crisis.[13]

At the centre of the constitutional debate between England and the American colonies was the nature of the legislative relationship between the metropolis and the colonies, specifically whether, and to what extent, America was to be legislatively subordinated to the British Parliament. The argument of the colonists for 'constitutional multiplicity' within the empire, for each of its constituents to be autonomous entities with their own legislatures, but under the British Crown, was unacceptable to the majority of people in England, who insisted on the indivisibility of sovereignty and asserted that, without the maintenance of legislative supremacy of the British Parliament over the colonies, the empire would cease to exist.[14] The American Revolution was the result of a direct clash between two legislatures, the British Parliament on the one hand and the colonial legislatures on the other, and as Greene points out, 'in the absence of any impartial tribunal to settle constitutional disputes between the center and the peripheries' of the empire, there was no means of resolving the conflict by law.[15]

[13] Greene, *Understanding the American Revolution: Issues and Actors*, pp. 72–3. Also see Bailyn, *Ideological Origins of the American Revolution*, and Reid, *The Concept of Representation in the Age of the American Revolution*.

[14] Onuf, (ed.), *Maryland and the Empire, 1773: The Antilon-First Citizen Letters*, p. 29.

[15] Greene, *Understanding the American Revolution*, p. 85.

At around the same time as the conflict between the British Parliament and American colonies was heating up, another affair in another corner of the world was beginning to occupy the attention of the English people. This involved the increasing financial and political influence in Parliament of the East India Company, a mercantile body that, on the basis of its trade monopoly in the East, derived from a charter from the British Parliament, had amassed enormous fortunes from India, over which it was also rapidly extending its political power.[16]

Registered with the London Stock Exchange, this trading company that had also become the government in India was effectively directed by a group of jobbers and brokers, who for all practical purposes had become legislators for India, determining policies for the Company's government on behalf of the shareholders of the company.[17] However, the Company, in order to avoid the responsibilities of rule in the colony, had consistently refused to acknowledge the fact that it was no longer simply a mercantile body, but had come to acquire state power in India.

The most important goal for this Company's government in Bengal, in keeping with the logic of the stock exchange was to make the maximum profit from the colony in the shortest possible time. The profit from India primarily came in two forms—(1) in the form of rent collected from cultivators at high rates, and (2) in the form of profits from often unfair trade practices. Since the government had established monopoly power over trade, it was in the position to fix prices on goods that the cultivators brought to the market after paying the rent, and then to sell them at high margins in European markets or to other European trading companies. The immediate consequences of this double squeeze on the cultivators in the form of rent and monopoly trading rights included large-scale devastation and pauperization of the Indian

---

[16] Mukherjee, *The Rise and Fall of the East India Company*, pp. 224–83. Other works on the East India Company include Sen, *Distant Sovereignty: National Imperialism and the Origins of British India*; Sutherland, *The East India Company in Eighteenth-Century Politics*; Keay, *The Honourable Company: A History of the English East India Company*; Lawson, *The East India Company: A History*; Marshall, *East India Fortunes: The British in Bengal in the Eighteenth Century*; Bayly, *Imperial Meridien: The British Empire and the World, 1780–1830*; Philips, *The East India Company, 1784–1834*.

[17] Philips, *The East India Company*, pp. 1–22.

peasantry, leading ultimately to famine, within the first fifteen years of the Company's rule.[18]

It was in the wake of these governmental practices that complaints against the East India Company's government and its oppression and plunder of the people of India started pouring into England from India. The prospect of a second empire in the East intensified the already vociferous debates about empire in England, particularly because the emerging colony in India was different from the American colonies in that it was not a settler colony, but was based on conquest, requiring new strategies of rule and new ideologies of governance and legitimacy. While there was an awareness that Indian wealth had become crucial to the economic stability of England, and some imperial theorists like Thomas Pownall even went to the extent of arguing that the loss of India might cause a 'national bankruptcy' and result in the ruin of the whole edifice of the British Empire, yet the old fear that an extended empire and the inflow of this vast wealth into the English system would corrupt institutions within England and eventually result in the collapse of the British Constitution and, with it, both empire abroad and liberty at home, was an equally powerful argument that resisted the drive towards imperial expansion.[19] In this new context, the constitutional implications of colonization and rule over a large alien population became a particularly urgent concern for metropolitan thinkers, who began to debate not only how the

[18] Mukherjee, *Rise and Fall of the East India Company*, pp. 299–385.

[19] Bowen, 'British Conceptions of Global Empire', p. 14. Parallels between the corruption that the East India Company's servants were introducing into England (particularly through the practice of buying seats in Parliament and thus threatening the existing political balance in the House of Commons), and the corruption in the days of the declining Roman Empire were not hard to imagine. Edward Gibbon in his book, *The Decline and Fall of the Roman Empire* that was published between 1776 and 1788, attributed the ruin of the Roman Empire to 'immoderate greatness,' specifically to the destruction of the virtue of the republic by the corruption that was the inevitable result of the acquisition of an extensive empire. It was the opportunity that empire provided to military commanders and economic speculators to acquire power that could not be controlled by law and conflicted with the virtue of equality, and the inevitable corruption that arose out the governance of the empire by military commanders, independently of the republic that ultimately resulted, in Gibbon's view, in the absorption of the city of Rome by the empire and thus in its ultimate decay. To contemporaries of Gibbon, the East India Company's emerging system of governance in the new colony in the East threatened to plunge the British state in a similar path of decline. See Gibbon, *The Decline and Fall of the Roman Empire*.

constitutional relationship between Britain and this new empire of conquest was to be constructed, but also the institutional framework within which the empire was to operate.

The first of the Parliamentary Acts that sought to impose restraints on the Company's authority in India and make it accountable to the British state was Lord North's Regulating Act of 1773. The primary goal of the Regulating Act was to create institutional barriers against the exercise of arbitrary power by the governor and the rampant corruption of the Company's servants by introducing a system of checks and balances in the Company's administration and establishing a proper mode of administering justice in India. With this purpose in mind, the Act created the institution of the Supreme Court, an independent judiciary under the direct authority of the British Parliament with the responsibility of acting as an effective external check against the absolute powers of the Company's administration in India. Bringing with it English common law, the Supreme Court was given jurisdiction over all persons in Bengal, Bihar, and Orissa and the power and responsibility to protect the 'natives' of India from the Company's officials by prosecuting all offenses by the latter, and even issuing summons against the Governor-General and council in the event of cases being brought against the Company itself. It was also given the right to review and veto all laws passed by the Governor-General's council, the supreme executive and legislative body in Bengal. Within the council itself, the Act placed severe restraints on the Governor-General's actions by the requirement that all executive and legislative decisions be sanctioned by a majority vote in the council (over which he had no power of veto).[20]

The Regulating Act however failed in its objective of making the Company's administration in India accountable to the British state, principally because the multiple levels of conflict over sovereignty that it unintentionally precipitated in India between the Governor-General and his council on the one hand, and between the Company's executive and the Supreme Court as an autonomous external judiciary on the other, effectively brought the administration in India to a standstill. The situation was rendered more confusing by the conflict between English common law that the Supreme Court brought with it to India and the native systems

---

[20] Setalvad, *The Rise of the Common Law*, pp. 1–62.

of law that already held sway in courts in the provinces of Bengal under the authority of the Governor-General and Council. These conflicts and contradictions made it imperative for the Parliament to intervene once again in the affairs of the Company in India by establishing a select committee of enquiry into the Bengal judiciary in 1781 under the guidance of Edmund Burke, and ultimately to two more Parliamentary Acts—Fox's India Bill of 1782 and Pitt's India Bill of 1784. While the first tried to resolve the fundamental conflict between the Company's trading interests and its responsibilities as a government by attempting to bring the administration of India under the direct control of the Crown, the second proposed that the Company retain control over the administration in India while at the same time creating a Board of Control in London, subordinate to Parliament, that was to supervise the activities of the Company in India.

However, both these bills in Parliament that aimed at bringing the East India Company's affairs under parliamentary control again could accomplish little in terms of controlling the Company's commercial and political power, even though they problematized, for the first time, the contentious relationship between the commercial interests of the East India Company and its political powers of governance in the newly emerging colony. While Fox's India bill was defeated in the House of Lords sealing the fate of his ministry itself, Pitt's bill accommodated all the demands of the East India Company and left it almost entirely intact, fanning the view that his ministry was, in fact, in league with the Company.[21]

It was in the aftermath of the loss of the American colonies and the failure of the Regulating Act of 1773, as well as the two India Bills in Parliament to bring about effective reform in the East India Company's administration in India that the impeachment trial of Warren Hastings began in 1788 in Westminster, charging the Governor-General of the East India Company's administration in India with corruption, bribery, high crimes, and misdemeanours. After impeachment in the Commons, the case finally moved to the House of Lords, the highest court of appeal in England, where Edmund Burke and his team of managers launched a prosecution for the final verdict.

---

[21] Sutherland, *East India Company in Eighteenth-Century Politics*, pp. 365–415.

THE DISCOURSE OF COLONIAL SOVEREIGNTY

I begin with an analysis of the arguments in defence of Warren Hastings that fundamentally challenged the very legal authority of the British Parliament to try him for crimes committed in India. The defence was constructed around two major claims about sovereignty. The first was based on an identification of the sovereignty that the East India Company exercised in India with its chartered rights, granted to it by the English Parliament.[22]

When Fox had introduced his Bill in Parliament, based on the principle that the Company's commercial affairs ought to be separated from its functions as a government, and therefore, its 'patronage' be taken away, the representatives and spokesmen for the Company had strongly opposed that Bill.[23] In all the debates in Parliament about its administration in India, the Company had insisted that the Bill was an encroachment on their chartered rights and their rights to private property, that it aimed at annihilating a body of commercial people and destroying their property and that it was, therefore, a despotic bill by its very nature. The Company had asserted that the territorial revenues of India could not be considered as belonging to the British government, any more than could the East India Company's commercial concerns be so considered, for both of these fell within the private property of the Company as a chartered body. In fact, they had argued that what was being attempted on the pretext of giving stability and permanency to the property of the inhabitants in India, was a destruction of the rights of Englishmen in England.[24] The defence of Warren Hastings in the impeachment trial continued this line of argument.[25]

---

[22] Philips, *The East India Company*, p. 20.

[23] Patronage referred to a system wherein the Directors of the East India Company had the right to dispose of appointments in the East India Company's administration in India, such as those of civil servants, writers, cadets, and assistant surgeons for the Company's armies, barristers, and attorneys for the Company's courts, etc. Each Director had at his disposal at least six or seven appointments in a year, and often, some Directors sold their patronage to buy and maintain seats in Parliament. See Philips, *The East India Company*, pp. 14–17.

[24] *The Parliamentary History of England from the Earliest Period to the Year 1803*, Vol. XXIII, p. 1210.

[25] This claim needs to be seen in terms of a long history of contentious debates in late seventeenth- and early eighteenth-century England between the supporters of English settlers and planters in America, intent on expanding British possessions in the new colony, on the one hand, and opponents of colonization of America on

The second and more radical claim was that the 'crimes' in India that Hastings was being tried for, such as aggressive offensive wars against 'native' rulers, treaty violations, abuse of judicial authority, etc., were, in fact, legitimate exercises of sovereign power in the new colony. When faced with a compelling account of the political nature of the Company's operations in India, Warren Hastings defended his actions as the Governor-General, making certain assertions about the source and nature of the sovereignty of the Company's administration in India.

Insofar as the *source* of this sovereignty was concerned, Hastings claimed that the Company had inherited the sovereignty over Bengal through a grant of the *Diwani* (the right to collect revenue) from the Mughal emperor.[26] Rejecting the legitimacy of the English Parliament's repeated attempts to bring the Company's administration in India under its control as reflected in the Regulating Act of 1773 and the two Parliamentary Bills of 1783 and 1784, Hastings asserted that since this sovereignty had nothing to do with the English Parliament, it was beyond its jurisdiction and

---

the other, who argued that, besides unfairly dispossessing the Native Americans of their land, colonization was enfeebling England, and even if allowed to continue, the colonies ought to be kept in a position of strict dependence to the mother country. See Arneil, *John Locke and America: The Defence of English Colonialism* and Tully, *An Approach to Political Philosophy: Locke in Contexts*. To a large extent the East India Company was reformulating the same contention in the context of the newly developing colony in India. This colonial claim that property rights in the new colony could not be interfered with by the Crown was closely tied to the Lockean argument that property was essentially grounded on man's labour and preceded the state. The state's only function was the protection and preservation of property and any attempt to interfere with property was an exercise in tyranny. See Locke, *Second Treatise of Government*, pp. 18–30, 65–8.

[26] This right to revenue collection, or Diwani, was obtained from the Mughal Emperor Shah Alam, at the conclusion of the battle of Buxar (1764) in which the East India Company's army under Robert Clive defeated the combined troops of the Mughal Emperor and the Nawab of Awadh. Rather than declare themselves the new sovereigns of Bengal and Awadh, the East India Company persuaded the Emperor to grant them the right to the land revenues of the province of Bengal on the payment of a small annual tribute, thus taking on the role of a tributary under the dejure sovereignty of the Mughal Emperor. As a result of this settlement with the Mughal Emperor, sovereign power in Bengal was split, with the East India Company, controlling the reins of power by controlling the machinery of revenue collection, and the puppet ruler of Bengal, continuing to bear the responsibilities of maintaining law and order and criminal administration. See Mukherjee, *Rise and Fall of The East India Company*, pp. 268–84.

had to be exercised in accordance with Mughal laws, customs, and conventions regarding sovereignty, not with those of the English.

The sovereignty which they (the soubahdars, or viceroys of the Mughal Empire) assumed, it fell to my lot very unexpectedly, to exert; and whether or not such power, or powers of that nature, were delegated to me by any provisions of any act of parliament, I confess myself too little of a lawyer to pronounce. I only know that the acceptance of the sovereignty of Benares, etc. is not acknowledged or admitted by any act of parliament; and yet, by the particular interference of the majority of the council, the Company is clearly and indisputably seized of that sovereignty. If therefore, the sovereignty of Benares, as ceded to us by the vizier, have any rights whatever annexed to it (and be not a mere empty word without meaning), *those rights must be such as are held, countenanced, and established by the law, custom and usage of the Mogul empire, and not by the provisions of any British act of parliament hitherto enacted.* Those rights, and none other, I have been the involuntary instrument of enforcing (emphasis mine).[27]

This claim about upholding indigenous customs, usages, and rights was not surprising given that Hastings, in his position as Governor-General in India, had been a staunch opponent of the imposition of English common law on the people of India, and one of the most enthusiastic patrons in the East India Company of indigenous learning, particularly in the field of law. As Governor-General, he had encouraged the systematization of different and often conflicting systems of law in India by commissioning some of the first translations into English of ancient Hindu and Muslim legal texts, and setting up educational institutions for the teaching of indigenous law.[28]

However, even as Hastings encouraged the systematization of India's legal traditions, that, he believed, was necessary for the administration of civil and criminal justice and the ultimate stability of British rule in India, he also asserted that these very traditions allowed for the exercise of arbitrary and exceptional power by the sovereign in the political domain as a matter of state necessity.

---

[27] Burke, *Speeches on the Impeachment Trial of Warren Hastings*, pp. 483–4. .

[28] Bernard S. Cohn has interpreted the emphasis given by Hastings to indigenous legal traditions as reflective of the fact that the East India Company's administration under Hastings in Bengal followed the model of a 'theocratic state.' See his 'Law and the Colonial State', pp. 65–7. Also see Brockington, 'Warren Hastings and Orientalism', pp. 91–108.

Moving from the *source* to the *nature* of sovereignty, Hastings, rather than deny the accusations of arbitrariness, argued that, in fact, in India, sovereignty in practice could mean nothing but despotism. According to him, this despotism that he inherited from the Mughals was provoked by the nature of the people themselves. It was a reaction to a permanently rebellious population, rather than a conscious choice on the part of the government:

The *Hindoos*, who never incorporated with their conquerors, *were kept in order only by the strong hand of power.* The constant necessity of similar exertions would increase at once their energy and extent, so that *rebellion itself is the parent and promoter of despotism. Sovereignty in India implies nothing else ... The whole history of Asia is nothing more than precedents to prove the invariable exercise of arbitrary power* (emphasis mine).[29]

What justified absolutism in India then, and necessitated the unhindered exercise of sovereign power (in contrast to England where it was illegitimate), was a set of exceptional circumstances, that could only be likened to the state of civil war, anarchy, and chaos, described by the political philosopher, Thomas Hobbes in his book *Leviathan*, as a stage antecedent to the emergence of the state.[30] Resorting to the familiar Hobbesian discourse of sovereignty, Hastings contended that, given this natural state of rebellion, since the sovereign's power alone could guarantee the security and preservation of life and property, it necessarily had to be unlimited and unquestioned, and notions such as justice and liberty could have no existence independent of his will.[31]

Painting a picture of a society in a state of perpetual war, Hastings articulated the state's relationship with the people in terms of a

[29] Burke, *Speeches*, pp. 484–5.

[30] Hobbes, *Leviathan*, pp. 185–6.

[31] In making this claim, Hastings was also asserting the need to remove the institutional checks that the East India Company had imposed on his authority by making his decisions as Governor-General subject to the approval of the members of the Council. In seeking the concentration of authority in his own hands, he claimed that as Governor-General, he was ultimately the representative of the British Crown, and therefore, had to exercise royal sovereignty in India in accordance with the interests of the King. These, he contended, were absolute, and subject neither to the interests of a commercial body, the East India Company, nor to Mughal power. See Sen, 'Warren Hastings and British Sovereign Authority in Bengal, 1774–80', pp. 68–70, and Marshall, 'The Making of an Imperial Icon: The Case of Warren Hastings', p. 5.

permanent conflict, where the people were 'rebels' and enemies of the state on an apriori basis. Thus, the wars that he had waged as Governor-General against native rulers and people or his breaches of faith and treaty violations were, Hastings argued, not 'crimes' but necessary and legitimate responses to rebellious governors and people, and to that extent were punitive in nature. With respect to the Rohilla wars, he asserted that they were necessary because the Rohillas had refused to pay for the protection that the Company's government has given them against invasion. 'We made war with them, on just grounds surely, unless any other process than that of the sword can be devised for recovering the rights of nations.'[32] Similarly, in referring to his policy towards the Marathas, Hastings asserted that he had pursued war because peace could be attained not by concessions and entreaties, but by the 'terrors of a continued War.'[33] Affirming 'as a fact unquestioned and unquestionable that we derive our original title to our possessions in Bengal from the sword alone,' Hastings contended that the new political base of the colonial state had to be force, as it had been for the Mughal state, for, without force, chaos, and anarchy would ensue and the very existence of the colonial state would be at risk.[34] Under the permanent threat of the dissolution of authority, the whole structure of the newly established colonial government could have but a single object, security, and the only bond between the subject people to the colonial government that of fear.

It was the necessity of fighting these perpetual wars against a rebellious population that also made it imperative, Hastings asserted, for the East India Company's officials in Bengal, to take bribes and presents that had been condemned as crimes by Burke and his prosecutorial team. Given the limited revenue available to the Company's state in India, other sources of funds had to be found in a 'time of most pressing Necessity, in order to relieve the Exigencies of the State' which were 'in such imminent Danger and Distress, that every little Aid of this Kind became an object of

[32] Hastings to D. Anderson (13 September 1786) in Glieg, *Memoirs of the Life of the Right Hon. Warren Hastings, first governor-general of India*, p. 303.

[33] Hastings to Sir John Macpherson (1 November 1781) in H. Dodwell, (ed.), *Warren Hastings' Letters to Sir John Macpherson*, pp. 99–100.

[34] *The Defence of Warren Hastings, Esq. (Late Governor General of Bengal) at the Bar of the House of Commons, upon the Matter of the several Charges of High Crimes and Misdemeanors, presented against him in the Year 1786*, p. 82.

National Consequence.'[35] Thus, Hastings argued in his defence that every policy that he has pursued in India had been dictated by the necessity of preserving the East India Company's state in India and not by his personal corrupt motives.

Sovereign power under the exceptional conditions in India had to be, as Hobbes had argued, absolute and unlimited. As the holder of this absolute power, Hastings had neither the obligations to respect previous covenants, nor was he bound by any laws. In opposition to theories of the natural freedom of the people that were relevant for England, it was the doctrine of the natural subjection of the people and patriarchal despotic power that was appropriate for India. The will of the sovereign was supreme and could not be subject to positive laws, and therefore, notions such as crime, punishment, and rights had little relevance.[36]

THE DISCOURSE OF IMPERIAL SOVEREIGNTY

It was against the 'colonial' discourse of sovereignty, based on the twin ideas of government as corporate property on the one hand, and arbitrary power on the other, that Edmund Burke developed what I have called the imperial discourse of justice. Faced with this unique logic of the colonial discourse of governance he had two distinct tasks. First, he had to prove that the East India Company in its role in India was not simply a mercantile corporate body, but operated as a government, and that, therefore, the logic of private property, as defined by the common law, was not sufficient to account for the Company's operations.[37] Second, he had to prove Warren Hastings' characterization of 'native' sovereignty false by arguing, on the one hand, that both the Mughal and Hindu rulers in India had well-developed systems of laws, which precluded the exercise of arbitrary power by the sovereign, and on the other, that Hastings' contention about a permanently rebellious population was historically and factually unfounded.[38]

As it turned out, Burke comprehensively developed both these lines of argument to great effect. He began his prosecution by

[35] *Journals of the House of Commons*, vol. 41, 1–2 May 1786, pp. 711–12.

[36] See the discussion of 'oriental despotism' in Charles de Secondat Montesquieu, *The Spirit of the Laws*, Cohler, Miller and Stone, (ed.), pp. 5.14–19.

[37] Burke, *Speeches*, vol. 1, pp. 58–95.

[38] Ibid., pp. 104–26.

establishing that the Mughal and Hindu kings of India were not arbitrary rulers. On the contrary, they ruled in accordance with established systems of jurisprudence that were in fact far more advanced than those in England and Europe.

> Those people lived under the Law, which was formed even whilst we, I may say, were in the Forest, before we knew what Jurisprudence was ... It is a refined, enlightened, curious, elaborate, technical Jurisprudence under which they lived, and by which their property was secured and which yields neither to the Jurisprudence of the Roman Law nor to the Jurisprudence of this Kingdom.[39]

He asserted that the rights of the people of India had been established long before the advent of the colonial state, and it was, therefore, obliged to protect the people in their rights.[40]

However, in so far as this trial involved two exclusive national/municipal systems of laws, customs, and jurisprudence, Indian and English, it presented a series of jurisprudential dilemmas. Under what jurisprudence could an English tribunal try one of its own subjects for violence and 'crimes' against an alien population? Could a subject of England be tried in the name of the laws of an alien land? How could those acts of violence be translated into the juridical language of crime and punishment? How was the Company's claim of corporate property, that was firmly based on English common law, to be delegitimated, while at the same time retaining the basis of the trial in some form of jurisprudence? Finally, how was the discourse of the will that was the basis of Hastings' defence, and also the basis of continental jurisprudence, to be firmly rejected in the discourse of empire?

---

[39] Marshall, *Writings and Speeches*, vol. 7, p. 285.

[40] In opposition to the Hobbesian theory of absolute sovereignty that discursively framed Hastings' defence, the political thinker John Locke had proposed that the state of nature, rather than being characterized by chaos and anarchy was a state in which people had property and rights. These rights were only conditionally surrendered to the monarch and the people had an obligation to obey only so long as the state worked for their good. In claiming that the rights of the people of India were prior to the state, Burke was resorting to this political tradition in England that prioritized the liberty of the people against claims of absolute power of the sovereign. As the King was subordinate to the law in England, as the Mughal and Hindu rulers in India were subordinate to the laws in India, so Burke argued, Hastings and the Company's government in India had to necessarily be subordinate to law. See Locke, *Second Treatise of Government*, pp. 101–24.

These series of dilemmas were made even more acute by the fact that impeachment involved a trial for public crimes that were political in nature, and therefore, directly engaged some of the fundamental questions of politics—sovereignty, rights of an alien population, rules of war, etc. Thus, as Burke pointed out, it was not simply Warren Hastings as an individual, or the specific criminal acts, that he and the government he headed might have engaged in, but the colonial state itself and the principles and maxims on which its discourse was founded, that were being indicted in this trial. The judgment given in this trial, therefore, would be crucial, because it would serve as a precedent and constitute the primary source of a critical discourse on colonialism in India. Emphasizing this point in no uncertain terms, Burke reminded the judges—'*According to the judgement* that you shall give upon the past transactions in India, ... connected as they are with the principles which support them, *the whole character of your future government in that distant empire will be unalterably decided* (emphasis mine).'[41]

Burke was well aware of the historical significance of this trial and the unprecedented nature of the dilemma that faced the judges. As he pointed out, this trial brought forth a new set of conditions for 'it has a relation to many things, it touches many points in many places wholly removed from the ordinary beaten orbit of our English affairs.'[42] This case could not be contained and tried within any of the exclusive municipal traditions since 'this cause is not what occurs every day in the ordinary round of municipal affairs.' As a consequence, the trial presented a rupture between the traditional national systems of legal discourses and the emerging reality of empire—'Hitherto we have moved within the narrow circle of municipal justice. I am afraid that, from the habits acquired by moving within the transcribed sphere, we may be induced rather to endeavour at forcing nature into that municipal circle, than to *enlarge the circle of national justice to the necessities of the empire we have obtained* (emphasis mine).'[43]

The necessities of empire made it imperative that the familiar world within which the East India Company's operations had been discussed so far be abandoned. Burke launched a vigorous attack

---

[41] Burke, *Speeches*, vol. 1, pp. 9–10.
[42] Ibid., p. 19.
[43] Ibid., p. 18.

against what he termed Hastings' 'plan of geographical morality' on the basis of which, the latter had claimed that two different territorial systems of laws and customs ought to be applied to judge the nature of the Company's affairs in India and his actions as the Governor-General—the common law, on the one hand, that protected the Company's chartered rights as a corporate body, and the tradition of arbitrary political rule as a phenomenon peculiar to India and the Asiatic state on the other, that the Company inherited from the Mughal Empire, granting them immunity from any judgments grounded in the standards of English common law.

These gentlemen have formed a plan of *geographical morality,* by which the duties of men, in public and in private situations, are not to be governed by their relative relation to the great Governor of the universe, or by their relation to mankind, but by climates, degrees of longitude, parallels not of life but of latitudes; as if, when you have crossed the equinoctial, all the virtues die ... *This geographical morality we do protest against. Mr Hastings shall not screen himself under it;* ... the laws of morality are the same everywhere (emphasis mine).[44]

But on what theory of jurisprudence was this new discourse of empire to be based, if not on municipal law? For this, Burke turned to a discourse of jurisprudence that over the last two centuries had become central to legal debates, particularly in Europe—the discourse of natural law.[45] 'There is but *one law for all*, namely that law *which governs all law, the law of our Creator, the law of humanity, justice, equity:—the law of nature and of nations.* So far as any laws fortify this *primeval law* ... such laws enter into the sanctuary, and participate in the sacredness of its character (emphasis mine).'[46]

The historiography on Burke has not adequately accounted for the irruption of the discourse of natural law in his speeches during the trial. Given Burke's status as one of the greatest and most articulate exponents of common law jurisprudence, the privileging of natural law over common law jurisprudence in this trial has been read by some scholars like John MacCunn and Leslie Stephen as a sign of

[44] Burke, *Speeches*, vol. 1, p. 94.

[45] Significant works on natural law include Tuck, *The Rights of War and Peace: Political Thought and the International Order from Grotius to Kant*; Buckle, *Natural Law and the Theory of Property: Grotius to Hume*; Strauss, *Natural Right and History*.

[46] Burke, *Speeches*, vol. 1, p. 504.

inconsistency and even political opportunism, while others like Charles Vaughan have dismissed it as a rhetorical digression.[47] Yet others like Peter Stanlis, while rightly recognizing and emphasizing the importance of natural law in Burke's thought, particularly in his speeches on India and to some extent Ireland, have tried to suture all the seeming disparities into one coherent whole by finding the jurisprudence of natural law at work in all of Burke's writings, thus ignoring the obvious shift from Burke's earlier writings on judicial and political issues.[48]

To understand why Burke created a sharp disjuncture between common law and natural law jurisprudence in this trial and privileged the latter in the context of the emerging empire in India, it is necessary to lay out the different senses in which the term common law was used in eighteenth-century England. First, it referred to a substantive system of territorial municipal laws specific to England, based on English customs and traditions. Second, it referred to a particular set of judicial procedures and practices such as adversarial rules of procedure, due process of law, trial by jury, judgment based on precedents, etc., that guaranteed protection against arbitrary power. Third, in a more general sense, common law jurisprudence referred to the process of making laws, locating the source of law in customs, tradition, and history, rather than in positive legislation based on the will of the legislator, or legal codes based on abstract rules.[49] Thus, implicit within common law jurisprudence were both universal normative principles of how laws were to be made and what procedures were to be followed in courts, principles that could be and were carried by British colonizers to different parts of the world in the process

---

[47] All these authors have interpreted the importance that Burke gave to 'expediency' as reflective of a form of conservative utilitarianism and a contempt for natural law. Vaughan, *Studies in the History of Political Philosophy Before and After Rousseau*, pp. 3–4; Maccunn, *The Political Philosophy of Burke*, p. 193; Stephen, *English Thought in the Eighteenth Century*, pp. 225–6.

[48] Stanlis, *Edmund Burke and the Natural Law*, pp. 231–3. Stanlis sees no inherent contradiction between Burke's appeal to common law on the one hand and to natural law on the other. Rather, in his interpretation, the two have a 'close reciprocal relationship' in Burke's thought. See his *Edmund Burke: The Enlightenment and Revolution*, p. 11. This interpretation prevents Stanlis from seeing the critical historical shift from common law to natural law in the impeachment trial, and the role it fulfilled in Burke's discursive construction of empire.

[49] Holdsworth, *A History of English Law*, pp. 330–583.

of building empire, and also particular claims about rights deriving from specific British territorial and municipal laws.

In the context of England, where the common law applied only to Englishmen, it was possible for legal scholars like Blackstone to argue for the compatibility of universal principles implicit in both common law and natural law jurisprudence, and to attempt to ground English common law in natural law and what he called the 'eternal principles of justice'.[50] However, in contrast, in the emerging Eastern empire, where the real challenge was determining the extent to which English common law and the rights that derived from it were universal and could be applicable to an alien people, it was the conflict and clash between the principles of universality and particularity in common law that had acquired critical importance. The central question was, could the people of India make an equal and universal claim with British subjects to the rights deriving from the principles implicit in common law, or was common law a particular territorial system of laws and procedures that only Englishmen, who had carried it with them to the colonies, could claim as their common inheritance?

The collective assertion of Englishmen in eighteenth-century India had been that the rights deriving from the substantive and procedural elements of common law was a particular English inheritance to which they had an exclusive right. Thus, in cases, for example, in which the Company's servants were accused of committing crimes against 'natives', they rejected the authority of 'native judges' in indigenous courts to try them and claimed that they had the special right to be tried by a jury of peers (that is, Englishmen) in an English court, a right granted exclusively to them by common law and not to indigenous people. This made it impossible to prosecute Company servants and Englishmen in general who had committed crimes against Indians.[51] Although the

---

[50] Blackstone maintained that there was a root connection between natural law and common law. 'For [God] has so intimately connected, so inseparably interwoven the laws of eternal justice with the happiness of each individual, that the latter cannot be attained but by observing the former ... The law of nature, being coeval with mankind and dictated by God himself, is of course superior in obligation to any other ... [No] human laws are of any validity, if contrary to this and such of them as are valid derive all their force, and all their authority ... from this original.' See Blackstone, *Commentaries on the Laws of England*, pp. 40–1.

[51] Setalvad, *The Rise of the Common Law*, pp. 1–62.

Supreme Court instituted by the Regulating Act of 1773 tried to remedy the fundamental injustice of the situation by introducing procedural principles of equality, making it possible for Indians to bring cases against the British, yet it failed to establish equality before the law as a universal principle in India, primarily because its jurisdiction did not extend to the courts in the provinces outside the Presidency town, over which the Governor-General and council had authority. Also, its attempt to introduce substantive elements of English common law (particularly in criminal cases) in India, where native systems of law already held sway made it unpopular with the people of India and was criticized by Burke himself as an unwarranted imposition on the colonized.[52] Thus, the claims by Englishmen in India to exclusive rights based on the procedural and substantive elements of common law continued well into the nineteenth century, depriving the people of India of any grounds on which they could claim impartial justice against the crimes of the colonizing English.

In contrast to the earlier British Empire in America, where the colonists, being largely English, had been able to claim the rights of Englishmen and make common law jurisprudence the source of impartial justice; in the case of India, the Indian population could not make any such claims, as the protections of English common law did not extend to them.[53] Thus, it was the inadequacy of common law jurisprudence as a substantive system of British laws to serve the needs of the newly emerging imperial formation in the East that made it necessary for Burke to privilege the discourse of natural law in this trial. In order to give the people of India an equal claim to justice with Englishmen, and make it possible to indict Warren Hastings and the East India Company's servants for their crimes against an alien population, it was imperative to turn from common law to the principles of natural law as a higher system of

---

[52] Speech on Bengal Judicature Bill in Parliament, 27 June 1781 in *Writings and Speeches*, pp. 140–2.

[53] This is why, in America, efforts by people like James Otis to ground colonial rights in natural law did not succeed. Colonists preferred to resort to the much stronger and more easily defended argument that they were protected by English common law. In making this argument, they excluded non-British inhabitants of North America such as slaves and native Americans from the claim to equal rights. See Otis, 'The Rights of the British Colonies Asserted and Proved', pp. 409–82. Also see Shannon, *Indians and Colonists*, p. 99.

law, that, in so far as it was supranational, could be the source of impartial justice for both colonizer and colonized.

It was to found the discourse of empire in the East on a deterritorialized notion of justice, humanity, and equity that Burke brought into play two synonymous notions of natural law and the law of nations, which not only had precedence over all positive/ municipal laws, but, in fact, constituted the ground on which the latter had to be justified. It was the conceptual split between the discourse of natural law and that of municipal law, that cracked open the space for a critical juridical discourse on arbitrary colonial practices, and allowed Burke to strategically deploy the discourse of natural law to reign in the discourse of sovereign arbitrary will and claims about the extra-legal nature of war, on which Hastings' defence had been based.

Natural law, in its modern form, was first comprehensively articulated by Hugo Grotius in the early seventeenth century precisely to limit the violence and plunder associated with the unlimited nature of war, at a time of incessant wars between nations, particularly in the context of colonial expansion.[54] The question that Grotius was trying to answer was whether nations were justified in waging wars on other nations, killing their people, and pillaging their wealth with impunity, or if there were limits to how far nations could go, even in war, and whether aliens had rights in war. Grotius' answer in no uncertain terms was that there were limits to what could and could not be done in a war, that wars needed to be justified.[55]

Grotius' most important achievement was the characterization of war in terms of justice, as just and unjust wars, whereby he brought the phenomenon of war within the range of the discourse of jurisprudence. War was no more the result of a total breakdown of the legal and the judicial, but could even be thought of as its

---

[54] Grotius, *On the Law of War and Peace, Three Books*. Also see Pufendorf, *The Law of Nature and Nations, Eight Books*, and de Vattel, *The Law of Nations, or, Principles of Law of Nature, Applied to the Conduct and Affairs of Nations and Sovereigns*. The idea of natural law had its beginning in Greek philosophy and was later taken up and transformed by the Roman Empire for its own purposes. Henry S. Maine gives a genealogy of the evolution of natural law from the ancient Greek philosophy through its modifications in the course of the Roman Empire in *Ancient Law: Its Connection with the Early History of Society and its Relation to Modern Ideas*, pp. 44–112.

[55] See the Prolegomena in Grotius, *On the Law of War and Peace*.

very extension and continuation, to the extent that it was a just war. To be characterized as just, wars had to fulfill certain criteria. Apart from the procedural requirement of a prior declaration, wars required just causes such as, self-defence and defence of property, and could not be fought simply for purposes of self-aggrandizement or plunder. Thus, Grotius set up a homology between war and judicial proceedings, thereby marking a break with all preceding discourse, in which war signified the moment of the dissolution of all laws with which one could judge actions.[56]

In making this argument, Grotius was challenging the existing discourse of sovereignty, founded on the writings of Bodin, in which war was the ultimate moment of the exercise of sovereignty, and any consideration of setting limits to war was a contradiction in terms.[57] Grotius, by bringing war within the domain of the discourse of justice, by the same token, brought sovereignty within its domain too. In making the concept of justice supranational and universal, the discourse of natural law made states initiating wars vulnerable to the charge of waging criminal wars, and therefore, under appropriate institutional conditions, indictable in a court of law. This opened up the space for a critical juridical discourse about war and its consequences to emerge.

In the event of the trial, Burke deployed the existing discourse of natural law to the colonial setting in India, thus creating a second strata of discourse from which colonial discourse articulated by the East India Company could be critiqued. Rejecting Hastings' claim that the wars that the Company had waged in India against native monarchs and people were a legitimate exercise of sovereign power against a habitually rebellious population, Burke deployed the discourse of natural law to argue that, on the contrary, it was Hastings and the Company's government that had waged criminal offensive wars against the people of India, leaving them no choice but to resist. Each case of rebellion that had broken out against the authority of the East India Company's government in India was provoked, Burke asserted, by the criminal policies, treaty violations and breach of trust, and violence perpetrated by Warren Hastings and the Company's government.

---

[56] Grotius, *On the Law of War and Peace*, p. 18.
[57] Bodin, *On Sovereignty: Four Chapters from the Six Books of the Commonwealth*, pp. 59–63.

The war against the Rohillas, in Burke's view, was one of the most flagrant examples of an unjust war waged against a peaceful people, for there was no proof that the latter had engaged in any acts of hostility or aggression against the Company or the King of Awadh, Nawab Shuja Dowla, with whom Hastings had entered into a criminal alliance for their extirpation. In the case of Benares, rebellion broke out when Hastings, in gross violation of the treaties and agreements of peace and friendship signed between the Company and the King, Chait Singh, guaranteeing the latter the protection of the East India Company on the payment of a regular tribute, not only attempted to criminally extort enormous bribes from him, but on his failure to pay, insulted and imprisoned the king, confiscated his property and tyrannically expelled him from those territories that he had held on the basis of repeated agreements with the Company. The 'Bloodshed, War and Confusion' that resulted from this 'unjust war,' Burke argued, was 'solely imputable to the Misconduct, Violence, Tyranny and culpable Improvidence of the said Warren Hastings.'[58] Finally, in Bengal, it was the exorbitant rents imposed by the Company's government on the peasants, and the cruel and inhumane methods deployed by their agents to extort payment, that ultimately resulted in unarmed rebellion in the districts of Rangpur and Dinajpur. In so far as all these rebellions were defensive and fought for the preservation of life and property, in Burke's opinion, they were just, legal, and legitimate.

In characterizing the widespread rebellions in India as just resistance, whose roots lay in the flagrant violation of treaties by the Company, Burke, while deploying the principles of natural law, was also marking a critical departure from earlier natural law theorists, who, until then, had debated the justice and injustice of wars primarily from the perspective of European colonizing states. The discourse of natural law had been developed in the period of expanding colonialism to govern relations between European states and to prevent wars between them, and many among the natural law writers had argued that the principles of natural law did not apply to nations and people lying outside Christian Europe, who, therefore, had no rights under natural law.[59] Even those natural law theorists who constructed rules that sought to

[58] Marshall, *Writings and Speeches*, p. 143.
[59] Tuck, *Rights of War and Peace*, pp. 40–6.

limit aggrandizement by European colonizers in the Americas and
Asia and wrote with sympathy about the rights of the colonized
(that is, the native Americans, in the American case) in the final
analysis, they too denied the 'natives' the absolute right to resist,
justifying the European acquisition of territory and property in
non-European lands on grounds of just war (if, for example, the
right of free passage and free missions were denied).[60]

In his speeches in the impeachment trial, Burke unequivocally
inserted into the history of natural law discourse and the domain
of just wars an alien and non-European colonized people's absolute
right to resistance against aggressive colonizing powers, whether
states or private companies. In so far as self-preservation was an
obligation imposed by nature, the colonized people, he argued, had
not just a right, but a duty to rebel against sovereign authority if
it was tyrannical. Asserting that the same Law of Nations prevails
in Asia as in Europe, Burke contended that the right of resistance
was not just a right reserved for the people of England and Europe,
but could be found to be a fundamental right written into the very
Constitution of Mughal rule in India. The Muslim ruler of India,
far from being arbitrary, had to be by the laws of the country 'a
protector of the person and property of the subjects and a right of
resistance is directly established by Law against him and even a duty
of resistance.'[61] Thus, if the people of India had resisted Hastings, in
so far as the right of resistance was written into their very laws, and
at the same time guaranteed by the universal law of nations and of
nature, their resistance was both legal and just.

In so far as Warren Hastings' discourse of sovereignty was
based on the will, Burke argued, it exceeded the domain of law,
and was, therefore, illegitimate and even criminal. For the idea of
the will in any form was a negation of the very idea of law. In sharp
contrast to continental political philosophy and jurisprudence of
sovereignty, which founded law variously on the notion of general
will and universal will, Burke deployed the discourse of natural

[60] Francisco de Vitoria was one natural law writer who had emphasized equality
between Christians and non-Christians in international law, in reference to the rights
of Indians in South America. See his *De Indis et de Iure Belli Relectiones*. However,
ultimately he justified the Spanish occupation and annexation of territory and the
subjugation of indigenous people on grounds of just war (if right of free passage and
free missions was denied).

[61] Marshall, *Writings and Speeches*, p. 275.

law to argue that any construction of laws, either on the basis of general will or metaphysical principles of reason was, by its very nature, illegitimate.[62] Man, in Burke's view, was not above law, but was always already subject to a preexistent law. As he asserted, 'man is born to be governed by law; and he that will substitute will in the place of it is an enemy to God.'[63] Insofar as Hastings had made his will the law, he had exceeded the bounds of legality, thus giving the people of India a natural right of resistance against his acts of aggression.

While arguing that the Mughal emperors were not arbitrary or despotic, Burke resorted to the discourse of natural law to contend, that even if some instances of arbitrary power could be found in Mughal history, all discourses of sovereignty based in the will were illegitimate. 'Those who give and those who receive arbitrary power are alike criminal, and there is no man but is bound to resist it to the best of his power, wherever it shall show its face to the world. Nothing but absolute impotence can justify men in not resisting it to the best of their power.'[64] Such a transfer of arbitrary power was a crime because 'no man (could) lawfully govern himself according to his own will, much less (could) one person be governed by the will of another.'[65]

The culmination of these just wars of resistance against Hastings and the Company's government, Burke was convinced, could be nothing but civil war, a state in which all bonds between the colonial government and the people would be broken, and the two parties would consider each other as enemies and acknowledge no common judge.[66] Such a state of affairs would surely imply the end of empire in the East as it had in the West. It was, therefore, imperative for the preservation of empire that a conceptual and institutional frame be constructed, that would provide for a just and impartial settlement of disputes between the new colonial rulers and their subjects and, thereby, foreclose the possibility of a recourse to arms. In opposition to the dyadic model of war in which the colonial

[62] Rousseau, 'On the Social Contract', p. 153; Hegel, *Elements of the Philosophy of Right*, pp. 54–5.
[63] Burke, *Speeches*, vol. 1, p. 101.
[64] Ibid.
[65] Ibid., p. 99.
[66] Vattel, *Law of Nations*, p. 542.

government and the people of India faced each other as enemies, a triadic model would have to be created in which the empire itself would occupy the third position of the judge, the position of justice, neutrality, and impartiality, and mete out necessary punishment to the perpetrators of crimes, even those committed by colonial rulers like Warren Hastings.

The American Revolution had clearly shown that the empire could not be maintained for long by the forcible subordination of the colony to Parliament and the municipal laws of the metropolis. Imperial justice, then, had to stand above the particular laws of different countries that formed the empire so that the empire and the nations within it would constitute a complex whole. In the new imperial discourse, the empire was not simply to imply a hierarchical relationship between nations, and the direct subordination of India to England. For it was not by subordinating the colonies to the laws of England, but precisely by deterritorializing the concept of justice from the soil of England and raising it above her national laws, laws of property, and rules of evidence that the discourse of the nation could be transformed into the discourse of empire.

The substantive elements of common law being municipal in nature were not adequate for imperial purposes, which had a larger and different field of operation. However, once the conceptual leap to natural law and imperial justice was made, the principles of common law jurisprudence once again came into play. The supremacy of the law over the will had been a rallying point for the Lords and the Commons for centuries in England in their struggle against the King, and had been an integral part of common law jurisprudence from Bracton through Coke to Blackstone.[67] The common law tradition in England identified customs, conventions, habitudes, etc. as the sources of law.

This (law) is a choice not of one day, or one set of people, not a tumultory and giddy choice; it is a deliberate election of ages and civilizations; it is a constitution made by what is ten thousand times better than choice, it is made by the peculiar circumstances, occasions, tempers, dispositions and moral, civil and social habitudes of the people, which disclose themselves only in a long space of time.[68]

---

[67] See Matthew Hale, *The History of the Common Law of England*; Maitland, *The Constitutional History of England: A Course of Lectures*; Holdsworth, *A History of English Law*.

[68] Burke, *The Works of the Right Honorable Edmund Burke*, pp. 146–7.

Placing himself in this tradition, Burke saw law not in terms of its deliberate construction by a process of philosophical reflection, or political decisions based on the notion of general will or the will of the monarch, but as immemorial custom that acquired its force and binding power from long usage. In Burke's view, laws could only be found and declared by political institutions like the parliament—'all human laws are, properly speaking, only declaratory.'[69]

The political implications of such an insistence on locating the source of law in longstanding customs was brought out by J.G.A. Pocock in his study on what he called 'the common law mind':

The attraction which the concept of the ancient constitution possessed for lawyers and parliamentarians ... Resided ... in its value as a purely negative argument. For a truly immemorial constitution could not be subject to a sovereign ... In an age when people's minds were becoming deeply, if dimly, imbued with the fear of some sort of sovereignty or absolutism, it must have satisfied many men's minds to be able to argue that the laws of the land were so ancient as to be the product of no one's will, and to appeal to the almost universally respected doctrine that law should be above will.[70]

Thus, a convergence took place in the trial between two independent traditions of jurisprudence—one, based on common law, and the other, based on natural law. On the one hand was the tradition of Brackton, Coke, Hooker, Blackstone, etc., and on the other Grotius, Pufendorf, and Vattel. One grew out of the historical struggle between the King and the Commons and developed along the idea of the supremacy of law, and the other, out of the necessity to rein in centuries of destructive wars between the nations of Europe. One developed as an exclusively national tradition. The other began as an international discourse intended to regulate international relations. However, what was common to both of them, and what made their convergence in Burke's discourse possible, was their common goal to set limits to the will of the sovereign, by locating the law in a 'time out of mind' rather than in the legislative command of the sovereign.

---

[69] Edmund Burke, *Works*, vol. 6, p. 145.
[70] Pocock, *The Ancient Constitution and the Feudal Law: A Study of English Thought in the Seventeenth Century*, p. 51.

THE COLONIAL AND THE IMPERIAL

Towards the Creation of a Supranational Tribunal

While recourse to natural law provided Burke with a supranational and deterritorialized discourse of justice, it was essential that this discourse be grounded in an institutional site that was not tied down by the discourse of national interests. There was a crucial antinomy between the conceptual and the institutional at the very heart of natural law theory, which, while constructing a discourse of universal justice over and above national interests, was unable to conceive of an institution that could enforce natural law against the will of individual sovereigns. The imperative of judicial neutrality and impartiality, that was fundamental to the jurisprudence of natural law, was rendered ineffective by the fact that the enforcement of justice was left by these theorists in the hands of national sovereigns, and thus defeated the very purpose for which the theory was developed in the first place. In practice, the international order as it had come to be constructed after the Treaty of Westphalia was predicated on the sovereignty of individual states and the sanctity of pacts and treaties. This antinomy of the institutional and the conceptual was noted by Kant in his 'Perpetual Peace', in which he objected to the idea of just wars, precisely on the ground that the absence of a suprastate legal body, which could take decisions in an impartial and neutral way, defeated the idea of just wars. In the absence of such a body, with clear rules and fixed procedures of taking decisions, any claim in the name of justice appeared voluntaristic, and, therefore, lost its required legitimacy.[71] This debilitating antinomy between the conceptual and the institutional had plagued natural law theory for many decades, and many treatises had been written on how it could be resolved.[72]

Burke sought to resolve this antinomy in the trial by grounding the imperial discourse of justice in the institution of the House of Lords in its judicial capacity centered on the King as imperial judge. For Burke, the King's role in the empire was to be not that of a national legislator but rather of a supreme impartial arbiter in all conflicts between the colonizers and the colonized. It was not the

[71] Kant, 'Perpetual Peace, A Philosophical Sketch', pp. 102–5.

[72] Liebniz, *Political Writings*, pp. 165–83. The only other natural law theorist to envision an ad hoc supranational authority capable of conducting collective sanctions against lawbreaking nations was Emmerich de Vattel. See his *Law of Nations*, p. 154.

will of the sovereign but rather his justice based on natural law that would hold the empire together. The King's judgments on all imperial matters were to derive their neutrality and impartiality from being based not on national laws reflective of narrow and parochial interests but rather on a pre-existing universal natural law grounded in the idea of the freedom of all. In so far as natural law stood above the King himself, he was as much subject to it as the people over whom he ruled.

To understand why Burke saw the King in the House of Lords as the only institution in England capable of performing the role of a supranational tribunal with regard to empire, it would be appropriate to look briefly at its role in British history.[73] In the course of British history, the House of Lords had come to acquire a unique position as an institution in which politics, even at the highest level, had been brought under the gaze of what Burke called 'Supreme Royal Justice,' not just in the domestic arena but also with respect to the empire.[74] This role derived from its historical position as the council of the Crown, who was both the ultimate source of justice within the realm (subjects had the right to appeal to his mercy and sense of equity when they felt that the

---

[73] British historiography has in the past payed little attention to the critical role of the House of Lords and the Crown in the creation and preservation of empire. This neglect can be attributed to what David Armitage has called the 'persistent reluctance of British historians to incorporate the Empire into the history of Britain.' See Armitage, *Ideological Origins of the British Empire*, p. 13. Also see Burton, 'Who needs the nation? Interrogating "British history"', pp. 137–53. British historians have assumed a separation between the British nation that is seen as domestic, and the empire that is viewed as external to the nation, and have either completely ignored the empire in their analysis of the growth of the British nation, or assumed that intellectual, political, and institutional developments in England occurred independently of empire and were not in any significant way affected by its existence. So that while the British state did formulate policies for its imperial possessions, it was not in any way seen to be constituted by empire. As P.J. Marshall put it, 'the needs of empire led to no structural reform of the British state. It developed on its own with little regard to what was happening in the empire.' See Marshall, 'Imperial Britain', pp. 382–3. Thus, while the role of institutions like the Crown, the Privy Council, the House of Lords, or the House Commons, has been studied exhaustively in relation to English politics, little is known about how these institutions responded to imperial needs or indeed of any attempts at reconstructing or realigning these institutions in terms of an empire.

[74] Edmund Burke's speech on Opening of Impeachment, 15 February 1788 in *Writings and Speeches*, vol. VI, p. 282.

courts of common law had failed them) and the supreme arbiter of justice in the empire.[75]

The House of Lords, as Turberville described it, was different from the House of Commons, in that it was a law-maker by two different methods—by the process of passing bills, which it shared with the Commons, and also by the process of interpreting the laws of the land as the supreme court of the land. [76] Commenting on what he called 'the union of the judicial and political character' in the House of Lords, Macaulay, the renowned historian of England, pointed out that it was 'not a mere accidental union.' 'The fact is,' he argued, 'not only that a Judge may be made a Peer, but that all the Peers, as Peers, are necessarily Judges ... The Supreme Court of the realm is a great political assembly; that to this assembly go up all appeals from all Courts of equity and law in this country, from the Courts in Ireland and Scotland.'[77]

As the highest court of appeal for Ireland and Scotland (which, together with England, formed part of the British imperial formation since the seventeenth century, as David Armitage has pointed out), the King in the House of Lords was already historically placed in the position of an supranational tribunal that was required to rise above narrow English national interests and play the role of an impartial judge in cases involving the conflicting interests of England, Scotland, and Ireland. [78] The Privy Council (earlier the King's Council and composed of members of the House of Lords) was responsible for addressing imperial appeals from all the dominions of the Crown, excepting Great Britain and Ireland.[79] This imperial role already placed the Crown and the

---

[75] For an extensive discussion of the relation between law and equity, and the Crown's importance as the source of justice as equity, see Chapter 2.

[76] Turberville, *The House of Lords in the XVIIIth Century*, p. 10.

[77] *Hansard's Parliamentary Debates*, p. 999.

[78] Armitage, *Ideological Origins of the British Empire*, p. 7; Holdsworth, *History of English Law*, vol. XI, pp. 6 and 26.

[79] Pike, *A Constitutional History of the House of Lords from Original Sources*, p. 308. The difference between the institutions of the House of Lords and the Privy Council was that while the House of Lords was a judicial body that included peers representing Ireland and Scotland, the Privy Council was a royal council, adjudicating on behalf of the Crown. The Privy Council's 'judgment' was more in the nature of a recommendation on which the Crown made the final decision. Also, a clear hierarchy was instituted between these two courts, with the Privy Council serving as the ultimate court of appeal for the colonies, while appeals from the

House of Lords in an ambivalent position in which any narrow consideration of national interests could be construed as a betrayal of imperial trust and responsibility, as it was in the American Revolution. Significantly, when the British Parliament had asserted its legislative authority over the American colonies, the colonists had claimed that what bound them to England was their loyalty and allegiance to the Crown, and not any form of subservience to the House of Commons.[80] By emphasizing the juridical role of the King and the Lords and dissociating them from any legislative role with respect to Empire, Burke was in fact seeking to realign British institutions in accordance with one of the most important lessons of the American Revolution—the need for a purely supranational institution that would stand above the narrow national interests of Britain and serve the needs of the Empire as a whole.

What made the institution of the King in the House of Lords particularly suited, in Burke's view, to take on the role of a supranational tribunal with respect to the empire was that, in so far as its members were not elected, it was not a representative body, having in Blackstone's words 'neither the same interests, nor the same passions as popular assemblies.'[81] So that, it was always in a position, unlike the House of Commons, to dissociate itself from popular nationalism and the discourse of national interests, and could, therefore, be deployed as the site for a deterritorialized discourse of imperial justice.[82] The unique ability of the British

---

United Kingdom itself were heard only by the House of Lords and were not subject to the jurisdiction of the Privy Council. See Swinfen, *Imperial Appeal: The Debate on the Appeal to the Privy Council, 1833–1986*, pp. 1–21.

[80] For the King's imperial role see Holdsworth, *History of English Law*, vol. X, pp. 340–76. Also see Pocock, 'Political thought in the English-speaking Atlantic, 1760–1790: The Imperial Crisis', p. 262.

[81] Blackstone, *Commentaries*, Vol. IV, Ch. 19: 258.

[82] The independence of the House of Lords has been noted by the foremost constitutional scholars of England. As Walter Bagehot noted, 'the House of Lords was more independent than the House of Commons because, having "no consituency to fear or wheedle", it was best placed to form disinterested judgements.' Walter Bagehot, *The English Constitution and Other Political Essays*, p. 180. Historians of the House of Lords have commented on the fundamental role that the upper House was seen to play in the mixed and balanced government of the eighteenth century by serving as the 'equipoise of the constitution.' See Weston, *English Constitutional Theory and the House of Lords, 1556–1832*, pp. 1–8; Turberville, *The House of Lords in the XVIIIth Century*, p. 33; McCahill, *Order and Equipoise: The Peerage and the House of Lords, 1783–1806*, pp. 12–38.

Parliament to appear in two configurations—one, at ordinary times when it played a legislative role, and the other, during times of impeachment, when the two Houses of Parliament split themselves into two institutional and enunciative personae, the House of Commons taking on the role of the accuser/pleader, and the House of Lords that of the impartial judge—allowed a possible discursive reconfiguration of English political institutions in reference to the newly emerging empire, so that, while the House of Lords with the King at its head could take on the position of impartial and neutral judge, the House of Commons could occupy the role of the petitioner/pleader on behalf of the colony, setting aside their respective legislative roles.[83]

The addressee of this imperial discourse of justice was the enunciative persona of an impartial judge. The institutional shift from a legislative assembly to a court of judicature was rendered essential, Burke told the Lords, because the House of Commons as an institution had failed to rise above the idea of national interests, which overdetermined its proceedings, and develop a comprehensive discourse of empire, thus rendering imperative 'the plenary justice'[84] of the House of Lords. Burke, therefore, reminded the Lords of this absolutely essential imperative of impartiality and neutrality:

It is feared that partiality may lurk and nestle in the abuse of our forms of proceeding. It is necessary, therefore, that nothing in that proceeding should appear to mark the slightest trace, should betray the faintest odour, of chicane. God forbid that when you try the most serious of all causes, that *when you try the cause of Asia in the presence of Europe, there should be the least suspicion that a narrow partiality utterly destructive of justice* should so guide us, that a British subject in power should appear

---

[83] Charles Howard McIlwain points out that Parliament as an institution itself developed as a judicial body, a high court, and it was only later in its history that the functions of adjudication and legislation were separated, with the House of Commons becoming primarily a legislative body, and the House of Lords continuing to have both a legislative and an adjudicative role. See his *The High Court of Parliament and its Supremacy: An Historical Essay on the Boundaries between Legislation and Adjudication in England.* This historical role made it possible in Burke's view for the Parliament to split itself into two judicial roles with respect to empire, the House of Commons taking on the role of a lawyer and the House of Lords taking on the role of an impartial judge.

[84] Burke, *Speeches*, vol. 1, p. 19.

in substance to possess rights which are denied to the humble allies, to the attached dependents of this kingdom (emphasis mine).[85]

In this discourse, the empire was to stand above the governments, both in England and in India, in its impartiality. The complex whole that was to comprise the empire was to be triadic, in the sense that the empire would emerge as the third person, standing above and in-between the two parties—the two nations, England and India. The space of impartiality was to be constituted in the discursive position of the third person, the judge.

What is striking about this argument for the displacement of the legislative by the judicial in the case of India is the sharp contrast with the American case, in which Parliament even went to war with the American colonies to assert its rights to exercise parliamentary sovereignty over America. J.G.A. Pocock has argued that the heart of the American problem for Britain had been less the maintenance of imperial control than the preservation of essentially English institutions, particularly the unity of the Crown and Parliament, which the colonists were calling into question by claiming allegiance to the Crown, but not to the legislative authority of the House of Commons. In the end, he contended, Britain preferred to lose her American provinces rather than modify her political institutions to accommodate them, for to give up on the unity of the Crown in Parliament was to give up on the idea and practice of liberty itself, which in British history had come to be indelibly tied to the existence of this institution.[86]

It was in this historical context of the loss of the American colonies that Burke sought to convince the political establishment in England that the preservation of empire in the east need not necessarily imply the repudiation of existing British institutions. Rather, the only way to preserve empire without giving up on liberty at home, and at the same time preventing rebellion in the colonies and ensuring that the rights of the colonized were preserved, would be to foreground the juridical dimension of the existing institutions of Parliament with respect to empire, and to create a confederation tied not by legislative subordination to the

---

[85] Burke, *Speeches*, vol. 1, p. 17.

[86] Pocock, 'Political thought in the English-speaking Atlantic, 1760–1790: The Imperial Crisis', pp. 246–82.

House of Commons, but by a judicial attachment to the Crown and the House of Lords.[87]

Whereas the American war was fought in the name of the sovereignty of Parliament, the possibility of such a war in the East was sought to be preempted by Burke through a judicial reconfiguration of English political institutions and the construction of a discourse of imperial justice in terms of natural law. Burke, who ruled out the viability of a judicial intervention in the case of America, spent fourteen years developing a comprehensive judicial discourse to situate India in the larger framework of the British Empire. Burke, the legislator (in the case of America) appeared in the enunciative persona of a lawyer to articulate the new imperial discourse of justice, while the people of Indian emerged, not as a people asserting their freedom, but as supplicants to justice at the bar of the House of Lords. 'Exiled and undone princes, extensive tribes, suffering nations, infinite descriptions of men, different in language, in manners and in rites—men separated by every barrier of nature from you, by the providence of God are blended in one common cause and are now become supplicants at your Bar.'[88]

This was a decisive moment in the history of empire, when, even as one phase of the British Empire had drawn to a close in America, the second phase was beginning to take shape, calling for a fundamental realignment of the highest political institutions in England in terms of its relationship with its new colonies.[89]

The institution of the House of Lords, Burke argued, needed to be constituted as that liminal space, that narrow space of exteriority

---

[87] Burke's proposition of reconstituting the House of Lords as a supranational tribunal, while not implemented in Britain in the eighteenth century, became a critical issue for the empire in the late nineteenth and early twentieth centuries. It was in this period that nationalists in Australia, Canada, and other colonies demanded that the distinction between the Privy Council and the House of Lords be abolished and a common imperial tribunal be created, that would include colonial representatives and render judgments impartially on appeals from the courts of all commonwealth countries including the United Kingdom itself. See Swinfen, *Imperial Appeal*, pp. 1–112, 178–218.

[88] Burke, *Speeches*, vol. 1, p. 16.

[89] Burke saw a clear connection between the loss of the American colonies and the need for preserving empire in the East. As early as 1777, criticizing the policies of the English Government and the East India Company in India, he writes 'Some people are great lovers of uniformity—they are not satisfied with a rebellion in the West. They must have one in the East: They are not satisfied with losing one Empire—they must lose another.' See Marshall, *Writings and Speeches*, vol. 5, p. 40.

outside the state, where politics and the state itself would be brought under the gaze of justice, or what Burke called state morality. Burke defined the nature of this institution and its jurisdiction: 'For this great end your lordships are invested with great and plenary powers: but you do not supersede, you do not annihilate, any subordinate jurisdiction; on the contrary, you are auxiliary and supplemental to them all.'[90] This supplemental discourse was to be the discourse of empire founded on the notion of state morality, and located in the House of Lords in its judicial aspect.

The discursive and institutional status that Burke gave to the judiciary found its sharpest formulation in his observations on the Revolution in France. In the course of criticizing the revolutionary government in France for abolishing the French *parlement*, which was an autonomous institution functioning as the highest court of appeal, and for bringing the judicature under the direct control of the national assembly in accordance with Rousseau's idea of the supremacy of the legislative 'general will', Burke argued:

Whatever is supreme in a state ought to have, as much as possible, its judicial authority so constituted as not only not to depend upon it, but in some sort to balance it. It ought to give a security to its justice against its power. It ought to make its *judicature*, as it were, something *exterior to the state* (emphasis mine).[91]

In sharp contrast to general political theory, that identified the judiciary as one of the three organs of the state, the legislature and the executive being the other two, Burke located the judicature not just exterior to the state, but as a balance against the power of the state.[92] What he brought out were two sets of antinomies—the conceptual antinomy between justice and power, and the institutional antinomy between the judicature and the state. In the Burkean scheme, justice and power were exclusive categories that had to be distinguished from contemporary political and constitutional phrases like judicial power. In Burkean discourse, power meant the power to dominate, and was synonymous with political domination. Since the concept of justice and the institution of the judicature were deployed against political

---

[90] Ibid., p. 11.

[91] Burke, *Reflections on the Revolution in France*, p. 242.

[92] Burke, *Speeches*, vol. 1, p. 58.

domination, they were exterior to the domain of power.[93] Justice thus was articulated in its critical difference from the power of the state.

By discursively situating the judicature exterior to the state, Burke's discourse sought to create a split between the idea of empire and England as a nation, where the empire would emerge as a supranational juridical formation, 'a refuge of afflicted nations' with its accompanying discourse of what he variously called 'superintending,' 'supplemental,' or 'imperial justice'.[94]

In discursively linking the idea of empire in India with a supranational deterritorialized discourse of justice in the impeachment trial of Warren Hastings, Edmund Burke proposed a radical alternative both to the dominant discourse of colonial sovereignty in eighteenth-century England based on notions of conquest and domination of the colonized, and the complementary discourse of the law of nations that had come to be predicated after the Treaty of Westphalia on the recognition of the absolute sovereignty of individual states. While the discourse of natural law had attempted to set limits to colonial aggrandizement by emphasizing the universal and transcendent principles of justice and equity, it too in the final analysis had come to be subordinated over time to the principle of national sovereignty and national interests of states.

It was clear to Burke that the discourse of international law grounded as it was on the discourse of national interests was proving to be not only inadequate, but, in fact, fatal to the future of empire in the East. The ruthless appropriation of property and wealth in the colonies that this discourse had inevitably given rise to was not only corrupting the political system in England and destabilizing the European balance of power as a whole, but was also provoking widespread resistance and rebellions on the part of the colonized in India, threatening the very existence of empire. If the empire was to be saved in the face of this growing resistance, it was imperative, in Burke's view, that the imperial authority recognize the rights of

---

[93] This explains why Burke refused to interpret the English Revolution of 1688 in political terms as a popular revolution which brought people to political power, but rather interpreted it in juridical terms as an attempt at the restoration of the Constitution that had been violated by the Crown. Burke, *Reflections on the Revolution in France*, p. 35. Also see Stanlis, *Edmund Burke: The Enlightenment and the Revolution*, pp. 216–50.

[94] Marshall, *Writings and Speeches*, vol. 7, p. 694; Burke, *Speeches*, vol. 1, pp. 58, 11, 17.

the colonized, particularly their rights of 'just resistance' against the oppression and violence of the colonial regime, and take steps to prevent its recurrence in the future. However, the crucial question that inevitably arose from such a recognition was, on what legal grounds could the empire continue to be justified and legitimized, and what steps could be taken to preserve the empire against threat of civil war and ultimate dissolution of all bonds between the rulers and the ruled?

Burke's proposal was that the empire becomes the site of a deterritorialized, universal justice that would rise above the national interests of Britain and serve as an impartial arbiter between the English colonial state in India and the colonized Indian society. The construction of this triadic discourse of supranational imperial justice was predicated on the possibility, that the imperial formation could split itself three ways into the enunciative personae of the plaintiff, the defendant, and the impartial judge. With the people of India as the plaintiff and the East India Company's Government as the defendant, the House of Lords in its judicial capacity centered on the King as impartial judge could take on the role of a supranational tribunal, a fair and impartial arbiter that would address the grievances and complaints of the colonized society against the colonizing state. This triadic imperial juridical formation, grounded on these three institutional and enunciative personae, would be constructed in opposition to a dyadic colonial political formation, in which the East India Company's government saw itself locked in perpetual conflict with its other, the 'rebellious population' of India. By deterritorializing the notions of law and justice from it national territorial moorings, the imperial discourse of justice would make possible the internalization of otherwise potentially violent conflicts and even civil war, while transforming them into juridical discursive conflicts between the colonized society as plaintiff and the English colonial state in India as defendant. In this model, colonial state power in India would no longer be the sole source of its own legitimacy, but would have to accede to the ultimate juridical sovereignty of the imperial.

The House of Lords, however, eventually acquitted Hastings on all counts in April 1795, thus failing in this case to rise, as Burke has proposed, beyond partiality and national interests to the position of a deterritorialized, imperial tribunal. The question that arises from this is, does this verdict diminish the historical significance of the trial and the Burkean discourse of juridical imperial sovereignty? Considering the nature of the case and its historical implications that unfolded over the next two centuries, I would argue that the question of Hastings' conviction or acquittal was of marginal importance to what the trial accomplished in a larger sense.

The crucial historical significance of Burke's efforts in the impeachment trial lies in that they were not aimed simply at seeking a judicial decision on the facts of Hastings' crimes in India. Indeed, Burke was aware even as he prosecuted the case, that the ultimate verdict on the facts of the case could go in Hastings' favor, in part due to the corruption and weakness of the judges, and in part due to what some judges could perceive as a lack of sufficient evidence from the standards of common law.[95] Thus, even as he sought to create 'a train of clear solid juridical Evidence, fit to establish the facts,' what was at stake for Burke in the larger sense was to lay out in the event of the trial the legal and moral parameters of a new discourse of empire for the future.[96] Insofar as there was no preexisting legal or political consensus, let alone a set of established laws, on the rights of an alien people in the colony against the arbitrary rule of the colonial state, the trial was much more than a regular judicial event. It was also a legislative moment in the history of British Empire in India, in which a framework and discourse of relevant laws and principles were for the first time sought to be articulated, that would make the colonial regime in India legally accountable for its policies and actions in the colony.

From this perspective, the very articulation of this discourse of imperial sovereignty and alien rights in the course of the trial was an event of enormous historical significance for the future of empire. Indeed, so effective were Burke's speeches in the trial in delegitimizing the colonial state in India, that it would take all the ingenuity of a James Mill and a John Stuart Mill, the founding and leading minds of British liberalism to mount a rescue operation in the nineteenth century to restore legitimacy and supremacy to the colonial state in India once again.[97] It was in the process of

[95] Edmund Burke to Henry Addington (8 January 1795) in McDowell, (ed.), *The Correspondence of Edmund Burke*, p. 110.

[96] Ibid.

[97] The major book in this regard was James Mill's *The History of British India* published in 1820 that became a textbook for British administrators in India in the nineteenth century and was to be the intellectual foundation of British colonialism.

contesting the Burkean discourse of empire that was firmly anchored in legal and moral principles, that James Mill was to construct an alternative discourse of empire based on the notion of a hierarchy of civilizations. In contrast to Burkean discourse that granted the colonial state in India legitimacy on the basis of how it carried out its legal and moral responsibilities towards the colonized society as the other, in Mill's discourse, the superiority of British civilization alone was to be established as a self-legitimating and self-evident principle that needed no further legal and moral arguments.

In the next chapter, I will show how the difference between the colonial and the imperial constructed in course of the impeachment trial came to play itself out in India in the late eighteenth century in the enduring conflict between the British East India Company's administration in India and the Supreme Court set up in Calcutta under the aegis of the British Parliament. I will argue that the discourse of imperial justice constructed in the impeachment trial had profound historical implications for the structure of British colonial political formation in India and the conceptual and institutional framework of empire in the eighteenth and nineteenth centuries.

See Mill, *The History of British India*. It is one of the ironies of history that while Burke, who has been characterized as a leading conservative thinker, sought to defend the rights of Indians against the arbitrariness of the colonial state, it was leading liberal intellectuals like James Mill and John Stuart Mill, who resolutely defended the absolutist nature of the East India Company's Government. This goes to prove how misleading a decontextualized and uncritical use of terms like 'conservative' and 'liberal' could be. For further discussion of the relationship between liberal thought and empire, see Parekh, 'Decolonizing Liberalism', pp. 85–103 and Uday Singh Mehta, *Liberalism and Empire*, pp. 46–114.

2

CONFLICT OF SOVEREIGNTY

The Judiciary, the Executive, and the Emergence of
the Indian Legislative Council as a Court of Law

In 1828 Raja Rammohan Roy, in an appeal to the King-in-Council,
made an observation that pointed to the critical importance of
the Supreme Court in the determination of sovereignty in India.

The idea of possession of absolute power and perfection is evidently not
necessary to the stability of the British Government in India since Your
Majesty's faithful subjects are accustomed to seeing private individuals
citing the government before the Supreme Court where the justice of
their acts is fearlessly impugned, and after the necessary evidence being
produced and due investigation made, the judgment not infrequently given
against the government, the judge not feeling himself restrained from
passing just sentence by any fear of the government being thereby brought
into contempt.[1]

The British Government in India, Roy claimed, was not an absolute
power, but one that was accountable to an external authority,
the Supreme Court, set up by the British King-in-Parliament in
1774, which would hear the grievances of the subjects and punish

---

[1] Rammohan Roy, 'Appeal to the King in Council on the Freedom of the Press' p.
110. For Rammohan Roy's thought see Bimanbehari Majumdar, *History of Indian
Social and Political Ideas from Rammohan to Dayananda*; Bruce Robertson, *Raja
Rammohan Roy: The Father of Modern India*; V.C. Joshi, (ed.), *Rammohan Roy and
the Process of Modernization in India*; Hirendranath Mukerjee, *Indian Renaissance
and Raja Rammohun Roy*. For an interesting recent article on Rammohan Roy's use
of the law 'as the new lever of power' to bring about changes in social customs and
habits see Anindita Mukhopadhyay, 'Rammohun Roy and the Conceptual History
of Governance and Law', pp. 876–90.

government officials for illegal acts. In Rammohan Roy's view, it was on this assurance that the stability of the British Empire rested. What is striking about Roy's observation is that not only did he directly contrast the notion of power with the notion of justice, but also placed imperial sovereignty in the idea of justice. Roy saw the question of sovereignty both in terms of an institution—the Supreme Court—and a category—imperial justice.

The dialectic of the colonial as the discourse and practice of power and governance, and the imperial as the discourse and practice of justice that I discussed in Chapter 1 took the institutional form in India of a conflict between the East India Company's government and the Supreme Court. It unfolded before the people of India as a grand spectacle in the Supreme Court where colonial power was subjected to public scrutiny and was forced to answer to imperial justice in the language of law. The figure at the centre of this spectacle was the English barrister who publicly critiqued and fearlessly questioned the government's authority in the name of justice, thus making the persona of the lawyer the most visible representative of the people against the power of government.[2] This spectacle of justice caught the imagination of Roy, as it did of many others in the nineteenth century. It is not surprising then that the Supreme Court as a theater of justice—and not the countless treatises on politics by the philosophers in the West—emerged as the primary historical source of much of Indian thinking about the state.

What gave the Supreme Court a critical position in the discourse of imperial justice was that it was located in a hierarchy of judicial institutions, at the apex of which stood the British House of Lords and the King, whose principal function was to hear the grievances of the people of India against the East India Company's administration and its officials. It is important to note that the appeal written by Roy was a petition to the British monarch articulating a specific

---

[2] It is important to note that the English barrister alone could plead in the Supreme Court at Calcutta. 'Native' lawyers could practice only in the Company's courts in the provinces. What made the Supreme Court distinctive and gave its proceedings the effect of a spectacle was that pleadings there were oral as opposed to written pleadings in the provinces. For a vivid description of the workings of the Supreme Court in Calcutta in the late eighteenth century from the point of view of a practicing attorney, see William Hickey, *Memoirs of William Hickey*. The only article-length work on the legal profession in the colonial period in India is Samuel Schmitthenner, 'The Development of the Legal Profession in India.'

grievance about the absence of freedom of the press under the East India Company's government in India. It assumed a crucial difference between the British Parliament and the Company's Government in India and was grounded in the hope that if the grievances of the people of India against the latter were lodged with the King-in-Council, that the King would inevitably render justice. In other words it was the existence of the King as impartial judge that made possible this critique of the East India Company's Government and grounded Roy's discourse in general.

It is important to note that the existence of a discourse of imperial justice in late eighteenth-century India did not mean the absence of power. In so far as power operates as much through discourse as through violence or coercion, it would be wrong to take literally the opposition of power and justice, and to see justice as lying entirely outside power, as anti-power. The conflict of colonial power and imperial justice could as easily be, and indeed was, made to operate as complementary forms of power. Roy continued in the same petition:

Public resentment cannot be transferred from the delinquents to the government itself while there is a prospect of remedy from the highest authorities; and should the highest in the country turn a deaf ear to all complaint, by forbidding all grievances to be ever mentioned, the spirit of loyalty is still kept alive by the hope of redress from the authorities in England. *The attachment of the natives of India must be as permanent as their confidence in the Honor and Justice of the British nation that is their last court of appeal next to Heaven.* But if they be prevented from making their real condition known in England, deprived of the hope of redress, they will consider the most peculiar excellence of the British Government as done away (emphasis mine).[3]

In this passage, Roy gave a glimpse of the strategic nature of the deployment of the discourse of justice: as long as there was the prospect of judicial 'remedy,' he contended, 'public resentment cannot be transferred from the delinquent to the government.' The theater of justice, in other words, provided a critical space in which much of the hostility against the colonial government could be fully vented, leaving the people of India still attached and loyal to the Empire. The resentment that might have erupted

---

[3] Rammohan Roy, 'Appeal to the King in Council on the Freedom of the Press'.

into violence against the colonial government could thereby be diverted into a labyrinth of discourse—the discourse of imperial justice.

The immense impact of this spectacle of justice in the Supreme Court on the public imagination in late eighteenth-century India was vastly disproportionate to its real effect on the working of the Company government. What Roy called the 'most peculiar excellence of the British Government' in fact consisted in its ability to split itself in India into two seemingly opposing visions of state that fascinated Indians, even as it trapped them. The struggle for independence from British rule that was to unfold in the twentieth century was in a way a narrative of India finding a way out of the labyrinth of the discourse of imperial justice.

In this chapter I explore the nature of the conflict between the colonial government and the Supreme Court in India that culminated in the founding of the first Legislative Council of India in 1853. Indeed, the Legislative Council owed its very origin to the efforts at resolving the enduring conflict between the colonial executive and the Supreme Court as an autonomous judiciary anchored in the figure of the King. Even as it functioned as a political institution, the Legislative Council, I contend, came to model itself—between 1853 and 1861—both in terms of its procedure and its telos or ultimate purpose— in the image of a British court of law. It was this newly constituted political institution of the Legislative Council that played a decisive role in the formation of a new juridico-political culture in late nineteenth-century India.

THE CONFLICT OF COLONIAL POWER AND IMPERIAL JUSTICE

The Supreme Court in Calcutta was established by Lord North's Regulating Act of 1773 in the British Parliament to restrain the colonial government's exercise of power in Bengal and to provide, in Burke's words, 'a strong and solid security for natives against the wrongs and oppressions of British residents in Bengal.'[4] The British East India Company that acquired the power of the de-facto sovereign of Bengal in 1757 had established its own system of courts in 1764 headed by the Sadr Adalats with jurisdiction over the entire province.[5] Placed under the direct authority of the Governor-

[4] Eric Stokes, *The English Utilitarians and India*, p. 2.

[5] For a comprehensive account of the East India Company's courts see Misra, *The*

General's Council—the chief executive and legislative body of the Company's government in India—these courts functioned as an arm and instrument of the executive without any judicial autonomy. In the event of a complaint against the Company's government, the people of Bengal had no recourse.[6] As narrated in the first chapter, the possession of absolute power by the Company's government in the first fifteen years of its rule in Bengal had led to widespread extortion and general oppression of the population by government functionaries. The introduction of the Supreme Court in Calcutta was intended to act as a check on the government's will and its ability to exercise power by subjecting it (the government) to the scrutiny of the Court, grounded in the authority of the King-in-Parliament.[7]

The jurisdiction of the newly established Supreme Court extended over all persons in Bengal, Bihar, and Orissa except the Governor-General and the members of his council. To maintain the autonomy of the Supreme Court from the colonial government in India, the judges were to be directly nominated and appointed by the English Crown, and not by the Court of Directors of the Company. The Court received the power and responsibility to prosecute offences committed by the officials of the government and

Judicial Administration of the East India Company in Bengal 1765–1782. Also see Morley, *The Administration of Justice in British India: Its Past History and Present State*.

[6] Significantly, in contrast to the Supreme Court where the Bar was extremely powerful, 'native' lawyers had very little power and independence in the provincial courts. The judge completely controlled the proceedings, deciding on both the material facts and the legal issues at stake. The lawyer's primary responsibility was to ensure the correctness of representations made to the court by his client. Thus the lawyer in the provincial court was reduced to being not an interpreter of law but a pleader for justice that depended to a large extent on the discretion of the judge. See Carrau, *The Rules of Practice of the Calcutta Sudder Court from 1793–1855*, p. 52. In sharp contrast to the Supreme Court, oral pleading was not allowed in the provincial courts. See Schmitthenner, 'The Development of the Legal Profession in India', p. 20. This foreclosed the possibility of the court being turned into a space for the public questioning of the government's authority. For the same reason, barristers from the Supreme Court were not allowed to plead in the provincial courts until 1846.

[7] For accounts of the Supreme Court's activities in India, see Setalvad, *The Rise of the Common Law*, pp. 1–62; Pandey, *Introduction of English Law into India: The Career of Elijah Impey in Bengal, 1774–1783*, pp.131–148; Robert Travers, *Ideology and Empire in Eighteenth-Century India: The British in Bengal*, pp. 181–206; Nasser Hussain, *The Jurisprudence of Emergency: Colonialism and the Rule of Law*, pp. 69–98; Lauren Benton, 'Colonial Law and Cultural Difference: Jurisdictional Politics and the Formation of the Colonial State', pp. 563–88.

generally to ensure that the Government's exercise of its power was in conformity with the spirit of the laws of England. In the event of a case against the Company, the Court had the power to issue summons even against the governor and the members of his council and to levy costs on the goods of the Company, if judgments went against the government. If deemed to be against the spirit of the laws in England, the Court had the right to veto laws passed by the Governor-General's Council. The Company, on the other hand, had permission to hire an attorney to defend it in the Supreme Court in actions brought against its officials.[8] All its servants, civil and military, were ordered to aid, assist, and obey the Supreme Court in all things and at all times. Appeals from the Supreme Court were to lie with the Privy Council in England.[9]

The Regulating Act, thus, laid the basis for an activist judiciary that, in so far as it was appointed by the King, was not only outside the authority of the East India Company's government in India, but by its very constitution, suspicious and hostile to its legislative and administrative authority, and eager to take on functional sovereignty in the colony. Armed with the power to disallow any regulation passed by the Governor-General and Council, the Supreme Court adopted an aggressive posture, actively deploying the discourse of justice to intervene in the administrative affairs of the Company, and demand accountability from its servants for their acts.[10]

Tensions emerged between the Supreme Court and the Company's administration within a few years of the Court's establishment, when it began to entertain suits brought by 'natives' against members of the provincial councils, the chief revenue and judicial bodies of the East India Company, which functioned under the authority of the Governor-General's Council, the final court of appeal. Refusing to recognize the authority of the company's judicial bodies to imprison 'natives' for defaults of revenue, the Court not only ordered the Council to pay damages to their accusers, but even had members of the Council arrested, when they failed to respond to its summons.

---

[8] Great Britain. House of Commons. 1804. *Reports on the Administration of Justice in the East Indies*, 1781–2, vol. 5, p. 63.

[9] Ibid., p. 67.

[10] See Derrett, 'Justice, Equity and Good Conscience', pp. 113–53. Also see Travers, *Ideology and Empire in Eighteenth-Century India*, pp. 181–206.

In the famous Patna cause, Nadarah Begum instituted an action of trespass in the Supreme Court against the judges (*qazis* and *muftis*) of the Patna provincial council (under the direct authority of the Governor-General's Council) for forcibly entering her house, for assaulting her servants and damaging her property in the course of enforcing a verdict against her. When the bailiff of the Supreme Court was sent to arrest the Company's judges for failing to respond to the summons of the Court, the Council was forced to post bail on their behalf. The Governor-General's Council also defended another suit instituted by Nadarah Begum against Ewan Law and other members of the Provincial Council at Patna. They were ordered the payment of 15,000 rupees as damages to Nadarah Begum.[11]

In a similar case, the Supreme Court, once again, had members of the Council arrested when they failed to respond to summons issued at the institution of a case for wrongful imprisonment by Kamaluddin, a revenue farmer who had defaulted on revenue payments to the Company. These cases became so numerous that members of the Governor-General's Council complained, in a letter to the Court of Directors in London, of the frequency with which farmers of revenue were escaping the 'just' demands of the government by seeking the 'protection' held out by the Supreme Court.

If we attempt to enforce our demands by confinement, a writ of Habeas Corpus immediately issues. The judges enter into the Merits of the Cause, declare our proceeding illegal, discharge the prisoner, and threaten our officers with fine and imprisonment if they presume to molest them.[12]

Despite these tensions the Governor-General's Council did resort occasionally to the Supreme Court for the opinion of the judges on points of law. On one crucial occasion, when John Clavering, a member of the Governor-General's Council, threatened to take over the garrison at Calcutta, oust Warren Hastings and assume, with the support of two other members of the Council—Colonel Monson and Philip Francis—the de facto position of the Governor-General, the Supreme Court was requested to give a judgment to bring

[11] Ibid., 4–15. See also Stephen, *The Story of Nuncomar and the Impeachment of Elijah Impey*, pp. 163–98.

[12] Extract of Minute from General Clavering, Colonel Monson and Mr Francis, dated Fort William, 21 November 1775 in *Reports on the Administration of Justice in India*, p. 90.

the conflict to a close, which it did in favour of Warren Hastings. Barwell, one of Hastings' supporters in the Council, stated in his evidence to the committee of the House of Commons, that if it had not been for the intervention of the judges, the power struggle in the Council would have seriously unsettled the Company's government in the colony.[13] Although Clavering and his supporters accepted the court's verdict this incident prompted them to write to the Court of Directors of the Company, requesting the appointment of an Advocate-General, who would apprise them of their rights, and ensure that they were safeguarded.

The insistence of the Supreme Court on the judicial principles of publicity and legal accountability was a continuous source of irritation. Complaining to the Court of Directors, the Governor-General in Council wrote:

The Declarations made by the Chief Justice from the Bench constitutes a precedent of the greatest consequence to the conduct of your affairs here ... According to the Doctrine delivered from the Bench, it is unlawful for your Governor and Council to refuse to produce in open court, any papers deposited in our Secretary's Office, whenever they shall be demanded by an Attorney as necessary for the information of the Court in any case depending before them. This Doctrine is general and indefinite ... It depends on the caprice or ignorance of any attorney to expose the transactions of your affairs in every branch and even your most secret instructions to us to the curiosity and comments of every by-stander in a public court, perhaps to the avowed enemies of the Company and nation.[14]

The existence of an activist judiciary claiming sovereignty in the colony combined with the increasing pressure in the British Parliament to whittle down the Company's power, indeed to even put an end to the Company's rule in India and incorporate the newly acquired territory as a national colony of Great Britain, were all seen as grave and imminent threats to the very existence of the Company's state in India. It was imperative under these conditions that the Company develop a parallel discourse of sovereignty that would bring legitimacy to its power and actions in India, and, at the same time prevent the Parliament and its primary instrument in India the Supreme Court from interfering in its efforts to profit from its activities in India.

[13] *Reports on the Administration of Justice*, p. 28.
[14] Ibid., p. 100.

This competing discourse was first articulated by John Day, the newly appointed Advocate-General of the East India Company in India, who advised the Governor-General's Council to openly resist the authority of the Supreme Court and question its jurisdiction in the provinces and over its revenue collectors on the basis of a new discourse that claimed sovereignty for the Council. Preservation of the state was the cornerstone of this discourse. Given that the Company's ability to collect revenue was the very life blood of the state in India, the argument went, any interference in its collection by the Court threatened the very existence of the state, including the structure of authority set up by the British Parliament in India. Therefore it had to be opposed: 'It was time to oppose any processes of the Court at the instant they operated to the prejudice of the revenue.'[15]

The *Cossijurah* case in 1778 brought these two contesting discourses of sovereignty to a dangerous confrontation, resulting in an armed showdown between the troops attached to the two institutions of the Governor-General's Council and the Supreme Court.[16] When Kashinath, a merchant at Calcutta and manager of Raja Soondernarain's zamindari of Cossijurah brought a suit of capias against the Raja in the Supreme Court, the Governor-General's Council, on the advice of the Advocate-General, sent notice to the Raja, that he was not under the jurisdiction of the Supreme Court and therefore not recognize its authority in any way.

This advice was based on the new interpretation given by the Advocate-General to the provision of the Regulating Act, which limited the jurisdiction of the Supreme Court to British subjects. In this interpretation, the 'native' zamindars in the provinces outside Calcutta were not subjects of the British Crown, but of the Mughal Emperor, and therefore did not come under the Court's jurisdiction. Only the Company as the *Dewan* or revenue collector—a power vested in them by the Mughal Emperor—had jurisdiction over them. The commander of the company's forces in Cossijurah was directed, in contravention of the requirements of the Regulating Act, not to render military assistance to the Supreme Court's officers under the Sheriff, but to report the case to the Council and await orders.

[15] Barwell in his evidence to the Select Committee of the House of Commons in 1782 reported Warren Hastings as declaring this in the Governor-General's Council. *Reports on the Administration of Justice*, p. 27.

[16] Ibid., pp. 22–6; Stephen, *The Story of Nuncomar*, pp. 209–20.

At the Raja's failure to respond to the summons of the Supreme Court's writ, the Sheriff was dispatched to Cossijurah to enforce a writ sequestering his property and possessions, and compelling his personal appearance in the Court, by force, if necessary. On hearing the news that the Sheriff's troops had entered the Raja's house and beaten and wounded his servants, the Governor-General immediately sent the Company's troops under Lieutenant-Colonel Ahmuty to defend the Raja, and confront and seize the Sheriff's officers. At the same time, the Governor-General also sent out a general notification to all zamindars of Bengal, Bihar, and Orissa, that not being subject to the jurisdiction of the Supreme Court, they should not appear, plead, or do any act that may amount to a recognition of the jurisdiction of the Supreme Court over them. In response, the Supreme Court issued attachments against William Swanston, Assistant at Midnapur, and Lieutenant Bomford for high contempt of court, for the part they played in the rescue of the property of the Raja of Cossijurah, and arrested North Naylor, attorney of the East India Company for contempt.

On a summons being served by the Supreme Court to the Governor-General in Council to answer to Kashinath Baboo on a plea of trespass, the Council articulated clearly its new discourse of sovereignty, openly declaring that the suits instituted against them by Kashinath was for acts done by them in their collective capacity as the Governor-General in Council. They asserted that their corporate acts as government of the Presidency, done in execution of the power vested in them by Parliament, were not cognizable in the Supreme Court of Justice and they were not answerable as individuals for the consequences of such acts. They gave a written declaration to the Supreme Court that they would not submit to any rule, process or judgment, or other Act, whatsoever of the Supreme Court in that suit, or any suit of the same nature, by which they may be made answerable to the Supreme Court as individuals, for the corporate acts of the Governor-General in Council, not cognizable by the Supreme Court.

The Governor-General in Council argued that any attempt to impose the authority of the Supreme Court and hold the government responsible in matters connected to the revenue, was a usurpation of the sovereignty of the East India Company. In a letter to the Court of Directors, 15 January 1776, the Council stated that:

It is plain, that the company's office of Dewan is annihilated; that the country government is subverted; and that any attempt on our part to exercise or support the powers of either, may involve us and our officers in the guilt and penalty of high treason; which Mr Justice Le Maistre ... expressly holds out in Terrorem to all the Company's servants, and others acting under our authority.[17]

While asserting its judicial sovereignty over the Company's government, the Supreme Court, in its turn, insisted on the difference between the public responsibilities of the Company's officials and their use of their official powers for private gain, actively prosecuted the officials of the East India Company, and claimed the right to review the proceedings of the Governor-General's Council and make these the ground for prosecution of members of the Council. Le Maistre, J declared that 'no true distinction in reason, in Law, or justice, can or ought to be made between the East India Company as a trading company and the East India Company as Dewan of these provinces.'[18] With respect to the management of the territorial revenue, he declared that according to the true interpretation of the Regulating Act, the control of the Governor-General in Council was not exclusive, but subject to the jurisdiction of the Supreme Court. It was equally penal, in his view, for the Company, or for those acting under it, to disobey the orders and mandatory process of the Supreme Court, in matters which merely concerned the revenues, as in any other matter whatsoever.[19]

Contrasting Visions of the State

The historic conflict between the Supreme Court and the Governor-General's Council that defined early colonial rule in India has been interpreted by contemporary writers and historians as primarily a clash of powerful personalities in an environment of insecurity and anarchy in the early days of the Company's rule. The positions that Warren Hastings, Philips Francis, Elijah Impey, John Hyde, and others took in this conflict are seen to be reflective of their mutual jealousies, and their hunger for power and profit in the new colony.[20] What this dominant historical interpretation fails

---

[17] *Reports on the Administration of Justice*, p. 91.

[18] Ibid.

[19] Ibid., p. 84.

[20] Macaulay, *Warren Hastings*; Busteed, *Echoes of Old Calcutta: Being Chiefly*

to explain, however, are the obvious patterns and regularities in these opposing discourses that cut across personal predilections and interests of the characters involved.

What comes through unmistakably in the comments and observations by the central figures in colonial affairs in late eighteenth-century India is that the contrasting arguments of the two sides, the colonial and the imperial, assume two contrasting visions—indeed, two contrasting philosophies—of the colonial state in India. What was at stake in this conflict was not just individual ambition, but two fundamentally different models of sovereignty and governance, with not only very different configurations of categories such as justice, property, rights, and representation but also very distinct alignments of these categories with institutions. One useful way to understand the nature of these two visions is to locate them in terms of the contrasting thoughts of two of the best-known British political philosophers in the early modern period—Hobbes and Locke.[21] While Hobbes' political philosophy corresponded with what I have identified as the colonial, Locke's corresponded to the imperial.

My intention here is not to prove any influence the two philosophers, Hobbes and Locke, may have had on the persons directly involved in the colonial affairs, but simply to bring out what was left unelaborated but nevertheless assumed in the opposing discourses of the Supreme Court and the Governor-General's Council over the issue of sovereignty. The possibility of continuities in the thoughts of these philosophers and the people engaged in running the colonial state in India cannot be ruled out. After all, it is no mere coincidence that these philosophers developed their thoughts on the state in the heyday of colonialism; their philosophies were as determined by history as the ideas of the men who were at the helm of the colonial state in India. It would be more adequate therefore to see the two philosophies as two contrasting political positions anchored in their times, rather than the creations of abstract and ahistorical theories.

---

the Reminiscences of the Days of Warren Hastings, Francis and Impey; Weitzman, Warren Hastings and Philip Francis; Stephen, The Story of Nuncomar and the Impeachment of Elijah Impey.

[21] What also needs to be noted is that there was much in Burke's vision of the state as reflected in his speeches during the impeachment trial of Warren Hastings that was in common with Locke's.

The institutional conflict between the Supreme Court, anchored in the figure of the King-in-Parliament, and the Governor-General's Council had its origin in what the Court saw as its primary function in the colony—to maintain the inviolability and sanctity of person and property as a fundamental principle and to judge all acts of the exercise of state power against this principle. In so far as the East India Company's officials in Bengal were deploying the power of the state to violate the natural right to property of the people of Bengal, the judges saw their task to be the restoration of the people's natural rights of property. In replying to the charges made by the Company that the Supreme Court had transgressed its lawful authority in India, Elijah Impey, the Chief Justice of the Supreme Court, claimed that by representing the people of India the Court had acted in complete accordance with the terms of the charter. In a long letter to Governor Johnstone dated 18 August 1778, Elijah Impey described the reasons for the popularity of the Court.

In and near Calcutta the Court has nearly had the complete effect of *giving security to the persons and property of the natives.* They feel themselves *entitled to the rights of humanity* in common with those Europeans, the meanest of whom they before considered as their lord, and they have now *courage and confidence* sufficient to assert those rights (emphasis mine).[22]

Impey assumed that his responsibility as a judge was essentially to give security to the 'person and the property of the natives.' The reason he assumed the rights of the 'natives' to be self-evident was because they were the 'rights of humanity.' In other words, the rights to security of person and property were 'the rights of humanity' and as such were natural rights; these rights were not dependent on legislation since they preceded the formation of the state and thus did not owe their existence to the state. In their claim to the rights of humanity the people of India were at par with the Europeans even if their country had become a colony. This notion of the 'rights of humanity' fell in the same category as the notion of natural law, deployed by Burke against Hastings in the impeachment trial.

This was also in conformity with the view of political philosopher, John Locke. For Locke, property was a genuine natural right

---

[22] Stephen, *The Story of Nuncomar and the Impeachment of Sir Elijah Impey,* p. 203.

because it had its origin in the labour of an individual as a member of the civil society, prior to the constitution of the state. The state was not the source of this fundamental right to property—the civil society was; the state was needed simply to protect the rights people were born with as the creators and owners of property in their civil society. The Lockean theory of the state precluded state voluntarism in matters of property and justified rebellion on the part of the people, if the state infringed on their natural right to property.[23] Given the a priori nature of these rights, the legislative function of the state was not as important as its judicial function; Locke assumed the primacy of the institution of the judiciary against the executive and the legislature. Indeed, in so far as the main function of the state was to simply maintain and protect already existing rights—not create new ones, the legislature itself appeared more like a judicial body.[24] The executive function of the state, in this view, was by definition limited to administering laws and protecting already existing rights subject to the supervision of the judiciary.[25]

In contesting the Supreme Court's vision of state based on natural rights to the security of person and property, the East India Company's Government offered its own competing notion of sovereignty which had been delegitimized in England itself but held a powerful attraction for the colonial state in India. This was the discourse of 'state necessity' grounded on the idea of self-preservation of the state, first articulated by Machiavelli, and later transformed into a legitimate legal concept in the late sixteenth century by Bodin.[26] In England it came to be reflected in the new

[23] Locke, *Second Treatise of Government*, pp. 18–83.

[24] It could be argued that John Locke's political philosophy was itself historically grounded on the practices of the English Parliament in the Middle Ages. Parliament in its early stages was essentially a judicial body, the King's Court, and the judicial business of hearing petitions and grievances of the people formed the nucleus of its proceedings. The House of Commons was merely the agency through which petitions were presented to the Crown, and legislative acts were in fact decisions of new cases. The idea that the prime purpose of Parliament was the dispensation of justice to the people persisted till the seventeenth century. See Haskins, *The Growth of English Representative Government*, pp. 89–108.

[25] Laski, *Political Thought in England from Locke to Bentham*, p. 9. Also see Lieberman, *The Province of Legislation Determined*, pp. 29–159.

[26] See Bodin, *Six Books of Commonweal*, 1576. According to Quentin Skinner, it is in this work that Bodin clearly articulates the idea of the state as a 'locus of power

discourses of state sovereignty in the sixteenth and seventeenth centuries, particularly in the political philosophy of Hobbes. In this discourse the state came before any law or rights. There were no laws or rights possible in the absence of the state. The state was the source of all laws and rights. If there were any laws or rights to be had, a state had first to be founded, maintained, and if need be, defended. How contrary this philosophy was to the one that was based on the notion of natural law could be gauged from the fact that in this philosophy the 'state of nature' meant a state of total chaos, lawlessness, and violence. In this theory, property was not prior to the state, but derived its inviolability from the very existence and power of the state. Therefore, justice and rights were not notions independent of the state, but rather emanated from the power of the sovereign and depended on it.

Since the state in Hobbesian philosophy was the very origin of laws, it could not be subjected to judicial prosecution for violating those laws. George Norton, the Advocate-General of Madras emphasized the point:

The duty of the judicial authority is to administer that as a law, and to declare that to be illegal, which the Government has pronounced (to be so). To bar any acts of a Government as illegal, is to assume to be the Government ... When the Court could bar any acts as illegal it is precisely because they are not authorized by Government, though they may be under the guise of acts so authorized.[27]

For Norton it was a contradiction in terms to claim that the acts of government could be deemed illegal. For the acts of government to be illegal, the laws would have had to have had an origin other than in the state, which was impossible.

The Court of Directors of the East India Company, writing to the Government of India, summed up the opinions of its officials:

A judicature utterly uncontrollable by the Government, and on the contrary controlling the Government, recognizing the highest authorities of the State only as private individuals, and the tribunals which administer justice in all

distinct from either the ruler or the body of people.' See Skinner, *The Foundations of Modern Political Thought, Vol. 2, The Age of Reformation*, p. 355.

[27] George Norton to Sir John Malcolm (Governor of Bombay) 1 January 1830, quoted in Sinha, *Indian Civil Judiciary in Making 1800–1833* (New Delhi: Munshi Manoharlal, 1971), p. 184.

its forms to the great body of the people only as foreign tribunals is *surely an anomaly in the strictest sense of the word* (emphasis mine).[28]

The Company officials, as is evident, were baffled by the sight of 'a judicature' not only 'utterly uncontrollable by Government,' but on the contrary 'controlling the Government' itself. If this condition appeared to be an 'anomaly in the strictest sense of the word', then that was because the Court assumed the existence of laws—natural laws and the 'rights of humanity'—outside of and prior to the state, to which the state had to adhere just like any 'private individual'.

In contrast the philosophy of the state that corresponded with what I have identified as the colonial saw laws more as an instrument of enforcing order and exacting obedience than a guarantee of rights and freedom. This philosophy operated in colonial India largely in the form of the doctrine of 'state necessity' and was clearly reflected in the East India Company's rejection of the Supreme Court's authority in Bengal. As George Rous, Counsel to the East India Company asserted in a statement written to the Court of Directors,

It seems to me, that in an unsettled State, where Dominion must be upheld by the Sword, and the Country regulated, as the Occasion requires, by a large discretionary Power, no Man ought to be responsible, as an Individual, for Acts done in any Department of Government ... much less ought his Conduct to be tried by the rigors of English Laws.[29]

The use of the expression 'unsettled State' is suggestive of visions of India being in the Hobbesian 'state of nature'—lawless and violent, where 'Dominion must be upheld by the sword'. Under such conditions the laws were nothing more than an instrument of the sword to enforce order and obedience in the population.

James Mill, the famous utilitarian philosopher and the Secretary of the East India Company's Board of Control, in his evidence to the Select Committee of the House of Commons in 1832 claimed,

[28] Char, *Readings in the Constitutional History of India, 1757–1947*, p. 278.

[29] Ibid., p. 208. In resorting to the Hobbesian theory of the state, the Governor-General's Council was also metaphorically attributing the characteristics of the state of nature to India. In so far as this state of nature was a state of perpetual war and insecurity, the colonial state had necessarily to be absolute and its sovereignty unquestioned. For a more detailed discussion, see Chapter 1.

much as Hastings had done at the impeachment trial, the need for absolute sovereignty and unquestioned authority of the government over its colonial subjects. It is interesting to note that Mill, an adherent of Benthamite utilitarianism and an advocate for the principle of the 'greatest good of the greatest number' as the basis of all laws in England, became the staunchest Hobbesian when it came to commenting on affairs in India. Mill argued that the Supreme Court in India was a redundant institution, given that an alternate structure of judicial tribunals—the one that functioned directly under the East India Company's government—was already present. When reminded that the Supreme Court had been set up in India to act as a bar to the illegal acts of the East India Company's Government, Mill responded that the East India Company's power with respect to 'native subjects' was absolute. The rights of Indian subjects were based solely upon laws enacted by the East India Company's Government in India, and therefore, the question of the government committing an illegal act against an Indian subject did not arise. Only Englishmen, whose rights and liberties were derived from the superior authority of the King-in-Parliament, could claim that the acts of the Indian Government were illegal in relation to the laws made by Parliament.[30]

In this colonial or Hobbesian model, the state's need for the consent of the people was indistinguishable from the need for their obedience; the people did not need to express their consent through representational practices such as elections. Any responsibilities of the government towards the people derived not from its legal accountability to the people, but from the moral sense of the ruler, or the state.[31] The rights of the people whether to their property,

---

[30] Evidence of James Mill before the Select Committee of the House of Lords, 29 June 1832, 77, pp. 119–21. For an analysis of James Mill's relationship with India see Majeed, *Ungoverned Imaginings: James Mill's The history of British India and Orientalism*.

[31] Warren Hastings is known for his interest in the customary laws, religions, and traditions of the 'natives' of India. The codification of Hindu law and its translation by Nathanial Halhed, the preparation of a grammar of the Bengali language were all undertaken in the late eighteenth century with his encouragement. Feiling, *Warren Hastings*. Some biographers of Hastings like Feiling have presented this fact as reflective of Warren Hastings' concern for the 'natives', his outrage at the imposition of English laws by the Supreme Court, and the representative nature of his government. However, it is important to point out that absolutist government in the Hobbesian model could be quite reconcilable with a paternal concern for

their customs, traditions, or religions derived solely from their obedience to the power and laws of the ruler and did not have any existence apart from the state. In this discourse, the very power of the British state to enforce order and security in India was its most powerful justification and therefore lawmaking had to follow the administrative needs of governance, not the fictional rights of the people. In so far as the colonial state was based on conquest, the East India Company was the absolute ruler and there could be no claims of illegality against the sovereign state.[32]

It is significant that even in the Lockean—or indeed Burkean—model in which the Supreme Court in India was anchored, the notion of the numerical representation of the people in and through elections was not essential. This is significant because even as the conflict between the Supreme Court and the Governor-General's Council was unfolding in India, the democratic idea that laws were legitimate only in so far as they were grounded in the people's freedom as expressed in their right to elect representatives to the legislature, had gained considerable ground in England and other parts of the West.[33] However, the legislative freedom of the people of India was not necessary as a precondition for the Supreme Court to defend their rights since the judges based their defence on the notion of natural rights or 'the rights of humanity'; these rights existed prior to elections as much as they existed prior to the state. In so far as legislation itself never emerged as a separate activity in either of these models, representation was primarily judicial, limited to consent as embodied in the customary law enforced in the law courts.

The idea of popular sovereignty and real representation of the people grounded in their freedom to make law was one that was absent in both the dominant models of the state that struggled

---

subjects. But this by no means implied that the government was a representative one, or accountable to the people in any respect.

[32] The discourse of state necessity and of the absolute power of the state was first articulated by Warren Hastings and further developed by James Mill and John Stuart Mill, John Strachey, J.F. Stephen, and others.

[33] As early as the seventeenth century during the English Civil War, the Levellers had urged popular representative government based on political equality. See Holorenshaw, *The Levellers and the English Revolution*. By the eighteenth century parliamentary sovereignty was clearly identified with the idea of the legislative freedom of the people. See Dicey, *Introduction to the Study of the Law of the Constitution*, pp. 41–8.

to determine the future of the colonial state. Thus the clash of sovereignty between the East India Company's government and the Supreme Court had less to do with their conflicting claims over representation of 'native' subjects in relation to English law, as Eric Stokes has argued, and more with the legitimacy and limits of the power of the colonial state.[34]

THE LEGISLATIVE COUNCIL AS A COURT OF LAW

The period between the two Charter Acts of 1833 and 1853 was of great significance in laying out the network of juridical categories, procedures, and discourses that were to overdetermine both the nature of political authority the East India Company was to exercise in India, and also the relationship between the Parliament in England and the Company's government in India. It was in this period that the primarily judicial role of the British King-in-Parliament with respect to India was institutionalized. Also, even as the East India Company was recognized as the sole legislative authority for British India, the Indian legislature itself came to be configured in 1853 in the image of a British law court based on the centrality of judicial procedures and personae, and also of juridical categories.[35] The specific alignment of categories and institutions that was set in place in this period was to have far-reaching implications for the development of anticolonial politics in India.

It was through the Charter Act of 1833 that the English Parliament recognized for the first time the sovereign legislative authority of

[34] E. Stokes has argued that the struggle between the Supreme Court and the Council had primarily to do with the question of anglicization of law and conflicting views over representation of the 'native' subjects with respect to English law. While the Supreme Court claimed to be delivering the people of India from the oppressive rule of its despotic monarchs and the arbitrary power of the East India Company's servants in India by spreading and implementing the principles of English law, the Company's Government insisted that the imposition of English law that was completely at odds with the religious beliefs and prejudices of the 'natives' was itself an injustice. Stokes, *English Utilitarians and India*, p. 35.

[35] For the most important works on the origin and development of legislative councils in colonial India, see Cowell, *The History and Constitution of Courts and Legislative Authorities in India*; Phillips, *Indian Legislation and Legislative Councils*; Char, *Centralized Legislation: A History of the Legislative System of British India from 1834–1861*; Sharan, *The Imperial Legislative Council of India*; Majumdar, *Indian Political Associations and Reform of Legislature 1818–1917*; Banerjee, *English Law in India*.

the East India Company in the colony and thereby resolved the anomalies and contradictions arising from the clash over functional sovereignty between an autonomous judiciary represented by the Supreme Court and the Company's government headed by the Governor-General's Council in India.[36] Even while abolishing the Company's trade monopoly in the colony, the English Parliament recognized the Company as the sovereign political authority in the colony and asserted in no uncertain terms the Supreme Court's institutional subordination to the Governor-General's Council. The directors of the company informed the Government of India that the 43rd, 45th and 46th clauses of the Charter Act gave the latter 'the privilege of sovereign legislation,' by providing that:

the laws and regulations, which you make under the Act are to bind all courts of justice, whether chartered by the King or not ... Your laws and regulations no longer require to be authenticated by registration in the Supreme Court, and they, notwithstanding, bind those courts, and must be noticed by them without being specially pleaded or proved.[37]

By the Charter Act of 1833 the Governor-General's Council was also converted into a legislative body, collapsing the separation of executive and legislative powers. An attempt was made to give the new institution a cover of legality by introducing a fourth legal member in the Council as a substitute for the sanction of the Supreme Court.[38] The Charter Act, as intended, strengthened the Governor-General's Council's position as an executive and legislative body with the absolute power to take administrative and legislative decisions in the colony unchecked by any other institution.[39]

---

[36] In this period there were efforts by individual Governors-Generals like Cornwallis and Bentinck to regularize the Company's judicial establishment as an independent system of courts. At the same time, the Company continued to emphatically reject the legitimacy of the Supreme Court as an institution exterior to the state itself. Stokes, *Utilitarians and India*, pp. 140–233.

[37] Desikachar, *Readings*, p. 278.

[38] This was reflected in a statement given by the Court of Directors in their dispatch to the Government of India (10 December 1834). In fact, the suggestion for a legislative council and a law commission had emerged out of the discussions between the judges of the Supreme Court and the Governor-General, Lord Bentinck in 1829–30. Stokes, *The English Utilitarians*, p. 175.

[39] The fourth member was in a position of subordination—any law could be passed without his concurrence or in his absence and he was a non-member in respect to issues in the political and secret Departments. The only difference between the

In an act of even more long-term significance, the Charter Act of 1833 institutionalized the position of the British King-in-Parliament as a purely judicial body with respect to the laws passed in India. It did this by discontinuing the provision of Pitt's India Act of 1784 that gave the home authorities in London the right to amend laws made in India. By retaining the power of the home authorities to disallow laws but not to amend them, the Charter Act left the power of positive legislation clearly in the hands of the East India Company's government in India.[40] Henceforth, legislation for India was to be effected in India on an ad hoc basis according to the contingencies of the colonial situation. However, even as the legislative role of the English Parliament with respect to India was curtailed, the judicial role of the King-in-Parliament was institutionalized in the creation of the Judicial Committee of His Majesty's Privy Council that was to hear all Indian appeals against the Company's Government.[41] The Privy Council as the King's Council was to remain the supreme judiciary for India until the end of the British Empire in 1947.

So far as the colonial government in India was concerned, it was only in 1853 with the formation of the Indian Legislative Council by the Charter Act that the first serious attempt was made to bring about a convergence of the two institutions of the Governor-General's Council and the Supreme Court that had for the last seventy-five years struggled for supreme authority in the colony. What was striking about the new Legislative Council as a major departure from the earlier Council was the inclusion of the Chief Justice of the Supreme Court along with one judge and a barrister—the fourth ordinary member—as the new members. No longer was legislative power to be exercised solely by the Governor-General and the three executive members. Rather the body was enlarged to have twelve members, including the judges and representative members from different presidencies. Ironically, the inclusion of judges in the Indian Legislative Council was taking place at a time when bills

---

operation of the old Governor-General's Council and the new legislative body was that, the discussions concerning lawmaking could no longer simply be authoritarian orders passed in secrecy but had to be made public. If publicity is seen as a principle that was original to judicial proceedings, it was this principle that was added to the Governor-General's Council in 1833 that was to have significant implications for the future. See Thornton, *India, State and Prospects*, p. 62.

[40] Desikachar, *Readings*, p. lxiv.

[41] Ibid., p. lviii.

were being proposed in the English House of Commons to exclude judges from the legislative assembly in England in order to uphold the principle of a separation of judicial and political realms.

The inclusion of judges in the Indian Legislative Council was intended to bring about a reconciliation between the Supreme Court of Law and the Council for reasons of legitimacy of the Company's rule in India, inaugurating yet another phase in the unfolding dialectic of the colonial and the imperial. This inclusion reflected an attempt to model the Legislative Council in part in the image of a court of law so as to give it much needed popular acceptability. The discourse and practice of legislation began to be reconfigured in light of the judicial procedures and juridical categories. Rather than being a mere committee of executive members secretive in its deliberations, the new legislature came to be constructed as a public body, with provision for the publication of bills for general discussion. The proceedings were thrown open to the public and the press, bringing increased public attention to all legislation, with newspapers dissecting every act being discussed and passed by the legislature. Members were not allowed to read written speeches but had to debate their opinions publicly.

Very soon, under the direction of the Chief Justice of the Supreme Court, Barnes Peacock, the Legislative Council from 1853–9 took on an activist judicial role, inquiring into grievances of the people against the government, calling for information and examination of the conduct of executive officers and demanding accountability at all levels of government. There was no longer any assurance that the proposals of the executive government would be accepted by the legislature as had been the practice in the Governor-General's Council for the last century. Rather the judges, making a constructive interpretation of their own powers and duties steadily undermined the executive's powers in India by raising embarrassing questions both for the administration in India and the home authorities. The proceedings of the council being open to the press and the public, these acrimonious debates received a wide publicity that had far-reaching implications.

The issues under debate covered a broad area of public concern. For instance, in March of 1855, in the discussion on a Bill concerning the Municipal Law of Bengal that proposed to give the Lieutenant-Governor of Bengal, an executive body, the absolute power to impose local taxes at his discretion, the Chief Justice and the other judges in the Legislative Council argued that the Indian Legislature alone—being open and more representative—could decide on matters of taxation for the benefit of the people; that this power of imposing pecuniary burdens on the people could not be delegated to the executive. Referring to the privileges and usages of the English Parliament and its refusal to delegate the powers of taxation to any other authority, Barnes Peacock, CJ argued that the Legislative Council was in a similar position. He claimed that what was true of the British Parliament must be true for the Indian Legislative Council—the power of taxation could not be delegated to an unrepresentative body like the executive. Justice Peacock's justification for this intervention by the Legislative Council is revealing: he asserted that the proposed Bill was in violation of the principles of the 'constitution of India' by which he meant the Charter Act of 1853. The Charter Act did not give any local government, the Chief Justice argued, the right to suspend any acts passed by the Legislative Council but this act proposed to do that. He argued that a uniform principle of legislation should be applicable to all such cases and that such an act should follow the precedent set in England by the Health of Towns Act.

What is striking, however, is that not only did the new Legislative Council, soon after its formation, assert its independence from the executive in India but it also declared that it was not subordinate to the Board of Control and the Court of Directors of the East India Company in England and could not be ordered to pass legislation in accordance with their wishes. When the directors of the Company disallowed the Administrator-General's Act in 1855 claiming that it had been legislated in contravention of its orders, Barnes Peacock, CJ, the Vice-President of the Legislative Council, argued that it was the Council's duty to act independently in the exercise of the important functions vested in them, and not be mere registrars of the decrees of the government. He declared, 'as long as I have the honor of a seat in the Council, I should claim the right to exercise within these walls a free and independent judgment and to abstain from giving any vote except after mature deliberation and according to my own conscience.'[42]

---

[42] Peacock, 'Speech on the Trade and Professions Bill', 30 August 1859 in *Proceedings of the Legislative Council of India for January to December 1859*, pp. 704–5.

A resolution declaring that the Court of Directors of the East India Company 'does not possess the right to require the Council to pass any law which the Court may think fit to direct' was passed unanimously by the Council on 8 December 1855 with Lord Dalhousie in the Chair.[43] Pointing to the Legislative Council's independence from the home authorities, Lord Dalhousie wrote to Charles Wood:

The Legislative Council is a separate body constituted by law ... You will find them asserting their legislative independence just as strongly as the 658 English gentlemen at Westminster ... if any demand be made upon them to submit, whether generally or specifically, their legislation for previous consideration in England, they will ... most decidedly refuse.[44]

Paradoxically, the assertion of institutional autonomy from the Home Government by the judges in the Indian Legislative Council was actively supported by the East India Company's government in India, which also wanted to claim unrestrained and unhindered authority in India, and not be subject to constant questioning either by the English Parliament or the Company's higher authorities. Arguing that neither the Board of Control nor the Court of Directors are the governors of the Indian Empire but that 'India is, and must be governed in India,' Macaulay asserted that 'the business of the Home Government is rather to judge what is past, than to give instructions for the future.' Pointing to his experience in the Government of India that 'every measure (in India) ... was taken without any authority whatever from home' and although disapproved by the Home Government, were never rescinded or annulled, he affirmed that 'the organization of the Government in India is really more important to the happiness of the people of that country than the organization of the Home Government.'[45]

Yet, despite the apparent convergence of interests between the Supreme Court's judges in the Legislative Council and the East India Company's officials in India vis-à-vis the Home Government, the justification for this independence in originating and passing laws for the colony came from radically different sources. While

[43] Lee-Warner, *The Life of the Marquis of Dalhousie*, p. 243.
[44] Moore, *Sir Charles Wood's Indian Policy: 1853–1866*, p. 51.
[45] Speech in the House of Commons at the second reading of the Government of India Bill, pp. 743–5.

the Company's government asserted that the peculiarities of rule and the contingencies of the colonial situation in India necessitated absolute unhindered power for the executive and legislative body in India, the judges in the Legislative Council argued that their powers were derived from the constitution of India—the Charter Act of 1853. Thus, while for the former, the claim for independence was coincident with a claim to absolutism, for the latter it was a claim in favour of an absolute law to which all authorities had to adhere.

In asserting the autonomy of the Indian Legislative Council, the judges of the Supreme Court were seeking to model the Council in the image of the British House of Lords in its judicial capacity and performing what they saw as their representative role. The autonomy of the institution of the Legislative Council was essential if it was to perform the function of acting as a check on the other branches of government, as a defense against corruption in high places and against arbitrary power. As the judges saw it, the purpose of the Legislative Council was to ensure that all executive powers of the Government were kept within the limits of the law by redressing the grievances of the people. In the process the Legislative Council was itself reconstituted discursively in the triadic model of a court of law, with the executive and the people in the enunciative positions of defendant and the accuser or plaintiff, and the legislators themselves in the enunciative position of the judge. Even as those members of the Council who were also members of the executive often spoke on behalf of the executive, the judges in the Legislative Council took upon themselves the responsibility to represent the cause of the people. In other words, the judges introduced into the Council the features of an adversarial system characteristic of the British law court.

This discursive and institutional construction of the Legislative Council in the image of a court of law was however a sharp departure from the discourse and practice of legislative sovereignty in England itself. By the middle of the nineteenth century there were fundamental transformations in the discourse and practice of political power in England, reflected in the emergence of the notion of legislative sovereignty as a dominant political idea, particularly with the growing importance of the political philosophy of utilitarianism as expounded by Jeremy Bentham and John Stuart Mill. Legislation had come to be seen as an activity that was essentially grounded in the expression of the people's will and had specific goals defined by the utilitarians as the 'greatest good of the greatest number'. The legislature, deriving its authority from the people's will, was the sovereign institution, while the judiciary and the executive merely interpreted and administered the laws that could not be challenged as they were made in accordance with the people's will and based on the principle of utility. Thus, Parliament was no longer concerned simply with the maintenance of a balance of power, organizing opposition to the arbitrary authority of the king, preserving peace, or redressing the grievances of the people, but had positive goals and a positive vision of the direction in which it wanted society to move. Legislation had come to be connected with ideas of economic productivity, growth, and social and political engineering and was grounded in the ideas of universality and equality and oriented towards the future rather than to the past.[46]

In sharp contrast, the Indian Legislative Council's claim for legislative autonomy and accountability from the executive between the period 1853–8 was articulated not in terms of the supreme legislative will and freedom of the people grounded in notions of utility and general good, but rather in terms of the judicial function of inquiring into grievances, of keeping the government within the limits of existing law and of maintaining a balanced constitution by resisting pressures from higher authorities like the Parliament and the Company's Board of Directors, and also from the populist demands of the people.[47] Operating within a predominantly judicial model and grounded on the juridical categories of impartiality and neutrality, there was no attempt by the Indian Legislative Council to rearticulate the laws in accordance with the concept of the will of the people or the legislative principles of universality, equality, and individual liberty. The inequalities inherent in customary law were not challenged, nor were universal procedural laws such as the habeas corpus established in the territory under the Company's jurisdiction.[48] The differential claims of European and 'native' subjects from the provinces to the protection of the Supreme Court was retained and there was no effort to establish the principle of equality as the principle of lawmaking by denying past inequalities.

---

[46] Ilbert, *Legislative Methods and Forms*, p. 212.

[47] According to the notion of virtual representation, representatives were responsible not to the people or communities that elected them but rather to the institution itself, and their primary duty was the preservation of institutional independence.

[48] See Hussein, *The Jurisprudence of Emergency*, pp. 69–97.

The formation of the Indian Legislative Council in 1853 as an attempt to reconcile the long-running confrontational relationship between the East India Company's executive and the Supreme Court proved to be too little and too late; it was unable to win the trust of the Indian public in the colonial government. Much of the Indian population continued to eye the Company government's use of the rhetoric of law warily as nothing more than an instrument for acquiring more power and wealth. Not surprisingly, in 1857 a major Revolt broke out threatening the survival of the colonial government and forcing Britain to fundamentally alter its discourse and practice of governance in India. With this began a new era of empire which is the focus of my next chapter.

3

INTO THE LABYRINTH

The Birth of Justice as a Discourse of Governance

In 1878 J.F. Stephen, the famous British legal historian and British Indian administrator, wrote a letter to the *Times* in which he reflected on the nature of the British Empire in India:

The British Power in India is like a vast bridge over which an enormous multitude of human beings are passing, and will (I trust) for ages to come continue to pass, from a dreary land, in which brute violence in its roughest form had worked its will for centuries—a land of cruel wars, ghastly superstitions, wasting plague and famine—on their way to a country ... which is at least orderly, peaceful and industrious, and which, for aught we to know to the contrary, may be the cradle of changes comparable to those which have formed the imperishable legacy to mankind of the Roman Empire ... Strike away at either of its piers and it will fall, and what are they? *One of its piers is military power: the other is justice; by which I mean a firm and constant determination on the part of the English to promote impartially and by all lawful means, what they (the English) regard as the lasting good of the natives of India.* Neither force, nor justice will suffice by itself. Force without justice is the old scourge of India, wielded by a stronger hand than of old. Justice without force is a weak aspiration after an unattainable end (emphasis mine).[1]

---

[1] Letter of J.F. Stephen to the *The Times*, 4 January 1878. James Fitzjames Stephen (1829–1894) was a famous British utilitarian thinker, legal historian, judge, and British Indian administrator. He served as law member on the Viceroy's Council in India from 1869 to 1872 and is known for his work on codification and law reform, particular the Indian Evidence Act of 1872. He articulated his utilitarian philosophy in the book *Liberty, Equality, Fraternity* (London, Smith, Elder, & Co., 1873). For J.F. Stephen's life and work in India see L. Stephen, *The Life of Sir J.F. Stephen, a Judge of the High Court* (London: Smith Elders and Co., 1845), pp. 237–76.

This is a remarkable passage both for its sweeping vision and its precise articulation of the imperatives that needed to determine the nature of the British Empire in India in the post-1857 period. Before we get to the metaphor of the bridge itself, what is to be noted are the two piers on which this bridge stands: military power and justice. This passage was an attempt on Stephen's part to reconcile power with justice. It was a clear recognition of the fact that the British Empire could not survive on force alone; that it had to construct a discourse of governance on the basis of the concept of justice. The last line of the passage seems to suggest that, for Stephen, power was only a means to justice as the ultimate end. Power was not an end in itself. Power in other words had to be subordinated to the discourse of justice. Or more precisely, military power had to be subordinated to the power of discourse.

Viewed closely, Stephen's metaphor of the British Empire as a bridge carried two visions of the colonial state, both based in the category of justice. The first suggested a passage for India and Indians from disorder to order. This discourse was grounded in the ontology of India as country of total disorder, violence, and chaos. In this view, as it had been in the views of Warren Hastings and James and John Stuart Mill, India was in a permanent Hobbesian 'state of nature' in which life was 'nasty brutish and short'. It was British rule that would provide India with the security required to bring her out of that state of nature into civilization. As is evident, much of what I characterized as the colonial discourse of governance in the period of the East India Company's rule in the first half of this chapter got incorporated into this discourse of justice as governance in the post 1857 period. In Stephen's articulation, justice meant 'a firm and constant determination on the part of the English to promote impartially and by all lawful means, what they (the English) regarded as the lasting good of the natives of India.' It is clear that Stephen deployed the category of justice not as part of a juridical discourse grounded in the Supreme Court—as was the case in pre-1857 India—but rather in the government itself. In other words, justice, for Stephen, was a discourse of governance and emphasized impartiality as the anchor of the government. If the British could be impartial in the affairs of India then that was because they were not Indians and as such had no stakes in the internal feuds of Indian society. In this view, the foreign origin of the British Empire in India was made its greatest strength and the very basis of the discourse of justice. Indian society in this view was nothing but a collection of warring communities and the role of British Empire was to be an impartial mediator between these communities.

The second vision embedded in the passage, however, was much grander, beyond the mundane goal of mere order, and even peace; something civilizational that brought to Stephen's mind the lasting contributions of the Roman Empire. In so far as the rule of law with all its attendant categories and institutions in much of the West was seen to be the most important and enduring Roman legacy, what Stephen was quite clearly referring to was the idea of liberty. Stephen's use of the phrase 'imperishable legacy' suggested something that would last long after the British Empire itself came to an end. It was as if he had in mind visions of a distant future the precise nature of which he dared not elaborate. The bridge as Stephen saw it, then, was also a temporal bridge: it offered the hope of taking India from a present of disorder to a future of liberty.

Stephen's letter summed up what, I argue in this chapter, came to be the twin discursive foundations of the British Empire in post-1857 India based on two distinct discourses woven around the category of justice—justice as equity and justice as liberty. This discursive reconfiguration was necessitated by the rupture caused by the political upheaval of the 1857 revolt that had threatened to bring British rule in India to an end. The transfer of the government of India from the Company to the imperial monarch in the wake of the Revolt resulted in major discursive and institutional realignments to put the empire on a new foundation and remove any possibility of similar upheavals in the future. With this transfer of power the colonial executive and the judiciary that had been in conflict for so long in India found themselves anchored in the same figure of the imperial monarch. As a result, the old conflict of the colonial and the imperial became internal to the figure of the monarch giving rise to the two discourses of justice as equity and justice as liberty.

I contend that this new dialectic of the two discourses of justice as equity and justice as liberty replaced the earlier dialectic of the colonial and the imperial, even as it also incorporated much of the substance of the earlier discourses. Justice as equity came to be the operational, administrative category of governance and was largely based on the discursive reconfiguration of India as a society of warring groups that needed an exterior and therefore neutral and impartial force to rule over it in the name of justice; it turned the foreign origin of the British Empire into an asset rather than a liability. This reconfiguration of India as a society of conflicting communities was the new ontology of India in the sense that it gave rise to a discourse about the very being of India that claimed to reveal the a-historical and a-temporal nature or timeless essence of it as a country and society.

Justice as liberty, on the other hand, took on the form of a teleology that was based on the promise that whatever India may have been in the past or continued to be in the present, it could still move toward a future of liberty and, indeed, even freedom. The teleology of justice as liberty gave rise to a new discourse of imperial pedagogy. The British Empire in India presented itself as a teleological pedagogical mission of taking India to the point of freedom and self-governance. In this discourse too the emphasis was sought to be shifted from the foreign origin of the colonial state: it was not the origin of the colonial state as foreign but rather its telos or pedagogical goal of 'liberty' and 'self-government' that was to be the basis of the Empire in India. It is important to note that this teleology of justice as liberty had long been in the making. Thomas Munro, one of the most important British administrators who had made a lasting contribution in developing the Company government's policy on land rights, wrote in 1824:

We should look upon India not as a temporary possession, but as one which is to be maintained permanently, until the natives shall in some future age have abandoned most of their superstitions and prejudices, and become sufficiently enlightened to frame a regular Government for themselves, and to conduct and preserve it. Whenever, such a time shall arrive, it will probably be best for both countries that the British Control over India shall be gradually withdrawn.[2]

Since India was not without government before the advent of Company rule, what Munro meant by Indians 'framing a regular government for themselves' was some form of self-government, in other words, liberty. In this vision, the British Empire in India was a pedagogical mission whose ultimate goal was to introduce the discourse and practice of liberty in its most visible form as self-government in India. This was the more precise articulation of what also came to be known as the 'civilizing mission'. It is significant

[2] Desika Char (ed.), *Readings*, p. 141.

that once a sense of mission was attached to British rule, a point of termination inevitably became a part of this vision. The being of the Empire was mapped along time and thus inevitably had to come to an end. A voluntary departure thus became an inevitable part of this vision of the Empire. It was this discourse of justice as liberty that allowed the British Empire to convert—with the consent of the Indian National Congress—its forced departure from India in 1947 into a voluntary 'transfer of power' in which the first prime minister of independent India received his oath of office from Mountbatten, the last Viceroy of the British Empire in India.

As is evident the two discourses were at odds with each other: even as the discourse of justice as equity painted India as a divided country at war with itself that had to have a foreign and therefore neutral and impartial state to enforce justice, the discourse of justice as liberty offered the hope of 'self-government'. For decades to come, India would remain trapped in the dialectic of these two opposing but also complementary imperial discourses meant to overcome the alien origins of the colonial state. This discourse of imperial justice as liberty will be the focus of my analysis in the next chapter where I discuss the nature, origin, and evolution of the Indian National Congress. It was in the rise and discourse of the Congress that the teleological aspect of the British Empire in India was most visible. In this chapter I focus specifically on the nature and deployment of the discourse of justice as equity as the dominant discourse of governance in the post-1857 period.

THE DISCOURSE OF IMPERIAL JUSTICE AS EQUITY AND LIBERTY

In the summer of 1857, northern India broke out into the most violent popular uprising that the colonial state had witnessed in its history. Beginning with a mutiny of soldiers in the Bengal army, this anticolonial insurrection quickly enveloped large sections of the general population shaking the very foundation of British rule in India. Thousands of British soldiers, military and administrative officers, and civilians were killed, British-owned factories were demolished, British police and revenue establishments were attacked, British government records, court-buildings, telegraph poles were destroyed, every symbol of British rule overturned.[3] Even

---

[3] Chaudhuri, *Civil Rebellions in the Indian Mutinies*; Mukherjee, *Awadh in Revolt, 1857–1858: A Study of Popular Resistance*; Stokes, *The Peasant Armed:*

as the Revolt was eventually defeated, it set off a series of major political changes that resulted in a fundamental reconfiguration of the colonial state with serious implications for the nature and evolution of the British Empire in India.

The most visible and immediate impact of the Revolt was the end of the East India Company's government in India. With the Royal Proclamation of 1858 the colonial government of India was transferred to the British Crown.[4] A new office of the Viceroy was added to the already existing position of the Governor-General, thus giving the head of the British Government in India a dual title. While, as Viceroy, he represented the monarch and her relationship to the princes and people of India, as Governor-General, he was responsible to the British Parliament through the Secretary of State for India, a cabinet minister in charge of Indian affairs in England.[5] Significantly, within days of the issue of the Royal Proclamation, Bahadur Shah Zafar, the last Mughal Emperor, was convicted by a British tribunal for treason because of his 'complicity' in the Revolt of 1857 and was banished to Burma, where he spent the rest of his days as a state prisoner.[6] This well-orchestrated event was designed to mark the other aspect of the post-1857 political transformation— the end of the hallowed Mughal monarchy.

It is important to recall that the East India Company until its very end had continued to operate, if only symbolically, under the sovereignty of the Mughal Emperor. Old and weak though it may have appeared, the Mughal Empire still sat at the center of popular political imagination in India, a fact brought home dramatically by the rebels of 1857, who declared the last Mughal their sovereign monarch.[7] The foregrounding of the British Crown through the

---

The Indian Revolt of 1857, Bayly. Bhadra, 'Four Rebels of Eighteen-Fifty-Seven'; Dalrymple, The Last Mughal: The Fall of a Dynasty, Delhi 1857; Nayar, (ed.), The Trial of Bahadur Shah Zafar.

[4] The Royal Proclamation was translated into the many languages and dialects in use in British India and read with 'proper ceremonial splendour' at every civil and military station and also 'in all the great centers of population.' See Cunningham, Rulers of India: Earl Canning, p. 171.

[5] For the often conflictual relationship between the Secretary of State and the Viceroy of India see Kaminsky, The India Office 1880–1910. Also see Kulke and Rothermund, A History of India, p. 256.

[6] See Nayar, (ed.), The Trial of Bahadur Shah Zafar.

[7] See Dalrymple, The Last Mughal: The Fall of a Dynasty, Delhi 1857, pp. 180–281.

Royal Proclamation in the immediate aftermath of the Revolt was an effort to emphasize continuity between the Mughal Empire and the new British Empire. The British government sought to demonstrate to Indians that the country was not really a colony under foreign rule, but simply a kingdom or empire as it had always been, and was most recently under the Mughals. The position of the first Viceroy and Governor-General of India was conferred on Charles John Viscount Canning, the Queen's cousin—an appointment that betrayed just how anxious and eager the Empire was to project the new government in India to be directly under the Queen. In a symbolic move of great significance for the future of British India, the Royal Titles Bill of 1876 passed in Britain under the new administration of Prime Minister Disraeli conferred the title of *Kaiser-i-Hind* or Empress of India on the Queen.

Moreover, a new and important routine of holding periodic durbars or royal courts was added to the function of the British monarchy with respect to India. In a grand Durbar held in Delhi in January 1877, Queen Victoria was proclaimed the 'Queen Empress of India'.[8] This Royal Durbar became an occasion for the ceremonial conference of titles, such as Nawab, Maharaja, Raja, Rai Bahadur, and Khan Bahadur, on 'native' rulers and members of the Indian elite, and care was taken to present them to the people of India and Britain as willing participants in the post-1857 British Indian Empire grounded in the figure of the imperial monarch. It is significant that the British Queen as Empress of India was placed at the top of a hierarchy of local princes and rulers, who were all classified and incorporated into the imperial framework.[9] This reflected the need felt by the Empire to make the British monarchy appear organic to the indigenous tradition of the monarchy; as if the Mughal Empire had been merely replaced by another that may not have been entirely indigenous, but still as organically linked. As Viceroy Lytton put it, the aim behind the Durbar was to conspicuously 'place the Queen's authority upon the ancient throne of the Moguls, with which the

[8] For a discussion of the symbolic significance of the Durbar of 1877, see Cohn, 'Representing Authority in Victorian India', pp. 632–82.

[9] For the most important works on the princely states and their role in the British Indian Empire see Fisher, *Indirect Rule in India*; Copland, *The Princes of India in the Endgame of Empire, 1911–1947*; Ramusack, *The Princes of India in the Twilight of Empire*; Bhagavan, *Sovereign Spheres: Princes, Education and Empire in Colonial India*; Jeffrey, (ed.), *People, Princes, and Paramount Power*.

imagination and tradition of [our] Indian subjects associate the splendour of supreme power.'[10] Interestingly, Viceroy Lytton also had a plan for an Indian Privy Council consisting of native princes in the likeness of British Privy Council.[11] Although this plan was eventually rejected, it betrayed, even in its failure, the desire to give form and substance—limited though it may have been—to the notion that the British monarchy was also an Indian monarchy. It revealed an attempt to erase, substantially if not entirely, the stigma of the British government being foreign and alien to India, a fact that had been emphasized by the rebels of 1857.

Henceforth, royal durbars became an institutional site for the display of the grandeur of the person of the British monarch as the imperial sovereign of India. The Durbar of 1877 was followed by two more royal durbars in 1903 and 1911—the first marking the coronation of King Edward VII and Queen Alexandra, and the second that of King George V and Queen Mary as the Emperor and Empress of India. These were also supplemented by durbars that the Viceroy held as representative of the British monarch in India. For example, soon after the Durbar of 1877, Canning held his own durbars in Kanpur, Agra, Ambala, Peshawar, Jabalpur, and Lucknow.[12]

The symbolic significance of the Queen's Proclamation and the royal durbars lay in that it allowed the British Empire to overcome part of its foreignness by presenting the monarchy as a deterritorialized and denationalized institution that stood above Britain as a nation, and thus maintain the discourse of imperial justice that was so vital for its survival. In the absence of the symbolic cover of the monarchy, there was always the possibility of a dangerous dynamic being set off between the colonizing nation and the colonized that could once again threaten the end of Empire, as in 1857. It is well known that the East India Company's rule in India was a rule by proxy in that the sovereignty of the Mughal Empire, symbolic though it was, was left intact. What is worth emphasizing, however, is that post-1857 India was as much an instance of proxy rule—even as India was ruled by England as a nation the imperial discourse of the empire came to be anchored in the figure of the

[10] Lytton to Queen Victoria, 21 April 1876, I.O.L.R., E218/518/1.

[11] Brumpton, (ed.), *A Selection from the India Office Correspondence of Robert Cecil, Third Marquis of Salisbury, 1866–1867 and 1874–1878*, pp. 219–22, 230–4.

[12] Cunningham, *Earl Canning*, pp. 178–84.

monarch who was presented as one who stood above England as a nation. In many ways it was this strategic importance of the British monarchy in constructing a denationalized discourse of the empire that kept it relevant in Britain itself well into the twentieth century.

At an obvious level, the transfer of power from the Company to the Crown may appear to have simplified the structure of the colonial state and solved some of its most enduring problems by replacing the feuding institutions of the Governor-General's Council and the Supreme Court on the one hand, and the weak Mughal Empire on the other with the direct rule of the British monarchy. Things, however, were much more complex. Even as the transfer of power seemed to solve some of the old problems, it also threw into disarray the discursive and institutional foundations of the Empire that had operated as a complex dialectic of colonial power and imperial justice. In so far as the Queen was now the head of the colonial state, the British monarchy could no longer be portrayed as exterior to the colonial state and a seat of impartial justice, as it had been in the pre-1857 era, when the colonial government had been under the East India Company. The British monarchy in India was now a colonial monarchy in that it was mapped onto the structure of an existing colonial polity. How then was the Empire to be reconfigured discursively and institutionally in this new era if it were to earn any legitimacy for itself in India?

In light of the 1857 Revolt, despite the use of the British monarchy to camouflage the nature of the colonial state in India, the foreign origin of the British Empire in India remained the toughest challenge to overcome. After all, a monarchy could be a national monarchy. Indeed it could even be the most powerful symbol of national identity and sovereignty. This fact was brought home dramatically by the 1857 Revolt. It was not Bahadur Shah Zafar, the last Mughal, who raised the banner of revolt against the Company and declared himself the real sovereign of India. Indeed, by most accounts he was rather reluctant to take command of the Revolt and very doubtful of its ultimate success. Rather, it was the rebelling soldiers who put Zafar back on the throne as the real sovereign and symbol of their national sovereignty against the Company's foreign rule.[13] In other words, national sovereignty

---

[13] For a fascinating account of the relationship between Zafar and the rebels see Dalrymple, *The Last Mughal*, pp. 134–98.

and the sovereignty of the people as reflected in the discourse of nationalism are two very different things. A country does not have to be a republic to also be a nation.

Thomas Munro, writing in 1824, long before the Revolt of 1857 broke out, was well aware of this shared element of national identity between a republic and a monarchy:

British India has none of these privileges [of liberty]; it has not even that of being ruled by a despot of its own; for to a nation which has lost its liberty, it is still a privilege to have its countryman and not a foreigner as its ruler. Nations always take part with their Government, whether free or despotic, against foreigners. Against an invasion of foreigners national character is always engaged, and in such a cause the people often contend as strenuously in the defence of a despotic as of a free Government. *It is not the arbitrary power of a national sovereign, but subjugation to a foreign one, that destroys national character and extinguishes national spirit.* When a people cease to have a national character to maintain, they lose the mainspring of whatever is laudable both in public and in private life, and the private sinks with the public character (emphasis mine).[14]

Munro in this passage pointed to the precise difference between a national monarchy and a colonial monarchy as two separate polities. Even if a country was deprived of its liberty under a monarchy, Munroe suggested, a monarchy could still be a national state, if not also a 'nation-state' as this term has come to be understood. A colonial state, on the other hand, was an alien state exterior to the nation and the society over which it ruled. Liberty was not the only thing a society lost under foreign rule. Indeed, if a society was already under a monarchy—as India was, liberty may not even have been the most important thing it lost. For Munro, in so far as the state became exterior not just to the people, but also to the culture of the people, the most important thing a society lost under foreign rule was the 'national spirit' and 'national character', in other words, its identity as a nation.

Given that the transfer of power to the Queen was not likely to be sufficient to overcome the foreignness of the colonial state, an urgent need was felt for a new discourse of governance and a new ground of legitimacy for the British Empire that would turn its foreignness into an asset rather than a liability. While many in the British administration argued that the only way to prevent

[14] Desikachar, *Readings*, pp. 139–40.

another Revolt was to strengthen the coercive apparatus of the colonial state, a significant part of the British ruling classes felt that any continuation of the old colonial ambition to seek absolute power through military power and cunning alone was likely to end in the destruction of the British Empire in India. It was the latter interpretation that was to carry the day and determine the nature of the post-1857 British imperial state in India.

Benjamin Disraeli, the leading spokesman of the opposition in the British House of Commons articulated on 27 July 1857 the earliest and most incisive analysis of the Revolt that would set the frame not only for Queen Victoria's proclamation of 1858, but also for later studies on the Revolt. In the aftermath of the war, amidst feelings of profound fear, consternation, and calls for vengeance that the Revolt had aroused in the British citizens both in India and in England, the immediate question for the British Parliament was—how could British power be reestablished and peace and security restored in the colony? The answer to this question, Disraeli contended, had necessarily to begin with an analysis of the causes of the war. For if the war was not merely a military mutiny but the manifestation of deeper discontents among the population of India as a whole, then a simple reform of the army would be inadequate in preserving British rule in India.[15]

In words reminiscent of Edmund Burke, Disraeli contended that what had been witnessed in 1857 was a 'national revolt' that was provoked by the Government of India's alienation of every class of the Indian population. In opposition to the claim that the British Empire in India was grounded in conquest, Disraeli constructed his own parallel narrative—or 'legal fiction' to use Bentham's phrase—that the British had been invited into India by native populations suffering under tyranny for the protection of their property and religion. This invented narrative of the origin of the British Empire in India—dubious as it was as a historical claim—was meant to give his discourse of justice a solid foundation. According to Disraeli the occupation of India had been preceded by solemn proclamations on the part of the British Parliament to respect and maintain inviolate the rights, privileges, laws, customs, property, and religion of the people.

Reiterating Burke's ideas of empire, Disraeli asserted that the source of the strength of the British Empire in India lay in the

---

[15] *Hansard's Parliamentary Debates*, 3d ser., vol. 147 (1857), cols. 536–41.

discourse and practice of justice, 'the strict observance of our treaties, the rigid maintenance of the laws and customs of the people, and, above all, a faithful respect for our guarantees of their land, and a scrupulous adhesion to our engagements not to tamper with their religion.'[16] The national revolt of 1857, argued Disraeli, was a result of the betrayal of these original principles of governance grounded in justice by the East India Company's government in India. The causes of the conflagration lay in the new policies of the Government of India that had resulted in 'the forcible destruction of native princes,' the 'disturbance of the settlement of property,' and 'tampering with the religions of the people.' In Disraeli's opinion, the events of 1857 constituted a national revolt for the restoration of the rights of property and religion that the Government of India had destroyed.

The principles on which this new discourse of governance was to be constructed was laid out by the Queen herself in her message telegraphed to the people of India gathered at the Delhi Durbar in January 1877. The Queen wrote, 'We trust that the present occasion may tend to unite in bonds of yet closer affection ourselves and our subjects; that from the highest to the humblest all may feel that under our rule the great principles of liberty, equity, and justice are secured to them.'[17] It is important to note that even as the Queen talked of her relationship with her subjects in personal terms as 'bonds of affection,' her speech also revealed that her relationship with her Indian subjects was to be mediated by the principles of liberty, equity, and justice. The foregrounding of these principles as the foundation of the new state and the source of its legitimacy revealed a determination to construct a discourse of governance. Conquest, or re-conquest, was not to be its own justification; there had to be a deeper and more enduring reason for British rule in India.

The relationship between the British monarchy and its Indian subjects then was to be as discursive as it was personal. It was as subjects to the principles of 'liberty, equity, and justice' that Indians became subjects of the British Empire. Significantly, the reverse was also true; it was as subjects of the British imperial monarchy that Indians would become subject to the principles of liberty, equity, and justice. In other words, the historical relationship of Indians

---

[16] Ibid.

[17] *Gazette of India*, Extraordinary, 1 January 1877, pp. 3–7.

as subjects to these principles came to be mediated through the figure of the Queen. Much of the British imperial political legacy in postcolonial India consists of the continuing relevance of this historical development. It was in their mediated form that these principles would soon become the foundation of the discourse and practice of the Indian National Congress. Indeed, as I contend in the last chapter on the Indian Constitution, it is in their imperially mediated form that the principles of justice, equity, and liberty continue to drive the postcolonial Indian polity even today. This imperial shadow has remained with India long after the Empire itself was brought to an end.

JUSTICE AS THE DISCOURSE OF GOVERNANCE

While exposing the fragility and vulnerabilities of the British Empire in India, the mass uprising of 1857 demonstrated very powerfully that despite internal differences, the population of India was capable of uniting in opposition to British rule, and, thereby, threaten its very existence. It also made clear that force alone would not suffice to maintain the British Indian Empire for long. Under these circumstances it became imperative for the very survival of the colonial state to construct a new discourse of legitimacy that would turn the alien origin of the British government into its strength rather than a provocation for future uprisings even as it would keep the Indian society fragmented to prevent another united revolt. It was in this historical context that, even as the absolute powers of the executive government began to be strengthened, the discourse of justice as equity was appropriated by the colonial administration in India as a strategy of colonial rule.

To understand the nature and specificity of the discourse of justice as equity in post-1857 British India and also postcolonial India, it would be essential to briefly trace the history of the concept and practice of equity in England. At the broadest level as thought, the notion of equity is meant to complement the idea of justice under law. Equity, as Aristotle articulated it over two millennia ago in Book V of *Nicomachean Ethics*, was not opposed to law or legal justice but 'corrected' and 'completed' it by recognizing the concrete particularities or specificities of a case that the law—grounded in the notion of impersonal universality and formal procedures—by its very nature could not:

All law is universal while there are some cases about which it is not possible to pronounce a general statement correctly; and so where it is necessary to speak in general terms, but impossible to do so correctly, the law takes account of that which occurs usually, though not aware that in this way errors are made. And the law is not wrong in so doing: for the error is not in the law nor in the legislator but in the nature of the object itself, since such is by necessity the subject-matter of actions.[18]

Insofar as the law aims at regulating a whole range of human affairs, its universal and formal provisions may not cover adequately the features presented by the concrete situations in which a particular case is embedded. This, Aristotle argues, is not the fault of the lawgiver, but is in the very nature of practical matters which cannot be captured by general rules in advance; the infinite variations of life, after all, exceed the formal universality of law. In that sense the law leaves gaps that must be filled by contextually appropriate judgments that aim not at strict retributive justice, but at a fair and sympathetic verdict by taking into account the innocent motives, good character, and personal histories of the offender as well as the circumstances of the offence that may serve to mitigate the severity of his crime. As opposed to justice under common law that is oriented to a legal and formal persona, equity is directed to the person in all his concrete complexity and uniqueness.

The concept of equity, however, also acquired a specific connotation in the historical context of sixteenth-century Europe as non-enforceable, as opposed to justice that could be enforced.[19] The non-enforceability of equity was related in theory to the fact that unlike justice under law that derived its legitimacy from the original freedom and autonomy of every individual and was accepted as valid either because it came through a legislative process that embodied the

---

[18] Aristotle, *Nicomachean Ethics*, Book V, p. 144.

[19] Major political thinkers of early modern Europe made this distinction between justice and equity. Pufendorf, the famous seventeenth-century German jurist and political thinker, posited that while justice consisted in the mutual respect for private property or in respect for persons as proprietors according to a clear and unambiguous system of positive law and was therefore enforceable, equity, also defined as charity or benevolence, was not. Kant similarly argued that equity was not a right but only an appeal to the moral duty of benevolence or beneficence and therefore, unlike justice, did not have the force of compulsion. While Leibniz, the continental philosopher of law, differed from the above thinkers in defining ideal justice as 'active benevolence', he too agreed that in practice charity and benevolence were not enforceable. See Riley, *Leibniz' Universal Jurisprudence: Justice as the Charity of the Wise*.

freedom or consent of all, equity fell in the domain of the benevolence of sovereign will. In other words, justice was related to the rights of individuals and was therefore owed to the subjects and, if denied, gave grounds for 'justified grievances' that they were wronged. Charity as the duty of the sovereign, on the other hand, was not correlated to the rights of the subjects and therefore could not be enforced.[20]

In the discourse of justice as equity, not just the plaintiff but the judge himself was assumed to be a person with a conscience and a sense of benevolence, and not just an office holder, bound by the formal logic of the law alone and applying it mechanically, if also correctly. In this discourse, insofar as the judge was a real person, justice became an aspect of his person, his sentiments. This conceptual disjuncture between justice as equity or charity and justice under common law found its institutional expression in the separation of Chancery courts from common law courts—while the Chancery courts were anchored in the person of the King and his benevolence or mercy, the common law courts were bound by formal legal rules and procedures in accordance with a system of positive law, equal and impartial to all, regardless of the consequences of its application. As the common law courts gained ascendance, equity courts were responsible for administering supplementary justice which continued to be grounded in the King's prerogative of mercy and benevolence rather than strict legal right under common law.[21] As John Fonblanque wrote in his 'A Treatise of Equity,' it was necessary to provide 'in every well-constituted government' a power for 'supplying that which is defective and controlling that which is unintentionally harsh in application of any general rule to a particular case.'[22]

The separate and distinct jurisdictions of the courts of common law and the courts of equity were carved out historically in the course of a long and contentious struggle between the King and the legal profession in seventeenth-century England over the right to

[20] See Allen, *Law in the Making*, pp. 383–425; Lieberman, *The Province of Legislation Determined: Legal Theory in Eighteenth-Century Britain*, pp. 71–87, 159–75; Baker, *An Introduction to English Legal History*, pp. 97–116.

[21] Parkes, *A History of the Court of Chancery; with Practical Remarks on the Recent Commission, Report, and Evidence, and On the Means of Improving the Administration of Justice in the English Courts of Equity*; Smith, *Lectures on Jurisprudence*, pp. 275–83.

[22] Fonblanque, *A Treatise of Equity*, pp. 74–5.

define law. While the King's advocates, most famous of whom were Bacon and Hobbes, argued that law was exclusively the command of the sovereign, the common law lawyers led by Coke asserted that the common law was the embodiment of the reason of the people that had been perfected over centuries and was therefore above the King himself. Judicial certainty and predictability, guaranteed by the common law through the doctrine of judicial precedent and the attendant formalities, technicalities, and rules of procedure associated with the adversarial system, were claimed by the common lawyers as indispensable for the defence of the rights of the individual against the arbitrary authority of the times.

However, it was precisely on the grounds that the system of common law had developed into a tangled labyrinth of judicial practices and forms of procedure that could only be manoeuvred by a professional body of lawyers and could easily result in the denial of substantial justice to the individual, that the justification for a separate jurisdiction for equity courts was found. The judicial doctrine and practice of equity in England claimed to be primarily a remedy against the tyranny of form in the common law courts. It owed its birth to the fourteenth-century practice of petitioning the King's conscience to do right for the love of God and 'by way of charity'. When the common law court seemed not to provide adequate remedy to a plaintiff, or its procedural requirements acted as obstacles in the path of justice, the King would call upon his Chancellor, most commonly a churchman—not surprisingly because of their largely shared notion of equity—to provide a remedy to his petitioner by summoning the litigants and 'laying it upon the conscience of the wrongdoer to do right'. As there could be no adequate definition of 'conscience,' the implication was that the Chancellor should exercise his discretion in deciding the particular case so as to provide substantial justice to the claimant. As Dicey describes it, 'equity originally meant the discretionary and arbitrary interference of the Chancellor for the avowed and often the real purpose of securing substantial justice between the parties in a given case and was essentially linked to the despotic prerogative of the Crown.'[23] Similar concerns about substantial justice and fairness also shaped the additional equity courts that developed in England after the Court of Chancery. Insofar as equity operated by taking

---

[23] Dicey, *An Introduction to the Study of the Law of the Constitution*.

into consideration the particular circumstances of individual cases, it came to be necessarily tied to judicial discretion, giving the judge the power to modify rules of law.[24]

It is important to note that the conflict between the notions of justice as equity and justice under common law in the modern period reflected in a deeper sense the conflict between the monarchy and the emergent ethos of a new democratic polity. The discourse of justice as equity was dominant in a monarchical polity where the laws had their origin in the person of the monarch and the people related to the monarch as his subjects. In contrast, in the new egalitarian political ethos of a democratic polity that was emerging in the late eighteenth and nineteenth centuries, the people and not the King were sovereign lawmakers. The increasing ascendancy of the common law courts over the Chancery courts in this period pointed precisely to the development of this new egalitarian polity. It was the absolute commitment to the equality of citizens before the law in the emerging democratic ethos that lay behind the commitment to the universality and formality of common law. Any breach in this universality would have undermined the fundamental principle of the equality of citizens. Justice either directed to a person or originating in a person would break the assumption of this formal equality. It is not surprising therefore that this new democratic ethos was against the system of jurisprudence of equity anchored in the monarchy.

Even as the discourse and practice of justice as equity had been reduced in Britain to a mere supplementary role in the face of the ascendancy of the discourse of common law reflective of the rising tide of democratic ethos, in India it was elevated to become the sovereign category in the wake of 1857 with the transfer of power to the British Crown; the discourse of justice as equity became the new discourse of colonial governance. It is important here to note some fundamental differences between the discourse of imperial justice in the period of the Company's rule in India and the discourse of justice as equity in the post-1857 period. The first was in the relationship of the monarch to law. In the period of the Company's rule in India, the figure of the King—as evident in the speeches of Burke and the institution of the Supreme Court—became the site for the introduction of the discourse of natural law into India to restrain

---

[24] Smith, *Lectures on Jurisprudence*, pp. 275–83.

the company government and force it to abide by those laws and values. It is important to note that in this period the monarch was no more than a judge; he was not the source of laws; the laws, since they were natural, were always already there. The only power and responsibility the King had was to apply those laws to protect the natural right of his subjects. The monarch's sovereignty amounted to the sovereignty of the principle of natural law. Justice consisted in the application of those natural laws. What had been assumed was the exteriority of the judiciary to the colonial government, if not the colonial state. The figure of the King in whom the institution of the Supreme Court was anchored, always appeared on the side of the people and the civil society against the Company state.

With the Queen's Proclamation in 1858, however, it was the figure of the British monarch that became the sovereign, the head of state. Now, sovereignty resided in the person of the Queen, not in natural law. The discursive change from justice under natural law to justice as equity reflected this major political change in post-1857 India. Unlike the earlier discourse of justice under natural law, justice as equity had its origin in the figure of the monarch; the figure of the monarch now became the source of both law and justice. Justice became an aspect of the monarch's person and as such was indistinguishable from the mercy and benevolence of the Queen. From being a principle, justice was reduced to a sentiment of the Queen. She stood above all laws, even as she became the source of all laws. Law was nothing more than the command of the monarch while justice itself was benevolence. As H.S. Cunningham put it in his biography of Viceroy Canning, the Royal Proclamation:

Had a good effect in placing before the many millions of Indian subjects, instead of the intangible and mysterious abstraction known as 'The Company,' the living personage of a Sovereign interested in their lot, desirous of their welfare, powerful enough to crush opposition, but inspired by sentiments of justice, and prompt to exercise the grand prerogative of mercy.[25]

While for Burke, the justice of the imperial monarch had to flow from the universality of natural law based on the notion of the equality and freedom of all, what was symbolically emphasized in the period after 1857 through the royal durbars was the person of

---

[25] Cunningham, *Earl Canning*, p. 175.

the imperial monarch, and her sense of benevolence and charity as the source of justice.[26] Imperial justice was now being tied not to the universality of law—natural or common—but rather to the notion of equity grounded in the personal discretion and compassion of the imperial monarch.[27] This rather subtle change in the image of the imperial judge, was to have far-reaching implications not just for the nature of the British Empire in India, but also for the nature of anticolonial politics under the Indian National Congress in the late nineteenth and early twentieth centuries.

The second crucial change in the post-1857 period was in the discursive positions to be occupied by the colonial government, the British Parliament, and the people of India in relation to the discourse of justice. For almost a hundred years after the establishment of the Company's rule in India, the dominant discourse of imperial justice under natural law had been triadic in nature and had posed the colonial government and the people of India as the defendant and the plaintiff respectively, and the British Parliament as the imperial judge. This triadic discourse of justice had sought to make the East India Company's administration accountable for its actions in India to the Parliament in England, and had prompted the people of India to present their grievances to the monarch in England against the colonial government. The resulting interference by the British King-in-Parliament in the affairs of the colonial government on behalf of Indian people had always been seen as a serious obstacle in the colonial bureaucracy's exercise of absolute power in India.

Not surprisingly, with the transfer of power to the British Crown in 1858, the colonial government in India had to be re-imagined in light of the new imperatives. The old triad of imperial justice in which the British Parliament had appeared as judge, the colonial administration as defendant, and colonized India as plaintiff was transformed into a new triad in which even as the colonial state in India came to occupy the position of judge, different communities

---

[26] Notably, the assumption of the title of Empress of India by the Queen was critiqued by Gladstone (now the leader of the opposition in the British Parliament) on the very Burkean grounds that it was 'dissociated from the regular control of the law, and associated with the undefined exercise of will.' Moore, *Liberalism and Indian Politics 1872–1922*, p. 23.

[27] At a personal level, Queen Victoria began to take a new interest in the Indian Empire and started taking Hindi lessons, even inviting Max Mueller to give lectures at the royal court. See Kulke and Rothermund, *History of India*, p. 256.

of divided Indian civil society in conflict with itself appeared as plaintiffs and defendants. This was a dramatic realignment of the discourse of justice and the major institutions of the empire; from being a defendant, the colonial government in India was repositioned as neutral and impartial judge who would distribute 'justice' between the warring communities it ruled. Justice, in other words, had become a discourse of governance.

It was Sir John Seely who clearly articulated the link between the lessons learnt from the Revolt of 1857 and the new discourse of governance. In his influential work *The Expansion of England*, Seely wrote:

The Mutiny was in a great measure put down by turning the races of India against each other. So long as this can be done, the government of India from England is possible, and there is nothing miraculous about it. But ... if the state of things should alter, if by any chance the population should be welded into a single nationality, then I do not say we ought to begin to fear for our dominion; I say we ought to cease at once to hope it.[28]

In Seely's view, the reason that the British Empire had survived the Revolt was because of its successful strategy of 'turning the races of India against each other.' The single most important lesson of 1857 for the British Empire then was that it could not allow the Indian population to 'be welded into a single nationality.' Despite the successful attempt to divide India against itself in the Revolt, Seely's diagnosis of the Revolt perceived that even if it was not absolute, there were enough sources of national unity and identity in India to threaten—as in 1857—the very existence of the British Empire in India. All the sources, therefore, of that national unity and identity—cultural, political, and historical—had to be systematically deconstructed and rendered meaningless; indeed, the very idea of India had to be rendered meaningless. Only then would the foreignness of the colonial state itself cease to matter; its oppression and exploitation of India would cease to find any voice making colonialism appear natural while also securing the permanence of the British Empire in India.

Henceforth, it was precisely within the splits and cracks between the communities of India that colonialism would locate itself; and it was by maintaining and consolidating differences and fostering

---

[28] Seely, *The Expansion of England: Two Courses of Lectures*, p. 270.

conflicts between communities, while claiming to stand above them, that colonialism would justify its presence in India.

The profound impact of this change was most visible in the imperial reconfiguration of Indian civil society. Viceroy Lord Dufferin's Minute of 1888 articulated best this recalibration of the discourse of imperial justice as equity in its strategic deployment by the colonial administration as the dominant discourse of governance.[29] While elaborating on the reasons why the principles of democratic representation could not be introduced in the provincial councils in India in the image of the British Parliament without endangering imperial rule, Lord Dufferin began by describing the specific nature of the British Indian Empire.

India is an Empire equal in size, if Russia be excluded, to the entire continent of Europe with a population of 250,000,000 souls. The population is composed of a large number of distinct nationalities, professing various religions, practicing diverse rites, speaking different languages while many of them are still further separated from one another by *discordant prejudices*, by *conflicting social usages* and even *antagonistic material interests* (emphasis mine).[30]

What Dufferin was emphasizing in this characterization was, of course, the diversity and heterogeneity of the Indian society that seemed like a cacophony of languages, rites, and religions without any unifying logic, but as importantly, the 'discordance,' 'conflicts,' and 'antagonisms' that were inherent in it.

Once the complete absence of any unity or identity in Indian society had been established as a self-evident fact, the next logical step was to deny that there was any being to the idea of India as a nation—there was no India. John Strachey, a prominent member of the British Indian administration, argued in 1888 that the first and most essential thing to learn about India was that 'there is not, and never was an India.'[31] India, he argued, was simply 'a name that was

---

[29] Lord Dufferin was Viceroy and Governor-General of India from 1884–8.

[30] See Lord Dufferin, Minute of 1888, Oriental and India Office Collections of the British Library, Dufferin Collection, MSS EUR F 130, 1199.

[31] John Strachey (1823–1907) was an important British Indian administrator who served in India from 1842 to 1880 with a brief interruption. He was a member of the Viceroy's Legislative Council in 1868 and became acting Governor-General for a fortnight after the assassination of Lord Mayo in February 1872. He also served as lieutenant-governor of the North-Western Provinces and as finance member in the Viceroy's Legislative Council in 1874.

given to a great region, including a multitude of different countries.' Unlike European countries, however, each of 'which is usually a separate entity, occupied by a separate nation more or less socially and politically distinct,' these countries in India were not nations of the modern European type either. Never having possessed 'according to European ideas any sort of unity, physical, political, social and religious' or the 'large measure of uniformity that characterized European civilization,' India could not legitimately make any claims to be a nation. 'The European observer,' asserted Strachey,

accustomed to the amassing of people in great territorial groups and to the ideas contained in such expressions as fatherland, motherland, patriotism, domicile and the like—has here to realize the novelty of finding himself in a strange part of the world where political citizenship is yet quite unknown and territorial sovereignty just appearing ... He gradually discovers the population of Central India to be distributed not into great governments, or nationalities, or religious denominations, not even in widespread races ... but into various and manifold denominations of tribes, clans, castes and sub-castes, religious orders and devotional brotherhoods.[32]

It is significant that Strachey felt compelled to re-affirm the non-existence of India as a nation in 1888, three years after the formation of the Indian National Congress in 1885. As we will discuss in the next chapter, the political discourse of the Congress was not based on the ideology of nationalism. Still, the words 'Indian National' in the name of the Party were alarming enough—it simply assumed the existence of India as a self-evident fact.

Having drawn a portrait of the Indian civil society in his Minute of 1888 as a random assortment of divided and conflicting communities, Dufferin went on to articulate the chief function of the colonial state in India, 'Its [India's] destinies have been confided to an *alien* race, *whose function is to arbitrate between a multitude of conflicting or antagonistic interests,* and its *Government is conducted in the name of a Monarch* whose throne is in England (emphasis mine).'[33] According to the Viceroy, the head of British Empire in India, the chief function of the colonial state was to arbitrate or ensure justice between a multitude of conflicting and antagonistic interests. In Dufferin's view, the reason that the colonial state was in a position to arbitrate

[32] Strachey, *India*, p. 2.
[33] See Lord Dufferin, 'Minute of 1888', 1199.

between the conflicting communities was because it was in the hands of 'an alien race.' It was the alien origin of the colonial state and of its administrators in India that allowed it to be neutral with regard to conflicting interests within the Indian society, and therefore capable of rendering impartial justice. The expression 'monarch whose throne is in England' is meant to emphasize the exteriority of the colonial state. In this new colonial discourse of governance grounded in the idea of justice as equity, the very exteriority or the foreign origin of the state to the Indian civil society was turned into the foundation of British Empire in India. Unlike in the pre-1857 era, the discourse of justice was not directed against the colonial government in India to an impartial imperial judge on behalf of the people of India; rather justice became a tool in the hands of the colonial government itself claiming to resolve conflicts within Indian society. The dramatic transformation of the government from being a defendant to the judge is clearly evident here.

It was because of 'the organic constitution of such an Empire as India, with it multifarious latent forces, its wondrous mosaic of nationalities,' Lord Dufferin asserted, that there was 'a constant *need of a strong, external,* and *independent* element to preserve a *just equilibrium between its heterogeneous constituent parts* and to counteract its innate disruptive tendencies' (emphasis mine).[34] As a divided society in conflict with itself, India, was not in a position to give birth to a state from within that could guarantee peace and justice, according to Dufferin—it needed an alien state. Thus, in and through justice as the discourse of governance, the foreign origin of the colonial state was transformed into its greatest ideological asset, indeed, the primary source of its legitimacy. If India were to have any semblance of unity and thus peace, it was claimed, it must learn to live under an alien state. India, in other words, needed the Empire more than the Empire needed India. India could never be a free country without destroying itself, without ceasing to be. In this discourse of justice as equity, the very being of India as a nation appeared to be derivative of the British Empire. In other words, India could be a nation only as a colony. It was only as British India that India could be itself.

In the citation above, Dufferin also uses an interesting phrase, 'just equilibrium,' to envision the ideal state of Indian civil society under the British Empire. What is interesting and revealing about

[34] Dufferin, Minute of 1888, 1199.

the phrase 'just equilibrium' is that it combines the strategic and discursive or ideological aspects of the idea of justice as equity; the strategic aspect consisted in keeping the Indian civil society in equilibrium or internally balanced by matching one community's strength against the other. The discursive aspect consisted in making this imperialist strategy appear as the greatest evidence of British imperial justice in action. It was to win legitimacy for the exteriority or the foreign origin of the colonial state that the discourse of India as a collection of communities in conflict with each other was constructed. Justice as the discourse of governance in post-1857 India became the other side of what has come to be known as the 'divide and rule' policy of the British Empire. Indeed, the strategy of divide and rule would have been impossible to deploy without the discursive hegemony of the idea of imperial justice as equity. As the 1857 Revolt had proved, mere political cunning was not enough to keep India divided. This discursive ideological hegemony of justice as equity allowed the British Empire to mobilize what came to be known as 'Indian Opinion' to its side.

In so far as the nature of the alien state was concerned, it necessarily had to be absolutist, it was claimed, because Indian society was incompatible with representative government based on the idea of freedom. Viceroy Dufferin concluded that because of 'the congeries of nations, religions, tribes, and communities, with the tremendous latent forces and disruptive potentialities that they contain' the representative principle based on a discourse of legislative freedom could not be introduced into the legislative councils in India.[35] In so far as the conflicts and antagonisms between communities in India rendered 'it absolutely unfitted to have its affairs administered by any ... modern democratic machinery' and 'no real "Representation" of the people (could) be obtained,' the British Indian Empire had by necessity to be a despotic empire and the Executive that represented Britain's imperium in India 'an Executive directly responsible, not to any local authority, but to the Sovereign and to the British Parliament.'[36]

In the discourse of justice as equity as a colonial discourse of governance, the alien origin of the British Empire and the principle of absolutism went hand-in-hand. Here is J.F. Stephen (who, as

[35] Ibid., p. 1192.
[36] Ibid., pp. 1199, 1202.

I cited earlier, had articulated the need for a discourse of justice as governance) laying out the foundations of British government in India:

It is essentially an absolute government, founded, not in consent but on conquest. It does not represent the native principles of life or of government, and it can never do so until it represents heathenism and barbarism. It represents a belligerent civilization, and no anomaly can be more striking or so dangerous, as its administration by men, who being at the head of a Government founded upon conquest, implying at every point the superiority of the conquering race, of their ideas, their institutions, their opinions and their principles, and having no justification for its existence except that superiority, shrink from the open, uncompromising, straightforward assertion of it, seek to apologize for their own position, and refuse, from whatever cause, to uphold and support it.[37]

For Stephen the idea of 'absolute government' necessarily derived from the idea of empire as based on conquest. It was also based on the idea of foreignness. In his view there was absolutely nothing in common between the two countries of Great Britain and India and their cultures; race, ideas, institutions, opinions, and principles were not just utterly different, but indeed opposed to each other. India was a 'belligerent' civilization. The British Empire had no other 'justification except [its civilization, military, and political] superiority.' As is all too evident, the representation of India as a land in the Hobbesian 'state of nature' that was part of the discourse of colonialism in pre-1857 India continued to be an essential part of the discourse of justice as equity in India under the Crown.

It is not surprising then that institutionally in post-1857 India the discourse of justice as equity went hand-in-hand with an absolutist executive.[38] Having incorporated the discourse of justice and the figure of the monarch as its own foundation, the colonial executive was much less dependent in this period on the judiciary for its own legitimacy. The Council Act of 1861 made the executive all-powerful and unequivocally subordinated the Indian Legislative Council to it.[39] The assertive and activist role played by the judges in the Legislative Council of 1853–8, their continuous public questioning of the executive

---

[37] Letter of J.F. Stephen to *The Times*, 1 March 1883.

[38] For a comprehensive narrative history of British administrative policy in India in the post 1857 period, see Gopal, *British Policy in India*.

[39] Ibid., pp. 20–1.

and demands for its legal accountability that had been a constant source of embarrassment to the Indian administration, were now seen as having undermined the legitimacy of British rule in the eyes of the native public. The Council Act of 1861 asserted in no uncertain terms the Indian Legislative Council's difference from the English Parliament, and declared that the council was not a representative or deliberative body and could not inquire into grievances, call for information or examine the conduct of the executive. It was merely a consultative body for executive departments and its function was to give opinions in cases and matters referred by the executive, such as the construction of statutes, cases involving legal principles, amendments of the law and notifications under any enactment. However, the executive was not bound to accept these suggestions. Moreover, all legislative proposals were to originate in the executive department and any differences of opinion among members of the government were to be exhausted in the executive and not voiced in the legislative council, where the act forbade any dissension.[40]

The supremacy of the executive government in legislative proceedings and its appropriation of the discourse of justice as a discourse of governance was best symbolized by the exclusion of the judges from the new council and silencing of the independent voice of the judiciary that had for so long been internal to the council. Sir Charles Wood wrote to Bartle Frere on 2 September 1860 that he was clearly against having judges in the legislative council.[41] Indeed the Councils Act of 1861 came to be known as the 'bill to extinguish Sir Barnes Peacock,' the Supreme Court judge who had tried to turn the earlier Council into a forum to record and address the complaints of the people.[42] The Indian legislature in the period immediately following 1857 was thus reduced to nothing but the executive acting publicly with minor checks and sanctions in matters that were otherwise beyond the competency of the executive government acting alone.[43]

Although non-official Indian members were now included in the new legislative council, their role was purely consultative. Indian

[40] Phillips, *Indian Legislation and Legislative Councils*, p. 20.
[41] Martineau, *The Life and Correspondence of the Right Hon. Sir Bartle Frere*, p. 331.
[42] Sharan, *The Imperial Legislative Council of India*, p. 29.
[43] Ibid., p. 30.

members of the Legislative Council of 1861 were not elected by the people but rather selected by the government on the basis of the social group to which they belonged. They had no legislative powers other than to suggest improvements in administration and advise the government on important decisions. The legislature was neither sovereign nor representative and was completely controlled by the executive.[44] In other words, the discourse and practice of legislation was reduced to nothing more than a tool of the executive. In C. Ilbert's opinion the newly formed legislative council of 1861 was 'as good a specimen of a bureaucratic legislature as can be found. The debates in the legislature were formal, unreal and soporific. The case of the intelligent, capable and public-minded official is effectively presented but one would like to hear more of what could be said by those on whom the law is to operate.'[45]

Having identified the warring communities as the basic units of Indian civil society, the colonial executive now turned the discourse of justice as equity into a legislative principle. It was not just the administering of law, but the making of law itself that became an act of justice as equity. Universality was dropped as the fundamental legislative principle which is common to most modern polities. Now law came to be directed to the particular, an essential feature of the notion of equity. Commenting on the necessity of the census, the Secretary of State argued in 1901:

The entire framework of native life in India is made up of groups of this kind, and the status and conduct of individuals are largely determined by the rules of the group to which they belong. For the purposes of legislation, of judicial procedure, of famine relief, of sanitation and dealings with epidemic disease, and of almost every form of executive action, an ethnographic survey of India and a record of the customs of the people is as necessary an incident of good administration as a cadastral survey of the land and a record of the rights of its tenants.[46]

As is evident in this passage, 'legislation' and 'judicial procedure' appeared with a litany of other duties—such as sanitation and

[44] Ghosh, *Comparative Administrative Law with Special Reference to the Organization and Legal Position of the Administrative Authorities in British India*, p. 84.

[45] Ilbert, *Legislative Forms and Methods*, p. 225.

[46] Resolution of the Government of India, Home Department (Public) no. 3919, May 23, 1901, Simla, National Archives of India.

famine relief—of governance, as if they were parts of the same continuum. This was characteristic of the general ethos under the colonial state in the post-1857 period that reduced all other aspects of the state—such as legislation and judicial procedures—to its core need of governance or exercise of executive power. What is also evident in this passage is the nature and origin of the colonial state's need to collect vast amounts of data based on identities; even as the Indian civil society was being divided up in the guise of catering to the needs of particular communities, it was the exteriority of the colonial state that was also being legitimized.

Thus Charles Wood's statement in course of the debate on the Indian Councils Bill of 1861, 'we have to legislate for different races with different languages, manners, and customs' was incorporated in the Lord Cross' Act of 1892 that, as Lansdowne saw it, would produce—rightly, in his view—Councilors 'who will represent types and classes rather than areas and numbers.'[47] It was because justice as equity had already been turned into a legislative principle directed to the particular that the only way Indians could be allowed into legislative councils was as representatives of 'types and classes,' in other words, as castes and communities, not as 'areas and numbers,' that is, as citizens. It was this legislative principle that later gave rise to the idea of 'separate electorate' that opened up a whole new domain of politics for communities scrambling to get representation in the legislative council proportionate to their actual number in the population. Particularization became the central legislative strategy of colonial rule in post 1857 India.

Justice as Equity and the Politicization of Caste

The mode and consequences of the deployment of the discourse of justice as equity as a strategy to fragment Indian civil society was most evident in the colonial administration's use of the category of caste in the post-1857 period. The connection in British India between the discourse of imperial justice and a new legal and administrative discourse about a divided India is evident in the fact that it was soon after the Queen's Proclamation of 1858 that set the stage for justice as the discourse of governance that the British legal and administrative policy came to be based on actively foregrounding

---

[47] Lansdowne's Speech, 16 March, 1893. Proceedings of the Legislative Council of the Governor-General of India, XXXII, 1893, pp. 105–11.

the caste system. Caste, the British colonial regime in India claimed, represented the essentially divided and conflictual nature of Indian society. As historians Susan Bayly, Nicholas Dirks, Ronald Inden, Thomas Metcalf, and others have pointed out, it was after 1857 that the British constructed caste as the most important category by which to understand and govern Indian society while ignoring other forms of social identification.[48] The British reified caste, scholars of caste have contended, by means of various colonial instruments, such as district manuals and gazetteers, imperial surveys, and finally the census of 1872, and made varna—the hierarchical ordering of castes into four groups with the Brahman at the top—the central idea behind the classification of Indian society.

What needs to be added, however, to the existing scholarship on caste under the British Empire in India is that it was the discourse of justice as equity that opened up the discursive space for various mechanisms—such as the census—to collect data on Indian civil society and give it meaning; what Dirks calls 'the textualization of social identity,' was framed by the notion of imperial justice as the discourse of governance.[49] The fact that the Census administrators were not interested in the academic description of Indian society but were driven by the ideological need to naturalize the absence of national unity and identity in India and then institutionalize it by integrating it into routine administrative decisions and policies is evident from the numerous statements of census commissioners like J.A. Baines (commissioner for the Census of 1891) and H.H. Risley (supervisor of the 1891 census for Bengal). Baines in the opening paragraph of the preface to the census wrote, 'it is well to begin by clearing out of the way the notion that in the Indian population there is any of the cohesive element that is implied in the term nationality. There is, indeed, an influence peculiar to the country, but it is adverse to nationality, and tends rather towards detachment without independence.'[50] Along the same lines, Risley commented in *The People of India* that Indians did not have the capacity to develop an idea of nationality, let alone rule themselves,

[48] Inden, *Imagining India*; Metcalf, *Ideologies of the Raj*; Bayly, *The New Cambridge History of India IV. 3. Caste, Society, and Politics in India from the Eighteenth Century to the Modern Age*; Dirks, *Castes of Mind: Colonialism and the Making of Modern India*.

[49] Dirks, *Castes of Mind*, p. 236.

[50] Baines, *General Report on the Census of India, 1891*, p. 121.

and this he ascribed primarily to the institution of caste. 'So long as a regime of caste persists, it is difficult to see how the sentiment of unity and solidarity can penetrate and inspire all classes of the community from the highest to the lowest.'[51]

It was the enumeration on the basis of caste in the 1872 census, historians like Sekhar Bandyopadhyay and Sumit Sarkar have claimed, that launched a whole new domain of public concern based on caste. Different caste groups alarmed about having their caste identity fixed forever in government documents started to petition the British census commissioners to have their claims to higher social or caste status recognized.[52] In Maharashtra various lower caste groups sought to be recorded as Ksatriya or Vaisya during the censuses of 1891 and 1901. The census commissioner in 1911 reported that hundreds of petitions appealing for a higher place in the caste hierarchy were received from different caste organizations which weighed as much as one and a half maunds (120 pounds).[53] Numerous texts began to be written by writers from lower castes offering historical evidence to justify their claims of higher caste status groups.

Once the essentially divided nature of Indian society based on caste and by implication the absence of national unity was made to appear natural, it then became the basis for Census supervisor Risley's political claim that Indian society was only compatible with ancient Indian monarchy or modern British 'benevolent despotism,' in other words, a state that was external to society and meted out justice to its conflicting parts from above.[54] The claim that the state in precolonial India was despotic was part of an imperial political manoeuvre to justify the presence of an alien and despotic colonial state by making it appear natural and organic to India. Commenting on the adjudicatory aspects of Risley's comments on caste, Dirks writes, 'One imagines that Risley would have set himself up as an ancient Indian monarch if only he could have, adjudicating competing claims over status with calipers in one hand and statistical tables

---

[51] Risley, *The People of India*, p. 287.

[52] Sarkar, *Writing Social History*, p. 376; Bandyopadhyay, *Caste, Protest, and Identity in Colonial India: The Namasudras of Bengal, 1872–1947*.

[53] O'Malley, *Report on the Census of India, Bengal, Bihar and Orissa and Sikkim*.

[54] Risley, *The People of India*, p. 281.

about nasal indices in the other.'[55] Yet the model for Risley was not so much an Indian monarch, but the Queen of England herself meting out imperial justice to her Indian subjects in the post-1857 period. Risley, in fact, was recasting Indian monarchs in the image of the British imperial monarch as she related to India. It is no surprise then that Risley was vehemently opposed to representative government based on the discourse of universality and freedom for India and was, quite predictably, a strong proponent for separate electorates based on religion and caste.[56]

The evidence of the success of the imperial strategy behind the discourse of justice as equity was not too long in coming. Predictably, given the number of castes running into hundreds, further divided along regional and linguistic boundaries, each group began to think of itself as a minority and as such felt afraid of a future without the British Empire that might expose them to domination by other groups. In 1916, the Justice Party—a very revealing name in the context of our discussion—came to be formed in Madras to represent the interests of non-Brahmans; it worked towards getting non-Brahmans a greater proportion of government jobs. The Justice Party refused to join the Congress campaign for Home Rule, viewing it as largely driven by Brahman interests. Indeed, it brought out a Manifesto that claimed that non-Brahmans supported the British Empire because of its commitment to *justice* for all castes and creeds (emphasis mine).[57]

On the other hand, the Indian National Congress, which did indeed have a disproportionately large number of Brahmans, was not interested in complete national independence either. The Congress goal of Home Rule, after all, was meant to gain more governmental autonomy for India even while remaining part of the British Empire. As powerful as the Brahmans were, given that as a caste they constituted only a small percentage of the Indian

---

[55] Dirks, *Castes of Mind*, p. 226

[56] Significantly, as Hermann Kulke and Dietmar Rothermund have pointed out, the Morley-Minto Reforms that granted separate electorates to Muslims were determined to a large measure by Risley who insisted on representation of communities rather than territorial representation. See Kulke and Rothermund, *A History of India*, p. 271.

[57] The Non-Brahman manifesto is printed as an appendix to Irschick, *Politics and Social Conflict in South India: The Non-Brahman Movement and Tamil Separatism, 1916–1929*; Baker, *The Politics of South India 1920–1937*; Dirks, *Castes of Mind*, pp. 242–3.

population, they too did not want to face a future without the British Empire, which could expose them to possible domination by numerically larger castes. The reluctance of the Congress to mobilize the masses against the British Empire came partly from the elite social base of much of its leadership. Any such large-scale mobilization that could stir up the masses was likely to spawn a new leadership that could threaten their dominance. Therefore, a slow movement through constitutional negotiations with the British Empire towards a purely administrative autonomy—stripped of any mass ideology such as nationalism—which gave the Brahmans and other elite groups more access to state power even as it kept the masses at bay became the preferred way. Home rule, as I will discuss in the next chapter, was an embodiment of this vision of a purely administrative autonomy. It was the discourse of imperial justice as liberty that would allow the Congress to pursue this goal.

The process of the politicization of caste began in earnest in the early twentieth century, a few decades after the first census. In Bengal, Sumit Sarkar points out, there was an explosion of caste politics between 1905 and 1920.[58] It was the discourse of justice that gave caste a voice and a language to speak in; social division along caste lines was sold to Indians in the name of justice. It was in the language of imperial justice that the empire constructed and addressed its subjects, and it was in the language of justice that the castes responded to the empire. The politicization of caste, in other words, began as the pursuit of social justice. The discourse of social justice, in turn, assumed the divided nature of the civil society and the need for the exteriority of the state to the civil society. To not take this language of justice into account in any exploration of the phenomenon of caste in modern times is either to miss the discursive framework in which it appears, or to de-historicize and thus naturalize it.

Under these historical circumstances, the possibility of a mass movement based on the discourse of political freedom with the goal of national independence appeared unlikely, if not impossible. Justice, not surprisingly, seemed like the only viable category for any political movement. As I argue in the next chapter, the Indian National Congress came to be firmly lodged within the epistemologico-juridical paradigm determined by the telos of what I

---

[58] Sarkar, *Writing Social History*, p. 376.

have identified as imperial justice as liberty. This juridical paradigm explains why the Indian National Congress, even as it critiqued the colonial government, continued to operate within an imperial juridical framework grounded in the figure of the monarch and thus failed to articulate a demand for complete national independence until Gandhi took over its leadership. With the limits of its military power exposed during the Revolt of 1857, the British Empire constructed labyrinths of discourse and offered it to Indians as a path to freedom, a path that became the very ground of the Indian National Congress. It was not until the non-cooperation movement led by Gandhi that a way out of this labyrinth towards national independence was found.

4

'VAKIL RAJ'

The Indian National Congress and the Birth of the Lawyer as Political Representative

While pleading for elected representation in the Indian Legislative Council in 1906, Madan Mohan Malaviya, a prominent leader of the Indian National Congress, argued:

In the reformed councils, the *government* will be exactly what they now are—the final arbiter of all questions that may be brought before the Council—in other words they will occupy the position of a *judge* in deciding all questions affecting our purses, our character, in fact, our whole being. The sole *privilege* that we are asking for is to be allowed *to choose* our own *counsel* to represent our cases and conditions before them ... The privilege of selecting one's own counsel is not denied even to the most abandoned of criminals under British rule. Why then should it be denied to the loyal and intelligent subjects of her Gracious Majesty? (emphasis mine)[1]

This passage is as striking as it is puzzling. It also lays bare the very foundation of the political philosophy of the Indian National Congress, the most powerful political party in colonial India; it contains the self-understanding of the Congress as a party, its view of the British Empire and expectations from it, and its understanding of India's place—and also hopes—in the Empire.

[1] Malaviya, *Speeches of Pandit Madan Mohan Malaviya*, p. 25. Madan Mohan Malaviya (1861–1946) was a prominent member of the Indian National Congress and was elected its President in 1909, 1918, 1932, and 1933. Trained in the law, he was a well-known journalist and educationalist. He founded the Benaras Hindu University, one of the premier educational institutions in India in 1916.

The first thing to be noted in the above passage is that Malaviya is pleading for popular elections to the Viceroy's Legislative Council in which the colonial executive had absolute power. Given that the practice of choosing one's representative to a legislative body is the very bedrock of modern democracy, what Malaviya is pleading for is freedom. What is surprising, however, is that this plea for freedom is addressed to the Queen—'her Gracious Majesty'—by her 'loyal and intelligent subject.' As is evident, the Congress discourse of freedom is anchored in the figure of the monarch. It was as subjects of the Queen that the Congress pleaded for freedom and hoped to receive it; it was as subjects of the British Empire that the Congress hoped that Indians would become free, not as citizens of India. How contrary this Congress understanding and pursuit of freedom is to much of modern history could be gauged from the fact that in most other major polities of the world freedom was won by either driving out the foreign colonial state or by putting an end to the monarchy. The Congress, on the other hand, hoped to receive freedom as a gift from a monarchy that was also foreign. What is evident is that the Congress discourse of freedom is in direct continuity with the discourse of imperial justice as liberty anchored in the figure of the monarch as we discussed in the last chapter.

What is also significant in the passage cited above is that Malaviya is pleading for freedom in the name of justice. The demand for freedom is not only grounded in justice, indeed freedom itself appears as a gift of justice. In the hierarchy of categories that constituted the political discourse of the Congress, the category of justice held the sovereign position and stood above that of freedom. The Congress could not think of freedom without also thinking of it as a gift of justice. It is important to note, however, that the category of justice as it was deployed in Congress discourse had a very specific connotation; it was a justice that was not anchored in law—either common or natural—but rather in the figure of the Queen. Justice stood above law just as the figure of the Queen in this discourse stood above any notions of law. This is the notion of justice as equity grounded in the benevolence and charity of the monarch to her 'loyal' subjects. It is not surprising, therefore, that for Malaviya, the freedom to elect one's own representatives to the Legislative Council was a 'privilege'—not a right. The Congress discourse of freedom was grounded not in the sovereignty of the people but rather in the sovereignty of the Queen. This specific understanding of freedom as a gift of justice set the Congress apart from most other modern movements for freedom.

It was because the Congress understood freedom as a privilege and a gift of the Empire that it pursued it through a politics of pleading and petitioning. In so far as the idea of armed struggle or even unarmed resistance is altogether incompatible with the understanding of freedom as a privilege, it is not surprising, that the very notion of resistance, let alone a violent one, was alien to the discourse and general ethos of the Congress. In this regard, the use of the word 'intelligent' in Malaviya's phrase 'loyal and intelligent subjects of her Gracious Majesty' is a revealing one. It was not an expression of Malaviya's vanity. Rather it contained a subtle message to the Queen and her Empire in India; the Congress was not so foolish that it would give in to temptations of an armed revolution, as people in other colonized countries had done. It was also Malaviya's way of publicly dissociating himself and the Congress from an emergent form of militant nationalism in the wake of the 1905 partition of Bengal by the colonial government. The Congress, it needs to be noted, was always aware of this other path to national independence and freedom, the path that called for a violent revolution to drive out the Empire from India, the path that it chose not to take. It was a choice that the Congress never failed to remind the British Empire of, not only to prove its loyalty and value, but also to win some concessions in return. Given the dominance of the Congress as the most important political organization for Indians, this discourse inevitably gave rise to a general political and intellectual ethos that looked askance at the ideas of resistance and revolt. The recourse to resistance and revolt in the pursuit of freedom was nothing but a sign of the absence of 'intelligence.'

What is also striking about Malaviya's argument for popular elections for the legislative council is that it was not just the concept of freedom that was subordinated to the concept of justice, it was also the legislative council as an institution that was being reconfigured in the image of the law court. Malaviya's statement runs counter to most accepted political theories of the modern state that often assume the separation and division of powers between executive, legislative, and judicial institutions as separate domains with their own networks of categories, functions, and procedures. Malaviya argued for the election of Indian representatives to the legislative council by first discursively reconfiguring the legislative council in the image of a court of law and then proceeding to logically derive his arguments in support of his demand. It was as if concepts, functions, and procedures could be de-territorialized from the institution of the law court and then re-territorialized on the legislative council, giving rise to an even more complex institutional configuration. It also reveals just how central the image of the law court with all its attendant discursive categories and rules was to the political discourse and practice of the Congress.

Let me begin by looking at the generalized topology that determines the functioning of concepts in the above statement, both in terms of the logical connections that are forged between different concepts and also the sequence of reasoning which leads from a certain premise to a conclusion. What is assumed in Malaviya's statement is a theory of political and legislative sovereignty—a government becomes the sovereign as a judge, 'the final arbiter'. Even as Malaviya conceded that 'the government will remain the same' as the undisputed center of power and authority, by investing the government with the persona of a judge he was forcing it to conform to the precepts and procedures of justice. In sharp contrast to the generally accepted ideas about the separation of powers, Malaviya's statement assumed the idea of a compound institution— a *legislative court*. In its new configuration, even as the function of the legislative council remained that of making laws and taking executive decisions, conceptually, structurally, and procedurally it would have to be reconstituted in the image of a court of law.

Having set up the image of a court of law at the origin of his discourse, Malaviya deductively argued that just as a judge could neither select the lawyers for the plaintiff and the defendant nor could he come to a judgment without them, the government as judge must also allow the people of India to choose their own representatives. This was a radical demand in so far as Malaviya was trying to introduce the idea and practice of *elected representation* for the first time into the institutional site of the legislative council. Until then Indian members in the council selected by the government were counsels to the government—not representatives of the people— advising it on the practices, customs, and opinions of the people. The demand that members be elected created, for the first time, the discursive space for a representative of the people in the legislative council. Malaviya, however, was not arguing for the elected majority of Indians in the council to form the government. Indeed, he was not even pleading for them to have voting rights in the council. All he was arguing for was that elected Indian representatives be heard in the legislative council before an executive decision was taken or a law passed. In other words, what Malviya had in mind were *legislator-pleaders*. It was only as a lawyer that an Indian could become a legislator in the political vision of the Congress.

However, even as Malaviya conceded the government much of its executive and legislative powers while restricting that of the public representative to mere pleading, he also radically, if subtly, tried to reconstitute the relation between the government and the people by introducing the judicial framework in the domain of legislative practice. In the reconstituted legislative council the government would no longer be the sole actor; it would have to operate in a transactional field whose operations were to be determined by a set of pre-given judicial rules such as publicity, strict rules of evidence, and the priority of judicial precedents; it would no longer be possible to continue with the system of arbitrary despotic rule by the executive that had characterized the practice of governance for so long.

Malaviya's passage gives a glimpse into one more aspect of the Congress that often goes unnoticed, but is of vital importance. While assuring the colonial government that much of its powers would remain intact in the reformed Council, Malaviya says: 'they [the government] will occupy the position of a *judge* in deciding all questions affecting our purses, our character, in fact, our whole being.' The terms to be noted here are 'character' and 'whole being'. It was as if Malaviya wanted to emphasize that in the nature of the colonial government and the discourse of justice and freedom much more was at stake than what is usually assumed to fall within the domain of governance, such as finance for example. What was at stake was the very being of the Indian as an Indian; not just what the Indian did not think, but *who* and *what* he was. The 'whole being' and the 'character' point to the birth of a new subjectivity—imperial subjectivity. This imperial subjectivity consisted in the Congress seeking freedom as if it was a new identity—British identity—that was being sought.

In the last chapter I discussed how notions of justice, equity, and liberty that were introduced in India by the British Empire in the wake of the 1857 Revolt were mediated by the figure of the monarch. This chapter focuses on how that historical mediation overdetermined the origin and nature of the Indian National

Congress, the most powerful political party in colonial India that came to be founded in 1888.

THE LAWYER AS ENUNCIATIVE PERSONA

The enunciative persona of a lawyer that Madan Mohan Malaviya took on in making this speech is not entirely surprising given that the Indian National Congress since its very inception was dominated by lawyers, barristers, and judges, many of whom were trained in London.[2] Of the group of nine men who formed the central leadership in the early Congress, as many as six—Pherozeshah Mehta, Badruddin Tyabji, W.C. Bonnerjee, Manmohan Ghose, Lalmohan Ghose, and Anandamohan Bose—were lawyers and two, Surendranath Banerjea and Romeshchandra Dutt, had received legal training.[3] Eleven of the sixteen Indian Presidents of the Indian National Congress between 1885 and 1909 were lawyers. Even amongst the delegates who were not in leadership positions, over one-third in the period 1885–1914 were lawyers. Indeed, the dominance of lawyers in leadership positions in the Indian National Congress continued even after this period, and included such prominent names as M.K. Gandhi, C.R. Das, Mohammed Ali Jinnah, B.R. Ambedkar, and J. Nehru.

The central role of lawyers in the Indian National Congress inevitably grew out of their importance in the politics of both Presidency towns and provincial towns. As Anil Seal has stated, 'in the Presidency capitals it was the successful high lawyer who was the backbone of politics; in the mofussil [districts] it was the pleader at the district bar.'[4] Historians of the Cambridge School have attributed the dominant role that the legal profession and other such professions played in national politics to patron-client relationships in this period, which, according to them, was vital to the growth of political association in India both at the local level and at the national level.[5] They argue that the Indian National

---

[2] See Misra, *The Indian Middle Classes; Their Growth in Modern Times,* p. 316; McLane, *Indian Nationalism and the Early Congress,* pp. 52–4; Seal, *The Emergence of Indian Nationalism: Competition and Collaboration in the Later Nineteenth Century,* pp. 123–130.

[3] See McLane, *Indian Nationalism and the Early Congress,* pp. 52–4.

[4] Seal, *Emergence of Indian Nationalism,* p. 130.

[5] Johnson, *Provincial Politics and Indian Nationalism: Bombay and the Indian National Congress 1880 to 1915*; Bayly, *The Local Roots of Indian Politics:*

Congress was not really nationalist but rather a body constituted by men who had little commonality of national goals, and pursued narrow local parochial ends and often the selfish advancement of their careers. Thus Anil Seal claimed that 'it is no longer credible to write about a [Congress] movement grounded in common aims, led by similar backgrounds, and recruited from widening groups with compatible interests. That movement now looks more like a ramshackle coalition throughout its whole career. Its unity seems a figment.'[6] Seal speculated that the main motivation behind the participation of Indians in the Indian National Congress despite their 'local rivalries' and 'glaring national differences' 'may well have been to strengthen their position inside their local societies.'[7] Thus, studies by the Cambridge School have focused on the socio-historical conditions for the rise of the profession of lawyers in cities and towns in nineteenth-century India only to argue that their participation in both national and local politics derived from their individual professional and class interests.

John McLane has also stressed the importance of the connection between the national and the local in his important work on early nationalism in India.[8] Thus, he argues that 'while the Congress seemed to be monopolized by lawyers, the lawyers were frequently linked through mercantile and landed patrons, as well as vakil clients, to a broad spectrum of society.'[9] This was due to the rapid expansion and growth of the legal profession in the nineteenth-century in India, specifically as a result of a substantial rise in litigation in the Presidency towns of Calcutta, Bombay and Madras, and also in the provincial towns brought about by new British agricultural laws and economic policies.[10] The difficulty of wading through new and complicated legal rules and procedures introduced by the British

---

Allahabad 1880–1920; Washbrook, *The Emergence of Provincial Politics, The Madras Presidency 1870–1920*; Seal, *The Emergence of Indian Nationalism*.

[6] Seal, 'Imperialism and Nationalism in India', p. 2.

[7] Seal, *The Emergence of Indian Nationalism*, pp. 112–13.

[8] McLane rejects the broader claim of the Cambridge school that the Congress was a movement of self-interested individuals, and stresses their commonality of purpose and broader collective vision. See McLane, *Indian Nationalism*, 7.

[9] Ibid., p. 9.

[10] For the use of Western legal discourse by the bhadrolok in Bengal to construct its identity as a class see Mukhopadhyay, *Behind the Mask: The Cultural Definition of the Legal Subject in Colonial Bengal (1715–1911)*.

made it almost imperative for land owners as well as commercial men to take the services of lawyers and 'vakils' trained in the British system.[11] The spread of legal education and rise of universities specifically devoted to the study of law in the nineteenth century meant that opportunities for participating in the legal profession were opening up to a large section of the English-educated middle class who had no difficulty finding employment.[12] Thus, it was no surprise, as Bipan Chandra Pal noted, writing about Bengal in the late nineteenth century, that lawyers were advancing rapidly into considerable power and influence over their countrymen in every district through their position at the Bar. This was the beginning of what came to be subsequently characterized as 'Vakil Raj' or the rule of the lawyers.[13]

While studies on the social origins of the groups that participated in the Indian National Congress do throw valuable light on the nature of the party and its politics, it is inadequate to study political discourse simply on the basis of speculations about the motivations of Congressmen deriving primarily from their class or personal interests.[14] In approaching lawyers as real or substantive persons what this approach misses is the persona of the lawyer and the discourse of imperial justice. These studies have not taken political discourse seriously, treating it simply as a mask to cover up 'real' interests that were often petty and personal. This methodology attributes far too much agency to individuals and groups, and ignores the larger discursive and institutional practices that brought about newer

[11] The term 'vakil' referred to intermediaries in the Mughal period who represented their clients' interests in various fields, legal and commercial. In the British period, 'vakils' came to take on the role of lawyers and represented their clients in the law courts. The term was used to denote lawyers of the lowest rung in the British Indian legal system. There have not been any full length studies of the role of the lawyers in Indian politics. The only article-length work on the legal profession is Schmitthenner, 'The Development of the Legal Profession in India'.

[12] As professional lawyers they were trained in the dominant legal philosophy of the day that was averse to ideas of popular representation and democracy. See Austin, *Lectures on Jurisprudence or the Philosophy of Positive Law*; Norton, *Topics of Jurisprudence or aids to the Office of the Indian Judge*; Maine, *Popular Government*.

[13] Bipan Chandra Pal, *Memories of my Life and Times*, p. xxxiv.

[14] This includes works written from a Marxist perspective. See Dutt, *India Today* and Desai, *Social Background of Indian Nationalism*.

forms of subjects and subjectivity in the colonial period.[15] It is not because these men were lawyers with personal connections at the local and national level that they came to participate in such large numbers in national politics, but rather because representational politics itself was grounded in a juridico-epistemological field and structured by the discursive methodologies, procedures, and practices of the British law court, that a space was created within which lawyers emerged as the model political representatives. The unity of the Indian National Congress derived specifically from it's grounding in this juridical discursive framework.

The anticolonial movement led by the early or pre-Gandhian Indian National Congress was neither driven by nationalism nor by class interest alone.[16] Its anticolonial campaign was anchored in the discourse of imperial justice—not in nationalism. Its demand for limited freedom was not based on the idea of the representative will of the people, nor indeed was it addressed to the people of India. Rather it was grounded in the category of imperial justice as equity and addressed to the Queen as imperial judge. Indeed, it was in the Congress' faith in the inherent justice of the empire emanating from the benevolence and mercy of the monarch rather than in the universality of law that its opposition to colonialism was grounded. This explains why the Indian National Congress was constrained

---

[15] For an important analysis of 'moderate nationalism' see Sanjay Seth, 'Rewriting Histories of Nationalism: The Politics of "Moderate Nationalism" in India, 1870–1905', *American Historical Review*, pp. 95–116. While the author focuses on the political thought of the early Congress, a look at some of the central categories that underpin his study, like 'loyalism', 'moderation of aims and goals', and 'obsessive concern with poverty' reveals that these are not so much discursive categories as psychological ones. Seth's frequent use of the term 'obsession' in crucial moments in the article confirms the psychological orientation of his study.

[16] There is a general agreement among historians of modern India that the Indian National Congress was a nationalist political formation, sometimes with the caveat that this nationalism was in its formative stage. See Sitaramaya, *History of the Indian National Congress*, vol. 1, 1885–1935; Chandra, Mukherjee, Mukherjee, Panikkar, Mahajan, *India's Struggle for Independence, 1857–1947*; Desai, *Social Background of Indian Nationalism*; Suntharalingam, *Indian Nationalism: an Historical Analysis*; Sarkar, *Modern India, 1885–1947*; Habib, *Essays in Indian History: Towards a Marxist Perception*; Masselos, *Indian Nationalism, a History*. For the most important works written by Subaltern historians, see Chatterjee, *Nationalist Thought and the Colonial World: A Derivative Discourse?*; Guha, *Dominance Without Hegemony: History and Power in Colonial India*. Also see Kaviraj, 'The Imaginary Institution of India', pp. 1–28.

to identify with the empire even as it opposed colonialism. The Congress, in other words, was an imperial political formation.

In what follows, I explore the construction of a juridical discursive framework within which Congress politics was lodged. I contend that the Indian National Congress as a representative body was constructed not in the image of the British House of Commons but rather that of the British House of Lords as the High Court of Appeal with the Queen as its central figure. That is why the Congress' mode of politics took the form of pleading and petitioning by a small group of educated elite led by the lawyer, who emerged as the quintessential political representative in the late nineteenth century. I focus not so much on the specificities of the demands of the Congress, but rather on moments in which speakers reflect on the very ground and conditions of the possibility of their discourse. I conclude the chapter by looking at the critique of the Congress discourse of imperial justice that came to be articulated in early twentieth-century India by leaders of a competing political movement grounded in a discourse of legislative freedom.

The Indian National Congress was born in 1885 as a representative forum for Indians in the absence of real representation in the Indian Legislative Council.[17] From its very inception, the Congress saw itself, not as a political party but as a virtual Parliament.[18] In a leaflet called the 'Tamil Catechism on the Indian National Congress' that

---

[17] The ground for its emergence was laid in many ways by the Indian vernacular press, that in the absence of representative institutions for Indians in the period 1861 and 1885, had come to occupy the discursive space of a representative body and had quickly become the principal forum where the administration was interrogated and called into account on a daily basis. The bitter conflicts between the executive and the press, as reflected in repressive acts like the Vernacular Press Act of 1872 that tried to throttle the vernacular press, and various sedition acts that severely restricted the freedom of the press to criticize the government, pointed to the deep apprehension of the colonial executive at the growing importance of vernacular newspapers as the primary representative forum, where public criticisms of the government could be launched. It is striking that the epistemological architecture of the newspapers in this period was itself based on that of the law court as evident in the editorials that were articulated from the enunciative position of a lawyer and criticized administrative acts in terms of judicial categories like neutrality and impartiality. Natarajan, *History of Indian Journalism.*

[18] For a comprehensive account of the formation of the Congress see Mehrotra, *The Emergence of the Indian National Congress.* Also see Majumdar, *Indian Political Associations and Reform of Legislature 1818–1917*; Majumdar and Majumdar, *Congress and Congressmen in the pre-Gandhian Era, 1885–1917.*

was attached to the appendix of the Report of the 1887 Congress, the reasons for the institution of the Congress were clearly laid out:

The councils in India resemble the Parliament of England only in name. They are called legislative councils. As at present constituted, the councils are mere shams and have no independent power. Their members are entirely powerless to regulate the expenditure of government, even to the extent of a single piece. Nor can they alter or cancel the laws that the Government has resolved to enforce.[19]

Under these conditions, the Congress was conceptualized as an alternate representative space where the real interests and grievances of the people of India would be represented. As the Congress Proceedings stated in 1885, 'Indirectly, the Conference will form the germ of a Native Parliament and, if properly conducted, will constitute in a few years an unanswerable reply to the assertion that India is still wholly unfit for any form of representative institutions.'[20] Two important aspects of the creation of the Congress need to be noted here. First, the Congress thought of itself as a Parliament, not as a party. Second, by proving itself a success the Congress wished to remove all doubts that Indians were not yet capable of forming and maintaining representative institutions. The latter view was based on the assumption that the British Empire's role in India was pedagogical in nature. It was as if Indians, by forming the Congress, were taking a test in the practice of representation, a successful completion of which would eventually result in equal rights for Indians within the Empire.

Even as the Congress projected itself as a representative institution, the image that it had of representatives was not of legislators representing the will and freedom of the people to make their own laws, but rather of lawyers pleading for justice from the government. This is evident in the appendix to the Report of the Third Congress in 1887, which includes a very important pamphlet that is written as a 'catechism' with the specific purpose of instructing the masses on the idea and practice of representation. This pamphlet is particularly significant because it points to the specificity of

[19] Report of the Third Session of the Indian National Congress held at Madras, 1887, Appendix II, All India Congress Committee Papers, Nehru Memorial Library, New Delhi, India.

[20] 'Origin and Composition of the Congress', Proceedings of the Indian National Congress, 1885.

the idea of representational practice that framed the Congress discourse at its very inception. This pedagogy of representation comes in the form of a conversation between Moulvi Farid-Ud-Din, an advocate, and Rambaksh, a villager of Kambakhtpur. It begins with Rambaksh's question to the Advocate 'Moulvi Sahib, there is a great talk nowadays of re-pre-sen-ta-tion and re-pre-sentative ins-ti-tutions, but what does it all mean?'[21]

In response to this inarticulate villager—who, presumably embodies the masses of India—stuttering out the critical words with such hesitation and difficulty, the advocate, rather than propose a definition of representation, drew a familiar image before him:

Don't you remember last year, when you and Matadin and Ramaprasad, and some thirty others of you had cases against Raja Harbans Rai ... and all the cases were quite alike, and you knew well about the matter, and had the best head of the lot, they all chose you and sent you in, to me, to the Sudder, to explain all the cases and get me to put in petitions for them as well as for yourself? Well, that is 'representation' and you were the 'representative.'[22]

What is striking about this attempt to convey the idea of representation through an everyday experience was its essential grounding in the law court, or the *sudder adalat*, and its vital connection to the person of the advocate. In the Congress' political pedagogy the idea and practice of representation was presented as fundamentally juridical, linked to the practice of petitioning one's complaints and grievances in a court of law. Moreover, in this chain of representation, the advocate himself played the indispensable role of mediating between the villagers and the judge. In other words, the practice of representation, as the Congress portrayed it, hinged on the existence of the law court, the paradigmatic representative institution and the persona of the lawyer, the quintessential representative figure in colonial India. If representation was not approached as an abstract concept, but was instead explained with the help of the image of the law court and the practice associated with it, then that was because the law court was the site of the

[21] 'A conversation between Molvi Farid ud Din, MA, BL, Vaquil (Barrister) of the High Court, Practising in the Zillah Court of Hakikatabad, and Rambaksh, one of the Mukaddams (chief villager) of Kambakhtpur', Appendix III of the Proceedings of the Indian National Congress, 1887, p. 205.

[22] Ibid.

origin of the discourse and practice of representation in colonial India. Representation did not come to India as an intellectual idea through the great works of political philosophy from the West; it came as a form of everyday discourse and practice anchored in the institution of the law court.

Thus, unlike in the House of Commons, the claim for representation by the Congress was not grounded on the idea of popular sovereignty or general will. Nor was it ever demanded that legislation for India would have to reflect the real interests of the people, or that the executive government would have to be accountable to the popular will. Rather, the demand was only that the representatives of the people be heard in the legislative council as lawyers articulating genuine popular grievances, as mediators between the government and the people. The final judgment on the public good would continue to rest with the executive.

It is important to keep in mind that the discourse of the Congress was addressed in the immediate colonial context to the Viceroy's Legislative Council that by the Council Act of 1861 had been made into a despotic body in which the colonial executive exercised absolute authority without any sense of accountability. What the Congress was pleading for was that the Council adopt the discursive structure of a court of law like its predecessor the Legislative Council of 1853, where judges had played such an important role in making the Executive accountable.

Congress leaders, taking on the enunciative persona of the lawyer, scrupulously adhered to the rules and systems of constraint that framed the discourse of the lawyer in the courtroom, so that the internal economy of their political discourse bore a remarkably close resemblance to that of judicial discourse within the courtroom. So, for instance, arguments against the British administration in India were given their strength not from a set of universal principles of freedom or liberty, or absolute political ideologies of popular sovereignty, but always proceeded by way of simile, metaphor, analogy, or example, remarkably akin to the methods of argumentation that lawyers use in the court, deploying, what in legal parlance are called 'judicial precedents' and 'illustrations.'[23]

[23] Allen, *Law in the Making*, pp. 161–366. Also see Baker, *An Introduction to English Legal History*. Even though one can see an affinity of ideas between the Indian Nationalists and the British Idealists, it is striking that nowhere in these speeches does one find an explicit reference to political doctrine or principle. Rather

Let me briefly examine the specific juridical practices, rhetorical strategies, and procedures that came to structure the Congress' political discourse. One of the most important discursive rules that determines the proceedings of a law court is the doctrine of judicial precedent, or the rule of 'stare decisis' in the English legal system, which lays down that a judgment issuing from a superior court is binding on any inferior court and must be followed in the future, unless it is overruled by a court higher than that from which the precedent originated. For the doctrine of judicial precedent to function effectively, it is essential that the court be organized into some proper system of hierarchy.

What is striking about early Congress political discourse is that political arguments against the administration invariably proceeded by conferring the status of 'judicial precedents' to the political statements and declarations of British statesmen and administrators, thus seeking to make them binding on all future government decisions and actions. All criticism against the government was launched in terms of its contravention of these past declarations that were constructed as legally binding, just as judicial precedents were in the law courts. Indeed, the crucial importance of these past declarations and pledges for the Congress can be seen from the fact that every year the front page of the Proceedings of the Indian National Congress consisted of an enumeration of some of the most important of England's pledges to India, including the Act of Parliament of 1833, The Queen's Proclamation of 1858, and speeches of different Viceroys, such as Lord Lytton, Lord Rippon, and Lord Dufferin.[24] These pledges constituted the very ground of Congress discourse and in so far as they were symbolically given the status of judgments, the Government, in its role as a 'court of justice' was required to fulfill them.

Gopal Krishna Gokhale, for example, in demanding the reduction of the Salt Duty in 1902, explicitly referred to statements made in the past by important British administrators and legislators like Sir James Westland, David Barbour, Lord Cross, and Lord George Hamilton, and contended that 'In view of these repeated

---

this discourse emerges out of the enunciative position of a lawyer and is framed exclusively by the rules and practices of the law court.

[24] Lord Lytton was Viceroy and Governor-General of India from May 1872 to April 1876, Lord Rippon from June 1880 to December 1884, and Lord Dufferin from December 1884 to December 1888.

declarations, it is a matter of intense regret and disappointment that the government have not taken the present opportunity to reduce a rate of duty, admittedly oppressive, on a prime necessity of life.'[25] Again, Rashbehari Ghosh, in demanding the separation of the executive and judicial functions of government, did not argue on the basis of principle, why this separation was absolutely imperative for the liberty of the subject, but rather made his demand incontrovertible by elaborately quoting the declarations of a host of administrators, like Harvey Adamson, Sir Frederick Halliday, Sir John Peter Grant, Sir Bartle Frere, Sir Cecil Beadon, and Sir Barnes Peacock, who had all condemned the mixing of the two functions in government.[26] Similarly, Dadabhai Naoroji, in contending before

[25] Gokhale, 'Budget Speech of 1902', in John S. Hoyland (ed.), *Gopal Krishna Gokhale, his life and speeches*, p. 76. Gokhale was a founding member of the Indian National Congress and was elected its president in 1905. A well-known educationist, he founded the Servants of India Society that became one of the most important social service organizations in the early twentieth century. He served on the Bombay Legislative Council in 1899 and the Imperial Legislative Council in 1902. For a comprehensive account of Gokhale's life and politics, see Nanda, *Gokhale: The Indian Moderates and the British Raj*.

Sir James Westland was a member of the Indian Civil Service and served in important administrative positions in India from 1862 till 1899, including Under Secretary to the Government of India in the Financial Department in 1870, and Secretary to the Government of India in the Department of Finance and Commerce. Like Westland, David Barbour served as an important member of the Indian Civil Service from 1863 to 1893 and held key positions, including Secretary to the Government of India, Financial Department in 1882, and Financial Member of the Supreme Council of the Governor-General from 1883–93. Lord Cross was Secretary of State for India from 1886–92. Lord George Francis Hamilton was Under Secretary of State for India from 1874–8, and Secretary of State for India from 1886–92. My notes on British administrators are taken from Buckland, *Dictionary of Indian Biography*.

[26] Rashbehari Ghosh, 'Speech in the Town Hall in Calcutta', given in April, 1919 in Zaidi (ed.), *Speeches and Writings of Dr. Sir Rashbehari Ghose*, p. 233. Sir Frederick James Halliday was a member of the Indian Civil Service and served as Secretary to the Government of Bengal in 1838 and Secretary to the Home Department of the Government of India in 1849. He was also a member of the Governor-General's Council from 1853 to 1854, and Lieutenant-Governor of Bengal from 1854 to 1859. Sir John Peter Grant served as a member of the Indian Civil Service from 1828 to 1859, occupying important administrative positions, including Secretary to Government of India in the Home and Foreign Departments (1852–4), and member of the Governor-General's Council from 1854–9. Sir Bartle Frere served as member of the Viceroy's Council in India from 1859–1862. A member of the Indian Civil Service, he was also appointed Governor of Bombay from 1862–1867

the House of Commons in England that the main features of British administration in the last century in India were gross corruption and oppression of the people of India, explicitly requested the House to observe that he would 'put his case (of the conditions of the people of India under the Government of India) in the words of Anglo-Indian English statesmen only and would not say a single word as to what the Indians themselves said.'[27] He then went on to quote the statements of Sir John Shore, Lord Cornwallis, Sir Thomas Monroe, Macaulay, and others, just as a lawyer would cite important judicial precedents to prove his case before a judge.[28] If Naoroji felt constrained not to cite speeches given by Indians, then that was because the words of an Indian did not carry the authority of a precedent.

'Unless history is a record of lies,' Rashbehari Ghosh asserted, in exhorting the people of India to be patient with constitutional agitation, 'Englishmen love freedom as their most cherished possession; but do not forget that the freedom they love is freedom broadening from precedent to precedent.'[29] In this statement the idea of freedom was clearly subordinated to the idea of procedural justice.

---

and member of the India Council from 1867–1877. Cecil Beadon was an important British administrator in India and served as Home Secretary to the Government of India in 1854, member of the Governor-General's Council from 1860 to 1862, and Lieutenant-Governor of Bengal from 1862–7. Sir Barnes Peacock was a legal member of the Governor-General's Council from 1852–9, Chief Justice of the Calcutta Supreme Curt from 1859–62, and Chief Justice of the Bengal High Court from 1862–70. He was also appointed member of the Judicial Committee of the British Privy Council in 1872.

[27] Dadabhai Naoroji, 'Speech in the House of Commons, 1894', in *Poverty and Un-British Rule in India*, p. 276. Dadabhai Naoroji (1825–1917) was a founding member of the Indian National Congress and was elected its President in 1886, 1893, and 1906. A famous educator and businessman, he was the first Indian to be elected Member of the British Parliament in 1892. He advocated the rights of Indians in the House of Commons and became particularly known for his economic critique of British rule. For a biography see Masani, *Dadabhai Naoroji: The Grand Old Man of India*.

[28] Ibid., pp. 276–80. Sir John Shore was Governor-General of India from 1793–1798 and member of the Board of Control from 1807–28. Lord Cornwallis was Governor-General of India from 1786–93. Thomas Babington Macaulay, famous British historian, poet, and Member of Parliament, served in India as the first law member of the Governor-General's Council from 1834–8. Macaulay was also responsible for the drafting of the India law codes.

[29] Rashbehari Ghosh, Report of the twenty-third Indian National Congress held at Surat on the 26th and 27th December 1907, p. xviii.

What is striking is that freedom appeared here not as an abstract principle or ideology but rather in reference to its grounding in judicial precedent. It was through a slow broadening of this judicial device of the precedent that much of modern British history itself came to be incorporated and deployed rhetorically as a model in the Indian anticolonial movement. It was as if there was no need for Indians to make history because all of the greatest political achievements of British history, including democracy itself, could be introduced into India one precedent at a time. Not surprisingly, what was missing in this discourse was any reference to political upheavals or revolution in England in the name of freedom. The Congress' discovery of the judicial precedent as a rhetorical tool rendered the pursuit of freedom through either resistance or revolution redundant.

Congress leaders were aware of the difference between the nature of the state in a country like Britain where people made their own history and in India where history was to be made through precedents. So, for instance, Gopal Krishna Gokhale, protesting against the speedy passing of the Land Alienation Bill in the Bombay Legislative Council without taking into account public opinion, argued:

Does anyone imagine that a measure of such far-reaching tendencies would have been introduced in England and passed through Parliament with so much precipitation in spite of the unanimous protests of the people? And I submit that the deliberation which becomes in England a duty of government, owing to the power of the electors, should also be recognized by the British government in India as a duty under a sense of self restraint.[30]

In this statement, Gokhale once again made his case on the basis of how the British Parliament worked. What is remarkable, however, were the contrasting reasons he presented for why the states in England and India had to function in the same way; while the government's duty to take public opinion into account in England was due to the 'power of the elector', in India, in contrast, the duty of the colonial state to heed public opinion was to come from 'a sense of self restraint'. In India it was not the power of the people that would force the state to exercise its power in a democratic way. Rather democracy would come through the self-restraint of the imperial state. That was, however, also to concede that the discourse of the Congress was not based on the power of the people. What, then, was it based

[30] Gokhale, 'Speech on August 23, 1901', in *Gokhale, his life and speeches*, p. 57.

on? What was left unstated but assumed in Gokhale's assertion was that the discourse of the Congress was based on the conscience of the state itself. If the Congress built a political discourse on the basis of its notion of the 'self restraint of the state' then that was because the Congress itself was a moment in the self-consciousness of the British imperial state; it inserted itself within the imperial political formation as a voice of the state's conscience, its true vocation in India. The Congress as an organization, in other words, was not grounded in the self-consciousness of the people of India.

Dadabhai Naoroji's claim for equal rights within the Empire is similarly built around a precedent:

We Indians have been free British citizens as our birthright 'as if born and living in England' from the first moment we came under the British flag ... The present Government ought fairly to be expected to act upon old principles, and to acknowledge and give effect to the birthright of Indians 'as if living and born in England'. England is bound to do this. Our British rights are beyond all question.[31]

Notice the repeated use of the phrase 'as if'. Indians could not be treated 'as if' they were born in England, unless India itself was treated as if it was England. The language of 'as if' acquired such centrality in Congress' discourse precisely because it was based on, to use Bentham's expression, a 'legal fiction'.

English historical precedents were also deployed in Congress discourse to promote certain modes of agitation among the people of India against the British government in India. Reminding Indians of events in England such as the emancipation of slaves, the enactment of the Catholic Emancipation Law, the repeal of the Corn Law, and the enactment of the Reform Law, Surendranath Banerjea argued that in England 'The noblest and most beneficent measures ... have been the outcome of constitutional agitation.'[32] Thus precedents from Britain and Europe were seen as laying down the law and the path along which agitation in India was to proceed, and the aim was to convince English statesmen to enact in India those laws that already prevailed in Britain.

[31] Naoroji, extract from 'Presidential Address of Dadabhai Naoroji at the twenty-second session of the Indian National Congress, Calcutta, December, 1906', in Majumdar (ed.), *Indian Speeches and Documents*, pp. 168–70.

[32] Banerjee, 'Presidential Address at the Eighteenth Session of the Indian National Congress', *Indian Speeches and Documents*, p. 204.

JUSTICE AS EQUITY AND
THE FIGURE OF THE IMPERIAL MONARCH

While the object of the discourse of the Congress was to convince the Indian Legislative Council to fulfill its role as a neutral judge and decide on issues affecting Indians only after hearing the lawyers on both sides, it was also clear that the executive in India as it functioned in the post-1857 period was despotic in nature and was unlikely to fulfill that role. As Lalla Hukum Chand of Lahore stated in the second Congress of 1886:

> No doubt, some form of representative government is required on all grounds. In every case before a *Court of Justice* both sides are heard and each side has the opportunity of proving to the *Judge* the justice of his own cause. *Here it is a court of injustice.* Government has it all its own way, and *we have no one to plead for us* and controvert the arbitrary claims of the government. They surround themselves with people who just repeat their opinions, and so nothing can be done for the good of the country and its people, who suffer in every way because they are never heard before the court.[33]

In light of the arbitrary nature of the colonial executive, the discourse of the Congress had necessarily to be addressed to a higher imperial judge who would stand above the two parties—the colonial government and the lawyers for the people of India—and arbitrate impartially between them.

In the discourse of the Congress, it was the imperial monarch who occupied the enunciative position of the supreme impartial judge and, therefore, the addressee of all its appeals against the colonial government. The figure of the imperial monarch as impartial judge thus came to be at the very foundation of the conceptualization of the Congress as an organization, and the essential condition for its existence as a representative institution. Indeed, without this figure, the Congress as a representative institution would be unthinkable. As Gokhale asserted in one of the annual meetings on the Indian National Congress:

> The Throne in England is above all parties—beyond all controversies. It is the permanent seat of the majesty, the honor and beneficence of the

---

[33] Report of the Second Indian National Congress held in Calcutta on the 27th, 28th, 29th, and 30th December 1886, p. 21.

British Empire. And in offering our homage to its illustrious occupants and their heirs and representatives, we not only perform a loyal duty, but also express the gratitude of our hearts for all that is noble and high-minded in England's connections with India.[34]

For the Indian National Congress, it was the throne of England that was the seat of imperial justice. What held India to England in its view was faith in the impartiality of the monarch as judge who extended her just rule over all subjects of the empire, irrespective of their nationalities. It is not surprising that in almost every annual meeting Congress delegates were eager to swear undying fealty to the person of the Queen and extol on the benevolence and magnanimity of the monarch, whom they saw as the source of the people's rights. The conclusion of annual meetings of the Congress with cries of three cheers to the queen—an enduring practice that continued well into the second decade of the twentieth century— reflected the Congress' recognition of the centrality of the figure of the monarch to its very existence.

What is striking about this discourse is that the justice of the monarch was tied not to the universality of law but rather to the monarch's personal conscience and sense of benevolence towards her subjects. When one looks at Congress discourse closely, it is evident that their claim for rights was grounded not on the universality of law but rather on the Queen's Proclamation of 1858 as a specific document that had pledged justice to the people of India. The Congress frequently referred to this Proclamation as the Magna Carta of their rights. In the annual meeting of the Indian National Congress of 1888, Madan Mohan Malaviya stated:

Permit me to refer for a moment to ... the Proclamation of 1858. It is not at all surprising to find speaker after speaker, from our worthy President downwards, referring to the great Charter of our rights and privileges. This is the keystone of the arch which supports all our demands. Therein our gracious Sovereign, under whose benign government we assemble year after year to deliberate upon our common wants and to formulate our common grievances,—our gracious Sovereign whose pictures now hang around us, shedding as it were, some faint reflection of her kindly and motherly influence on our deliberations (loud cheers);—therein, Gentlemen, our

[34] Gopal Krishna Gokhale, Report of the *Twenty-first Indian National Congress*, held at Benares on the 27th, 28th, 29th, and 30th December 1905, p. 6.

most noble Queen of England and Empress of India solemnly extended to us pledges the fulfillment of which we now pray for.[35]

All acts to improve the condition of the people of India like the Proclamation then would necessarily spring from the benevolence of the monarch.

To all his Majesty's subjects inhabiting his wide dominion of India, it is well known that his Majesty takes a keen interest in their welfare and is always anxious to ameliorate their condition by acts of beneficence which befit the Sovereign on whose kingdom the sun never sets. Our hearts are too full now to adequately express our deep gratitude to his Imperial Majesty for the gracious boons conferred upon us.[36]

It was in the Queen's pledge or promise that the Congress' discourse was anchored. The fact that the British colonial government in India was also under the figure of the same Queen seemed to have presented no noticeable problem to the Congress. How was it possible to reconcile the imperial and the colonial into a single discourse? The solution lay in mapping the two earlier discourses of the colonial and the imperial along a temporal line that connected the present with the future; even as the present continued to be colonial, the future came to be anchored in the imperial promise of justice as liberty. Thus the Congress discourse of justice as liberty took on the form of a teleology that was based on the assumption that whatever India may have been in the past or still was in the present, it could still move towards a future of liberty and, indeed, even freedom. The concept of justice anchored in the figure of the monarch was 'the keystone of the arch,' to use Malaviya's phrase, that connected the present of foreign rule with the future of liberty. The discourse of justice was now a teleological pedagogical mission of taking India to the point of self-governance.

It is significant that the Queen's Proclamation of 1858 that the Congress claimed as India's Magna Carta had come in the wake of the 1857 Revolt that had almost brought the British Empire in India to an abrupt end. Even as the Revolt had been crushed,

[35] Report of the Fourth Indian National Congress held at Allahabad on the 26th, 27th, 28th, and 29th December 1888, p. 64

[36] Muralidhar Ray, Report of the twenty-sixth Indian National Congress held at Calcutta on the 26th, 27th, and 28th December 1911, pp. 43–4.

it had brought home to the Empire the fragility of the East India Company's rule in India; it had forced the Empire to construct a discourse through which it could communicate and engage with Indians and win much needed legitimacy for its future stability, indeed its very survival. The deployment of the discourse of imperial justice as a new discourse of governance in the Queen's proclamation was then a direct outcome of the revolt that is often dismissed as a failure. In other words, the discursive space in which the Congress came to locate itself was more a victory of the revolt than a gift of the Queen. Yet, given the nature of the political discourse of the Congress—based as it was on the rejection of resistance as a means to freedom—it remained completely silent on the 1857 Revolt, even as it attributed its so called 'Magna Carta' to the Queen's magnanimity to the wild cheers of the Congressmen. 'In 1858 our Queen gave you your great Charter, unasked (loud cheers), with wondrous and sagacious magnanimity, thus affording a signal and illustrious example of how to invest a gift with a deep and abiding value.'[37]

The Congress' disavowal of the 1857 Revolt was a deliberate act of forgetting and of dissociation not just from resistance or revolution but also from a political discourse based on nationalism. Any acknowledgment of the revolt would have put the agency of historical change in the people of India. That would have been contrary to the fundamental principle and general ethos of the Congress which believed in the 'self restraint of the state' as the source of liberty in India.

In the Congress' discourse it was the imperial monarch alone— not the British administration—who would right the wrongs that had been perpetrated on the people of India as an act of charity. One of the most significant of these acts that Congressmen rarely failed to point out was the annulment of the Partition of Bengal that was announced at the time of King Edward's visit to India which ended years of mass agitation.

The might and justice of his rule have been fully demonstrated to us by his Majesty, conferring several boons, which will at all times to come be remembered with gratitude by us, the greatest of which is his gracious act of the annulment of the Partition of Bengal, which as an act of grace has enshrined him on the hearts of the Bengali population and which, I

---

[37] Report of the Fourth Indian National Congress, 1888, p. 29.

am sure, will spread peace and contentment where unrest prevailed, and exterminate the stray weeds of anarchism that had unfortunately grown up of late.[38]

Once again the Congress credited the annulment of the Partition of Bengal to a generous boon from the imperial monarch, not to the years of mass agitation that had given birth to militant nationalism in India. Indeed the mass movement that had compelled the Empire to annul the partition was referred to in the above citation as 'the stray weeds of anarchism' and betrayed the deep antipathy of the Congress towards any form of public participation in a political cause against British colonialism in India. 'What repressive laws, proscriptions, persecutions, and deportation have failed to achieve in six years,' asserted A.C. Mozumdar in the annual meeting of the Indian National Congress in 1911, 'the kindly touch of the Royal prerogative has accomplished in one minute.'[39]

What is also striking about this discourse is that it was addressed specifically to the person of the Queen rather than to her status as the head of the British parliamentary system. The Empire was held together, in the Congress' view, not by the British constitutional system but rather the personal benevolence of the monarch, who, despite the constraints of parliamentary form, sought to do justice to her Indian subjects as a matter of charity and benevolence. Ultimately it was this royal generosity that elicited undying loyalty from her subjects, and it was this bond of loyalty and gratitude that tied the people of the Empire together:

Inside (the Congress Hall) hung pictures of her Majesty, no part of the original design, but bought thither, at different times, by their owners, unexpected, unsolicited tributes of their loyalty. Great as was the enthusiasm in regard to Mr. Gladstone, it was as nothing to that exhibited in regard to the Queen, every mention of whose name, every allusion even to whom, was uplifted on the cheers of the entire gathering. Nor was this mere lip service, toadyism, or idiotic reverence for a great unknown: *it was the heartfelt expression of genuine love awakened in the entire country by the knowledge that, constitutional Sovereign as she is, fenced in by a thousand traditions and debarred from anything like a free and full expression of her own personal*

---

[38] Muralidhar Ray, Report of the twenty-sixth Indian National Congress, 1911, p. 44

[39] A.K. Mozumdar, Report of the twenty-sixth Indian National Congress, 1911, pp. 45–6.

feelings, it was to her Majesty personally, and not to either of the two great English parties, that India owes her Magna Carta (emphasis mine).[40]

The Congress' emphasis on the person of the monarch and his benevolence as the source of justice, rather than on the universality of law is rather puzzling. As lawyers trained in the British system, Congressmen could not have been unaware of the fact that one of the most significant historical achievements of the English Revolutions had been to permanently subordinate the King to the law. Did these constant references to the mercy and charity of the monarch as the source of people's rights not run counter to the fundamental axiom of British legal discourse and practice that placed the law above the king? The answer to this lies in the fact, that even while the Indian National Congress saw imperial justice as the telos of its politics, the justice they sought was grounded not on the universality of law but rather on the notion of equity. As I discussed in Chapter 2, the discourse and practice of equity as it had developed through English history was essentially tied to the idea of substantive justice and particularity on the one hand, and to the benevolence of the monarch on the other.

In emphasizing the person of the imperial monarch as the source of justice, the Indian National Congress was configuring the Indian polity around the imperial discourse of justice as equity. All petitions of the Congress therefore took on the nature of pleas addressed ultimately to the magnanimity, benevolence, and conscience of the monarch. Even as the Congress took on the enunciative persona of a lawyer, no assertions were made about the absolute rights of subjects based on the universality of law. Rather they prayed in the ultimate analysis for the discretion of the King as judge who, keeping in mind the particularities of their case, would render an equitable justice between the colonial administrators and the people of India.

HOME RULE AND THE DISCOURSE OF JUSTICE AS LIBERTY

One of the earliest and most forceful articulations of the Congress' telos of imperial justice was Dadabhai Naoroji's book *Poverty and Un-British Rule in India*, published in 1906, that was to be crucial

---

[40] Report of the Fourth Indian National Congress held at Allahabad on the 26th, 27th, 28th, and 29th December 1888, p. lv.

to an understanding of the economic consequences of the colonial state in India. As the first detailed theoretical and critical analysis of the economic and administrative policies of the British government in nineteenth-century India, this book related widespread poverty in the subcontinent to the drain of wealth from India to England, and to the destruction of India's indigenous industry.[41] What is striking about this critique of British colonialism in India is that it was lodged in the imperial discourse of justice as liberty.

The primary purpose of Naoroji's critique, as the title *Poverty and Un-British Rule in India* suggests, was to expose colonial governance in India as 'un-British rule'. But the deployment of the term 'un-British' raises a critical question: Why did Naoroji make a critique of British colonial government in India as being 'un-British,' since, by 'un-British,' Naoroji could clearly not have meant rule by a non-British people? How could the government be British and 'un-British' at the same time? It is clear that by the term 'un-British', Naoroji was not referring to the people in charge of the government (who were British), but the actual *mode* of governance. The term 'British,' therefore, referred to the fundamental principle on which, he thought, the colonial state ought to have been based, but was not. Naoroji's critique assumed a homology between the terms 'un-British' and 'unjust'. British rule meant the rule of justice, and any deviation from this principle would transform it into an instance of 'un-British' or unjust rule.

Thus, in the discourse of Naoroji and the early Indian National Congress, the term 'British' did not simply refer to the territorial or national identity of a people, but was elevated to the status of a principle. In fact, Naoroji was precisely critiquing the tendency of the colonial government to identify British rule in India with rule by the British people, thereby reducing the colony to the status of mere property in the hands of the latter. In this discourse, on the one hand, Britain came to be deterritorialized as a particular nation (geographical political unit) and became reconstituted in justice as a principle. On the other hand, justice itself was deterritorialized from the context of English common law as a system of national laws

---

[41] Naoroji, *Poverty and Un-British Rule in India*. For works on Dadabhai Naoroji's critique of British economic policies in India see Ganguli, *Dadabhai Naoroji and the Drain Theory*; McLane, 'The Drain of Wealth and Indian Nationalism at the turn of the century', pp. 70–92; Chandra, *Rise and Growth of Economic Nationalism in India*. Also see De (ed.), *Essays in Honour of Professor S.C. Sarkar*.

and reconstituted in the idea of empire as a universal principle. The discourse of the Indian National Congress, in effect, denationalized the British Empire and turned it into a principle, or more precisely a telos of justice. It was as if the British Empire was a mission—a mission of justice.

Imperialism, then, in the discourse of the early Congress, 'in the best and truest sense, does not mean privilege and supremacy, but good government and equal rights.' Rashbehari Ghosh claimed that 'It was this spirit which inspired Chatham when he pleaded for the government of India and Ireland. It was this spirit which sustained Burke in that trial which made his name familiar as a household name in India.'[42] Within this discursive formation constructed within the horizon of imperial justice, words like nationalism, imperialism, corruption, and exploitation took on very different connotations from those that were given to them by later nationalists and radicals. What came to be termed 'exploitation' by later nationalists and radical politicians was seen as administrative malpractices and corruption, more cases of injustice and 'un-British' acts of the executive, rather than the inevitable and logical consequences of imperialism. In fact, the early Congress spoke not of 'exploitation' but of 'financial injustice' and the 'breaking of pledges.' What was assumed as part of this discourse was that if these instances of malpractice on the part of the colonial state were to be brought to the notice of the higher authorities of the Empire in England, they would surely be addressed. Congress discourse, in other words, was a moment in the self-consciousness of the Empire. What the Congress, in effect, was doing was to remind the Empire of its own teleology, the imperial teleology of justice as liberty. In the Congress, the Empire heard the echo of its own teleology.

The Indian National Congress adopted the two related but also distinct discourses of imperial justice as equity and imperial justice as liberty, which I have discussed in Chapter 2 as its own twin

---

[42] Ghosh, 'Speech in the Indian National Congress in 1906', in *Speeches and Writings Delivered on Various Occasions*, p. 203. Burke's writings and speeches were extremely popular with Indian nationalists in the late nineteenth and twentieth centuries, so much so, that the British colonial administration in India, believing that his works encouraged disloyalty, interdicted his writings at Calcutta University. Many of Burke's famous speeches were memorized by leading Indian National Congress members and frequently recited in political meetings. See Prashad, 'Whiggism in India', pp. 412–31.

foundations. These twin discourses overdetermined all aspects of the Congress. England in this discourse was not a colonizer, but a 'deliverer, who had come to India, with the ready acquiescence of the people, to heal and settle, to substitute order and good government for disorder and anarchy.'[43] This statement by Rashbehari Ghosh, an important Congress leader, is almost an exact reproduction of the imperial discourse of justice as equity that came to be constructed in the wake of the 1857 Revolt. Here India before the British Empire is shown as a Hobbesian 'state of nature', a land of complete 'disorder and anarchy' that needed a powerful external force like the British Empire 'to heal and settle' it. It also reproduced the imperial 'legal fiction'—used much earlier by Disraeli in British Parliament in the wake of the 1857 Revolt—that the British Empire came to India 'with ready acquiescence of the people', thus brushing aside the history of a century of conflict and warfare that started in 1757 and came to an end only with the suppression of the 1857 Revolt.

Elaborating on the imperial discourse of justice as liberty Ghosh claimed that 'it was the political and sacred mission of the English nation to raise two hundred millions of fellow subjects to the rights of fellow citizenship.' What Ghosh terms the 'political and sacred mission' of the British Empire in India was precisely what I have identified as the teleological discourse of imperial justice as liberty. According to Ghosh, only when Indians showed themselves 'fit for such responsibility [of self-governance] would the English nation retire from India, their task completely accomplished and their duty done.'[44] The emphasis here is not on the English nation 'retiring' but on the 'accomplishment' of England's 'task' and 'duty' to give India a system of self-governance. For the Congress, the freedom of India did not consist in driving out the British, but in allowing them to complete their pedagogical mission of introducing the discourse and practice of self-governance in India. The freedom of India, in other words, was neither the duty nor the right of the Indians, but entirely a British imperial duty and prerogative. Not surprisingly 'retiring' from India was also a British prerogative, because as rulers they alone could determine when India was ready to govern itself.

---

[43] Ghosh, 'Speech at the Calcutta Congress of 1906', *Speeches and Writings*, p. 19.

[44] Ghosh, 'Budget Speech for 1907–1908', *Speeches and Writings*, p. 139.

The political discourse of the Indian National Congress delinked the question of national freedom from the question of the departure of the British from India. Indeed, given the nature of its discourse the Congress could as easily plead for the permanence of British Empire in India. Here is Surendranath Banerjea in his presidential address to the eighteenth session of the Indian National Congress:

We plead for the permanence of British rule in India. We plead for the gradual reconstruction of that ancient and venerated system, which has given to India law and order and the elements of stable peace. We plead for justice and liberty—for equal rights and enlarged privileges—for our participation in the citizenship of the Empire; and I am sure we do not plead in vain.[45]

In so far as the possibility of the British leaving India abruptly was remote, these pleas were Banerjea's way of declaring, as the president of the Indian National Congress, his faith in the British Empire and expressing gratitude for its pedagogical mission in India. Also, note that for Banerjea freedom meant the ability of Indians to participate 'in the citizenship of the Empire'. How common this sentiment was in the Congress at the time could be gauged from the fact that Ghosh, in the previous citation also defined freedom as 'the rights of fellow citizenship' for Indians. For the Congress national freedom was indistinguishable from the citizenship of the Empire. In other words, India's freedom consisted in getting more closely integrated with the Empire rather than separating from it. As far as the Congress was concerned, it was not as the citizens of India that Indians were going to become free, but as citizens of the Empire.

The Congress' view of freedom as 'citizenship of the Empire' was best articulated in its goal of Home Rule, which became the slogan of the Congress in 1917 with the election of Annie Besant, the founder of the Home Rule League, as the president of the Indian National Congress.[46] The Congress' goal of Home Rule, or autonomy within the empire, had self-governing dominions like Canada and Australia as its model. When the Congress presented its idea of freedom as citizenship of the Empire, what it hoped for was that Indian subjects would become like citizens of the dominions

[45] Banerjea, 'Presidential Address at the Eighteenth Session of the Indian National Congress', in *Indian Speeches and Documents on British Rule, 1821–1918*, p. 205.
[46] Owen, 'Towards Nation-Wide Agitation and Organization—The Home Rule Leagues, 1915–1918', pp. 159–95.

who alone were recognized as 'autonomous nationals of an Imperial Commonwealth'. As far as the Congress was concerned, its goal of Home Rule was the culmination of the imperial teleology of justice as liberty.

The Congress' demand for Home Rule (also referred to as dominion status) can be understood more adequately by placing it within a larger historical context set by the publication of the book *The Problem of the Commonwealth* in 1916 by Lionel Curtis.[47] Written at a time of war and uncertainty, Curtis's book and his invention of the term 'commonwealth' was a strategic discursive move to prolong the British Empire by redefining it and thus ensuring support for it from all parts of the Empire. While the term dominion, in its difference from the term dependency, had until then been reserved only for white colonies that were self-governing as expressed in the Colonial Conference of 1907, this narrow racial definition was by the second decade of the twentieth century looking increasingly inadequate in serving the needs of Empire.[48] On the one hand, the rise of rival imperial powers like Russia, Germany, and Japan resulting in war necessitated the garnering of substantial military and financial support for Britain from distant parts of the empire, many of which had predominantly non-white populations. On the other hand, the rise of violent nationalism as a powerful force in many colonies made it unlikely that such support would be forthcoming unless the empire redefined its relationship with the colonies and acknowledged the legitimacy of aspirations for self-determination, while at the same time accommodating

[47] Curtis, *The Problem of the Commonwealth*. This book was available for private circulation in 1915.

[48] Writing in 1910, Valentine Chirol pointed in unambiguous terms to race as the essential marker of difference between the dominions and other dependent parts of the empire:

There can never be between Indians and Englishmen the same community of historical traditions, of racial affinity, of social institutions, of customs and beliefs that exist between people of our own stock throughout the British Empire. The absence of these sentiments which cannot be artificially forged makes it impossible that we should ever concede to India the rights of self-government which we have willingly conceded to the great English communities of our own race ... We must continue to govern India as the greatest of the dependencies of the British Crown.'

See Chirol, *Indian Unrest*, pp. 332–3.

these aspirations within the larger framework of empire.[49] The very real threat of imperial disintegration that arose from the emergence of these forces in the beginning of the twentieth century made it imperative that the British Empire re-invent itself in order to survive.

The central discursive goal of the Commonwealth idea then was to accommodate but also subordinate the aspiration for self-government to the discourse of imperial justice as equity by uniting the colonies around the idea of a common allegiance to the King as impartial arbiter. Curtis suggested that the British Commonwealth be constructed as an imperial federal state with a parliament and government for the whole Empire to deal with defence, foreign affairs, and other important common matters, while national parliaments dealt with national matters.

The discursive trap that the Commonwealth idea proved for the Indians became evident in the First World War when Indians enthusiastically lent their support to British imperial forces in Europe in the hope that India would ultimately be conferred self-government with the other dominions. Against all predictions in England that 'India would burst into rebellion' the moment England got into serious trouble elsewhere and thus would have to be reinforced with troops from England at the time of war, India sent over one million men to the battlefield in Europe, East Africa, and the Middle East and contributed 146 million pounds towards the cost of war.[50] The annual meeting of the Congress in December 1914 expressed its 'profound devotion to the Throne,' and noted 'with gratitude and satisfaction' the dispatch of Indian troops to the Western front. The Congress offered to the Viceroy

---

[49] It is significant that Lionel Curtis came up with term 'Commonwealth' in 1909 while discussing a solution to the rise of violent nationalism in India with his friend Marris. Curtis recounted later that it was during this discussion that he ceased to think of self-government as an institution 'peculiar to the peoples of Europe' but rather as a goal for all societies ruled by the British, 'It was from that moment that I began to think of the British Commonwealth as the greatest instrument ever devised for enabling the principle to be realized, not merely for the children of Europe but for all races, kindreds and peoples and tongues.' See Mehrotra, *India and the Commonwealth 1885–1929*, p. 80, quoting Lionel Curtis, *Papers Relating to the Application of the Principle of Dyarchy to the Government of India to Which Are Appended the Report of the Joint Select Committee and the Government of India Act, 1919*.

[50] Mehrotra, *India and the Commonwealth*, p. 65.

it's 'most heartfelt thanks for affording to the people of India an opportunity of showing that, as equal subjects of his Majesty, they are prepared to fight shoulder to shoulder with the people of other parts of the Empire in defence of right and justice, and the cause of the Empire.'[51]

In 1916 a joint demand was put forward by all sections of the Indian National Congress and the Muslim League asking that 'in the reconstruction of the Empire India should be lifted from the position of a dependency to that of an equal partner in the Empire with the self-governing Dominions.'[52] As a result of India's participation in the war, it was admitted to the membership of the Imperial Conference of 1917 that redefined the British Empire as the British Commonwealth, even as it rejected Curtis' idea of an imperial federation and affirmed complete autonomy for dominions. Most importantly, however, the Conference rejected India's plea to be included in the group of self-governing dominions within the Commonwealth. Moreover, India was also excluded from the discussions of the next Imperial Conference of 1926, when the Balfour Committee met to clarify the idea of dominion and its relation to the British Government. The Committee asserted that:

Members of the Commonwealth were autonomous communities within the British Empire, equal in status, and in no way subordinate to one another and in any aspect of their domestic and external affairs, though united by a common allegiance to the Crown and freely associated as members of the British Commonwealth of Nations.[53]

It is clear from these discussions that racial difference was ultimately the reason behind the refusal of white self-governing dominions to accept India as an equal member; racial difference had come in the way of the imperial teleology of justice as liberty putting an end to the re-imagining of a new imperial sovereignty in which 'all would be equally subject and in which all would be equal sharers.'[54]

[51] Report of the Proceedings of the Twenty-Nineth Indian National Congress held at Madras on the 28th, 29th, and 30th December 1914, pp. 1–2.

[52] The Times of India, 30 December 1916 and 1–2 January 1917.

[53] See 'Appendix' in Marshall, 'The Balfour Formula and the Evolution of the Commonwealth', in The Round Table: The Commonwealth Journal of International Affairs, p. 550.

[54] Hancock, Survey of British Commonwealth Affairs, vol. 1, p. 32.

The Congress, however, remained undaunted in the face of what seemed like an end to its claim for Home Rule. The inability of the Indian National Congress to break out of the imperial teleology of justice as equity and liberty, and its grounding in the figure of the imperial monarch is evident from the fact that despite these repudiations, the Congress continued to see dominion status as its ultimate goal as reflected in the Nehru Report of 1928, which was one of the first attempts by the organizational leadership of the Indian National Congress to devise a constitutional plan for India. Taking its definition of the commonwealth and of 'dominion status' from the Balfour Committee in the Imperial Conference of 1926, the report proposed as its objective 'establishing' for 'the commonwealth of India ... what is called a dominion form of government' by which was meant 'autonomous communities within the British empire, equal in status ... united by a common allegiance to the crown, and freely associated as members of the British commonwealth of Nations.'[55] Significantly, the constitution that Motilal Nehru proposed saw as its goal the linking of India, which is itself described as a commonwealth (not a nation), to the Commonwealth of the British Empire, in a single chain forged together by a common allegiance to the Crown.[56] The discussions about India's path to self-government at the Round Table Conferences that followed continued to evolve within this larger framework of imperial justice as liberty that ultimately culminated in the Indian Constitution.[57]

CRITIQUE OF THE CONGRESS DISCOURSE OF JUSTICE

The deployment of the category of justice as an imperial strategy for the maintenance of colonial rule did not go unnoticed by some sharp contemporary observers both in Britain and in India. In 1907 the writer George Bernard Shaw, pointing to the fundamental incompatibility between justice as a discourse of governance in the colonies and that of democracy or freedom (legislative and executive) at home in England, stated incisively, 'If the justice of the Englishmen

[55] Nehru, *The Nehru Report: An Anti-Separatist Manifesto*, p. 2. Also see the 'Appendix' to the Report, p. 183.

[56] Ibid.

[57] I discuss the grounding of the Indian Constitution in the discourse of justice as equity in Chapter 5.

is sufficient to ensure the welfare of India or Ireland, it ought to suffice equally for England. But the English are wise enough to refuse to trust to English justice themselves, preferring democracy.'[58]

For Shaw, one of the most vocal critics of British policy in Ireland, this discourse of freedom at home and justice abroad was at the heart of British imperial ideology. Shaw contended that while these categories had been made to appear as part of the same continuum by the empire, they were in fact incompatible:

English Unionists, when asked what they have to say in defence of their rule of subject peoples, often reply that the Englishman is just, leaving us divided between our derision of so monstrously inhuman a pretension, and our impatience with so gross a confusion of the mutually exclusive functions of judge and legislator. For there is only one condition on which a man can do justice between two litigants, and that is that he shall have no interest in common with either of them, whereas it is only by having every interest in common with both of them that he can govern them tolerably. *The indispensable preliminary to Democracy is the representation of every interest: the indispensable preliminary of justice is the elimination of every interest. When we want an arbitrator or an umpire, we turn to a stranger: when we want a government, a stranger is the one person we will not endure* (emphasis mine).[59]

In Shaw's view, the category of justice ran into a fundamental contradiction as soon as it went beyond its native institution of the law court and took over the functions of legislation and governance. Whereas justice required neutrality and impartiality on the part of the judge towards the people, governance and legislation on the other hand required the legislator and the government to represent and execute the interests and the will of the people. While justice was helped by the alienness or exteriority of the figure of the judge with respect to the parties, legislation and governance on the other hand could not but be grounded in a complete identification with the people.

Shaw went on to expose the imperial discourse of justice as nothing more than an ideology deployed as a cover by England as a nation for its colonialist exploitation of India:

[58] Shaw, 'Preface for Politicians', in *John Bull's Other Island and Major Barbara: Also How He Lied to Her Husband*, p. xxvii.

[59] Ibid., pp. xxvi–xxvii.

The Englishman in India, for example, stands, a very statue of justice between two natives. He says, in effect, 'I am impartial in your religious disputes, because I believe in neither of your religions. I am impartial in your conflicts of custom and sentiment, because your customs and sentiments are different from, and abysmally inferior to my own. Finally, I am impartial as to your interests, because they are both equally opposed to mine, which is to keep you both equally powerless against me in order that I may extract money from you to pay salaries ad pensions to myself and my fellow Englishmen as judges and rulers over you. In return for which you get the inestimable benefit of a government that does absolute justice as between Indian and Indian, being wholly preoccupied with the maintenance of absolute injustice as between India and England.'[60]

As is evident in the above statements Shaw was able to see the exact nature of the deployment of what I have identified as the discourse of imperial justice as equity. It was through this discourse that the British Empire was able to turn its foreign origin into an asset in India claiming that it alone could be a neutral and impartial judge in conflicts between the warring communities of India. Shaw also noted that this discourse of justice allowed the colonial state to cloak its exploitation of India.

Within India, an equally sharp critique of the incongruity of the Indian National Congress operating within the imperial teleology of justice as liberty had already begun to emerge by the last decade of the nineteenth century (almost fifteen years before Shaw's writings were published). By 1893, growing disillusionment with the Congress politics of petitioning and pleading had led to the emergence of a new group of political thinkers and activists who launched a radical critique of the discourse of imperial justice and the enunciative persona of the lawyer as political representative, primarily in the provinces of Maharashtra, Bengal, and Punjab. Grounded in an alternative discourse of legislative freedom as the right to make laws for oneself and self-government, and not simply to passively receive justice—and advocating 'purna swaraj' or complete freedom from British rule, this new discourse was based on a radical rearticulation of the primary contradiction that characterized the colonial situation and a rethinking of the methods for its resolution. In this discourse, the fundamental conflict was not between the pledge of imperial justice as liberty and the reality of colonial power, on which the

---

[60] Ibid., p. xxvii.

discourse of the Congress had been based, but between two separate nations, England and India, and their irreconcilable conflict of interests.[61] The teleology of imperial justice was beginning to come up against its limits and run into crisis.

The historical conditions for the emergence of a discourse of legislative freedom lay in the general disillusionment of a large section of the educated middle class with the Congress and anger against the colonial government.[62] The famine of 1896–7, combined with repressive political measures by the British administration like the anti-plague policies in Bombay, and the frequent imprisonment, and even deportation of popular leaders had aroused deep resentment among the larger Indian populace. This long gathering resentment and anger took on a particularly potent form during the mass movement in Bengal in 1905 against Lord Curzon's proposed scheme for partitioning the province, a scheme that the British saw as an effective way to curb the rising tide of anticolonial activities in an increasingly restive region.[63]

[61] In the language of the dominant leadership of the Congress since taken on by a majority of Indian historians, these new leaders were referred to as 'Extremists'. They have been seen generally as part of the Indian National Congress. It is true that in the course of the early twentieth century, there were alliances between the dominant leadership of the Congress and some of these new leaders; there were even instances of adoption by the Congress of their tactics of agitation such as economic boycott. However, in my view, in light of their discourse of overt resistance to empire based on the notion of legislative freedom, this group was fundamentally in conflict with, and, in the ultimate analysis, exterior to the dominant discourse of the Indian National Congress which remained firmly anchored in the discourse of imperial justice as liberty. I will, therefore, treat them as separate from the Indian National Congress.

[62] My intention here is limited to briefly setting the Congress teleology of imperial justice off against an emergent teleology of legislative freedom in the early twentieth century to situate it within the field of historical possibilities as it obtained at the time. A comprehensive inquiry into this teleology of legislative freedom that culminated in Subhas Bose's declaration of independence in 1942 in Singapore—a moment of immense significance in its meaning and political impact—is beyond the scope of this chapter. For biographies of Subhas Chandra Bose see Gordon, *Brothers Against the Raj: A Biography of Indian Nationalist Leaders Sarat and Subhas Chandra Bose* and Getz, *Subhas Chandra Bose: A Biography*. Also see Pelinka, *Democracy Indian Style: Subhas Chandra Bose and the Creation of India's Political Culture*; Chakraborty, *Subhas Chandra Bose and Middle Class Radicalism: A Study in Indian Nationalism 1928–1940*.

[63] For the Swadeshi Movement see Sarkar, *Swadeshi Movement in Bengal 1903–1908*; Broomfield, *Elite Conflict in a Plural Society: Twentieth Century Bengal*; Ray, *Social Conflict and Political Unrest in Bengal, 1875–1927*; also Cronin, *British*

This mass movement, the first of its kind, spawned new forms of anticolonial resistance, dramatically different from Congress' long familiar ways of pleading and petitioning—boycott of British goods, workers' strikes in major industries like railways, ironworks, jute mills, on the one hand, and the mushrooming of secret societies, armament factories, and arsenals of arms, explosives and ammunitions across much of North India in defiance of the official policy of the Congress. It seriously alarmed the colonial bureaucracy, that saw all this as signs of a 'conspiracy to wage war against the King-Emperor' and a threat to the very foundation of British rule in India.[64]

Aurobindo Ghose, one of the leaders and intellectuals of this new emerging ethos of legislative freedom in Bengal, was also one of the first to launch a critique of the idea of imperial justice that constituted the ground of Congress' political discourse.[65] As early as 1893, within eight years of the formation of the Congress, Ghose wrote in the newspaper Indu Prakash:

We constantly find it asserted that the English are a just people and only require our case to be clearly stated in order to redress our grievances. It is more than time that some voice should be raised—even though it may be the voice of one crying in the wilderness—to tell the Press and the public that this is a grave and injurious delusion, which must be expunged from our minds if we would see things as they really are ... if we are indeed to renovate our country, we must no longer hold out supplicating hands to the English Parliament, like an infant crying to its nurse for a toy, but must recognize the hard truth that every nation must beat out its on

Policy and Administration in Bengal: Partition and the New Province of Eastern Bengal and Assam 1905–12.

[64] Tripathi, The Extremist Challenge: India between 1890 and 1910; Majumdar, Militant Nationalism in India and Its Socio-Religious Background, 1897–1917; Ker, Political Trouble in India 1907–1917; also see Majumdar and Majumdar, Congress and Congressmen in the pre-Gandhian Era, 1885–1917.

[65] In this discussion, I will focus primarily on the writings of Aurobindo Ghose between 1893 and 1910 when he played an active and leading role in the anticolonial movement. Ghose wrote extensively on various issues after his retirement from active politics while in his ashram in Pondicherry. There were important transformations in his ideas in this period, but since he was not active in politics, I will leave them out of the discussion. For a recent biography see Heehs, Sri Aurobindo, a Brief Biography. Also see Sri Aurobindo and the New Thought in Indian Politics. Being a study in the ideas of Indian nationalism, based on the rare writings of Sri Aurobindo in the daily Bande mataram during the years 1906–1908; Mitra, Sri Aurobindo and Indian Freedom.

path to salvation with pain and difficulty, and not rely on the tutelage of another (emphasis mine).[66]

Ghose's characterization of his own dissent from the Congress' by now standard discourse as 'the voice of one crying in the wilderness' betrayed his sense of helplessness and also revealed just how dominant the Congress and its discourse was. His reference to 'pain and difficulty' in the 'path to salvation' was also suggestive of the need for struggle and resistance—anathema to the Congress—on the way to freedom.

The Congress' faith in imperial justice, in Ghose's view, found reflection in a judicial mode of politics that derived not just its inspiration but also its essential practices from the British law courts, where most of the Congress politicians had been trained. It was this very judicial mode of politics that was responsible for the failure of the Congress, for it necessarily prevented the Congress from being a popular body:

The Congress fails, because it has never been, and had made no honest endeavour to be, a popular body empowered by the fiat of the Indian people in its entirety ... He (Mr. Pherozshah Mehta) is quite averse to the dictum that by not transgressing the middle class pale the Congress had condemned itself, as a saving power, to insignificance and ultimate sterility ... wider activity and a more intense emphasis would be in his view highly unadvisable and even injurious ... In plain words a line of argument is adopted amounting to this: *'The Congress movement is nothing if not a grand suit-at-law, best described as the case of India vs. Anglo-India, in which the ultimate tribunal is the British sense of justice, and Pherozshah Mehta, Mr. Umesh Chandra Bonerji and the other eminent leaders of the bar are counsel for the complainant. Well, then, when so many experienced advocates have bound themselves to find pleas for him, would it not be highly rash and inopportune for the client to insist on conducting his own complaint?'* ... So far there has been nothing at all to prevent me from denying that the analogy of the law-court holds; this sort of vicarious effort may be highly advantageous to judicial matters, but it is not, I would submit, at all adequate to express the reviving energies of a great people (emphasis mine).[67]

A more incisive and vivid characterization of Congress discourse in all its complexity that also exposed its political limits would be

---

[66] Ghose, 'India and the British Parliament', in *Indu Prakash*, 26 June 1893 in Sri Aurobindo, *New Lamps for Old*, pp. 2–5.

[67] Ibid., pp. 26–30.

hard to find in the writings of this period. Describing the Congress movement as 'the grand suit-at-law', Ghose laid out the entire cast of characters that constituted the political theater of the Congress at the time: the Congress leaders as counsels, India as the plaintiff, Anglo-India as the defendant, and the British sense of justice as the judge. In this political theater, the people of India were reduced to nothing more than mute recipients of justice as the clients of the Congress.

Ghose articulated with great precision exactly what the political implication of Congress politics was in terms of the possibilities that it excluded. By 'bringing the methods of the Bar into politics' and taking on the enunciative position of the lawyer pleading for his client's cause, the Congress, Aurobindo Ghose contended, was in effect denying the people of India the right to speak for themselves.[68] Clearly Aurobindo assumed the existence or possibility of two different, and under certain circumstances, mutually incompatible and exclusive discourses and practices of representation; representation based on justice, and representation based on freedom. For Aurobindo representation based on the concept of justice could exist only at the cost of representation based on the idea of freedom. In so far as the essential separation between the lawyer and those he represented was constitutive of the very nature of judicial representation, the Congress' mode of politics necessitated that the masses remained passive and silent observers rather than active participants. In Ghose's view, the Congress was, therefore, in its essence and by its very nature anti-democratic, and derived its status as a representational body paradoxically from a denial of real representation to the people of India. As Bipan Chandra Pal, Aurobindo Ghosh's close associate put it, it was essential to break up the 'old lawyer rings' of the Congress and plant new seeds of democracy from which would flower a new leadership.[69] The Congress' mode of politics had to be rejected because it was foreclosing the possibility of the emergence of a discourse and practice of legislative freedom in India, both by prolonging the rule of the foreigner by its discourse of imperial

[68] Ibid., p. 14.

[69] 'Bande Mataram', 17 September 1906, reprinted in Haridas and Uma Mukherjee, *Bipin Chandra Pal and India's Struggle for Swaraj*, and Pal, 'The Shell and the Seed', pp. 134–5.

justice and by preventing the 'proletariat' from coming into their own internally. 'The proletariat among us is sunk in ignorance and overwhelmed with distress,' wrote Ghose. 'But with that distressed and ignorant proletariat ... resides, whether we like it or not, our sole assurance of hope, our sole chance in the future.'[70]

It is important to recognize, however, that Ghose would not have been able to see through the Congress teleology of imperial justice as liberty, had he himself not been located within the discourse of legislative freedom. Ghose's critique of the Congress must be seen as a critique of the teleology of imperial justice as liberty launched from the ground of the teleology of legislative freedom. 'Freedom (*swadhinata*) is the goal of our political efforts,' claimed Aurobindo Ghose. In defining political freedom in the newspaper *Dharma* in 1909, Ghose wrote:

Political freedom is only one aspect of swaraj—it has two sides, external freedom and internal freedom. Complete independence (*sampurna mukti*) from the rule of the foreigner is external freedom; democracy (*prajatantra*) is the ultimate express of internal freedom. So long as rule by the other remains, no nation (*jati*) can be called a free nation that has attained swaraj. So long as democracy is not established, the people internal to the nation cannot be called a free people. We want complete freedom (*sampurna swadhinata*), complete independence (*mukti*) from the foreigner's command (*aadesh*) and bondage, internally complete rule by the people, these are our political goals.[71]

By defining freedom as consisting of two sides—external and internal—Ghose delinked the idea of national independence from the idea of self-government or democracy. While external freedom or national independence meant freedom from foreign rule, internal freedom meant self-government or democracy. It is in this teleology of legislative freedom that the idea of foreign rule came to be seen as the absence of freedom. In Ghose's view India could have national independence without having democracy; these two sides of freedom needed to be distinguished and then dealt with separately. This was a repudiation of the Congress view that privileged democracy or self-government over national independence. As the Congress saw it, national independence was not necessary for self-government;

---

[70] Ghose, 'New Lamps for Old', p. 57.

[71] Ghose, 'Swadhinatar Artha', in *Dharma*, no. 8, 1909 in Sri Aurobindo, *Writings in Bengali including editorials from Dharma*, vol. IV, pp. 148–9.

democracy was compatible with Empire. It was this view that found
its articulation in the goal of Home Rule.

The primary goal of the new political discourse of legislative
freedom in twentieth-century India was to construct the India–
Britain relationship as one that was essentially based on the
distinction between the self and the other. It rejected Congress
discourse that sought to deterritorialize and denationalize the
British Empire by setting up a homology between British Empire
and justice. Aurobindo Ghose argued in 1906 that there was no
difference between the 'British nation across the sea' and the British
administration in India in that both were equally interested in
perpetuating despotism in India:

The conviction has taken a deep root in many minds ... that British
Liberalism will never be strong or sincere enough to accept India as a co-
sharer in the great British Empire, standing on terms of perfect equality with
its other parts; but that so long as this British connection lasts, India must
hold a subordinate and more or less dependent position in the federation of
that Empire ... Radicals and Conservatives (British) are thus alike conscious
to perpetuate the present despotism in this country. This conviction is fast
growing among our people, and it has, naturally commenced to turn our
eyes not only from the Government of India, but also simultaneously from
the British nation across the sea.[72]

Unlike Dadabhai Naoroji, who saw a contradiction between
the principle of justice on which British rule was based and
the despotic acts of the administration, and for whom politics
consisted of the gradual attenuation of this contradiction, for
Ghose, the oppression of the people of India was an inevitable
consequence of the alienness of British rule. The British Empire
was an alien power that had strategically used the discourse of
justice and benevolence over the last two hundred years to serve
its colonial interests. The logic of self-interest that operated under
cover of the discourse of justice and benevolence, therefore, had
to be unmasked:

Pax Britannica has been established in this country in order that a foreign
government may exploit the country ... We believed in the benevolent
intentions of the Government, but in politics there is no benevolence ... We

---

[72] Ghose, 'Bande Mataram', 21/22 August 1906 in *Sri Aurobindo: Supplement*,
vol. 27, pp. 4–5.

were in those days deceived by the apparent benevolent intentions under which rampant self-interest was concealed.[73]

For Ghose, the British Empire was no more to be invoked as a neutral and impartial third party. It was the primary adversary against whom a struggle for freedom had to be launched. In contrast to what Burke had pleaded for, the empire in reality was not an impartial arbiter, de-territorialized from national interests and standing above the colonial state, to which grievances could be presented, but was one with it. The primary political task, therefore, was to displace the triadic juridical relationship on which the empire was predicated by a dyadic struggle between two fighting collectivities.

Bipan Chandra Pal, another leader and intellectual of this new discourse of the legislative freedom, claimed that 'it is not in human nature to rest eternally contented with a state of subordination' because 'freedom is constitutional in man.'[74] He emphasized the ineradicability of conflict in the political struggle for freedom:

The knowledge of *Swaraj* is absolutely impossible without a consciousness of the presence of *para-rashtra*. The knowledge of the self is absolutely impossible unless the self comes in contact and conflict with the not-self ... *Para* is directly against *swa*. It is in the conflict between the self and the not-self, in political affairs, that the conception of real self-government grows; and in proportion as keen becomes the conflict between the self and the not-self, in political matters, in that proportion strong becomes the desire for *Swaraj*. Therefore the *conflict must be kept up* (emphasis mine).[75]

In the above passage Pal articulated his notion of freedom in terms of a conflict between the self and the other. Significantly, for Pal the source of self-government or democracy lay in the intensity of nationalism as a sense of identity against another rival identity. It was the political momentum that would be built in the process of driving the British out of India that would lead to self-government within India. Democracy, in other words, would come out of the struggle for national independence. In Pal's view nationalism was the very core of democracy. If democracy was to develop in India,

[73] Ibid., p. 555.

[74] Pal, 'That Sinful Desire', in 'Bande Mataram' on 18 September 1906, quoted in Appendix of Chapter 1 in *Memories of My Life and Times*, p. 638.

[75] Pal, 'Swadeshi and Swaraj', in *The Rise of New Patriotism*, p. 190.

'conflict [with the British Empire] must be kept up.' Once again, this idea was in sharp contrast to the core notion of the Congress that self-government or democracy was not only compatible with the British Empire, but indeed a gift of the British Empire.

Despite the emergence of the discourse of legislative freedom and the political ascendancy of Gandhi in the second decade of the twentieth century, the deep and abiding ethos of the top leadership in the Congress remained firmly anchored in the imperial teleology of justice as liberty which was revealed in countless negotiations with the British Empire over various issues, mostly constitutional in nature. This core ethos of the Congress was not hidden from Charles Freer Andrews, an Englishman who had made India his home and grew to be a close friend of Gandhi and Tagore, and who also knew the top leadership of the Congress very well.[76] Andrews found this ethos puzzling and made an extensive and passionate critique of it as conflicting with the national interest of India as a British colony. The primary target of his critique was the discourse of imperial justice as liberty that had become a deep and abiding part of the general ethos in the Congress.

Andrews' critique of the Congress ethos was two fold—on the one hand, in opposition to the Congress that clung to the denationalized notion of the British Empire, Andrews insisted on exposing its foreign or alien nature and origin. On the other hand, he also critiqued the inability of the Congress to think of India as a nation under foreign rule. In a series of books, speeches, articles, and pamphlets written in the 1920s, Andrews argued that 'the goal of Indian freedom' must inevitably lie 'outside the British Empire.' Emphasizing the 'humiliation' of being 'regarded as a conquered nation' and asserting that 'foreign rule and foreign exploitation' is a 'common disgrace which we must all feel,' he sought to convince Indians that dominion status within the British Commonwealth would only perpetuate India's subjection and would never lead to perfect equality of status with the other dominions, as most Indians hoped.

For, in the ultimate sense, he asserted, the British Empire was 'an Empire of kinsmen' in which Indians 'were foreigners, and

---

[76] By this time, Aurobindo Ghose had retired from politics. Pal took on a much moderate stance supporting the idea of Home Rule. See Andrews and Mukerji, *The Rise and Growth of the Congress in India.*

must always remain foreigners.' [77] Despite the smooth and pleasing speeches at the Imperial Conference in London in July of 1917, he pointed out, 'white' race dominion and the rejection of racial equality was 'being sedulously preached in nearly every part of the British Empire.' [78] 'India was already for all practical purposes outside the Empire,' Andrews asserted, for the white dominions had 'ignominiously hurled India by their savage exclusion laws and white race policies outside the Empire.' [79] Even if India was ultimately granted self government with the other dominions, it would never mean equality within the Empire, for 'blood relations would combine against the outsider, the foreigner, India' and she would be outvoted on almost every vital issue, [80] 'India is and must remain a foreigner in relation to the British Commonwealth,' [81] Andrews contended, and could never 'become an integral part of an Empire which must always remain peculiarly and centrally British.' [82]

Given the nature of the Empire, Andrews found it inexplicable why so many Indians regarded the goal of complete independence with suspicion and why there was such a deeply rooted 'obsession' among Indians that 'whatever might be happening in other countries, British rule in India is permanent.' He pointed out that future historians would find it difficult to explain why leading Indians 'were actually hugging the chains that fastened them to the British Empire; how they took pride in the fact that they were British subjects and British citizens ... at a time when Indians were being treated like helots and outcastes' in British dominions such as South Africa, Natal, and Kenya. 'It will surely appear inconceivable to such historians,' Andrews asserted, 'that Indians would have sunk so low in character as to boast, even in such days as these, of the fact that they were "British".' [83]

Andrews was aware that what attracted some 'advanced social thinkers' in India to the British Empire and the Commonwealth was the 'high humanitarian ideal of the federation of all races' and their

---

[77] Andrews, *Indian Independence: The Immediate Need*, pp. 6, 18.

[78] Ibid., p. 8.

[79] Andrews, *How India Can Be Free*, p. 10.

[80] Ibid., p. 23.

[81] Ibid., p. 26.

[82] Ibid., p. 25.

[83] Andrews, *The Claim for Independence*, pp. 10–11.

detestation of 'the common bigotry of "nationalism".' He conceded that like Indian political leaders he had himself been fascinated with the idea that the British Empire might lead to the 'Parliament of Man'. However, he had come to be convinced particularly after the First World War that Empires could never lead to the Parliament of Man and that if India 'remained within the Empire', it would inevitably mean a sacrifice of the ideals of India to the central ideal of Empire which was essentially geared towards British goals. [84]

However much 'Home Rule within the British Empire' might be substituted for the present despotic power of the Viceroy and Council, I was quite certain, as an Englishman,—knowing my countrymen, as no Indian could possibly understand them,—that there would always be some residuum of subjection in India's position; some remaining mark of dependence; some patronage from the imperial center; something wholly foreign, and not Indian at all. And such dependence and patronage, however disguised and kept out of sight, would perpetually lead to ... national deterioration.[85]

What exasperated and bewildered Andrews about the Congress was the refusal and even inability of its leaders to think of themselves as Indians, as separate from the people of Britain, despite being subjected to extreme forms of racial and other humiliations.

It would be useful here to recall Malaviya's statement cited at the beginning of this chapter where he unambiguously recognized the British Empire's authority as judge to determine the 'whole being' of Indians. For the Congress the reach of the Empire extended farther than government policy, or indeed even the Indian mind; it reached into and determined the very being of an Indian. This 'being' that Malaviya referred to was in fact a new subjectivity. The Congress was not just a Party or Parliament, it was also a form of subjectivity—an imperial subjectivity. If it could not think of the British Empire as foreign, then that was because the Empire was at the core of the very being of this subjectivity. If the Congress could not think of an Indian identity, then that was because it was as citizens of the British Empire that Indians were going to become free. It was as if the gift of freedom could come only as part of the gift of a new identity, British identity. For the Congress, becoming British was the ultimate solution to all the humiliation that appalled Andrews but

---

[84] Ibid., p. 23.
[85] Ibid., pp. 34–5.

only stiffened its own resolve. What the Congress saw in the British Empire was not a source of Western thought, but the hope—or illusion, as Aurobindo Ghose might have said—of a new being.

It was not until Gandhi took on the leadership of the Congress and grounded political discourse on a new category of renunciative freedom that the Congress turned to mass mobilization and also articulated the demand for complete national independence. The ascendance of Gandhi in the second decade of the twentieth-century marked the displacement of the discourse of imperial justice as liberty anchored in the figure of the monarch by a radical new discourse of freedom, struggle, and conflict that Aurobindo Ghose had argued for, albeit with a completely different network of categories and also a radically different telos.

5

FROM IMPERIAL JUSTICE TO TRANSCENDENTAL FREEDOM

The *Samnyasin* as Leader in the Movement
for National Independence

In 1921 Mahatma Gandhi launched the historic nonviolent non-cooperation movement against British colonial rule in India with a call for the boycott of all British law courts, and a ban on practicing lawyers from participating in and leading the struggle for national independence. Asserting that it was through the law courts that the British Empire had maintained and perpetuated its power in India, Gandhi warned that allowing lawyers to continue leading the nation would be nothing short of committing 'national suicide'.[1]

In this chapter I explore the process through which the enunciative persona of the lawyer as the quintessential political representative in the Indian National Congress gave way to the persona of the *samnyasin* or renouncer as the new figure of the leader in the movement for independence from British colonial rule.[2] This change in the mode of leadership was symptomatic, I contend, of the displacement of the discourse of imperial justice that had framed the political goals of the early Indian National Congress and also determined its mode of politics as pleading and

[1] Gandhi, 'Practicing Lawyers' in Young India of 30 March 1921. *Young India, 1919–22*, p. 367.

[2] The honorific 'Mahatma' has been used variously to refer to a saint, renouncer, or one who has dedicated himself to the service of mankind. For a discussion of how the title came to be fixed on Gandhi see Conrad, 'Gandhi as Mahatma: Political Semantics in an Age of Cultural Ambiguity'.

petitioning. With this displacement began the ascendance of a new discourse of transcendental freedom and a mass movement under the new persona of the renouncer as the leader. While independence from British colonial rule was the primary objective of the Gandhian movement, the Gandhian discourse of freedom on which the practice of non-violence was grounded was not derivative of Western notions of legislative and judicial freedom based on the concepts of individual rights, representative government, national identity, and nation-state, but rather was genealogically connected with traditional Indian (Hindu, Buddhist, and Jain) spiritual discourses of transcendental or renunciative freedom, which is a translation of the Sanskrit words *samnyasa, moksha, nirvana,* or *mukti,* and their respective ascetic practices.

There were crucial differences between these two discourses, which, significantly, Hegel in his *Philosophy of Right,* the classic work on the Western idea of political freedom, recognized as alternative and competing discourses of freedom, and not just a reflection of the opposition between religious and secular ideas.[3] Fundamental to the Western discourse of political freedom that had come to be based by the nineteenth century on the twin foundations of the state with institutions of representative government and democracy on the one hand and private property, individual rights, and free market on the other, was the concept of identity, both national and individual. As Mortimer J. Adler pointed out in his classic study, what united the diverse reflections on freedom in the modern West through its history was the critical difference between the self and other.[4] In sharp contrast, in India, where the categories and goals of freedom and liberty had historically been part not of political discourse and practice, but of spiritual and religious discourse and practice, the discourse of freedom was based not on identity deriving from distinctions between the self and the other, but rather on the renunciation of the self and, therefore, of identity in general.

It was because the Gandhian movement was oriented towards the ultimate goal of renouncing the self itself, that Gandhi was able to raise the discourse of freedom above any political discourse based on identity, even as he brought it to bear upon the immediate goal of political independence. It was this discourse of renunciative

---

[3] Hegel, *Elements of the Philosophy of Right,* pp. 38–9.
[4] Adler, *The Idea of Freedom,* p. 15.

freedom that allowed the Gandhian movement to overcome the fragmentation of Indian society that had been an essential part of the British colonial discourse of governance based on justice as equity in the post-1857 period and bring in people of diverse religious, ethnic, and caste backgrounds into the movement, whether they were Hindu, Muslim, Sikh, or Dalit. The British colonial state's largely successful division of India into a society of minority identities had effectively foreclosed the possibility of a mass movement for national independence based on a discourse of political freedom. The significance of the Gandhian discourse of renunciative freedom was that it provided a way out of the labyrinth of the politics of identity and made possible a large-scale mass movement for national independence based on non-violence, an essential pillar of this discourse of renunciative freedom.

In this chapter, I problematize the cultural and historical genealogy of the discourse and practice of freedom in twentieth-century India.[5] Specifically, I focus on the genealogy of the problematization of freedom in nineteenth- and twentieth-century India and explore how a culturally specific Indian discourse of freedom came to combine with political resistance to colonialism under Gandhi's leadership. I argue that the discourses of renunciative freedom underwent two fundamental transformations in modern India. In the first mutation, which occurred in the first half of the nineteenth-century as a result of the encounter with the Western discourse of freedom brought by British colonialism, the pursuit of renunciative freedom, which was traditionally an individual pursuit and involved a complete renunciation of the world and an ascetic retreat from it, was transformed into an ethical engagement with the world in the form of social service or service to humanity as a whole. In the second mutation, which occurred with Gandhi's declaration of the

---

[5] The only author who has explored the genealogy of this culturally specific discourse of freedom is Dennis Dalton. See his *Indian Idea of Freedom: Thought of Swami Vivekananda, Aurobindo Ghose, Mahatma Gandhi, and Rabindranath Tagore*. For an interesting recent article on the theme of freedom in India, see Kaviraj, 'Ideas of Freedom in Modern India', pp. 97–143. Unlike Dalton, Kaviraj does not take the Indian idea of renunciative freedom seriously arguing that freedom makes sense only in the context of societies. Because Kaviraj's definition of freedom is inherently Western, he misses the significance of the contest between the Western concept of political freedom and the Indian concept of renunciative freedom in modern India. He also overlooks the centrality of the discourse of renunciative freedom in the Gandhian movement of nonviolent non-cooperation against British rule.

non-cooperation movement against British rule in 1920, this pursuit of spiritual freedom through ethical engagement with the world was transformed once more, this time into a political engagement with the world involving active confrontation and conflict with the established political system. The Gandhian revolution in the discourse of spiritual freedom consisted in a novel combination of an ethics of service to society and an ethics of resistance to the state. With this mutation in the discourse of renunciative freedom, I argue, a new enunciative persona was constituted on the Indian political scene, the persona of the *samnyasin* or renouncer as political leader.

THE INDIC DISCOURSE OF FREEDOM AND THE COLONIAL CHALLENGE

Mahatma Gandhi, like many of his educated contemporaries who were active in public life, was trained as a lawyer. He was educated at the Inner Temple in London and, after an indifferent practice in Kathiawar and Rajkot in India, sailed to South Africa in 1893 as a legal advisor to Dada Abdullah and Company. In 1894 he enrolled as a barrister in the High Courts of Natal and Transvaal despite the opposition of European lawyers, and he continued to practice his profession actively in South Africa until 1914.[6] His experiences in South Africa, particularly in relation to the British government and the existing legal system, were profoundly disturbing to Gandhi. As an Indian who had lived in England in the 1880s, Gandhi was no stranger to legal, political, national, and racial discriminations. Yet what he saw and experienced in South Africa profoundly altered his expectations of the government and the legal system.[7]

What was striking about South Africa was not just the existence of various kinds of discrimination between subjects of the empire but the fact that the inequalities were written into the laws. South Africa at this time had innumerable laws that denied equal rights to all subjects of the empire, and a judicial system that overlooked, without compunction, the oppression of the coloured races by the

---

[6] Huttenback, *Gandhi in South Africa: British Imperialism and the Indian Question, 1860–1914*; Brown and Prozesky, (eds), *Gandhi and South Africa: Principles and Politics*; Maureen Swan, *Gandhi: The South African Experience*; Troit, 'The Mahatma Gandhi and South Africa', pp. 643–60.

[7] Brown, *Gandhi: Prisoner of Hope*, pp. 5–137.

white population. The laws were not only discriminatory but all-encompassing regulating even the most trivial aspects of life. Indians, together with other coloured people in the Transvaal, were not allowed to own land and had no franchise. Under the special law for 'Asiatics', Indians could not walk on public footpaths or move out of doors at night without a permit.[8] Yet, as an Indian lawyer, Gandhi was responsible for helping with the proper execution of the laws.

This challenging political environment drew a dualistic, even a conflicted response from Gandhi—on the one hand juridical, on the other ethical, marked by the beginning of a lifelong experiment with an ethical and ascetic lifestyle. Along with the defence of his individual clients in the law courts, Gandhi began an intense campaign to mobilize public opinion and bring the British government's attention to the plight of the Indians in Africa. He led the Indian community in Natal in petitioning the Natal Legislature and imperial authorities against discriminatory laws such as the Disenfranchising Bill of 1893 and the bill to tax indentured labour in 1894. In May 1894 he was instrumental in founding the Natal Indian Congress, which held regular meetings to voice Indian opinion, collected funds, and carried out propaganda to acquaint the English in South Africa, England, and India with the real state of things in Natal.[9] This campaign was carried out within what I call a juridical paradigm where the primary object was to appeal to imperial justice against unjust acts of the local government by organizing petitions to Parliament for the redress of grievances.

This juridical paradigm that Gandhi was operating with had been constructed as early as the 1780s in England, when Edmund Burke in his prosecutorial speeches in the impeachment trial of Warren Hastings, had decisively linked the telos of justice to the idea of empire.[10] In the course of the trial, Parliament was asked to relinquish its executive and legislative responsibilities over India and instead assert its judicial supremacy. This institutional and conceptual realignment discursively created a triadic imperial political formation modeled on the British court of law with

---

[8] Guest, 'Indians in Natal and Southern Africa in the 1890s', pp. 7–20.

[9] Gandhi, *Autobiography: The Story of My Experiments with Truth*, pp. 78–307.

[10] For a general account of the trial see Marshall, *The Impeachment of Warren Hastings*. Also see Carnall and Nicholson, (eds), *The Impeachment of Warren Hastings: Papers From a Bicentenary Commemoration*.

the Indian people as plaintiff, the local colonial government as defendant, and the British parliament, specifically the House of Lords as the 'neutral' and 'impartial' judge.[11] Gandhi in the course of his agitation in South Africa pointed to the importance of this triadic discourse of imperial justice:

> we have no hesitation in saying that one of the greatest secrets of the success of the Empire is its ability to deal out even-handed justice ... it makes up for many a defect in the legal administration in the various British possessions. It serves as a beacon-light to tell Indians ... that they need not be without hope, so long as the fierce sun of pure justice beats on the chill surface of broken promises.[12]

More interesting is the second response that this political challenge in South Africa provoked in Gandhi. Along with the juridical form of mobilization, Gandhi began to experiment early on in South Africa with a completely new and unique lifestyle, setting up a farm outside the boundaries of the city and settling there with his family and other close friends and followers. Tolstoy Farm reflected Gandhi's deliberate retreat from and even renunciation of modern city life. It was on this farm that he began what turned out to be lifelong experiments with celibacy, with fasting, with education of children, with manual labour to produce most if not all of life's necessities, and with various dietary and medical practices like insistence on using natural and herbal remedies.[13]

Given that Gandhi had complete faith at this time in the promise of imperial justice, the juridical response of petitioning for the removal of common grievances is quite understandable in the given historical circumstances, as was insistence on non-violence that logically followed from this faith. However, as a response to what was obviously a political challenge faced by a colonized people, Gandhi's retreat to a rural ascetic and ethical lifestyle seems a curious move indeed. What explains Gandhi's intriguing recourse to a whole set of practices that could only be termed spiritual or religious?

This second response, however, was not entirely unique or unprecedented. With the advent of colonialism in late eighteenth-

---

[11] See Mukherjee, 'Justice, War, and the Imperium: India and Britain in Edmund Burke's Prosecutorial Speeches in the Impeachment Trial of Warren Hastings'.

[12] M.K. Gandhi in Indian Opinion, 31 March 1906 in *The Collected Works of Mahatma Gandhi*, p. 250.

[13] See Gandhi's *Autobiography*, pp. 179–87, 235–8, 281–307.

and nineteenth-century India, issues of subordination, inequality, and of freedom for the colonized had become critical for Indian thinkers even before Gandhi. Strikingly, these thinkers often, if not invariably, responded in precisely the same conflicted, dualistic way. Why? Why did the search for freedom invariably take an ethical, ascetic, and spiritual turn, while the relationship of the people with the government continued to be articulated in terms of justice rather than political freedom?

In some senses one could argue that at this historical juncture Gandhi himself lacked a discourse that could make his ethical practices intelligible. In other words, his actions preceded a discourse in terms of which they could be explained. The genealogy of the irruption of these practices can be explained by the fact that while the categories and goals of freedom and liberty had been part of political discourse and practice in the West, in India they had traditionally been a part of spiritual and religious discourse and practice.

While historians have rightly pointed to the heterogeneity of Western notions of freedom, and the national and contextual specificities and peculiarities of such notions, in general by the nineteenth century, what has been identified as a distinctly Western discourse of political freedom had come to be based on the idea of individual rights deriving from the sanctity of private property on the one hand and the idea of collective national sovereignty enshrining the people's right to make laws on the other.[14] Historically the idea of political freedom as self-government had gained ascendance in the West in the struggle against the monarchy launched by both religious and secular institutions and movements to carve out spheres of autonomy for themselves.[15] Ultimately, it was with revolutions of the

[14] Isaiah Berlin has called these 'negative' and 'positive' freedoms respectively. See Berlin, 'Two Concepts of Liberty'. Also see Pitkin, 'Are Freedom and Liberty Twins': pp. 523–52; Arendt, *On Revolution*, p. 142. For a comprehensive work on the development of ideas of freedom in the West, see Adler, *The Idea of Freedom*. There has been considerable work on the national specificities of ideas of freedom within Europe. See, for example, Krieger, *The German Idea of Freedom: History of a Political Tradition*; Kley (ed.), *The French Idea of Freedom: The Old Regime and the Declaration of Rights of 1789*; Baker, *Inventing the French Revolution: Essays on French Political Culture in the Eighteenth-Century*; Konig (ed.), *Devising Liberty: Preserving and Creating Freedom in the New American Republic*.

[15] While secular institutions like medieval towns, law courts, and parliaments had played a central role in resisting monarchical power and emphasizing the freedom of the individual both to produce and exchange goods and also to be protected from

late eighteenth and nineteenth century that the Western discourse of freedom came to be decisively linked to the modern nation-state and its ideology of nationalism and national identity on the one hand, and individual rights and identity on the other.[16]

In contrast in India, the category of freedom has historically always been part of spiritual discourse and was common to most religions born in India, including Hinduism, Buddhism, and Jainism. Contrary to the popular perception of Hinduism as a religion of personal gods, there is a very strong and parallel tradition in Hinduism that has no conception of God, personal or otherwise. In this tradition, the term that is used in the place of God is *Brahman*, which is indefinable and generally translated as the absolute or infinite. *Moksha* or liberation, which is described as the telos of life in this tradition of Hinduism, is to become one with the absolute or *Brahman*, losing one's identity, individuality, and specificity.[17]

Note the contrast between this Indian category of liberation and the Western political category of freedom or liberty. Whereas in the West historically, and more specifically as part of democratic discourse, freedom was based on national and individual identity,

capricious authority, the Church had not only resisted the assumption of despotic power by the state, but had also provided models for representative institutions by adopting Roman traditions of popular elections. The religious wellsprings of the western discourse of freedom are particularly evident in the Renaissance and Reformation that emphasized individual potential while also promoting ideas of resistance to temporal authority, ideas that found resonance in the revolutions of the late eighteenth and nineteenth centuries. See Weber, *The Protestant Ethic and the Spirit of Capitalism*; Hexter (ed.), *Parliament and Liberty: From the Reign of Elizabeth to the English Civil War*; Burns and Goldie (eds), *The Cambridge History of Political Thought, 1450–1700*; Grell and Scribner (eds), *Tolerance and Intolerance in the European Reformation*; Helmstadter (ed.), *Freedom and Religion in the Nineteenth Century*.

[16] See Woloch, (ed.), *Revolution and the Meanings of Freedom in the Nineteenth Century*; Lucas (ed.), *The French Revolution and the Creation of Modern Political Culture*; Bailyn, *The Ideological Origins of the American Revolution*; Palmer, *The Age of Democratic Revolution*. Representative works on nationalism include Anderson, *Imagined Communities: Reflections on the Origin and Spread of Nationalism*; Gellner, *Nations and Nationalism*; Hobsbawm, *Nations and Nationalism since 1780*; Colley, *Britons: Forging the Nations 1707–1837*; Bell, *The Cult of the Nation in France: Inventing Nationalism 1680–1800*; Mosse, *Confronting the Nation: Jewish and Western Nationalism*.

[17] Radhakrishnan, *Indian Philosophy*; Dasgupta, *A History of Indian Philosophy*; Mohanty, *Classical Indian Philosophy*. Also see Klostermaier, *Hinduism, A Short History*, p. 160.

in India it meant exactly the opposite: losing any and all forms of identity altogether. The logical and historical implication of such an understanding of moksha was a complete renunciation of the world.

In pre-modern Indian society, life was conceptually organized around the pursuit of four goals, known in Sanskrit as *Purusharthas*: *dharma* or the pursuit of the good constituting the domain of ethics and law, *artha* or the pursuit of power, constituting the domain of politics, *kama* or the pursuit of pleasure and happiness, constituting the domain of sexuality, and finally moksha or the pursuit of freedom, constituting the domain of renunciative, ascetic, and meditative practices. Each of these domains had its textual and discursive tradition, the *dharmasastra*, the *arthasastra*, the *kamasutra*, and also the texts belonging to various religious schools and sects pertaining to ascetic and meditative practices respectively.[18] However, a hierarchy was assumed in terms of the relative importance of each of the four goals, with the pursuit of moksha ranked the highest and pleasure, the lowest. It is as part of this philosophical tradition that renunciation emerged as a principle of crucial importance in the development of Indian religions, and the persona of the samnyasin or renouncer as the seeker of moksha or spiritual freedom came to be one of the principal figures in Indian life.[19]

Significantly, in this framework freedom and politics as the pursuit of power, constituted two exclusive and mutually incompatible domains. Whereas politics as the pursuit of power involved governance and warfare, freedom, on the other hand, required complete renunciation of the other three goals, including that of power. Given this perspective, it is not surprising that Gandhi's involvement in the anticolonial resistance movement in the twentieth century was marked simultaneously by a commitment to spiritual freedom as the highest goal on the one hand and a critique of the Western discourse of freedom as being partly an exercise of power on the other, most evident in colonialism.

[18] Derrett, *Dharmasastra and Juridical Literature*; Law, *Studies in Ancient Hindu Polity, Based on the Arthasastra of Kautilya*; Boesche, *The First Great Political Realist: Kautilya and His Arthasastra*; Vatsyayana, *The Kama Sutra of Vatsyayana: the Classic Hindu Treatise on Love and Social Conduct*.

[19] For works on renunciation in pre-modern India see Olivelle, *Samnyasa Upanisads: Hindu Scriptures on Asceticism and Renunciation*; Dumont, 'World Renunciation in Indian Religions', pp. 33–62; Heesterman, *The Inner Conflict of Tradition: Essays in Indian Ritual, Kingship, and Society*.

It was the advent of British colonial rule in India and the challenge posed by the introduction of the Western discourse of freedom that brought the discourse of moksha or renunciative freedom to the center of modern Indian thought.[20] As a parallel indigenous discourse of freedom, the Indian discourse of renunciative freedom had a certain sense of kinship, but more significantly a strong sense of rivalry with the Western discourse of political freedom. An encounter between the Western discursive tradition of political freedom and the traditional Indian discourse of renunciative freedom was, therefore, inevitable.

An acceptance of the Western notion of political freedom would have created two fundamental problems for thinkers in early modern India. On the one hand, they would have had to abandon a very significant part of their religious and spiritual traditions that had developed around the concept of renunciative freedom. On the other hand, they would have been compelled to see the position of the British colonial government, a government by a foreign people, as untenable and contestable, and would therefore also have been compelled to develop a discourse of resistance against colonialism. In short, there were three options available to Indians at this juncture of colonialism. They could either continue with the traditional pursuit of renunciative freedom unmindful of the colonial political system, or they could adopt the Western notion of political freedom and endeavour to lay the foundations of a political discourse of resistance against the British colonial government in India. The third option was to build a bridge between the two traditions of freedom without abandoning either entirely.

From the Discourse of Personal Renunciation to Ethical Freedom

It was the third option that Indian thinkers in the nineteenth century—Rammohan Roy, Vivekananda, Bankim Chandra Chatterjee, and Tagore, among others—chose by creating a discourse of *ethical freedom* as a bridge between the imperatives of renunciative freedom and political freedom. Unlike renunciative

[20] Political thinkers of the West like Hobbes, Bacon, Hume, and Locke were studied in British educational institutions in India. See Basu, *History of Education under the Rule of the East India Company* and Basu, *The Growth of Education and Political Development in India 1898–1920*.

freedom which required one to withdraw from the world completely, ethical freedom allowed one to engage with the world without losing the telos of freedom. The way to do this was to lose one's individual identity and interests altogether by dedicating oneself to the service of society and humanity at large. This ethical turn allowed Indian thinkers in the nineteenth century to avoid a direct political confrontation with the colonial government, whose role they continued to articulate in terms of the discourse of imperial justice, a discourse that was quite in line with the rhetoric of the colonial government itself.[21]

It was Rammohan Roy who brought the discourse of spiritual liberation to the center stage of Indian thought by founding a new religion in 1830 called the Brahmo Samaj based on the ancient Upanishadic ideas of Brahman and moksha.[22] Marking a break from the past, however, Roy argued that the pursuit of moksha or spiritual freedom did not require one to renounce the world. Rather, one could now pursue spiritual freedom by dedicating oneself to social service.[23] It is important to note that this ethical compromise of social service as the new way to spiritual freedom stopped far short of engaging with the affairs of the state.

The split between juridico-political liberty and the discourse of transcendental freedom is also evident in the late nineteenth-century writings of Bankim Chandra Chatterjee. Chatterjee argued in numerous essays that the juridical discourse of liberty, which presupposed the individual as the subject of law, with rights given or not given to him by institutions of political society, was a

---

[21] As the British colonial government was still in the process of consolidation, and, given the level of political consciousness among the Indian people, a mass resistance movement against the colonial government at this time would have been an unlikely project; this was a pragmatic compromise.

[22] Roy, 'The Abridgement of the Vedanta', pp. 4–14. For the life and work of Rammohan Roy see Joshi (ed.), *Rammohan Roy and the Process of Modernization in India*; Crawford, *Ram Mohan Roy: Social, Political and Religious Reform in 19th Century India*; Robertson, *Raja Rammohan Ray: The Father of Modern India*; Chatterji, *Rammohun and Modern India*. For accounts of the significance of the Brahmo Samaj for Hindu social reform see Kopf, *The Brahmo Samaj and the Shaping of the Modern Indian Mind* and Heimsath, *Indian Nationalism and Hindu Social Reform*.

[23] *Essential Writings*, pp. xxix–xxxi. Also see his discussion of the *Mundaka Upanisad* in *Selected Works of Raja Rammohun Roy*.

Western import.[24] The real telos of Indian life as handed down by the ancient civilization of India was not political liberty, defined as the instrumental use of freedom as rights for the pursuit of material ends, but freedom from desire or *mukti*/moksha, which was an end in itself.[25] Significantly, moksha or the pursuit of spiritual freedom was for him, indistinguishable from what he called 'dharma' defined as ethical conduct in the service of humanity. In Chatterjee's view, politics was exterior to the pursuit of real freedom, which was moksha. The political domain was not the domain in which freedom could be exercised or realized; at most it could help to create conditions under which one had the choice to pursue moksha. It is therefore not surprising that Bankim Chatterjee never quite opposed British rule in India as an alien rule by a foreign power that had deprived the people of their political freedom. Within his discourse there was no need for opposition or resistance to foreign rule because the category of politics itself was foreign to the pursuit of moksha as real freedom. As long as the political system did not interfere in people's pursuit of their dharma, which in the case of Hindus was moksha, it did not matter that the political system was controlled by foreigners. The goal of a national independence under which people could exercise their freedom as legislators by making laws for themselves in their own name fell outside Chatterjee's concerns.

It was Swami Vivekananda, however, who had the most lucid insight into the nature of the challenge the Indic tradition of spiritual freedom faced in the wake of the British Empire and contact with Western intellectual and political traditions. Vivekananda precisely articulated the difference between the West and India as fundamentally one between their respective notions of freedom, and not just between Indian spirituality and Western materialism, a generalization that was common in the writings of that period. In a lecture entitled 'Hindu and Greek', he stated:

The Greek sought political liberty. The Hindu has always sought spiritual liberty. Both are one-sided. The Indian cares not enough for national protection or patriotism, he will defend only his religion; while with the Greek and in Europe (where the Greek civilization finds its continuation)

---

[24] Chatterji, 'Dharmatattva', p. 609. Also see Kaviraj, *The Unhappy Consciousness: Bankimchandra Chattopadhyay and the Formation of Nationalist Discourse in India.*

[25] Chatterji, *Bankimracanavali*, p. 586.

the country comes first. To care only for spiritual liberty and not for social liberty is a defect, but the opposite is a still greater defect. Liberty of both soul and body is to be striven for.[26]

What is evident in Vivekananda's writings is the urgency of the need to build a bridge between the two notions of freedom, the need to find a middle way between the two. As for Rammohan Roy and Bankim Chatterjee, for Vivekananda too, the resolution of this fundamental conflict between the Western discourse of political freedom and the Indian discourse of renunciative freedom lay in bridging the two by developing a discourse of ethical freedom in which moksha could be attained by ethical service to humanity.

Redefining true renunciation as unselfish work and work without the desire for results, Vivekananda stated 'the ordinary *Samnyasin* gives up the world, goes out and thinks of God. The real *Samnyasin* lives in the world, but is not of it. Those who deny themselves, live in the forest and chew the cud of unsatisfied desires are not true renouncers. Live in the midst of the battle of life ... Stand in the whirl and madness of action and reach the Center.'[27] The goal for the real samnyasin, then, as Vivekananda reconceptualized it, was ethical service to humanity.

The true *samnyasins* forgo even their own liberation and live simply for doing good to the world ... The *Samnyasin* is born into the world to lay down his life for others, to stop the bitter cries of men, to wipe the tears of the widow, to bring peace to the soul of the bereaved mother, to equip the ignorant masses for the struggle for existence, to accomplish the secular and spiritual well-being of all through the diffusion of spiritual teachings and to arouse the sleeping lion of Brahman in all by throwing in the light of knowledge.[28]

Vivekananda exhorted his disciples to immerse themselves as samnyasis in the work of educating the masses, particularly women, and also in charitable activities to remove poverty and illiteracy.[29] Indeed, it was the goal of ethical freedom that inspired him to establish the order of the Ramkrishna Mission, a network of charitable institutions run by samnyasis whose primary aim was

[26] Vivekananda, *The Complete Works of Swami Vivekananda*, p. 51.
[27] Ibid., p. 50.
[28] Ibid., pp. 466–7.
[29] Ibid., p. 444.

the service of humanity.[30] Here too, as is evident, Vivekananda's attempt to find the middle way between the two notions of freedom stopped far short of what could be recognized as political.

The most vivid illustration of the nature of this ethical pursuit of the spiritual liberation and the historical–political circumstances under which it was invented can be found in Rabindranath Tagore's novel *Gora*.[31] Tagore, who won the Nobel Prize in literature in 1913, was, in his intellectual importance and influence on modern Indian culture, second only to Gandhi.[32] The novel *Gora* or the *White Boy* is named after its central character, an extremely conservative Brahmin Hindu leader, who leads a Hindu nationalist movement against British colonial rule, a movement that is also hostile to Muslims. Brought up by Brahmin Hindu parents, Gora discovers in the prime of his political career that his real parents were Irish and had left him in the care of his Hindu family in the wake of the 1857 rebellion against British rule.[33] This discovery that he was Irish by birth shatters Gora, for now it becomes impossible for him to continue to lead an independence movement based on Hindu religious and national identity. Gora suddenly finds himself to be neither a Brahmin, nor a Hindu, nor indeed even an Indian. At the same time, he has lived the life of a Hindu for far too long to find his way back to his Irish and Christian identity. It was as if an abyss had opened up right under Gora's feet.

Interestingly, it is at this point of the complete loss of identity that Gora discovers his true ground for selfless service to India and to humanity at large. In Tagore's eyes this is the moment of Gora's real freedom. With this discovery, however, the novel ends, implying that with the attainment of Gora's true freedom, the political project of national independence from British rule has been abandoned. In effect, Tagore like his predecessors failed to reconcile the pursuit of

[30] See Beckerlegge, *The Ramakrishna Mission: The Making of a Modern Hindu Movement*.

[31] Tagore, *Gora*.

[32] For the life of Rabindranath Tagore see Thompson, *Rabindranath Tagore: Poet and Dramatist*; Kripalani, *Rabindranath Tagore: A Biography*; Dutta and Robinson, *Rabindranath Tagore: The Myriad Minded Man*; Dasgupta, *Rabindranath Tagore: A Biography*.

[33] Chaudhuri, *Civil Rebellions in the Indian Mutinies*; Mukherjee, *Awadh in Revolt, 1857–1858: A Study of Popular Resistance*; Stokes, *The Peasant Armed: The Indian Revolt of 1857*; Bhadra, 'Four Rebels of Eighteen-Fifty-Seven'.

moksha as ethical engagement with the world with a discourse of anticolonial resistance.[34]

At an obvious level, the novel *Gora* reflected Tagore's engagement with a new form of nationalism based on Hindu national identity that was emerging in India in the early twentieth century. However, given that this form of Hindu nationalism was essentially derivative of the modern discourse of political freedom with its three pillars of national identity, nationalism, and the nation-state, Tagore's novel was at a deeper level a critique of the discourse of political freedom as such. If the question of identity lay at the heart of the novel, that was because, for Tagore, the modern discourse of political freedom was based on a fundamental division between the self and the other, a division that was at the root of much of the conflict that accompanied the rise of nationalism in the modern world.

In the discourse of ethical freedom defined as service to society or humanity as a whole any kind of identity, individual or collective, not only signified the absence of freedom, but was, in fact, a positive bondage.[35] From the perspective of the Indic understanding of freedom, the modern notion of political freedom was indeed a contradiction in terms.

REPUDIATING THE DISCOURSE OF IMPERIAL JUSTICE

Just as the discourse of spiritual freedom seemed unable to get past the ethics of social service, political discourse in India in the pre-Gandhian period was as moribund. Trapped in a discourse of imperial justice, it had been unable to find its way out towards national independence. While Gandhi's ethical practices in South Africa were genealogically affiliated with, what was by now, a century-old effort at reconciling the imperatives of renunciative and political freedom, in so far as the colonial government was concerned, all these thinkers had articulated the responsibilities of

---

[34] Tagore was very conscious of the difficulties inherent in trying to reconcile the two discourses of freedom: 'I sometimes detect in myself a battle ground where two opposing forces are constantly in action, one beckoning to peace and the cessation of strife, the other egging me on to battle.' See Ghose, *Rethinking Tagore: Three Lectures*, p. 4.

[35] For incisive analyses of nationalism and humanitarianism in Tagore see Nandy, *Rabindranath Tagore and The Illegitimacy of Nationalism*; Nussbaum, 'Patriotism and Cosmopolitanism', pp. 3–17. For a related discussion also see Banerjee, 'The Work of Imagination: Temporality and Nationhood in Colonial Bengal', pp. 280–322.

the colonial state towards the people of India within the discourse of imperial justice, which implied that although the people in India had no legislative power, they had access to the judiciary in the colony and in England and could bring legal claims against the local colonial government.

It is significant that even Gandhi himself, until as late as 1918, framed his political discourse in terms of the goal of imperial justice. After his return to India from South Africa in 1914, even while leading some of the most extensive peasants' and workers' movements in Champaran, Kheda, and Ahmedabad, Gandhi continued to see these movements primarily in terms of the imperial juridical paradigm as essentially pleas for justice. In a letter to the viceroy during the First World War, Gandhi interpreted the movements he led in Champaran and Kheda as his personal contribution towards proving to the Indian people the ultimate good and justice of the British Empire:

In Champaran by resisting an age-old tyranny I have shown the ultimate sovereignty of British justice. In Kheda a population that was cursing the government now feels that it, and not the government, is the power when it is prepared to suffer for the truth it represents. It is, therefore, losing its bitterness and is saying to itself that government must be a government for people, for it tolerates orderly and respectful disobedience when injustice is felt. Thus Champaran and Kheda are my direct, definite and special contribution to the war.[36]

With the passage of time, however, the long held and surprisingly widespread hope of imperial justice was beginning to appear to the people of India more like a political trap intended to keep India as a British colony indefinitely.[37] Yet, while the inadequacy of the discourse of justice was becoming clear, the Indian discourse of freedom, having abandoned the renunciative path, had come only so far as an ethical engagement with the world. What was felt to be urgently required was a discourse of resistance.

---

[36] Gandhi, *Autobiography*, p. 168.

[37] The exploitative nature of British rule was particularly emphasized in the early twentieth century by a radical nationalist faction within the Indian National Congress called the 'Extremists' in Indian historiography. See Tripathi, *The Extremist Challenge: India between 1890 and 1910*. Also see McLane, *Indian Nationalism and the Early Congress*; Seal, *The Emergence of Indian Nationalism: Competition and Collaboration in the Later Nineteenth Century*.

The underlying violence of British rule was brutally brought home to Gandhi with the massacre at Jallianawala Bagh in the Punjab in 1919.[38] This massacre of large numbers of Indians, including old people, women, and children, was conducted by the British army at a protest meeting, held as a response to a call by Gandhi to protest the Rowlatt Act.[39] By this act the British government in India had acquired the right to arrest individuals without warrant and hold them in prison without trial, hold special trials without jury, and completely disarm the Indian population. The Jallianawala Bagh massacre had a particularly shattering impact on Gandhi and the Indian population at large because of the deliberate nature of the massacre and the brutality with which it had been carried out. The walled compound in which the people had gathered had a single entrance that had been blocked by British troops who had fired at the gathering indiscriminately. A large number of people, finding no escape route, had come directly in the line of fire, while others had jumped into a well in the compound to protect themselves, thus dying in the process.

This massacre and the British government's refusal to punish General Dyer, who had ordered it, finally shut the window of hope that the discourse of imperial justice had offered to Gandhi and others in the Indian National Congress for the last two decades.[40] It was at this moment that Gandhi departed radically from his earlier juridical modes of agitation, such as petitioning, signature campaigns, and handing memoranda to the government, and began a new era of open resistance and confrontation with the British government. The possibility of any reconciliation between the Indian people and the British government now appeared to him illusory. This departure is marked by the noncooperation movement in 1920, the Civil Disobedience Movement in 1930, and the Quit India Movement in 1942.

In the wake of the Jallianawala Bagh massacre and specifically in order to consider the report of the commission set up by the

---

[38] Good accounts of the Jallianawala Bagh massacre include Furneaux, *Massacre at Amritsar*; Dutta, *Jallianawala Bagh*; Fein, *Imperial Crime and Punishment: The Massacre at Jallianwala Bagh and British Judgement, 1919–1920*; Draper, *Amritsar: The Massacre That Ended the Raj*.

[39] For the movement against the Rowlatt Act, see Kumar (ed.), *Essays on Gandhian Politics: The Rowlatt Satyagraha of 1919*.

[40] Collett, *The Butcher of Amritsar: General Dyer*.

government to inquire into the massacre, the Indian National Congress convened a special meeting in 1920. In this meeting Gandhi and his supporters, finding the commission's report callous and unresponsive to the outrage that the massacre had provoked in the masses, passed a resolution of noncooperation with the government. A new era in the movement for independence had begun. With it a new discourse of resistance was also beginning to emerge.

The noncooperation resolution had three components. The first was a boycott of imported goods especially from England. Gandhi called for public burning of imported goods, and bonfires of foreign clothes were organized on a large scale all over India. The second was the boycott of all government institutions including law courts, schools, and councils. The boycott of British law courts with their juridical discourse was now necessary because the law courts were seen to be not only complicit in colonial oppression but in fact constituting the very ground of it. During Gandhi's 1922 trial for causing disaffection to the government, Gandhi, recounting his experiences in South Africa, stated:

Even as I discovered early on that I had no rights as a man because I was an Indian, my faith in the British Empire sustained the belief that the treatment of Indians was an excrescence upon a system that was intrinsically good. I therefore gave the empire my enthusiastic service in the Zulu rebellion of 1906 and the First World War in the hope that the colonized peoples would ultimately be granted equal rights and equal participation in the empire.[41]

However, Gandhi concluded during the same trial that his subsequent experiences, particularly the Jallianawala Bagh massacre had proven that the colonial

government established by law in British India was carried on for the exploitation of the Indian masses and for prolonging her servitude. I hold it to be a virtue to be disaffected towards a government which in its totality has done more harm to India than any previous system.[42]

The third and final element of the noncooperation resolution was a ban on participation by practicing lawyers and legal professionals in the struggle for national independence. Describing the people's hopes from the British law courts as a hallucination, Gandhi wrote:

[41] Gandhi's written statement in the trial of 1921. Gandhi, *The Law and the Lawyers*, pp. 114–19.
[42] Ibid.

So long as we regard with superstitious awe and wonder the so called palaces of justice we cannot gain the desirable status (as free people). If we were not under the spell of lawyers and law courts and if there were not touts to tempt us into the quagmire of the courts and to appeal to our worst passions, we would be leading a much happier life than we do today.[43]

Until this time, lawyers and legal professionals had constituted the overwhelming majority in the leadership of the Indian National Congress. Now, to continue with their leadership positions in the Indian National Congress, they had to quit their legal practices.

It was at this point that Gandhi decisively abandoned the discourse of imperial justice and the politics of petitioning, and initiated a new phase of active resistance against the government and its policies. With this abandonment of the discourse of imperial justice, he also abandoned the essential triadic structure of imperial justice, which required a neutral and impartial judge (the British Parliament) to determine the truth between the plaintiff (the colonized people) and the defendant (the colonial administration). For Gandhi now, truth was accessible only to the parties involved in the dispute. Rather than being advantageous, the position of the judge as a so-called neutral and impartial third party was an impediment to the determination of truth. Gandhi went so far as to say that even while it was preferable to come to a compromise peacefully on a dispute, if that was not possible, then it was better to resolve the conflict through violence rather than resort to the intervention of the third party, the judge, the British legal system.[44]

The Renouncer as Leader of Political Resistance

Time then had arrived for the creation of a new order of discourse. It is not surprising that after his arrival in India, even as Gandhi began to grapple with the questions of the day, he also began to move, largely unaware, towards the figure of the renouncer. For, through much of Indian history, while renunciation had been the condition for truth in society, the enunciative persona of the renouncer had been the agent of truth. It is important to note here that unlike the thinkers discussed above who were scholars of the renunciative tradition, Gandhi came to the tradition of spiritual

---

[43] Gandhi, 'The Hallucination of the Law Courts', *Young India*, 6 October 1920, p. 350.

[44] Gandhi, 'Hind Swaraj', p. 260.

freedom in search of an answer for a political question. It was as a political activist that Gandhi became a renouncer.

Gandhi stepped into the enunciative position of the samnyasin or renouncer at a historical juncture when the limits of the discourse of imperial justice stood exposed. What made this move so significant historically is that, by so doing, Gandhi took on the position of an enunciator of truth with the power to challenge the discourse of the British Empire. Even as late as the nineteenth century it was the samnyasin alone who was seen as the enunciator of truth in Indian society. Vivekananda, who had himself become a samnyasin, had asserted that to speak of politics in India, one had to speak the language of religion.[45] And it was the renouncer alone, who, in the view of the masses of India, spoke the true language of religion; when one 'preached as a householder,' Vivekananda pointed out, 'the Hindu people will turn back and go out. If you have given up the world, however, they say, "He is good, he has given up the world".'[46]

As one who had detached himself from the affairs in the world and had identified himself with the cosmos, the renouncer stood outside society, and it was precisely that position of disinterestedness and impartiality towards the affairs of the world that made him the enunciator of truth. Vivekananda had even suggested that the power that the samnyasins commanded as enunciators of truth in Indian society be put to the service of politics: 'This tremendous power in the hands of the roving *samnyasins* of India has got to be transformed, and it will raise the masses up.'[47] In a sense, then, the emergence of Gandhi, and the discursive position that he came to occupy, can be said to have already been anticipated in the discursive context of late nineteenth- and twentieth-century India where the discourse of renunciation had come to be tied to the discourse of ethical service to society.[48] It was because Gandhi spoke from the

---

[45] Vivekananda, 'My Life and Mission', p. 77.

[46] Ibid., p. 89.

[47] Ibid., p. 90.

[48] In their studies of the Gandhian movement, historians like Shahid Amin have analysed the different and often conflicting perceptions among the peasantry of Gandhi as a 'mahatma' or renouncer. What is significant from my perspective is not so much how Gandhi was perceived by people participating in the movement as how his emergence can be said to have been foreseen to a large extent in the historical and cultural context of twentieth-century India. See Shahid Amin, 'Gandhi as Mahatma.'

enunciative position of the samnyasin or renouncer that his discourse was accepted and recognized as the discourse of truth.

When Gandhi donned the garb of a renouncer and spoke about politics, the traditional discourse of transcendental freedom, previously grounded on the explicit rejection and exteriorization of politics, came to intersect with the historical concern for independence from British rule and the idea of resistance. In this lies the core of Gandhi's revolutionary innovations in the field of political strategy. Gandhi declared in unambiguous terms the subordination of the telos of independence to that of moksha. 'For me the effort for attaining swaraj is a part of the effort for *moksha* ... I would not be tempted to give up my striving after moksha even for the sake of swaraj.'[49] Freedom was not to be thought of in terms of law, which is motivated by an imperative to normalize and wipe out difference. The end was not the overcoming of the other through appropriation by the self, but the transcendence of desire itself. Therefore, intrinsically tied to the goal of moksha was the ideal of *anasakti* or nonattachment. Attachment led to worldly involvement and was a major obstacle to moksha. The aspirant towards moksha therefore had to cultivate a total absence of desire.

In Gandhian discourse, the idea of freedom was located outside Hegel's dialectic of master and slave, for Indians, while refusing to be slaves, would also renounce the desire to be masters. The self was to become a cipher where truth could reside. 'When the sense of "I" has vanished, we cease to feel that we are subject to anyone's authority. He who feels himself to be a cipher experiences peace in all conditions of life.'[50] Freedom then was indistinguishable from renunciation, renunciation of desire and of identity. In contrast to the discourse of justice grounded in the presupposition of mutual reciprocity, Gandhi's discourse was based on the idea of actions in excess of the bounds of reciprocity. Actions were not to be reduced to the dictates of a moral law and the obligation to perform a moral duty at the beckoning of a categorical imperative. In a life of transcendence, the grammar of norm and law was to be replaced by the grammar of love and sacrifice.

Within this discursive framework, the method of resolving the fundamental conflict between the colonizer and the colonized must

[49] Gandhi, 'Striving after Moksha', p. 15.

[50] Gandhi, in a letter to Vasumati Pandit, written on 21 August 1930. Ibid., 2, p. 625.

be not petitioning and pleading, but struggle. Yet the struggle itself could not be based on violence, which would merely reproduce the violence of colonialism, and transform the *satyagrahi* into a mirror image of the colonizer, but must be based on non-violence and the power of truth. 'I am endeavouring to show my countrymen' Gandhi declared in his trial, 'that violent non-cooperation with evil only multiplies evil, and that as evil can be sustained by violence, withdrawal of support for evil requires complete abstention from violence.'[51] To Tilak's principle of conflict, *shath prati shathyam* (wickedness unto the wicked), Gandhi responded *shath pratyapi satyam* (truth even unto the wicked).[52]

In this new discourse of transcendental freedom, the internal organization of the individual self and the external organization of the social and political were both parts of a single web. This notion of freedom was introspectively political in that freedom from the self coincided with freedom from the other. Thus, the enunciative position from which political discourse could henceforth be articulated was necessarily that of the samnyasin who had renounced desire, anger, and passion. But whereas the traditional religious definition of *samnyasa* meant the renunciation of all worldly activities, Gandhi redefined samnyasa as renunciation only of those activities that were prompted by desire.

Samnyasa does not mean the renunciation of all activities; it means only the renunciation of activities prompted by desire and of the fruits of action performed as duty. This is real freedom from activity. That is why one must learn to see inactivity in activity and activity in inactivity.[53]

In Gandhi's definition, it was essential for every individual participating in political life to scrupulously adhere to the principle of *ahimsa* (non-violence).

In this age, only political *samnyasis* can fulfill and adorn the ideal of *samnyasa*, others will more than likely disgrace the *samnyasin's* saffron robe. No Indian who aspires to follow the way of true religion can afford

---

[51] Gandhi's written statement in the trial of 1921 in Kher, (ed.), *The Law and the Lawyers*, p. 119.

[52] Gandhi, 'Note on Tilak's Letter', *Young India*, 28 January 1920. See Iyer, (ed.), *Moral And Political Writings*, p. 379.

[53] Gandhi in a letter to Narayan M. Khare in Iyer, (ed.), *Moral and Political Writings*, p. 627.

to remain aloof from politics. In other word, one who aspires to a truly religious life cannot fail to undertake public service as his mission and we are today so much caught up in the political machine that service of the people is impossible without taking part in politics.[54]

For the life of the political samnyasi or *satyagrahi* there were certain renunciative practices that were mandatory. 'Self effacement is *moksha*,' wrote Gandhi in his autobiography, 'and whilst it cannot, by itself, be an observance, there may be other observances necessary for its attainment.' The practices of *brahmacharya* (celibacy) vows, fasting, *aparigraha* (non-possession), and especially ahimsa (non-violence) were essential to the life of a *satyagrahi*. 'Satyagraha' Gandhi declared at the commencement of the movement around the Rowlatt Act, 'is a process of self-purification, and ours is a sacred fight, and it seems to me to be in the fitness of things that it should be commenced with an act of self-purification. Let all the people of India, therefore, suspend their business on that day and observe the day as one of fasting and prayer.'[55]

This struggle for each satyagrahi then was a deeply personal one, where each person's search for transcendental freedom would inevitably coincide with the struggle for national independence. In this vision it was not the collective identity that was the subject of the history of independence, as Partha Chatterjee argues, but millions of singularities, out on personal quests for freedom.[56] It was from this perspective that the discourse and practice of freedom in India came to be tied to the concepts of duty, responsibility, and conscience, rather than to that of individual rights.

However, Gandhi's declaration of non-cooperation with British rule also marked at the same time a break from the nineteenth-century ethical discourse of moksha, or the pursuit of spiritual freedom as social service. For it was in the Gandhian discourse that one can see a complete articulation of the conjuncture between the discourses of transcendental freedom and political resistance. The idea of tying political resistance to the discourse of samnyasa was not entirely a Gandhian political innovation. It had been articulated

---

[54] Ibid., p. 138.

[55] Gandhi, *Autobiography*, pp. 414–15. Also see *The Collected Works of Mahatma Gandhi*, p. 143.

[56] See Chatterjee, *Nationalist Thought and the Colonial World: A Derivative Discourse?*

in the late nineteenth century most powerfully by Bankim Chatterjee in his novel *Anandamath* which depicted the picture of a national rebellion led by patriotic samnyasins.[57] In some sense this novel can be seen as a transitional phase in Indian intellectual history signaling a move from the discourse of ethical freedom to that of resistance grounded in the idea of renunciation. However, in general, in Bankim Chatterjee's writings, this idea of tying the discourse of renunciation and the discourse of resistance was still nebulous and ambivalent, and was subordinated to his larger project of redefining renunciation as ethical freedom and refraining from engaging with the political domain. Indeed the novel *Anandamath* even ends with the rebellious samnyasins submitting to British rule and acknowledging the importance of the British legal order.

It was only in the Gandhian movement that the conjuncture between the discourse of renunciation and that of political resistance found its fullest and most radical articulation and came to be firmly grounded in the discourse of non-violence or ahimsa. Even though Gandhi's movement was based on what he called satyagraha or truth force and not on the force of violence, it did involve confrontation. Indeed Gandhi understood his non-violent resistance as a war. He frequently used the term 'soldiers of non-violence' to describe the participants in the Satyagraha movement.[58] Several times in prison he turned down the proposals of his fellow prisoners to demand the privileges accorded to political prisoners on the grounds that they were prisoners of war, and it would be undignified on the part of the prisoners to ask for such privileges.[59]

The radical nature of the shift from the peaceful ethical pursuit of freedom to a confrontational albeit nonviolent politics of resistance is evident in Tagore's public critique of Gandhi's politics.[60] Gandhi had always insisted on the subordination of the telos of national independence to that of moksha, which, for him, meant the effacement of the consciousness of the self or the ego. In Tagore's eyes Gandhi's declaration of non-cooperation and the initiation of active resistance were symptomatic of his abandonment of the

---

[57] Chatterji, *Ananadamath*, p. 700.

[58] Gandhi, *Collected Works*, 18: p. 133, 24: p. 142, 28: p. 434, 36: pp. 25–6.

[59] Gandhi frequently used metaphors of war and battle to describe *Satyagraha*. See Iyer (ed.), *Moral and Political Writings*, 1: p. 401, 2: pp. 413–14 and 3: pp. 67, 76.

[60] Tagore, 'The Cult of the Charkha', pp. 482–4 and 'Tagore's Criticism of Non-Cooperation', pp. 485–7.

primacy of the discourse and goal of renunciative or spiritual freedom over national independence.[61]

As a thinker who shared Gandhi's commitment to the ideals of renunciative and ethical freedom Tagore found the idea of non-cooperation one of hostility and even hatred, and the rejection of everything foreign exclusivist and, therefore, unacceptable. Moksha, reconstructed in its ethical form had come to mean identification with all of humanity rather than a retreat into national or communal identity. Tagore found Gandhi's call for non-cooperation divisive and provocative, inevitably leading to disharmony, conflict, and hostility between nations and peoples.[62]

The idea of non-cooperation is political asceticism ... It has at its back a fierce joy of annihilation which at its best is asceticism, and at its worst is that orgy of frightfulness in which the human nature, losing faith in the basic reality of normal life, finds a disinterested delight in unmeaning devastation, as has been shown in the late War and on other occasions ... No in its passive moral form is asceticism and in its active moral form is violence. The desert is as much a form of *himsa* (negligence) as is the raging sea in storm; they both are against life.[63]

The philosophical thought that underlay Tagore's criticism of Gandhi's non-cooperation derived from a commitment to the Upanishadic idea of *advaita* or non-dualism, which did not allow any division of the world into self and other. This idea, however, preempted any attempt at construction of a political discourse of opposition, confrontation, or resistance, which is necessarily articulated in terms of self and other. 'The infinite personality of man (as the Upanishads say) can only come from the magnificent harmony of all human races,' Tagore wrote:

[61] In Ashis Nandy's view, the difference between Tagore and Gandhi were only a matter of emphasis. What united them was a critique of nationalism and a refusal to recognize the nation-state as the organizing principle of Indian civilization. See Nandy, *The Illegitimacy of Nationalism*, pp. 1–4. For other discussions of the differences between Gandhi and Tagore, see Dalton, *Mahatma Gandhi*, pp. 67–78; Rukmani, 'Tagore and Gandhi'; Bhattacharya, 'Introduction' in S. Bhattacharya (ed.), *The Mahatma and the Poet: Letters and Debates Between Gandhi and Tagore, 1915–1941*, pp. 1–37.

[62] Tagore, 'Criticism of Non-Cooperation' in *Collected Works of Mahatma Gandhi*, Appendix 4, 23, pp. 485–87.

[63] Ibid., p. 485.

My prayer is that India may represent the cooperation of all the peoples of the world. For India, unity is truth, and division evil. Unity is that which embraces and understands everything; consequently it cannot be attained through negation. The present attempt to separate our spirit from that of the Occident is an attempt at national suicide ... No nation can find its own salvation by breaking away from others. We must all be saved or we must all perish together.[64]

Gandhi's response to Tagore was to assert the importance of rejection in arriving at truth; '... rejection is as much an ideal as the acceptance of a thing. It is as necessary to reject untruth as it is to accept truth ... we had lost the power of saying "no." It had become disloyal, almost sacrilegious to say "no" to the government.'[65] Referring to the *Upanishads* (*Brahmavidya*) again, he reminded Tagore that the pursuit of freedom necessarily required a series of rejections, since the ideal of transcendental freedom could not be defined positively and pursued directly. Gandhi pointed out that what he called Tagore's 'horror of everything negative,' including resistance, was not exactly representative of the *Upanishadic* approach to renunciative freedom. The philosophers of the Upanishads had, after all, attempted to define the Brahman or the absolute not in terms of its positive attributes, which could have been limiting and would have turned the Brahman into a finite entity or identity, but rather by rejecting all positive definitions; '... the final word of the *Upanishads* (*Brahmavidya*),' asserted Gandhi, 'is "Not." *Neti* was the best description the authors of the *Upanishads* were able to find for *Brahman*.'[66] However, this did not mean that non-cooperation was an exclusive doctrine based on identity:

Our non-cooperation is neither with the English nor with the West. Our non-cooperation is with the system that the English have established, with the material civilization and its attendant greed and exploitation of the weak ... Indian nationalism is not exclusive, nor aggressive, nor destructive. It is health-giving, religious and therefore humanitarian.[67]

[64] Tagore, *Modern Review*, November 1921.

[65] Gandhi, 'The Poet's Anxiety' in *Collected Works*, 23, p. 220.

[66] Gandhi, 'The Poet's Anxiety', p. 220. For other responses by Gandhi to Tagore's criticisms see Gandhi, 'The Poet and the Charkha', in *Collected Works*, 33, pp. 196–201; 'The Great Sentinel' in *Collected Works*, 21: 287–91.

[67] Gandhi, 'The Great Sentinel' in *Collected Works*, 21, p. 291.

Even while Gandhi cited the Upanishadic principles of negation to defend the resistance movement against the British Empire, clearly he was extending the logic of that negation as it had historically been understood. Negation as renunciation and negation as resistance are two very different kinds of acts. Whereas negation as renunciation involves withdrawing oneself from the world, negation as resistance implies an active engagement with the world in order to change it. The Upanishadic ideal in its traditional form had involved renunciation or samnyasa leading to a complete ascetic withdrawal from the world. For such a renouncer active political non-cooperation would have been unimaginable.

This unprecedented and revolutionary transformation of the renunciative tradition to include direct confrontation with an unacceptable political establishment was necessitated, in Gandhi's own view, by the historical conditions of modern society itself in which politics and the state pervaded every domain of life. When asked how he reconciled his 'idealization' of samnyasa with his struggle for national independence or *swaraj*, Gandhi replied:

If the *samnyasins* (renouncers) of the old did not seem to bother their heads about the political life of society, it was because society was differently constructed. But politics, properly so-called, rule every detail of our lives today. We come in touch, that is to say, with the State on hundreds of occasions, whether we will or no. The State affects our moral being. A *samnyasin*, therefore, being well-wisher and servant par excellence of society, must concern himself with the relations of the people with the State, that is to say, he must show the way to attain swaraj. Thus conceived, swaraj is not a false goal for anyone ... A *samnyasin*, having attained swaraj in his own person, is the fittest to show us the way. A *samnyasin* is in the world, but he is not of the world.[68]

In Gandhi's view then, in contrast to the past, when society was autonomous in relation to the state, politics in the present was so all-pervasive and overpowering that nothing was allowed to remain exterior to it. The omnipotence of the state was accompanied paradoxically by a doctrine of political freedom that was grounded on the idea of the state and the discourse of rights and identity. It was imperative, under these conditions, to launch a struggle to retrieve the earlier discourse of renunciative freedom that had been colonized by political discourse, along with the struggle to regain

---

[68] Gandhi, 'The Correspondent's Dilemma' in *Collected Works*, 31, pp. 376–7.

the autonomy of society from politics. The most appropriate leader for such a movement was necessarily the samnyasin who embodied that marginalized discourse of renunciative freedom. Indeed, in so far as the samnyasin was 'in the world, but not of the world,' his presence in the movement, in Gandhi's view, was a constant reminder that real freedom could not be achieved within politics. The renouncer then had a dual function—ethical service to society and ethical resistance to the state. He was to involve himself with politics on behalf of the society against the state.

By emphasizing the discourse of renunciative freedom and the figure of the samnyasin as the leader of the movement, Gandhi, even as he launched a movement of opposition to the British, was also preempting the emergence in India of a modern Western discourse of freedom based on the state and identity. What was at stake was not just independence from British rule but the imperative to foreclose the possibility of the emergence and dominance of a discourse of freedom in modern India that was grounded in the nation-state as the all-powerful arbiter of the destiny of people and society, and its corollary the discourse of identity.

This chapter has been an exploration into the Gandhian discourse of freedom in its difference from Western discourses of political freedom and the implications of this difference for the nonviolent anticolonial struggle. What makes this difference over the notion of freedom extremely significant is the centrality of this notion to both Indic and Western cultures; while in Indic intellectual traditions the pursuit of spiritual freedom was historically regarded as the supreme goal, in the West the notion of political freedom had over time come to be recognized as its highest political and intellectual achievement. Indeed, it was as a place where the historical telos of political freedom came to find its fulfilment that the modern West presented itself as the ultimate measure and standard for other cultures, societies, and their histories, as evident in the works of Hegel, one of the greatest philosophers of the West. In so far as the Gandhian nonviolent revolution in India was grounded in a competing discourse of freedom, the West faced in it much more than just another anticolonial resistance movement against the British Empire; it faced a challenge to its core notion of political freedom.

It was one of the remarkable features of nineteenth- and early twentieth-century British liberalism that even as it held the goal of freedom to be the highest a man or a society could aspire to, it was also the flag bearer of British colonialism. British liberals saw no contradiction in fighting for democracy or self-government at home and waging war for colonies abroad.[69] For Gandhi this reflected the essential nature of the Western discourse of political freedom in which there was no contradiction between freedom of the self and domination over the other. In Gandhi's view it was precisely because this notion of political freedom was grounded in the idea of the self that when faced with the other it turned into an exercise in domination or power. Thus, power, the Gandhian movement demonstrated, was the hind part of the Western discourse of freedom. Remarkably, Hegel, the philosopher of 'the end of history,' had foreseen—almost a century before the arrival of Gandhi—the possibility of the Indic discourse of spiritual freedom turning its attention to the real world with the intention of changing it. Indeed, sure of his dialectical method, Hegel had even boldly predicted the nature and implications of this possibility were it to come to pass. When this abstract and negative freedom, Hegel asserted, referring to the Indic notion of spiritual renunciative freedom:

turns to actuality (the concrete world), it becomes in the realm of both politics and religion the fanaticism of destruction, demolishing the whole existing social order, eliminating all individuals regarded as suspect by a given order ... Only in destroying something does this negative will (or freedom) have a feeling of its own existence ... its actualization can only be the fury of destruction.[70]

However, contrary to Hegel's predictions of 'the fury of destruction,' the tradition of renunciative spiritual freedom introduced to the world a whole new kind of politics—the politics of non-violence. If Hegel's prediction was proved wrong in such a dramatic fashion by history then that was because he encountered in the notion of spiritual freedom the exteriority of another tradition of thought whose logic escaped his all-encompassing dialectics.

[69] See Mehta, *Liberalism and Empire: A Study in Nineteenth Century Liberal Thought*; Parekh, 'Decolonizing Liberalism', pp. 85–103.

[70] Hegel, *Philosophy of Right*, p. 38. Note that Hegel compares the Hindu idea of renunciative freedom to the idea of abstract freedom in the French Revolution that resulted in the Reign of Terror.

Although the Gandhian nonviolent resistance movement against colonialism was largely responsible for India's independence in 1947, once the process of legislating and framing the constitution for the future nation-state began, Gandhi dissociated himself from it completely. Indeed he went on to suggest that the Congress should disband itself, now that the goal of independence had been achieved. That, of course, did not happen, but this parting of ways between the Congress as a legislative political party and Gandhi demonstrates the nonlegislative nature of the Gandhian discourse and practice of freedom. In his own words, real freedom is an ethical state of enlightened anarchy where every individual is guided by his inner truth or conscience.

The power to control national life through national representatives is called political power. Representatives will become unnecessary if the national life becomes so perfect as to be self-controlled. It will then be a state of enlightened anarchy in which each person will become his own ruler. He will conduct himself in such way that his behavior will not hamper the well-being of his neighbors. In an ideal state there will be no political institution and therefore no political power.[71]

In that sense one could call the Gandhian innovation a form of nonlegislative and negative politics with enlightened anarchy as its telos. This is what essentially distinguishes the Gandhian movement from the politics of Hindu nationalism that seeks to legislate on the ground of organized religion.

In 1947 as news of the partition of India and a transfer of populations became public, large-scale Hindu versus Muslim riots began to break out in different parts of the country, the Calcutta riots being the most devastating. While the members of the Indian National Congress were busy in Delhi celebrating independence and taking the reins of power, Gandhi spent his last days visiting one riot prone area after another. It is told that his fasts for peace had the moral power of single-handedly bringing many of the riots to a spontaneous halt. During the Calcutta riots, when Gandhi was fasting for peace, a Hindu man came to him to speak of his young son who had been killed by Muslim mobs, and of the depth of his anger and longing for revenge. And Gandhi is said to have replied: 'If you really wish to overcome your pain, find a young boy, just as

[71] Gandhi, 'Enlightened Anarchy: A Political Ideal', p. 602.

young as your son, a Muslim boy whose parents have been killed by Hindu mobs. Bring up that boy like you would your own son, but bring him up with the Muslim faith to which he was born. Only then will you find that you can heal your pain, your anger, and your longing for retribution.'

The only way to overcome the cycle of revenge, in Gandhi's view, was to reverse and thereby shatter the logic of identity. In the Gandhian frame of things, it was the loss of identity, not its assertion that would bring true freedom. It is not surprising then that Gandhi was assassinated by a Hindu nationalist whose idea of freedom based on national identity, nationalism, and nation-state found itself at loggerheads with the Gandhian discourse of freedom that went beyond identity.

6

AN IMPERIAL CONSTITUTION?

Justice as Equity and the Making
of the Indian Constitution

The Indian Constituent Assembly met between December 1946 and December 1949 in New Delhi to draft a constitution that was finally adopted on 26 January 1950.[1] In this chapter I will offer a historical reading of the forces and legacies that shaped the Indian Constitution. What one sees in the Indian Constitution is the ultimate triumph of the juridico-epistemological framework of empire, grounded in the discourse of imperial justice as equity with its accompanying figure of the monarch as judge. It is in the Constitution that one can see the mutation of imperial justice as equity from a critical category of anticolonialism to the sovereign legislative category of Indian politics and the final marginalization in the post-independence political formation of the Gandhian discourse of transcendental freedom under which the struggle for independence had been largely carried out. However, I contend that even as the Gandhian discourse of transcendental freedom came to be marginalized, its legacy survived in the form of an unqualified recognition of universal adult franchise in the Indian Constitution.

THE IDEA OF CATEGORICAL SOVEREIGNTY

In making a constitution a state not only sets an overarching goal for itself, but also decides how and under whose guidance it will

---

[1] For the most comprehensive account of the framing of the Indian Constitution see Austin, *The Indian Constitution: Cornerstone of a Nation*. For some interesting recent interpretations, see the collection of articles in Hasan, Sridharan, and Sudarshan, (eds), *India's Living Constitution: Ideas, Practices, Controversies*.

pursue that goal. Given the inherent complexities of a society like India, the decision on the goal and the modality of how to pursue it had necessarily to be a choice between multiple, competing, and often conflicting alternatives. In making these choices, the framers of the Indian Constitution were also answering the crucial question of sovereignty.

One of the important ways to bring out the specificity of constitutional democracies is to study the different ways in which they answer the question of sovereignty. The question of sovereignty has been posited primarily in terms of a discourse of possession, the central question being, *who* holds absolute power in the state, rather than *how* it is exercised as a form of practice that evolves historically.[2] With differences in the theoretical perspectives of different schools of thought, the figure of sovereignty has also varied: it could be an individual (a monarch), a people (a nationality), an institution (the parliament), or a class (the bourgeoisie, the proletariat, or the peasantry). Most recently, however, theorists like Carl Schmitt and Georgio Agamben have formulated the question of sovereignty in terms of circumstances that require measures exceeding the bounds of legality.[3] Sovereignty, in the view of these theorists, is linked to the necessity to make exceptions to the general rule in concrete circumstances, and the sovereign is *who*ever decides *what constitutes an exception.*[4]

What is common to all these perspectives is a legal and theoretical approach that elaborates an ideal state, rather than analyses complex historical developments of political values, concepts, and institutions in their interconnectedness. While the first approach remains by and large theoretical, rarely engaging with concrete historical instances of the exercise of sovereignty, the second approach is too narrow, concentrating only on

[2] This mode of problematization has reduced sovereignty to the status of property, belonging to a subject. For classic works on the question of sovereignty see Hobbes, *Leviathan*; Rousseau, *The Social Contract and Discourses*; Locke, *Two Tracts of Government*; and K. Marx and F. Engels, *Collected Works.*

[3] Schmitt, *The Crisis of Parliamentary Democracy*; Schmitt, *Political Theology: Four Chapters on the Concept of Sovereignty*; Agamben, *Homo Sacer: Sovereign Power and Bare Life*. Also see Agamben, *State of Exception.*

[4] Schmitt and, following him, Agamben have drawn on the initial formulation given by the sixteenth-century theorist Bodin. See Schmitt, *Crisis of Parliamentary Democracy*, p. 43. See Bodin, *The Six Bookes of a Commonweale*. Also see Franklin, *Jean Bodin and the Rise of Absolutist Theory.*

exceptional situations, leaving the vast field of everyday legislative and executive policy decisions unaccounted for. The question is, given the numerous choices and alternatives that nations face, by what criteria and under what imperatives are particular legislative or policy judgments and decisions preferred over others? Every such normal day-to-day decision involves a clear understanding of what constitutes an overriding imperative that must be applied and with which there cannot be any compromise. Scholars who problematize the question of sovereignty in terms of exceptions tend to ignore the fact that the logic of exception operates at the everyday level in all constitutions.

Moreover, the role of political discourse is often ignored in a discussion of the question of sovereignty. In the dominant approaches, the issue of sovereignty has been studied overwhelmingly in terms of the sovereign's will and his power to coerce, an approach that betrays assumptions that have their origins in monarchical polities.[5] Behind these approaches is an understanding of sovereignty as power that is exterior to discourse. However, as recent theorists and historians have shown, and as has also been borne out by my analysis of the nature and evolution of British Empire in India, modern power operates as much through discourse as through violence. Indeed, it is as truth that power in the modern world often presents itself. The question of sovereignty, therefore, is also a question of meaning, or truth, and thus discourse.

This need to study sovereignty as a historically constituted discursive formation becomes particularly important in a democratic polity that requires constant consensus building on vital issues through public debates and discussions. In a democracy sovereignty depends as much on the ability of the state to persuade as the ability to coerce. If a democratic polity fails to develop a broadly recognized discursive mechanism of persuasion, it is likely to run into serious problems of legitimacy, risking its power of coercion in the process. More often than not, it is through slow changes in the structure of the discourse, rather than through violence, that a democratic polity evolves. It, therefore, requires an infrastructure of persuasion as much as an infrastructure of coercion. The infrastructure of persuasion is constituted in the general discursive formation within

---

[5] See Foucault, *Power/Knowledge: Selected Interviews and Other Writings, 1972–77*, p. 121.

a polity, particularly in the dominant political discourse with its specific network of categories.

Rather than looking at sovereignty, then, simply in terms of the institution or the person that possesses final authority in a state, the better approach may be to see it as a complex discursive formation involving ever-shifting alignments of conceptual networks and institutional practices that evolve historically and as such vary, often in subtle ways, from one polity to another.[6] The existing approach to the question of sovereignty in terms of exceptions assumes it to be an instance of arbitrary will, altogether free of any constraints. Exceptions, however, are not stripped of discourses altogether. Rather, a category itself can take on the position of an exception suspending all other categories that may appear to come in its way in the face of a challenging crisis. In other words, the question of 'who' decides on what constitutes the exception can very well be derivative of the sovereignty of a category itself. Thus, the issue of how a particular constitution answers the question of sovereignty can be more appropriately studied in terms of a

[6] The fundamental question of sovereignty differs widely from country to country. The most telling comparison is that between the United States and the United Kingdom. It could be argued that in America, sovereignty is constitutional, in so far as the text of the constitution itself is sovereign. As the first written constitution, which not only laid out the institutional organization of the state, but also delineated the hierarchy of categories that were to be involved in the process of decision-making, it is the text of the American Constitution itself, in its independence from the institutions and the people who framed it, that has historically emerged as sovereign in America. Thus the Constitution cannot be superseded under any circumstances and any violation of the provisions of the Constitution renders all authority null and void, and results in conceptual chaos. The differential power of institutions in America is also derivative of the sovereignty of the Constitution itself, so that the overriding powers of the Supreme Court are derivative of its right to interpret the Constitution. In contrast, in the United Kingdom, in the absence of a written Constitution, it is the institution of the Parliament that has come to exercise sovereignty in the name of legislative freedom, with the category of justice and the institution of the judiciary occupying a subordinate role, not comparable to the power of the judiciary in the United States. Although there are conventions and customs that the British Parliament follows, yet historically it is the institution of the Parliament itself that determines what those are. This is, however, not to suggest that that there are no controversies in America or England about the nature of sovereignty and the hierarchy of categories and institutions and their role in the polities. The question of sovereignty is a complex issue and one can only talk of overdetermining political traditions.

See Kelly and Harbison, *The American Constitution: Its Origins and Development*. Also see Yardley, *Introduction to British Constitutional Law*.

discursive configuration anchored in a sovereign category in its precise alignment with existing institutions, and not just in terms of 'who' decides on the exception.

The Categorical Sovereignty of Justice as Equity in the Indian Constitution

If one acknowledged Aristotle's definition that every constitution must have some vision of the national good towards which it strives, the question that confronted the framers of the Indian Constitution was what was this national good or telos going to be for India?[7] A close look at the hierarchy of categories that frames the Indian Constitution reveals that the category of justice occupies a preeminent position. This is clear in the Preamble of the Constitution itself, which I reproduce in its exact format:

WE, THE PEOPLE OF INDIA, having solemnly resolved to constitute India into a Sovereign Democratic Republic and to secure to all its citizens:

JUSTICE, social, economic, and political;
LIBERTY of thought, expression, belief, faith, and worship;
EQUALITY of status and of opportunity; and to promote among them all
FRATERNITY assuring the dignity of the individual and the unity of the Nation:
IN OUR CONSTITUENT ASSEMBLY, this twenty-sixth day of November, 1949, so HEREBY ADOPT, ENACT AND GIVE TO OURSELVES THIS CONSTITUTION.[8]

The Preamble is a critical part of the Indian Constitution in that it contains the philosophy of the Constitution framers. While the rest of the Constitution is focused on the rules and institutional details of governance, it is in the Preamble that one finds articulated a network of political categories hierarchically ordered and meant to guide the constitution makers and future legislators in their decisions. Unlike the Federalists and Anti-Federalists in America, the Indian Constitution framers did not debate and discuss publicly the

[7] Aristotle, *The Politics and the Constitution of Athens*, pp. 106–7.

[8] The Preamble to the Constitution of India cited from Basu, *Commentary on the Constitution of India (Being a comparative treatise on the universal principles of Justice and Constitutional Government with special reference to the Organic instrument of India)*, p. 42.

philosophical foundations of the Indian Constitution.[9] Therefore, it is in the Preamble alone that one can get an insight into the fundamental philosophical assumptions that guided their crucial decisions in the making of the Constitution.

The Preamble of the Indian Constitution clearly institutes justice, rather than freedom or individual rights, as its foundational and overdetermining category, bringing the social, the economic, and the political domains within its jurisdiction. Note that the category of liberty or freedom is second in importance to justice. What is also significant is that this freedom is limited to the freedom of thought, expression, faith, and worship, and as such does not extend to the domains already covered by the category of justice. Equality and fraternity occupy positions further down in the hierarchy. As one can see in the very formatting of the text of the Preamble, by capitalizing the major categories and then setting them in order of precedence, the framers were giving the sovereignty of justice in the hierarchy of categories a visual and self-evident form.

To bring out the significance and implications of the political philosophy of the Constitution framers based on the sovereignty of the category of justice, I will set it off briefly and schematically against alternative political philosophies based on the sovereignty of the category of freedom. I will look specifically at the political philosophies of two of the most important thinkers in the modern West, Jean Jacques Rousseau and John Locke, whose works reflect the ethos of some of the most important constitutions in the West. This comparison becomes particularly relevant because the making of the Indian Constitution was a self-conscious endeavour in which important members of the Constituent Assembly like B.N. Rau meticulously studied the constitutions of different countries and even visited these countries in order to develop the most appropriate model for India.[10] The constitution framers in India had various options in the form of several very famous and widely known and admired national constitutions that had been in existence for over a century. There was a clear sense among Indian Constitution framers that they had an opportunity to incorporate what they

[9] Madison, Hamilton, and Jay, *The Federalist Papers*. For the Anti-Federalists see Storing, *What the Anti-Federalists Were For*; Duncan, *The Anti-Federalists and Early American Political Thought*.

[10] Rau, *Constitutional Precedents*; Also see Rau, *India's Constitution in the Making*.

had learned from the existing constitutions of other democracies in the West.

Democracy, Rousseau had argued in *The Social Contract*, is founded on a series of correspondences between the people, territory, state, unity, freedom, and legitimacy. 'To be free you must belong to a people; to be a people you must have a common identity burnt into you; to be a flourishing people you must exclusively inhabit a contiguous territory; to flourish freely as a territorialized people you must stringently limit contact with the foreign.'[11] In Rousseau's theory of democracy, therefore, the pre-existing communal or national identity becomes the ground of the state, and the polity in general. In this definition, the idea of democracy is tied to the will of the majority, and the individual derives his status as an equal and free citizen in the state as a member of a particular community or nationality, not from his own individuality, property, or his ability to labor. He is equal and free because he belongs to a particular community. The individual is subordinated to the nation or community; he has no existence outside the community and all his rights, including the right to property, are subordinate to the will of the majority that is expressed through elections and laws. It is in and through one's community or nation that an individual becomes free; by himself he has no rights. Here the notion of freedom is anchored in the community or communal-national identity, not in the individual. In this model, the legislative organ of the state, in so far as it embodies the freedom of the collectivity to determine its own future, is supreme. The judiciary is subordinate to the legislature and merely administers and executes this collective will that is expressed as the law of the land. Thus, what is critical in this constitutional model is the idea of positive or legislative freedom, that is, the power of the collective to make its own law, and justice is defined only in terms of what the collective wills as law. [12]

The other model that was available to Indian Constitution framers was that of grounding the Constitution on the individual and the primacy of the idea of private property. In Locke's theory of

---

[11] Rousseau, *The Social Contract*, p. 130.

[12] It is in this sense that Carl Schmitt argues that democracies are necessarily tied to the idea of homogeneity, the idea of a collective will that is reflected both in the democracy's external relationship with other nations, and also in the form of domination that marks the internal relationship of the state to its people. Schmitt, *The Crisis of Parliamentary Democracy*, p. 9.

government, private property—not communal or national identity as in Rousseau—comes prior to the formation of the state.[13] For Locke, therefore, private property is a natural right. Man is free in his ability to labour and his ownership of private property. Man does not become free in the state; he is already free in the civil society. Man needs the state only to protect his freedom that is economic in nature and as such belongs to the civil society. The individual as the owner of private property is the primary unit of the state, not the communities and groups. The market system would be the ultimate guarantor of this freedom. Locke's ideas found expression most clearly in the American Constitution. As Kenneth Burke points out, what provided the American Constitution with a larger purpose were the interests of property, business, economic freedom, competition, and productivity.[14] That is not to say that national or collective identity did not matter in this model, only that it was subordinated to the idea of individual as the producer and owner of private property. Justice in this model flowed from the law that derived from the freedom of man grounded in private property and his ability to labour.

In sharp contrast to Western constitutions based on the category of freedom, anchored either in collective identity or individual property, the Indian Constitution was grounded, as the Preamble makes clear, on the category of justice as the sovereign legislative principle. The primacy of justice over freedom was not, however, just a philosophical matter for the framers of the Indian Constitution. They laid out how the category was to be deployed in practice in very precise terms in Part IV of the Constitution, a section called the Directive Principles of State Policy that was to be the framework of the entire legislative practice of the postcolonial Indian state. Holden Furber noted in an article written in 1949 that the list of directive principles should have formed part of the Preamble since it reflected 'the social philosophy of the Congress Party,' the main force behind the Constitution.[15] On the contrary, what the directive principles reveal is the determination of the Indian National Congress to convert its philosophy as already expressed in the Preamble into a practical guide for legislation in the future.

---

[13] Locke, *Second Treatise of Government*, pp. 5–68.

[14] Burke, *The Grammar of Motives*, p. 377.

[15] Furber, 'Constitution-Making in India', p. 87. Also see Vaidyanathan, 'The Pursuit of Social Justice', pp. 284–305.

The first and most fundamental of the Directive Principles of State Policy requires the state to work towards a 'social order in which justice, social, economic and political shall inform all institutions of national life.'[16] In the economic domain, the state is required to direct its policy towards securing that 'ownership and control of material resources is so distributed as best to serve the common good' and that 'the operation of the economic system does not result in the concentration of wealth and means of production to the common detriment'—justice as fair distribution. In the social domain the state is directed to secure justice 'not only among individuals but also amongst groups of people residing in different areas and engaged in different vocations' and to 'protect weaker sections from social injustice'—justice as compensatory discrimination. In the domain of international relations, the Directive Principles require the state to maintain and pursue 'just and honorable relations between nations' and 'encourage settlement of international disputes by arbitration' in opposition to the 'power politics' of the cold war—justice as neutrality and impartiality.[17]

The Directive Principles are crucial to an understanding of the Constitution in so far as they were meant to guide the work of legislation as a whole. Directive Principles, in short, were the legislative principles in the Indian Constitution. If these principles were not made justiciable—a fact often brought up to prove their insignificance—then that was because they were not laws; they were the principles of lawmaking or legislation, in short, meta-laws. Justice itself—as it appeared in the Indian Constitution—was not a law; it was the law of all laws; the source and measure of all laws. Justice, in other words, constituted the ontology and the teleology of law.

At the very outset, then, one can see the difference between the Lockean and Rousseauean understanding of legislation and that of the Indian Constitution: unlike Rousseau and Locke for whom freedom had to be at the origin of legislation, the Indian Constitution framers anchored the idea and practice of legislation in the notion of justice. In elevating the notion of justice to the sovereign legislative principle, the Indian Constitution made justice the very source of law. In modern Western democracies with freedom

[16] Basu, *Shorter Constitution of India*, p. 272.
[17] Basu, *Commentary on the Constitution of India*, pp. 392–404.

as their sovereign legislative principle, justice comes after the law or justice under the law; in the Indian Constitution, on the other hand, justice in its sovereign form does not consist in the application or the enforcement of law, but rather comes before the law. In so far as justice was elevated to the position of a sovereign legislative principle by the Indian Constitution framers, law has its origin in justice, not vice versa.

Justice, however, cannot precede or become the basis of law unless the one who makes the law in the name of justice also precedes the law; in other words, one who, as the figure of justice, stands above the law. The polity in which such a figure has been historically present is monarchy; in a monarchy justice lies in the person or the conscience of the monarch who stands above law even as he is the source of all laws. The placing of justice before the law by the Indian Constitution framers betrays the fact that the specific concept of justice that they were operating with was justice as equity—a monarchical principle—not justice under the law which is based on the notion of universality and impersonality of law and legal procedures. Justice as equity is anchored in the figure or the person of the monarch and his personal conscience, neutrality, and impartiality.[18] The impartiality and neutrality of the monarch requires that he or she either not be identifiable at all, or be least identifiable with any of the groups he rules over. What gives legitimacy and authenticity to the figure of the monarch is precisely his—and therefore the state's—exteriority to the people he rules over. To put the presence of the monarchical principle of justice as equity and the exteriority of the state in the Indian Constitution in historical perspective it may be useful to recall that the political revolution in the modern West consisted precisely in the destruction of this monarchical exteriority of the state and the advent of the nation-state that brought about a relationship of identity—complex and varied though it was—between the civil society or nation and the state.

Unlike common law justice anchored in the universal and the formal, justice as equity is aimed at the particular and seeks to provide substantial justice by making exceptions to the universality of law and the uniformity and formality of procedural requirements. Unlike the common law courts in England—grounded on the

---

[18] See Chapter 2.

notion of the universality and rationality of an impersonal law, with rigorous formal procedures, equity courts, which grew out of the King's prerogative, were based on moral principles like duty, trust, and conscience, and were addressed to the compassion and mercy of the judge, who received his authority ultimately from the monarch. Justice as equity thus assumed the sovereignty of the person of the monarch and not of an impersonal system of laws, and as such is necessarily discretionary. What was distinctive about the historical development of equity jurisprudence in England was that it did not claim to be an independent system of rules but rather sought to supplement common law justice.

The specificity of the deployment of the idea of justice as equity in India is evident in the fact that unlike in England, where equity continues to be a judicial category and comes in only to supplement the main system based on common law that is universal and general in its scope, in the Indian Constitution justice as equity has become the sovereign legislative principle. Whenever the legislature encounters a conflict between the legislative imperatives of universal law and discretionary equity, the Constitution empowers the imperative of justice as equity to override the imperative of universal law. In this view of legislation, the state comes before the law or the community over whom it rules. The state is the source of all the laws, not the people. The state—not the people—is also, therefore, the source of the Constitution.

Given the exteriority of the monarchical state, the discourse of justice as equity was historically anchored in the duty and compassion of the monarch, in opposition to the modern revolutionary discourse of the rights of the citizens deriving from the universality of law. It was not surprising then that grounded as it was in the discourse of justice as equity, the directive principles were specifically defined in terms of the duties of the state rather than as rights of the individual. As the preamble to the section on directive principles states, these principles were 'fundamental in the governance of the country' and 'it shall be the *duty* of the state to apply these principles in making laws.'[19] It is critical to note that these principles could not be enforced by any court and individuals could not claim them as legal rights. Their enforcement was dependent entirely on the discretion and conscience of the state.

---

[19] Basu, *Shorter Constitution of India*, p. 158, emphasis mine.

The grounding of the Indian Constitution on the category of justice as equity as its sovereign legislative principle throws up an extraordinary paradox: the constitution of a democratic polity is anchored in a monarchical principle of legislation. The historically remarkable nature of this paradox becomes evident when juxtaposed against the fact that even Burke, who pleaded in the House of Lords—an institution centred on the figure of the King—on behalf of the people of India, based his arguments on an already existing system of natural law, not the compassion or mercy of the king alone. Burke, even as he addressed the king for justice, did not assume the king to be the source of law; the king was only a judge; the laws were part of the system of natural law that preceded the king. The king was expected to only administer those a priori natural laws. To place the king above the law would have been, for Burke, an act of turning the country over to 'arbitrary power'.[20]

EQUITY AND THE INSTITUTIONAL SOVEREIGNTY OF PARLIAMENT

The legislative sovereignty of the category of justice as equity, however, did not mean that the category of freedom was completely absent from the Indian Constitution. Indeed, without the category of freedom the Indian Constitution could not legitimately have called itself the Constitution of a democratic polity. However, given the legislative primacy of the category of justice, freedom was bound to come in conflict with it. This conflict of the categories of justice as equity and freedom is not just at the very heart of the Indian Constitution but also the Indian polity as a whole. The Indian Constitution sought to resolve this conflict in favour of justice by making freedom operate under the legislative sovereignty of the notion of justice as equity; freedom has to operate within the limits set for it by justice. In other words, while justice operates as a sovereign legislative category, freedom operates as a subject category. The primary mode in which the notion of justice as equity exercises its sovereignty over the notion of freedom in the Indian Constitution is evident in its power to suspend or override freedom when the latter is deemed to be coming in the way of justice.

The notion of freedom operates in the Constitution in the form of fundamental rights. The best way, therefore, to see the relative power of the notions of justice and freedom is to see how the fundamental

---

[20] See a more elaborate discussion of this in Chapter 1.

rights fare in the face of the sovereignty of the category of justice. In the Indian Constitution fundamental rights are divided into seven parts—The Right to Equality, the Right to Freedom, the Right against Exploitation, the Right to Freedom of Religion, Cultural and Education Rights, the Right to Property, and the Right to Constitutional Remedies. The function of the Fundamental Rights in the Indian Constitution, as in other constitutions, was the protection of the individual from encroachment by the state, which John Elster considers the most critical function of any constitution.[21]

The sovereignty of the concept of justice as equity in the Indian Constitution is invested in its authority to override Fundamental Rights—or individual rights—grounded as they are in the notion of freedom, the very bedrock of modern democracy. What separates the Indian Constitution from most other modern constitutions is the logic of exception embedded in it—even as it lays out rules regulating the interrelationship between the different branches of the government and institutes the Fundamental Rights of citizens, at the same time the Constitution makes way for exceptions to the otherwise universally applicable rules. These exceptional situations, however, include not just periods of national emergencies brought about by external aggression and war or domestic disorder, but also everyday situations when the Parliament could decide that the suspension of some essential and universal constitutional provision was necessary in the interests of bringing about a more equitable society.[22] The Constitution gives the Parliament the power to suspend and limit these rights under certain conditions, including while legislating. Even while laying out a set of rights, the Constitution is explicit that Fundamental Rights are not to prevent the state from suspending individual rights in the name of justice as equity. Thus unlike national emergency provisions in other constitutions, which can only be applied in exceptional situations,

---

[21] See Elster's 'Introduction', p. 2. Jon Elster has argued that all constitutions are necessarily anti-majoritarian, implying that the primary function of a constitution is to protect individual rights. It is quite clear that in making this theoretical proposition Elster projects the American Constitution as a universal model for all democracies. Ulrich K. Preuss, rather than make a similar universalist claim, has contended that constitutions can be either 'radical democratic' or institutional. See Preuss, 'Constitutional Powermaking for the New Polity: Some Deliberations on the Relations Between Constituent Power and the Constitution', p. 145.

[22] Pant, *Constituent Assembly Debates, Official Report*, p. 85.

in the Indian Constitution the logic of exception is not dependent on external emergencies but in fact is written into the Constitution as a permanent tool that can be deployed in any situation by the Parliament in the name of equity.

To make sure that these rights—fundamental though they may have been—were not interpreted as absolute and as such binding on the state, the Constitution framers invented another technique of adding qualifications to each right. Attached provisos circumscribed individual rights to such an extent that one of the members of the Constituent Assembly, Somnath Lahiri, argued in a memorable phrase that the rights had been framed 'from the point of view of a police constable.'[23] As Austin, the constitutional scholar, points out, this 'particular aspect of personal freedom was whittled down until on paper at least it was non-existent ... in the end they (the Constituent Assembly members) pinned their faith upon the mercy of the legislature and the good character of their leaders.'[24] If the 'faith upon the mercy of the legislature and the good characters of their leaders' became the assumed guarantors of these rights then that was because within the discourse of justice as equity rights as such were seen as privileges granted by the state as a gesture of its compassion towards the people; rights were a sign of the 'duty' and 'self-restraint' of the state.

One of the consequences of the legislative sovereignty of the category of justice as equity and the subordination of the category of freedom was that the power and authority of the Supreme Court was undermined. Even with a written constitution, the Supreme Court's absolute right to review parliamentary legislation in terms of their constitutionality—as it is in the United States—was drastically limited, if not altogether removed by the framers of the Indian Constitution. While the Constitution did provide for judicial review in the domain of Fundamental Rights and the relation between the central and state legislatures, severe restrictions were placed on the nature of review. As the noted scholar of the Indian Constitution, S.P. Sathe, points out, 'maximum care was taken to avoid making judicial review censorial of legislative policy as it had been in the United States.'[25] D.D. Basu, the well-known constitutional

---

[23] Lahiri, *Constituent Assembly Debates*, Vol. III, p. 384.

[24] Austin, *The Indian Constitution*, p. 112.

[25] Sathe, *Judicial Activism in India: Transgressing Borders and Enforcing Limits*,

scholar, pointed out the essential difference between the American Constitution and the Indian Constitution:

While the declarations in the American Bill of Rights are absolute and the power of the State to impose restrictions upon the fundamental rights of the individuals ... had to be evolved by the Judiciary, in India, this power has been expressly conferred upon the Legislatures by the Constitution itself in the case of the major fundamental rights.[26]

The Constitution framers further undermined the Supreme Court's authority by rejecting the 'due process' clause as a fundamental procedural element in the constitution, inspite of overwhelming public demand for it.[27] John Elster has argued that the supremacy of the judiciary over the legislature and the executive, and the practice of due process are the institutional means of guaranteeing the protection of individual rights from electoral majorities and powerful factions that might infringe on these rights.[28] By giving the courts the power to judge in a case where an individual's rights may have been infringed upon by the legislature or the executive, the right to due process safeguards fundamental rights from the excesses of the state; in the absence of the right to due process one would have nowhere to turn to for help against the state. Arguing that 'to fetter the discretion of the Legislature would lead to anarchy,' Govind Ballabh Pant, B.N. Rau, Jawaharlal Nehru, and others contended that in the interests of law and order, the prevention of violence and the imperatives of social justice, the due process clause needed to be dispensed with, and Parliament given the absolute power to override the rights of the individual.[29] In words reminiscent of the British colonial administration, Rau warned the Constituent Assembly that

p. 36. Also see Seervai, *The Position of the Judiciary Under the Constitution of India*; Mehta, 'The Inner Conflict of Constitutionalism: Judicial Review and the Basic Structure', pp. 179–206.

[26] Basu, *Introduction to the Constitution of India*, p. 70.

[27] Ambedkar acknowledged that 'no part of our draft constitution was so violently criticized as Art 15' that rejected due process. See *Constituent Assembly Debates*, IX, p. 1497. The classic statement on the right to due process is given in the Fifth Amendment of the American Constitution 'nor shall any person ... be deprived of life, liberty, or property without due process of the law; nor shall private property be taken for public use without just compensation.'

[28] See Elster, 'Introduction', in Elster and Slagstad, (eds), *Constitutionalism and Democracy*, p. 2.

[29] Pant, *Constituent Assembly Debates* (16 December 1946), vol. I, p. 85.

'The Courts, manned by an irremovable Judiciary not so sensitive to public needs in the social or economic sphere as the representatives of a periodically elected legislature, will, in effect, have a veto on legislation exercisable at any time.'[30]

Thus, while the authority of the Supreme Court as the guardian of the Constitution was undermined by the Constitution framers, it was the institution of the Parliament itself that was given the right to take exceptional policy decisions in the name of the overriding category of justice as equity which could, in fact, go against the fundamental provisions of the Constitution itself.[31] Moreover, Parliament had the right to amend the fundamental provisions of the Constitution if the court's decisions conflicted with its own sense of justice as equity. Thus, frequent amendments of the Constitution became an institutionalized way of dealing with judicial independence and asserting the legislative will of the Parliament, even when legislations were declared to be unconstitutional by the Supreme Court.[32]

Although the Court was given the power to issue prerogative rights to enforce Fundamental Rights, the emergency provisions gave the executive the authority to deny the right to the prerogative rights for long periods of time. Parliament also had the right to remove judges, a tool that could be used to bring intractable judges in line with the wishes of Parliament.[33] Most importantly, Parliament could modify or abolish any of the powers of the Courts by constitutional amendments that could be initiated by the introduction of a bill in either house of Parliament. The Bill

---

[30] Rau, *Constitutional Precedents*, pp. 17–18.

[31] This was due to the fact that Indian Constitution framers found themselves faced in 1947 with the historical task of reconciling two very different political formations, the British Westminster model with its system of parliamentary sovereignty and the American model of a written constitution, with its system of constitutional sovereignty.

[32] There were as many as seventeen amendments to the Constitution when Nehru was prime minister. See in particular First (1951), Fourth (1955), and Seventeenth (1964) Amendment Acts in Basu, *Shorter Constitution of India*. Notably, the First Amendment of the Indian Constitution in 1951, that came as early as within a year of the adoption of the Constitution, instituted the Ninth Schedule that protected from judicial review legislation that were clearly unconstitutional and in violation of Fundamental Rights. See Austin, *Working a Democratic Constitution: The Indian Experience*, pp. 71–98. Also see Baxi, 'Preface', in Sathe, *Judicial Activism*, p. xi.

[33] Basu, *Commentary on the Constitution of India*, 1, pp. 742–3.

would have to be passed by each house by a majority of the total
membership of that house and by a majority of not less than two-
thirds of the members of that house present and voting and finally
assented to by the President. In so far as the essential provisions of
the Constitution were concerned, Parliament could alter and even
eliminate any of these without recourse to the people so long as the
appropriate majorities could be obtained in the two houses.

The relatively easy process of amendment to the Constitution
also reveals that the Congress did not see the Constitution as a
permanent sovereign text that would endure through the ages. 'No
Supreme Court and no judiciary,' declared Nehru 'can stand in
judgment over the sovereign will of the Parliament, representing the
will of the entire community ... Ultimately the whole Constitution
is a creature of Parliament.'[34] By designating the Constitution as
'a creature of Parliament' what Nehru did in effect was to put the
Parliament both above the Supreme Court and the Constitution
itself. This understanding effectively abolished any notion of
the sovereignty of the Constitution as a unique document that
anchored the entire polity, and reduced it to the status of a regular
act of legislation. For the text of the Constitution to acquire the
aura of sovereignty—and by implication for the Supreme Court to
acquire autonomy as its final interpreter—it was essential that the
moment of constitution framing be symbolized as an extraordinary
moment, distinct from routine acts of legislation.[35] For example,
the American Constitution, coming in the train of the revolutionary
struggle for independence, became a sovereign document marking
not just the independent existence of America as a nation separate
from the British Empire, but also a fundamentally new relationship
between the people and the state. This fact is also borne out by the
rarity of amendments to the United States Constitution.

[34] Jawaharlal Nehru in the *Constitutuent Assembly Debates*, IX, pp. 1192–5.
As undisputed leader of the Congress and the first Prime Minister of India, Nehru's
views were some of the most important in the Constituent Assembly and reflected
the discursive framework within which the Congress operated. For Nehru's views
on India's past and future, see in particular *The Discovery of India* and *The Unity
of India, Collected Writings 1937–1940*. Also see Gopal and Iyengar, (eds), *The
Essential Writings of Jawaharlal Nehru*. For a classic biography of Nehru, see Gopal,
Jawaharlal Nehru: A Biography. Also see Wolpert, *Nehru: A Tryst with Destiny*.

[35] Bruce Ackerman has emphasized the importance of a distinction between
normal politics and constitutional politics in 'Neo-Federalism?', pp. 162–3.

It is not surprising then that when the Supreme Court did presume to take on the position of the guardian of the Constitution in the postcolonial period, the power of amendment that was in the hands of Parliament was used time and again to defeat it. The Supreme Court, in effect, lost the most powerful guarantee of its institutional autonomy—the absolute right to overturn an act of legislation of the Parliament in the name of the Constitution. Given that the text of the Constitution itself was not invested with any form of sovereignty having been subordinated to the institutional sovereignty of the Parliament, it was only logical that the judiciary itself as an institution came to be subordinated to the Parliament.

The 'sovereignty' of Parliament, however, is derivative in nature; it has its origin in the categorical legislative sovereignty of justice as equity. It is this category of justice as equity that constitutes the 'exceptional,' and the institutional sovereignty of Parliament flows from it. In this sense it is inadequate—while trying to determine the nature of sovereignty in a polity—to simply focus on *who* decides on the exception, as Schmitt has argued, while ignoring the nature of *what* constitutes the exception. In the case of the Indian polity, the *who*—the Parliament—derived its power of making exceptions from the *what*—the category of justice as equity. The discursive sovereignty of the category of justice as equity is more important in laying bare the nature of sovereignty in India than the institutional sovereignty of the Parliament.

In 1955 Nehru made an observation that reveals in clearest terms both the nature and the origin of the Parliament's sovereignty. 'There was an inherent contradiction,' Nehru argued, 'between Fundamental Rights and the Directive Principles of State Policy' and 'it is up to the Parliament to remove the contradiction and make fundamental rights *subserve* the Directive Principles of State Policy (emphasis mine).'[36] This statement reveals a clear understanding on the part of Nehru of the inherent contradiction between the Directive Principles anchored in the category of justice as equity and fundamental rights anchored in freedom. The way to remove the contradiction was by making 'fundamental rights subserve the directive principles of state policy'—that is by making freedom 'subserve' justice. The use of the word 'subserve' is very significant. Nehru did not ask

---

[36] *Lok Sabha Debates*, 14 March 1955; cited in Austin, *The Indian Constitution*, p. 101.

for the removal of fundamental rights expressive of freedom, but its 'subservience' or subordination to justice as articulated in the Directive Principles. Justice, in other words, was the sovereign legislative category and freedom the 'subservient' category. The categorical or discursive sovereignty of justice as equity operated in the Constitution through a logic of exception, which is invested in the Parliament's ability to suspend any and all other provisions, privileges, and rights based on the notion of freedom were they to come in the way of justice. The institutional sovereignty of the Parliament over both the Constitution and the Supreme Court, thus, is derivative of the categorical sovereignty of justice as equity. Thus, what legitimized this concentration of power in the Parliament's hands and justified not making individual rights absolute was that it was the institution of the Parliament—like the British colonial state before it—that would be the primary agent of a new society, where the people themselves were merely passive recipients of the beneficence of the state rather than agents of their own future.

JUSTICE AS EQUITY AND THE COMMUNITY

While the institution of the Parliament configured in the image of the imperial monarch was the source of justice, the recipient of justice as equity for the framers of the Indian Constitution was not the individual, but the community, the group. This derived from the fact that the Constitution saw the community as the fundamental unit of the nation, not the individual. The discussion of justice as equity in the Indian Constituent Assembly is notably distinct from its Western counterpart in that it is deployed not for the benefit of the individual—as in the historical juridical deployment of equity—but rather to provide substantial justice to the larger group—whether community, caste, tribe, ethnic, or linguistic group. In effect, Parliament was being given the power to suspend or override the universal provisions in the Constitution relating to the individual rights in favour of substantive equity to the community.

Indeed, looked at closely, what seemed like individual rights in the Constitution were in fact, at least partly, group rights. It is important to note that the Nehru Report of 1928, the Karachi Resolution of the Indian National Congress of 1931, and the Sapru Report of 1945—three documents from which the Constitution derived many of its clauses—all looked at the question of rights

200 INDIA IN THE SHADOWS OF EMPIRE

not so much with the individual's freedom in mind, but rather as a safeguard to create a sense of security among members of different communities.[37] The Sapru Report, for example, had stated that the Fundamental Rights of the new Constitution would be a 'standing call' to all that:

What the Constitution demands and expects is perfect equality between one section of the community and another in the matter of political and civil rights, equality of liberty and security in the enjoyment of the freedom of religion, worship, and the pursuit of the ordinary applications of life.[38]

Clearly, individual rights were seen in terms of protecting the rights of one group from the possible encroachments by other groups, not by the state. Thus one of the most important rights included in the section on Fundamental Rights, the freedom of conscience and religion was initially conceptualized not in individualistic terms, but rather to prevent one community from dominating another. In other words, part of what came to be known as Fundamental Rights was directed not to the individual as a citizen of the nation but as a member of his community.

A statement by Jawaharlal Nehru in the Constituent Assembly in 1949 brings out in unambiguous terms the dominant legislative ethos that inspired the framers of the Constitution regarding individual rights. Articulating what he thought ought to be the right way to think about the community–individual relationship and to measure their relative value while taking legislative decisions in independent India, Nehru argued, 'No individual can override ultimately the rights of the community at large. No community should injure and invade the rights of the individual unless it be for the most urgent and important purposes.'[39] Notice Nehru's use of the words 'cannot' and 'should not' to describe the relative power of the individual and the community, proxy for state; while the individual 'cannot override' the 'rights of the community', the community 'should not' hurt the rights of the individual unless it must. The 'should not' that sets the limit to the power of the community is an ethical injunction that could be set aside in exceptional circumstances. The community, which is to say the state, is bound by its own sense of

[37] See Austin, *Indian Constitution*, pp. 52–8.
[38] Sapru et al., *Constitutional Proposals of the Sapru Committee*, p. 260.
[39] Nehru, *Constituent Assembly Debates*, pp. 1192–5.

ethics—not law—in not injuring the rights of an individual. On the other hand, the 'cannot' that limits the power of the individual has the force of law; there are no exceptions to this universal law.

This statement clearly reveals that for Nehru, individual rights had their source in the state's sense of ethics, its ethical magnanimity towards the individual. The legislators in the Indian Parliament as representatives of their communities then were bound not by the Constitution but their own sense of ethics in granting or protecting individual rights even as legally they had all the legal and political power to 'injure and invade the rights of the individual' 'for the most urgent and important purposes'. In the dominant legislative ethos anchored in the state, the so-called individual rights were not rights at all; they were a privilege, a gift granted by the Parliament to individuals. Since individual rights are the most visible aspect of freedom in the modern discourse and practice of democracy, freedom itself, it turns out, was a privilege, a gift in postcolonial India.

The discursive indispensability of the notion of justice as equity in the Indian polity comes into full view when seen against the eventual failure of a powerful attempt to replace it with the notion of socialism. It is often assumed that because the Directive Principles of State Policy were addressed at substantive justice rather than formal equality, what motivated their inclusion in the Indian Constitution was the ideology of socialism that had acquired substantial currency in this period in India. The view that the ideology of socialism was at the origin of some of the most important feature of the Indian Constitution has proved to be a major distraction preventing scholars from getting to the real historical origins of it in the nature of the British Empire and the Indian National Congress in pre- and post-Gandhian periods. While it is true that socialism was an intellectual inspiration for certain sections of the Congress, especially for central figures like Nehru and Ambedkar, yet in the ultimate analysis, it did not acquire the significance or political weight to allow it to challenge the primacy of the concept of justice as equity, let alone replace it. The fact remains that the concept of socialism did not find a place in the Objectives Resolution or in the Directive Principles of the Indian Constitution at the time of its framing.[40]

---

[40] In 1976 the concept of socialism was indeed introduced into the Preamble of the Constitution, but that is a later development that would require a separate historical investigation.

However, the reasons for the Congress leadership's attraction to general ideological socialism is not far to seek; there are large areas of compatibility between the notion of justice as equity and the idea of socialism, most importantly that both are directed at substantive equality as opposed to the formal or abstract equality under law, promised by democratic polities. It was because the discourse of justice as equity historically framed the larger discussions of the Constituent Assembly, that both socialists (of which there were many kinds) and non-socialists in the Constituent Assembly could agree that the basic principle of substantive equality as opposed to the formal equality under the law should be underlined in the Constitution through the section on the Directive Principles of State Policy. In other words, even while the term socialism was useful for ideological purposes, the Directive Principles did not require an explicit discourse of socialism because the discourse of substantive equality was already intrinsic to the discourse of justice as equity.

The second area of compatibility between the discourse of justice as equity and that of socialism lies in the fact that both share similar notions of the state; both believe in the primacy of state over civil society and see the state as the primary agent of social and political transformation. Deriving from this belief is their shared view of the necessity of the state control of the economy and general distrust of the market economy. Finally, the discourse of justice as equity and that of socialism also share a deep distrust of the notion of freedom and its manifestation in the economic domain and individual rights. That was why the Congress and its leading figures felt much closer to the socialist communist Soviet Union even as the Indian democratic polity seemed to share, at least on the surface, much more with Western democracies.

The discourse of justice as equity and the discourse of socialism, however, were not homologous: the discourse of socialism could not be completely mapped on to the discourse of justice as equity. The most important difference between the two discourses was that while in socialism legislation and law were based on the principle of universality that assumed the unity and uniformity of the civil society, the discourse of justice as equity did not have universality as its legislative principle; it was crafted for a society that was assumed to be divided into communities that needed legislation and law to be tailored to their specific needs. This central difference was largely the reason why socialism could never replace the notion of justice as equity as the foundation of the dominant political discourse in India, even as some gestures were made a few decades later to give it some legal expression. What, however, is revealed in the ultimate failure of socialism to replace justice as equity as the sovereign legislative principle, is how indispensable the notion of India as a collection of random communities in conflict with each other was to the discourse of justice as equity. The pervasive political ethos that postcolonial India was made up not of citizen individuals, but rather of communities, as reflected in the framing of the Indian Constitution was not a construction of the Indian National Congress. Rather it was the Congress' imperial inheritance.[41] Indeed, the continuities between the British Empire and the Indian Constitution—with the Indian National Congress as the bridge between the two—are so fundamental that it would not be an exaggeration to claim that the Indian Constitution in some of its major aspects is imperial in nature.[42]

The imperial continuities in the Indian Constitution derived partly from the fact that it was based on the British Parliament's Cabinet Mission Plan of 1946, which in turn derived its most essential features from the Government of India Act of 1935.[43] In a conversation with Alan Campbell-Johnson the press attaché of Lord Mountbatten, B.R. Ambedkar, the principal drafter of the Constitution, acknowledged that some two hundred and fifty clauses of the Government of India Act had been directly incorporated into the new Constitution.[44] The Directive Principles, as Ambedkar pointed out in the discussion on the draft constitution in the Constituent Assembly, were in fact the Instruments of Instructions which were issued to the Governor-General and to the Government

[41] Scholars who have seen the community as the ground of British colonial governmentality include Chatterjee, *The Nation and its Fragments: Colonial and Postcolonial Histories*; Scott, 'Colonial Governmentality'.

[42] For a contrasting view that see the making of the Constitution as a 'revolutionary' moment see Mehta, 'Indian Constitutionalism: The Articulation of a Political Vision', pp. 13–30.

43 Banerjee, *The Making of the Indian Constitution*, pp. 137–50. Also see Coupland, *The Constitutional Problem in India*.

[44] Campbell-Johnson, *Mission with Mountbatten*, pp. 319–20. For Amdedkar's works, see Moon, (ed.), *Dr Babasaheb Ambedkar: Writings and Speeches*. For biographies of Ambedkar see Omvedt, *Ambedkar: Towards an Enlightened India*; Jaffrelot, *Dr Ambedkar and Untouchability: Analysing and Fighting Caste*; Keer, *Dr. Ambedkar, Life and Mission*.

of the Colonies and to those in India by the British Government under the 1935 Act.[45]

The Government of India Act, however, was more than just a legal document; in it was embedded the British imperial conception of India as a colony. What was most important about the discursive framework that anchored the Government of India Act—and the terms of the transfer of power from the Government of British India to the Government of India—was the colonial construction that India was not a nation, but rather a heterogeneous collection of random communities locked in their irreconcilable conflicts with each other. If India was united and in peace, then that was because the British colonial state as a foreign and, therefore, neutral and impartial judge was able to enforce it in the name of justice.

Indeed, the very discourse and practice of legislative representation came to be anchored in this colonial construction of India as a collection of warring communities. In the system of legislative representation instituted by the British in India in the late nineteenth century, Indian members were nominated by the colonial government into the legislative council based on their social and religious identity. This system of group or communal representation in the legislative council later came to be institutionalized in the idea of separate electorates for different communities, articulated in the Morley-Minto Reforms of 1909, the Government of India Act of 1935, and the Cabinet Mission Plan.

The general ethos of legislative representation grounded in group identities came to be reflected in the composition of the Indian Constituent Assembly itself.[46] The composition and the debates of the Indian Constituent Assembly bear out in clearest terms the implications of this imperial representational principle; overwhelmingly, members participated in debates not as representatives of India as a nation but rather as representative of specific religious communities, caste groups, and tribes. While elaborating on the aims and objectives of the Constitution, Sri Biswanath Das, a member of the Constituent Assembly, pointed out the nature of the Assembly in December in 1946:

---

[45] Ambedkar, *Constitutional Assembly Debates*, vol. VII, p. 41. Also see Prasad, *Ideas and Men*, p. 62.

[46] See Jennings, 'The Constitution of India'.

We have in this great Assembly not only the representatives of the Hindu majority provinces but also the representatives of Hindu minorities in Muslim majority provinces. We have also the representatives of Scheduled Castes, Christians, Sikhs, Parsis, Anglo-Indians, and of Tribal and partially-excluded areas. We have amongst us also the representatives of the great Muslim community barring the leaders of the Muslim League.[47]

Comprising of 389 members, the majority of the Assembly was elected not by adult suffrage, but by members of provincial legislatures who were themselves elected in 1945 on the basis of a restricted franchise—set up by the sixth schedule of the 1935 Act—which excluded the large body of peasants, small shopkeepers and traders, and many others on the basis of tax, property, and educational qualifications.[48] Even more importantly, however, the members of the provincial legislatures—who elected the members of the Constituent Assembly—had been elected as representatives of their respective religious communities—Hindu or General, Muslim, and Sikh. The number of seats in the provincial legislature granted to the three major religious communities was fixed in proportion to their percentage in the total population of a province.[49] Members of the constituent assembly, therefore, represented their communities, not the nation. The enunciative position of these members of the provincial legislatures and the Constituent Assembly, in other words, was anchored in their respective communities, not in the nation.

The elections to the Provincial Legislatures in 1945 had given the Indian National Congress about 85 per cent of the 'General'— mostly Hindu—seats and the Muslim League most of the Muslim seats in the provinces. Thus, when elections to the Constituent Assembly took place in July of 1946 Congress candidates filled 203 of the 210 General seats, the Muslim League members won 72 of the 78 seats reserved for Muslims, and 16 seats went to the Sikhs, the Scheduled Castes, and other smaller groups.[50] The Princely states had 93 representatives and the Chief Commissioners' Provinces had

[47] *Constituent Assembly Debates*, vol. I, p. 121

[48] According to the constitutional scholar Granville Austin, only 28.5 per cent of the adult population could vote in the provincial assembly elections of 1946. See Austin, *The Indian Constitution: Cornerstone of a Nation*, p. 10.

[49] Ibid., p. 5.

[50] The Akali Sikhs and the Unionists of the Punjab had three seats each, the Communists and the Scheduled Castes Federation one each, and independents has eight seats. See Austin, *The Indian Constitution*, p. 10, fn 36.

4 representatives. It is also important to note that although elections to the Constituent Assembly took place with the cooperation of the Muslim League headed by Mohammed Ali Jinnah in July of 1946, the Muslim League boycotted the Constituent Assembly soon after the elections. Thus when the Constituent Assembly convened for the first time in December of 1946, representatives of the Muslim League were not present, giving the Congress an effective absolute majority. After the Partition and the formation of the two independent nation-states of India and Pakistan in August 1947, Muslim League members who remained in India did join the Constituent Assembly occupying 28 seats, while the Congress occupied 82 per cent of the now reduced number of 299 seats.

The discourse and practice of legislative representation as it developed over the colonial period culminating in the Constituent Assembly was clearly grounded in the community, not in the individual. In the politics of electoral representation in India the British Empire had discovered a new domain for its imperial statecraft. By introducing representative or electoral politics the British Empire could fulfill two seemingly conflicting imperial aims at the same time. On the one hand it could claim that it was fulfilling its longstanding promise as part of its general pedagogical mission in India to slowly introduce the elements of political freedom or self-governance, valorized as the highest achievement of the Western civilization. On the other hand, by anchoring the discourse and practice of representation in the community, rather than the individual, it could at the same time divide Indian civil society even more deeply at the broadest level along communal, sectarian, ethnic, caste, and linguistic lines. This division was intended to preempt any possibility of now ever-proliferating communities from coming together to demand national independence from the British Empire. More 'freedom' meant deeper divisions between the communities and therefore more dependence on the British Empire to unite them; more freedom, in other words, necessitated a stronger empire. India's status as a colony, paradoxically enough, was presented as its only way to 'self-governance.' It was only as a colony that India could win 'freedom' for itself. It was as if the Indians could have their 'self-government' and the British their empire at the same time. Such was the logic of the British Empire in India.

In other words, the introduction of the discourse and practice of electoral representation or self-governance in India was meant to achieve exactly the opposite goal—keep India as a permanent British colony with the help and consent of Indians. The historical circumstances and the mode in which legislative representation was deployed in colonial India changed the very meaning of the category of freedom—freedom came to be defined not so much in relation to the state, but in terms of one community's relation to another. In the domain of legislative representation, freedom came to mean freedom from another community. As Somnath Lahiri stated in another memorable phrase in the Constituent Assembly, 'there is no freedom in this country ... we have freedom only to fight amongst ourselves.'[51] So far as the communities' relation with the state was concerned, justice remained the sovereign operational category.

Given that this discourse and practice of freedom as reflected in electoral politics in the late nineteenth and twentieth centuries only exacerbated the divisions between communities and turned them all into minorities precluding the possibility of national independence, it also helped reinforce the discourse of justice as equity as the sovereign imperial principle. Divided Indian society looked at the British Empire as their only hope. Even as the communities pursued their freedom separately, together justice was all they could hope for. Whereas 'freedom' seemed to accelerate the process and extent of social and religious divisions, justice as equity seemed to offer a point of unity in the figure of the imperial monarch. It was in this precise historical and political context of India as a British colony that the notion of freedom came to concede its claim to categorical sovereignty to justice. By anchoring the discourse and practice of elected representation in the communities, the British Empire found a way to subordinate freedom to the discourse of imperial justice; freedom was made to operate within the commanding limits of imperial justice—the ideological foundation of the British Empire in India.

The extent of confidence that British imperial strategists like Churchill had in their ability to deploy the discourse of justice to divide India against itself could be gauged from the fact that they suggested deploying it at a critical time in the 1940s, when India seemed as good as lost, to outflank the movement for national independence led by Gandhi by getting the Indian masses over to the side of the Empire. Indeed, Churchill, the arch imperialist, well

[51] Somnath Lahiri, *Constituent Assembly Debates* (19 December 1946), I: 134.

known for his antipathy towards socialist and Marxist thoughts and movements, was ready to deploy the discourse of justice to mobilize Indian peasants and workers against their oppressors, the Congress. 'It would really *pay* us,' Churchill stated, 'to take up the cause of the poor peasant and confiscate the rich Congressmen's lands and divide them up.'[52] In Churchill's scheme, the discourses of socialism and justice could be deployed to 'pay' imperialist dividends. Cripps was even more elaborate:

If the British Government could enlist the sympathy of the workers and peasants by immediate action on their behalf, the struggle in India would no longer be between Indian and British upon the nationalist basis, but between the classes in India upon an economic basis. There would thus be a good opportunity to rally the mass of Indian Opinion to our side. It is most important that the Indian workers and peasants should realize that it is British initiative which is working for them against their Indian oppressors; this would entail a proper publicity service in India.[53]

The strategic nature of the imperial discourse of justice is clear in this statement—justice was the other side of the divide and rule policy. Once the Indian civil society had been fragmented, even the ideology of socialism could be mobilized to defend and maintain the British Empire.

THE IMPERIAL VISION IN THE INDIAN CONSTITUTION

The Indian Constitution, as Mahavir Tyagi, a member of the Constituent Assembly, put it succinctly in 1949, was a 'one party constitution.'[54] In so far as the Constituent Assembly was indistinguishable from the Indian National Congress, the vision that the Assembly had for the future of India cannot be understood in isolation from that of the Congress and its history. As the constitutional scholar J.L. Austin put it, 'the Constituent Assembly was a one-party body in an essentially one-party country. The Assembly was the Congress.'[55] After the partition, the Congress majority constituted as much as 82 per cent of the Constituent Assembly. At the same time, the Congress was also

---

[52] Hutchins, *India's Revolution: Gandhi and the Quit India Movement*, pp. 284–5.

[53] Hutchins, *India's Revolution*, p. 285

[54] *Constituent Assembly Debates*, vol. IX, p. 1656.

[55] Austin, *Indian Constitution*, p. 8.

the overwhelmingly dominant presence in the Indian Parliament and provincial legislatures, and thus national and state governments. The four leaders of the Indian Constituent Assembly—Jawaharlal Nehru, Patel, Rajendra Prasad, Maulana Azad—were also the leaders of the Indian National Congress and members of its highest council, the Working Committee. Even as the Constitution was still being written, Jawaharlal Nehru became the Prime Minister of the Union Government in 1947, Patel the Deputy Prime Minister, and a number of important figures in the Constituent Assembly prominent ministers in the Congress government. To quote Austin again, 'the Assembly, the Congress and the government were like the points of a triangle, separate entities, but linked by over-lapping membership.'[56]

In so far as the Congress was grounded in the imperial teleology of justice, it also had to assume the British characterization of India as a society of communities in perpetual conflict to be the truth. As B.R. Ambedkar stated in the Indian Constituent Assembly, 'I know today we are divided politically, socially, and economically. We are a group of warring camps, and I may go even to the extent of confessing that I am probably one of the leaders of such a camp.'[57] It is not surprising therefore that the national independence having been won, the Congress claimed for itself the same role that the British Empire had played in India; it claimed to be the source of unity for a nation divided into innumerable communities. Investing Parliament with the role of the impartial judge under the sovereign legislative discourse of justice as equity, in effect, meant investing the Congress party with that role. The Congress alone, it was claimed, could offer the neutrality and impartiality that was needed to sustain the discourse of justice as equity. Purushottam Das Tandon, in speaking to the aims and objectives of the Constituent Assembly, articulated in no uncertain terms in the Constituent Assembly in 1946 what he saw as the ground of India's unity:

Congress is the only body in which Hindus, Muslims, Parsees, Jains and Buddhists can unite. In politics, it refuses to recognize any difference on account of religion. To say that such and such sections be separated from the country on a religious basis is not religion but pure politics—politics which will destroy the unity of the country.[58]

[56] Ibid., p. 9.
[57] *Constituent Assembly Debates* (17 December 1946), vol. I, p. 100.
[58] *Constituent Assembly Debates* (13 December 1946), vol. I, p. 68.

Characterizing ideological discourse based on religion as 'pure politics' that undercut the unity of the nation, Tandon argued that the unity of India could only be grounded in the Congress, because it alone stood above the politics of group identity.

What Tandon's statement reflected was a fundamental paradox at the very heart of the Indian Constitution—even as constitutional discourse itself came to be grounded on the idea of heterogeneity of Indian society, using categories derived from sectional, religious, regional, and caste identities, yet any form of representational politics that claimed to identify with these interests became projected as a threat to the very unity and integrity of India. How could the Parliament or the Congress represent different communities, and also stand above them and be neutral towards them at the same time? Parliament could not mediate between the communities if it also represented those communities.

How then was this contradiction to be resolved? The British imperial legacy to India was that given its inescapable social divisions, if India were to have peace and unity, and of course freedom, it must not attempt to give birth to a state from within its own civil society for the simple reason that a divided society could not offer a position of neutrality and impartiality needed to mediate between the communities; given its nature, India was not fit to be a 'nation-state'. It was only as subjects of a state exterior to the civil society that Indians could become free. India must therefore either accept a state from outside or at least have a conception of the state as exterior to the civil society. In pre-Gandhian colonial India, it was after all around the figure of the Queen as Empress of India and impartial judge that the Congress had brought all communities together. The discourse of justice as equity that was seen as the guarantor of peace and unity of India was unsustainable without the figure of the monarch exterior to an Indian civil society made up of conflicting communities.

But how was the exteriority of the state to the civil society to be maintained now that the British Empire had departed? It therefore followed that if the Congress were to remain anchored in the discourse of justice as equity in the absence of the impartial monarch in postcolonial India, it would have to reinvent itself: it had to elevate one of its own to occupy the now vacant position of the monarch in the wake of the British departure from India. It is not surprising then that as soon as the British left, the Congress, by the sheer force of the discourse of justice as equity on which it was based, slowly began to elevate one of its own, Jawaharlal Nehru, to occupy the imperial position of the monarch as impartial judge. Parliament, which is to say the Congress, reconfigured itself as a court of equity centered on Nehru as the new monarch. The emergence of the Nehru dynasty was derivative of this discourse of justice as equity.

UNIVERSAL FRANCHISE AS A GANDHIAN LEGACY

Remarkably, the Indian Constitution contained one provision that ran counter to the dominant discourse of justice as equity on which it was grounded—universal adult franchise based on the idea of the freedom of the individual as a citizen, the colonial idea of separate electorates for the communities having been completely abandoned. It is striking that the Constitution of India is more radical with regard to the franchise than other contemporary constitutions in so far as it places no restrictions on adult franchise on the basis of property, taxation, education, income and such; in a constitution otherwise full of qualifications attached to individual rights, this was one right left without any qualification. The entire adult population of India numbering 210 million, according to the 1961 census, was given the unqualified right to exercise their freedom to vote and elect their representatives to the Parliament and state legislatures in postcolonial India.[59]

The Indian Constitution, therefore, carried a conflict at its very heart: the discourse of imperial justice as equity as a discourse of governance that was anchored in the figure of the monarch and directed to groups or communities, and the democratic electoral polity with universal adult franchise based on individual freedom of the citizen were two very contrary, indeed opposite, principles. Even as the discourse of justice as equity grounded on the representation of communities came to anchor the polity at large, the principle of universal suffrage based on the representation of the individual as a citizen rejected the colonial notions of separate electorates and communal representation. It was as if Indians could become citizen-individuals and as such equal, irrespective of the communities they belonged to, only during elections. Moreover, while the discourse of governance based on the idea of justice as equity assumed the

---

[59] Basu, *Commentary on the Constitution of India*, p. 70.

presence of a monarch as the sovereign figure who would render impartial justice between communities, the necessity of five-year national elections assumed the sovereignty of the people.

The crucial question that arises is what was at the origin of this contradiction at the heart of the Indian Constitution? Under what imperatives did the Constitution framers introduce universal franchise when it ran counter to the very fundamentals of the discourse of governance based in the category of justice as equity? It is important to note at the very outset that the debates in the Indian Constituent Assembly between 1946 and 1949 reflect a marked absence of enthusiasm in the majority of the members towards the idea of universal adult franchise. Strikingly, universal franchise was not part of the aims and objectives discussion in the constituent assembly. Indeed, even the term democracy was left out of the discussion and only included later in the draft preamble. The attempt by Ambedkar to include universal adult franchise in the chapter on Fundamental Rights was rejected by the draft committee and left for inclusion 'in some other part of the constitution'. Ultimately, it was grafted on to the Constitution towards the end of the document as Article 326 of Part XV—this too on the initiative of Ambedkar.[60]

The decision by the Constituent Assembly not to ratify the draft constitution by universal franchise is another reflection of the opposition of a majority of the Assembly members to the idea of the direct participation of the people of India in constitutional decision making. Indeed when some members of the Assembly suggested that there was a need to legitimize the Constitution by ratification on the basis of adult suffrage, it was immediately brushed aside by a majority of the members. This decision stands in sharp contrast to other major democratic constitutions that were seen as the reflection of the people's will. Thomas Paine, in defining the word constitution, famously said that 'A constitution is not the act of a government, but of a people constituting a government.' As Hannah Arendt pointed out, it is for this reason that constituent assemblies and special conventions were set up in France and in America solely for the purpose of drafting a constitution, and the need was felt 'to bring the draft home and back to the people and have the Articles of

[60] Rao, *The Framing of India's Constitution: A Study*, pp. 460–2, 471. Also see Sarkar, 'Indian democracy: The Historical Inheritance', p. 37.

Confederation debated, clause by clause, in the town-hall meetings and, later, the state congresses.'[61] While the Indian Constitution framers gave the impression of putting the Constitution directly in this tradition by including in the Preamble the words 'We the people of India give to ourselves this constitution,' in reality they saw the Constitution as a gift of the state, not a reflection of the will of the people.

The ambivalence on the part of a majority of the Constitution framers for the idea and practice of universal franchise can be explained by the fact that the conflict at the heart of the Indian Constitution was the result of two competing historical legacies that framed it. While the Constitution as a discourse of governance was an imperial legacy that survived in the Congress party and the Nehru dynasty, in which the people were nothing but passive recipients of justice, the necessity of elections as fundamental to democratic practice was a legacy of the Gandhian mass movement against colonialism and other democratic movements for rights that emerged in its wake. The presence of universal adult franchise as a powerful democratic principle in an otherwise imperial polity is connected fundamentally with the nature of Gandhian mass movement that led to India's independence. Even though the contradiction was negotiated in favour of the discourse of imperial justice as equity in the Indian Constitution, it remains the driving force of the postcolonial Indian polity.

As I have shown earlier in the book, the pre-Gandhian Indian National Congress grounded in the imperial discourse of justice as equity had not been able to develop a discourse of complete national independence until the rise of Gandhi. It was Gandhi who exposed and shattered the carefully built imperial pedagogical discourse that the ultimate telos of the British Empire in India was to set it free once the people in India had learnt the ways of self-government. By mobilizing the masses in large numbers against the British Empire, rather than pleading for its justice and benevolence as the pre-Gandhian Indian National Congress had done, the movement led by Gandhi helped develop a democratic ethos in which people came to see themselves as sovereign; the masses saw their freedom as emanating from their own actions, in their ability to resist and control the state. For the first time the state's legitimacy was linked

---

[61] Arendt, *On Revolution*, pp. 143–4.

to its ability to serve the people. Ultimately, by introducing universal adult suffrage and five-year elections, however reluctantly, into the Constitution, the framers were accommodating this Gandhian legacy that was too powerful to ignore.

What is remarkable about the making of the Indian Constitution is the complete absence of Gandhi from it. Seen superficially, it is extremely puzzling that the man who had been the leading figure in the movement for independence would retreat from an opportunity to give an enduring form to a hard won independence. The explanation for Gandhi's absence from constitutional discussions lay in the nature of the Gandhian discourse of freedom itself. If Gandhi had nothing to do with the making of the Constitution as the template of governance in independent India, that was because his discourse of freedom had nothing to do with matters of governance. It was only as resistance that the Gandhian discourse of freedom related to the state. Freedom in the Gandhian sense meant freedom from the state and the discourse of governance as such. It is not surprising then that Gandhi called on the Congress to disband itself at independence. Rather than heed his advice, the Congress resurrected the discourse of imperial justice as equity historically anchored in the figure of the monarch and put it at the center of the Constitution as the discourse of governance.

The recognition of universal suffrage by the Constitution framers was not a proof of the Constitution's magnanimity, as is often assumed, but rather of its limit. It was a direct legacy of the power and popularity of the Gandhian mass movement and other democratic movements for rights against colonialism; the power of democracy was too strong for the Constitution makers to deny the people the right to universal adult franchise. It is not surprising then that it was Ambedkar, the leader of one of the most important democratic movements for rights of the Dalits or lower castes, who was also the strongest advocate of universal franchise in the Constitution.[62] Also, the framers' ultimate decision to include it in the Constitution was in no small measure attributable to the fact that the Congress was the single most dominant party in the country at the time of independence, and therefore universal adult franchise

---

[62] Nagaraj, *The Flaming Feet: A Study of the Dalit Movement*; Omvedt, *Dalits and the Democratic Revolution: Dr. Ambedkar and the Dalit Movement in Colonial India*; Prashad, *Untouchable Freedom: A Social History of the Dalit Community*; Dirks, *Castes of Mind*; Zelliot, 'Congress and Untouchables: 1917–1950'.

posed no real threat to it or its discourse of imperial justice at the time of the making of the Constitution. It is extremely significant to note finally that even as the Constitution framers were compelled to recognize universal adult franchise, they were determined to prevent the electorate from exercising any political function by their direct vote. All devices of direct democracy, such as the Referendum, Recall, or Initiative, were meticulously avoided in the Indian Constitution.[63] The people of India could not exercise their direct vote for ordinary political or for constitutional purposes. The legislative function could only be exercised by the representatives of the people elected in the general election. As K.T. Shah, one of the members of the Constituent Assembly expressed it:

The right to consult the people by means of a Referendum, or the power of the people to initiate radical legislation to make the Constitution really democratic ... have all been negatived. The excuse that has been given is that we are not yet ready for such methods of working democracy in all its fullness. We would need, we were told, greater experience, better education, and more wide-spread consciousness of political power in the masses as well as its responsibilities, to be able to work with success such radical forms of democratic government. I am afraid ... I cannot quite accept and endorse such a view of our people's capacity ... The ability to work a democracy comes by having the responsibility to do so, not by paper professions in its name, and practical negation of its forms. Had we agreed to such arguments in the past, had we accepted the suggestion of the British that the people of India were not educated enough and aware enough of their rights and obligations to be able to work a democratic Government of their own, we should never even now have obtained our independence ... Because you are still unable to trust in full the people; because you are still unable to realize that it is only by working a democracy that democracy will really be established in this country, you have not accepted those suggestions of mine ... which wanted ... such instruments and devices to be introduced in the Constitution.[64]

In this incisive critique of the draft constitution, what Shah was pointing to was the discursive continuity between the British Empire and the Constitution framers in their distrust of the people of India and of democracy as such. Despite the fact that independence had

[63] Basu, *Commentary on Constitution of India*, 3rd edn, 1, p. 47.
[64] Shah, *Constituent Assembly Debates* (17 November 1949), XI, p. 619.

been won by a mass struggle, the people were still to be denied an active part in political decision making in postcolonial India. Clearly, for the Constitution framers, the gap between the representative and the represented had to be maintained at all times. The juridical model of representation in which the representative as advocate would plead for his clients before the imperial judge continued to dominate the thinking of the leaders of the Congress as they met to frame the Constitution. In the manner of the imperial state before it, the Constituent Assembly saw the people of India as passive recipients of the justice and benevolence of the state, not as active agents of their own future.

Even as the Gandhian legacy of mass movements survived in the form of the necessity of adult franchise and elections in the Indian Constitution, it was the imperial discourse of justice as equity that came to anchor the Indian polity at large. Indeed, there was so much continuity between the Indian Constitution and the administrative structure of the colonial period that Ambedkar, the principal draughtsman of the Constitution, had serious doubts about the very need for a Constituent Assembly:

I cannot see why the Constituent Assembly is necessary to incubate a Constitution. So much of the Constitution of India has already been written out in the Government of India Act of 1935 that it seems to be an act of supererogation to appoint a Constituent Assembly to do the thing all over again. All that is necessary is to delete those sections of the Government of India Act 1935, which are inconsistent with Dominion status.[65]

The use of the phrase 'dominion status' as the standard against which the existing colonial laws needed to be measured before they could be recognized as the laws of independent India betrays that even at the time of its independence India continued to be seen by the Congress under the category of 'dominion status' or its equivalent 'Home Rule'.[66] National independence meant nothing more for the

[65] Quoted in Chavan (ed.), *The Makers of India Constitution: Myth and Reality*, pp. xxxii–xxxiii.

[66] It is important to note that it was V.P. Menon, one of the important leaders of the Congress, who suggested to the Secretary of State in January 1947 that the transfer of power from the British Government to the Indian state be on the basis of dominion status, so that there would be no need to wait for the Constituent Assembly to reach agreement on the new political structure of the postcolonial state. See Menon, *The Transfer of Power in India*, pp. 346–64.

Congress than the realization of the old demand for 'dominion status' in which ultimate sovereignty lay with the British Crown. It is noteworthy in this context that the Constituent Assembly ratified a declaration that Nehru had unilaterally signed at the Conference of Commonwealth Prime Ministers in London on 27 April 1949 making India a member of the British Commonwealth under the Crown.[67] It would be hasty to dismiss these statements and actions as meaningless given that the British did, after all, leave India. What they betray at a deeper level is the need felt in the highest leadership of the Congress to maintain a discursive continuity with the British Empire. Even as the British left India, much of the discursive infrastructure of the British imperial polity was left intact as an enduring legacy—a fact nowhere more evident than in the Indian Constitution.

Hardly had Ambedkar put the final touches to a work that still sits at the center of a raging storm that a fear came over him briefly. He told the Constituent Assembly in his last speech:

In India, bhakti [devotional form of Hinduism], or what may be called the path of devotion or hero-worship, plays a part in its politics unequaled in magnitude by the part it plays in the politics of any other country in the world. Bhakti in religion may be the road to the salvation of a soul. But in politics, bhakti or hero-worship is *a sure road to degradation* and to *eventual dictatorship* (emphasis mine).[68]

The triumphant moment of the completion of the Constitution of India as an independent country seems an odd time for a leading member of the Constituent Assembly to voice anxieties about the possibility of a general political 'degradation' and 'eventual dictatorship'—the Constitution of a democratic polity is, after all, one of the most important safeguards against any such possibility. Looked at closely, Ambedkar's statement consists of two parts—a fear about the possibility of dictatorship accompanied by a thought about the cultural source of the possibility of dictatorship. Ambedkar's fear was not unfounded. Where Ambedkar, however, went astray was in his thought about bhakti being at the source of that possible dictatorship. After all, Gandhi, the man who had led

[67] See *Constituent Assembly Debates* (16 May 1949), VIII, p. 2.
[68] Ambedkar, *Constituent Assembly Debates*, vol. XI, 25 November 1949, p. 1205.

India to independence and to whom bhakti mattered more than most others in the Congress, walked away from power even as others scrambled to find a place in the new government. The source of the possible dictatorship that was the object of Ambedkar's fear lay more precisely in the imperial legacy of the discourse of justice as equity as the sovereign legislative discourse of governance that was not viable in the absence of the figure of the monarch. If dictatorship is defined as a system in which an institution or a figure that makes laws seems at the same time to stand above it, then a monarchy, seen from the perspective of modern democratic polities, would appear to be a permanent form of dictatorship. Yet, the discourse of justice as equity that sits at the heart of the Indian Constitution cannot function without the figure of the monarch and the exteriority of the state to the civil society.

It was modern India's democratic legacy of anticolonial mass movements that sensitized and alerted Ambedkar to anticipate and articulate a very real danger of 'dictatorship' as he concluded his work on the Constitution. However, the discursive force of the British imperial legacy—deeper and more pervasive than often thought—prevented him from thinking his way to its origin. This was not just Ambedkar's story—it is the story of postcolonial India itself. Not long after his work on the Constitution was completed, Ambedkar left government a disappointed, indeed a disillusioned, man, to launch another chapter in India's history of mass movements, even as Nehru, his one time colleague in the Constituent Assembly, now the Prime Minister, began to reinvent himself in the shadows of an ever-departing but never-departed Empire.

7

INDIA AFTER INDEPENDENCE

A Tale of Conflicting Legacies

One of the curious things about Indian independence from the British Empire is that it has not been consecrated with the designation of revolution.[1] This stands in stark contrast to all major events of national freedom in world history, either from colonialism or from native monarchies that have been characterized as revolutions. Why then was Indian independence any less of a revolution than other moments of national freedom? After all, it came at the end of one of the largest and most disciplined mass movements in history, spanning decades. What is more, it was the only instance in world history where the mass movement that led to independence was based on the idea and practice of non-violence.

Behind the absence of the designation of revolution lies buried an aspect of India's emergence as an independent country that often goes unnoticed—it reveals the triumph of the British imperial narrative of its history in India. The absence of the narrative of revolution in India—including in Indian historiography—assumes a discourse of freedom without resistance. This freedom without resistance is nothing but the ideology that presented the British Empire in India as a pedagogical mission as articulated in the discourse of justice as liberty. In this imperial discourse, India's national independence was the fulfilment of the avowed imperial mission; national independence was an imperial gift to India. As I have shown in Chapters 2 and 3 of this book, the Indian National

---

[1] One of the few scholars to call the Indian independence movement a revolution is Franchis G. Hutchins. See his *Spontaneous Revolution: The Quit India Movement*, pp. 1–2.

Congress itself was anchored in this imperial discourse. With the withdrawal and then death of Gandhi—the driving force of the anticolonial movement—and the return of the Congress to its pre-Gandhian discursive moorings, the notion of resistance slowly fell out of the historical narrative, making revolution appear an unlikely designation for Indian independence.[2]

This disavowal of resistance has had a profound impact on studies of the postcolonial Indian polity. The proliferation of paradoxes in reference to postcolonial India that I alluded to briefly in the introduction has its roots in the triumph of this imperial narrative of the British Empire as a pedagogical mission. It is in this context that one can understand why the birth of constitutional democracy in India has been understood not as the outcome of a complex development of culturally specific and historically contingent discourses, institutions, practices, and conflicts, but rather in terms of the transfer and communication of a set of ideas (such as freedom, liberty, equality, and justice), and institutions, western in origin, to a traditional eastern society. This transfer and communication of western ideas to India as a methodological premise of such studies assumes the pedagogical model that robs the postcolonial polity of its history. Paradoxes (such as modern but also traditional, western but also eastern, industrialized but also poor, urban but also rural) arise from a tendency on the part of scholars to see the postcolonial Indian polity in ahistorical terms as a simple juxtaposition of different and disparate—but also inert—elements, without any meaningful connection between them.

This largely theoretical—and pedagogical—approach to the study of Indian constitutional democracy has two problems. First, the theoretical–pedagogical approach makes differences between western and non-western democracies appear as digressions, deviations, and signs of inadequacy or lack, rather than as the outcome of complex histories of discourses and institutions through time.[3] Contemporary political scientists have referred to postcolonial India as a 'transitional'

[2] In many ways the birth of Subaltern School of historiography with its focus on peasant insurgencies was a reaction to the dominant Congress ethos based on the general disavowal of resistance.

[3] The absence of a historical approach to Indian democracy has been pointed out by Sumit Sarkar in his chapter 'Indian Democracy: The Historical Inheritance', in *The Success of India's Democracy*, pp. 23–46.

or 'follower' democracy, not only assuming the theoretical sameness of democracies everywhere, but also presupposing that the essential structure and the set of abstract categories that define democracy can be simply communicated or transferred from one author-nation to others.[4] It is not surprising that while most historians of modern India terminate their research at 1947, the year of India's independence, assuming postcolonial political development to be inaccessible to historical research, most studies by political scientists have taken 1947 as their point of departure, as if the postcolonial political formation had emerged fully formed without any history.[5] In the absence of an understanding of the historical processes through which what appear as contraries have nevertheless come together, the postcolonial Indian polity is likely to continue to appear as nothing more than a bundle of paradoxes.

Second, the theoretical–pedagogical approach, by focusing on the transference of ideas from England to her colonies, is indifferent to questions of power, domination, and the cultural and historical conditions behind the production of knowledge that have become so much a part of cultural history today. In the case of postcolonial nations, such an emphasis on a benevolent transfer of ideas means that the specific histories of conflict and movements of opposition to colonialism through which democracies have become realities in erstwhile colonies are also ignored. If the emergence and success of democracies were simply a matter of transferring categories and institutions from the metropole to the colonies, how would one explain the fact that the postcolonial histories of nations like India, Pakistan, Bangladesh, and other Asian and African nations have diverged so radically despite having the same British colonial past? My contention is that the evolution of democracy in particular and of political formations in general in postcolonial nations depended not just on British imperial institutions and acts, but also to a significant degree on the legacy of the specific nature of the anticolonial resistance movements they inherited.

[4] Kohli, 'On Sources of Social and Political Conflicts in Follower Democracies'. For general theoretical works on democracy see Benhabib (ed.), Gutman and Thompson (eds), *Democracy and Disagreement*; M. Rosenfeld (ed.), *Constitutionalism, Identity, Difference and Legitimacy*; Elster and Slagstad (eds), *Constitutionalism and Democracy*.

[5] Sarkar, 'Indian Democracy: the Historical Inheritance', p. 23.

Seen in light of its historical origins, the Indian polity in the wake of independence came to be constituted by two primary historical legacies—the Congress discourse of imperial justice and the Gandhian legacy of non-violent mass movement. It is the dialectic of these two legacies that has determined the nature and dynamics of postcolonial politics in India. In so far as the Congress—in the wake of independence and Gandhi's death—fell back on its original discourse of imperial justice as equity which was anchored in the figure of the monarch, it lacked the conceptual resources or political incentive to give rise to the discourse and practice of democracy in postcolonial India based on principles of popular sovereignty and universal suffrage from within itself.

At the same time, it was because the discourse of imperial justice was historically anchored in the figure of the monarch that the Congress soon developed its own version of it—the dynasty. One of the glaring omissions in the scholarship on the nature and history of postcolonial Indian polity is the absence of any attempt to problematize the intriguing presence of a dynasty at the helm of the Congress and, consequently, the Indian state for much of India's years as an independent democratic country. Indeed, the postcolonial Indian polity has followed the model of 'constitutional monarchy' more closely than Britain, the original home of this polity. As is evident from the research presented in the course of this book, the dynasty is the other side—the institutional side—of the discourse of justice as equity that has anchored much of the democratic polity of postcolonial India, as it did the post-1857 British Empire.

If the Congress still recognized universal suffrage as an unqualified right in the Constitution, then that was because of the force of the Gandhian legacy. The democratic features of the postcolonial Indian polity are anchored in the Gandhian legacy of mass mobilization that turned the people of India from passive recipients of imperial justice to active and sovereign subjects of history. Despite the fact that the Gandhian movement—grounded as it was discursively in the Indic traditions of renunciative freedom—failed to construct a legislative discourse of governance, it did manage to extract the crucial concession of universal suffrage or the political necessity of elections from the Congress, a concession that has come to be the mainstay of Indian democracy.

Some scholars have argued that democracy in postcolonial India has come to be limited to elections, implying that it does not extend to governance.[6] The reason lies in the fact that the political necessity of elections and the discourse of governance have had their origins in two different, even incompatible, legacies that I have traced in my study. If democracy does not, or appears not to, extend to governance then that is because governance continues to be anchored in the imperial legacy of the discourse of justice as equity addressed to the figure of the monarch. The political necessity of elections, on the other hand, owes its origin to the Gandhian legacy of mass resistance. In so far as the Gandhian movement did not have a legislative discourse of governance, it could take democracy only as far as the elections. In the absence of the sovereign discourse of legislative freedom, the postcolonial Indian polity as a whole draws much of its dynamism and indeed its future possibilities from this necessity of elections; it is this democratic necessity of elections that has increasingly brought vast sections of the Indian civil society disenfranchised for long onto the centerstage of Indian politics.

It was the inherent and essential conflict between the Indian National Congress as the bearer of the imperial legacy of justice as the discourse of governance and the Gandhian democratic legacy of disciplined mass resistance that was the main driving force behind the major developments in the first three decades of postcolonial Indian politics. In the decades after independence, even as the Congress fell back on its imperial discourse of governance under the increasingly dynastic leadership of the Nehru–Gandhi family, it also grew increasingly intolerant of the Gandhian democratic legacy. What kept the essential fissure between the two legacies within the Congress from erupting in the open in the immediate aftermath of independence was the momentum built up over three decades of sustained mass movement by the Congress under Gandhi in the colonial period. However, as the Congress, driven by the very logic of its origins, began to increasingly resemble a royal court under its dynastic leadership, a slow but inevitable alienation set in amongst the section of the leadership within the Party which identified with the Gandhian legacy. This alienation led to a split in the Party, and eventually to an open conflict between the two legacies.

The essential difference between the two legacies came out into the open and turned into an active confrontation, most vividly, in the period immediately preceding and following the declaration of

---

[6] Khilnani, *The Idea of India*, p. 48.

emergency in 1975 by Indira Gandhi, the daughter and successor of Jawaharlal Nehru, the first prime minister and leader of the Congress. This was a dramatic moment in the history of postcolonial India in which the imperial side of the discourse of justice as equity came in public confrontation with the Gandhian legacy of mass movements. What is most striking about the imposition of dictatorial rule during the emergency that suspended the fundamental rights of the citizens while giving the Prime Minister absolute power as the head of the state, was that it was done precisely in the name of justice as equity. The fundamental rights or freedom of the people had to be suspended, Indira Gandhi declared, in order to give the government the power it needed to alleviate the hardships of the poorer sections and the middle classes by the 'better distribution of goods.'[7] Thus the declaration of emergency by Indira Gandhi starkly exposed the imperial lineage of the discourse of justice as equity.

It was not surprising, then, that in the ensuing resistance movement against the imposition of emergency, almost all the well-known Gandhians, including Jayaprakash Narayan and Morarji Desai, found themselves arrayed against the embodiment of the imperial legacy, Prime Minister Indira Gandhi. In the response that the emergency provoked, the future of constitutional democracy in India was permanently affected. For the first time in thirty years of India's independence, the Indian National Congress had to concede power to a new party, the Janata Party in 1977. Moreover, it was through this popular resistance against the Emergency that whole new sections of the Indian population that had hitherto remained politically disengaged were brought into the mainstream of Indian politics, fundamentally changing the very nature of the Indian polity, particularly in the states. Once again the legacy of Gandhian resistance had come to the rescue of a beleaguered democracy.

What happened in the aftermath of the electoral defeat of the Congress, however, also exposed once again the limits of the Gandhian legacy that had come to the fore in the wake of national independence. Even as the new Janata government succeeded in dealing a serious blow to the imperial side of the discourse of justice

---

[7] *Prime Minister's Broadcast to the Nation on Proclamation of Emergency*, New Delhi: Government of India Division of Audio-Visual Publicity, 1975.

by mobilizing the masses, it not only left the discourse of governance grounded in the idea of justice as equity itself untouched, indeed it even claimed that discourse as its own. It was not surprising, then, that this new experiment was only a fleeting success, soon falling apart. The Janata Government was an impossible experiment in governance to begin with: it was an attempt to maintain the discourse of justice as equity without the central figure of a monarch to whom it necessarily had to be addressed. In the absence of a monarch-like figure, the government formed by the Janata Party ended up becoming a coalition of disparate and fractious groups that could not survive the contrary pulls for more than a couple of years, leaving the door open for the Congress to make a triumphant return. In this failure, however, what stands starkly revealed is how essential the figure of the monarch or the dynast is to the discourse of justice as equity.

Even as the powerful Gandhian legacy—that continues to operate in and through popular electoral practices and the general ability for mass mobilization—militates against the imperial legacy visible in the figure of the dynast, the continued reliance of the Indian polity on the discourse of justice as equity needs the same figure of the dynast as its anchor. In the absence of this dynastic anchor, a national government in India—if at all possible—has proved to be, and is likely to continue to be, unstable, because parties formed in the provinces in the name of justice as equity by their very nature claim to represent a part—a province, community, caste, language, or ethnicity—and must depend on the dynast to turn the fragments into a whole to give themselves national unity. On the other hand, the Indian National Congress with the dynast at its center—by its very nature—must continue to reproduce and also enforce the old colonial image of Indian civil society as a collection of warring fragments that the monarch alone can unify.

Through much of its years as an independent country, the Indian polity has been caught in this cycle of opposing political legacies. The postcolonial Indian polity, therefore, is very different from western democracies where an identity of the state and the civil society, albeit complex and uneven, is often assumed—a fact reflected in the idea of the 'nation-state.' Given that in the postcolonial Indian polity—as in the colonial polity before it—the state and the civil society continue to find themselves to be exterior to each other, it is not surprising that they often appear to prey upon each other without limit. It is sobering, though not surprising, given the colonial legacy, to recall that much of the widespread and gruesome violence in postcolonial Africa took place, and continues to take place today, in the pursuit of justice.[8]

---

[8] See Mamdani, *When Victims Become Killers: Colonialism, Nativism, and the Genocide in Rwanda.*

BIBLIOGRAPHY

PRIMARY SOURCES
Unpublished Works

Government of India Proceedings, National Archives of India, Delhi.
Home Department (Public Branch) Proceedings, 1800–1947.
Home Department (Miscellaneous Branch) Proceedings, 1800–1947.
Home Department (Judicial Branch) Proceedings, 1800–1947.
Home Department (Political Branch) Proceedings, 1800–1947.
Indian National Congress. *Report of the (First to Fifty-Sixth) Indian National Congress*, 1886–1950.
All India Congress Committee Papers, Nehru Memorial Library, New Delhi, India.
Manuscript and Private Papers at the India Office Library, London.
Indian Legislative Consultations.
Home Miscellaneous Collections.
Public and Judicial Department Records.
Political and Secret Correspondence.
Private Collections of Viceroys of India in European Manuscript Collection.

Published Works

Great Britain. Parliament. *Parliamentary Papers* (1772–1947)
Great Britain. Parliament. *Hansard's Parliamentary Debates*. 1st Series (1803–20).
Great Britain. Parliament. *Hansard's Parliamentary Debates*. 2nd Series (1820–30).
Great Britain. Parliament. *Hansard's Parliamentary Debates*. 3rd Series (1830–91).
Great Britain. Parliament. *Parliamentary Debates*. 4th Series (1892–1908).
Great Britain. Parliament. *Parliamentary Debates*. Commons. 5th Series (1909–80).

Great Britain. Parliament. *The Parliamentary History of England from the earliest period to the year 1803, from which last-mentioned epoch it is continued downwards in the work entitled 'Hansard's parliamentary debates'.* London: T.C. Hansard, 1806–20.

Great Britain. Parliament. House of Commons. *Reports on the Administration of Justice in India* (1775).

Great Britain. Parliament. House of Commons. *Second Report from the Select Committee on the Administration of Justice in the East Indies* (1781–2).

Bengal, Supreme Court of Judicature. *Reports of Cases Argued and Determined in the Supreme Court of Judicature at Fort William in Bengal with a table of cases and index of principal matters.* Calcutta: P.S. D'Rozario, 1845.

Great Britain. Parliament. House of Commons. *Journals of the House of Commons*, 41, (1786).

East India Company. *Fort William—India House Correspondence and Other Contemporary Papers Relating Thereto.* Delhi: Published for the National Archives of India by the Manager of Publications, Government of India, 1957–85.

Bengal (India). Legislative Council. *The Bengal Legislative Council Proceedings.* Calcutta, 1862–1944.

India. Imperial Legislative Council. *Proceedings of the Legislative Council of India.* Calcutta: F. Carbery, Military Orphan Press, 1856–61.

India. Imperial Legislative Council. *Proceedings of the Legislative Council of India.* Calcutta: Military Orphan Press, 1862–1920.

India. Legislative Assembly. *The Legislative Assembly Debates.* Simla, 1921–47.

India. Constituent Assembly. *Constituent Assembly of India Debates: Official Report*, 12 vols (1946–9). Delhi: Manager of Publications, Government of India Press, 1966.

Other Published Works

Acharyya, B.K. *Codification in British India.* Calcutta: S.K. Banerji, 1914.

Allen, C.K. *Law in the Making.* London, Oxford, New York: Oxford University Press, 1964.

Andrews, C.F. *Indian Independence: The Immediate Need.* Madras: Ganesh and Co. Publishers, 1921.

——. *How India Can Be Free.* Madras: Ganesh and Co. Publishers, 1921.

——. *The Claim for Independence Within or Without the British Empire.* Madras: Ganesh and Co., 1921.

Andrews, C.F. and Girija Mukerji, *The Rise and Growth of the Congress in India.* London: G. Allen & Unwin Ltd, 1938.

Appadorai, A. *Documents on Political Thought in Modern India.* Bombay, New York: Oxford University Press, 1973.

Aristotle. *Nicomachean Ethics*. Terence Irwin(trans). Indianapolis: Hackett Publishing Company, 1985.

————. *The Politics and the Constitution of Athens*. Stephen Everson (ed.). Cambridge: Cambridge University Press, 1996.

Auber, Peter. *An Analysis of the Constitution of the East-India Company, and of the Laws passed by Parliament for the Government of their Affairs, at Home and Abroad: To which is prefixed, a Brief History of the Company, and of the Rise and Progress of the British power in India*. London: Kingsbury, Parburg, and Allen, J.M. Richardson and Harding and Co., 1826.

————. *The Law Relating to India and the East-India Company*. 2nd edn. London, W.H. Allen, 1841.

Austin, John. *Lectures on Jurisprudence or the Philosophy of Positive Law*. Robert Campbell (ed.). London: J. Murray, 1885.

Bagehot, Walter. *The English Constitution and Other Political Essays*. New York and London: D. Appleton and Company, 1911.

Baines, J.A. *General Report on the Census of India, 1891*. London: Printed for the Indian Government, 1893.

Bandyopadhyay, B. *Samvadpatre Sekaler Katha*. 2 vols. Calcutta: Bangiya Sahitya Parishad.

Banerjea, Surendranath. *A Nation in Making; Being the Reminiscences of Fifty Years of Public Life*. London, New York, Oxford University Press, 1925.

Basu, Durga Das. *Shorter Constitution of India*. New Delhi: Prentice-Hall of India Private Ltd, 1988.

Blackstone, William. *Commentaries on the Laws of England*. 4 vols. Facsimile of the First Edition of 1765–9. Chicago: University of Chicago Press, 1979.

Bodin, J. *The Six Bookes of a Commonweale*. Cambridge: Cambridge University Press, 1962.

Bolts, William. *Considerations on India affairs; particularly respecting the present state of Bengal and its dependencies. With a map of those countries, chiefly from actual surveys*. London: printed for J. Almon, P. Elmsley, and Richardson and Urquhart, 1772–5.

Bond, E.A. (ed.) *Speeches of the Managers and Counsel in the Trial of Warren Hastings*. London: Longman, 1859.

Bose, Amrita Lal. *How to Be a Great Orator*. Calcutta: Bengal Medical Library, 1910.

British Indian Association. *Petitions and Letters of the British Indian Association to the Legislative Council and Other Public Authorities of India*. Calcutta: Stanhope Press, 1853.

Brumpton, Paul R., (ed.). *A Selection from the India Office Correspondence of Robert Cecil, Third Marquis of Salisbury, 1866–1867 and 1874–1878*. Lewiston, Queenston, Lampeter: Edwin Mellen Press, 2002.

Buckland, C.E. *Dictionary of Indian Biography*. London, Sonnenschein, 1906.

Buckland, Charles Thomas. *Constructions of the Sadar Diwani Adalat of the Lower and North Western Provinces, 1793–1856*. Calcutta: Thacker, Spink and Co., 1856.

Burke, Edmund. *The Works of the Right Honorable Edmund Burke*. 6 vols. London: George Bell and Sons, 1877.

———. *The Correspondence of Edmund Burke*. R.B. McDowell (ed.). Cambridge: Cambridge University Press, 1969.

———*Reflections on the Revolution in France*. T.H.D. Mahoney (ed.). Indianapolis: The Bobbs–Merrill Company, Inc., 1976.

———. *Speeches on the Impeachment Trial of Warren Hastings*. 2 vols. Delhi: Discovery Publishing House, 1987.

———. *The Writings and Speeches of Edmund Burke*. 7 vols. Paul Langford (ed.). Oxford: Clarendon Press; New York: Oxford University Press, 1981–2000.

Busteed, H.E. *Echoes of Old Calcutta: Being Chiefly the Reminiscences of the Days of Warren Hastings, Francis and Impey*. London: W. Thacker and Co., 1908.

Campbell, George. *India as it May be; An Outline of a Proposed Government and Policy*. London: J. Murray, 1853.

———. *Modern India: A Sketch of the System of Civil Government. To which is prefixed some account of the natives and native institutions*. London: J. Murray, 1852.

Campbell-Johnson, Alan. *Mission with Mountbatten*. London: Robert Hale Limited, 1951.

Carnall, Geoffrey, and Colin Nicholsan, (eds). *The Impeachment of Warren Hastings: Papers from a Bicentenary Commemoration*. Edinburgh: Edinburgh University Press, 1989.

Carrau, J. *Reports of Summary Cases determined in the Presidency Sudder Court. Comprising reports from 1834 to 1852 with an index*. Calcutta: Bengal Military Orphan Press, 1853.

———. *Rules of Practice of the Presidency Sudder Court 1793–1855*. Calcutta: Military Orphan Press, 1856.

Chakravarty, Bholanath. *Sei ek din ar ei ek din, arthat banger purbba or barttaman abastha*. Calcutta: Adi Brahmo Samaj, 1876.

Chunder, Bholanauth. *Raja Digambar Mitra, C. S. I., His Life and Career*. Calcutta: Hare Press, 1893.

Chirol, Valentine. *Indian Unrest*. London: Macmillan and Co., 1910.

Clark, C. *Rules and Orders of the Supreme Court of Judicature at Fort William*. Calcutta: Thomas Jones, 1824.

Coupland, Reginald. *The Constitutional Problem in India*. London: H. Milford, 1944.

Cowell, H. *The History and Constitution of Courts and Legislative Authorities in India*. Calcutta: Thacker Spink and Co. Ltd, 1872.

———. *A Short Treatise on Hindu Law as administered in the Courts of British India*. Calcutta: Thacker, Spink and Co. Ltd, 1895.

Cunningham, H.S. *Rulers of India: Earl Canning*. Oxford: Clarendon Press, 1891.

Curtis, Lionel. *The Problem of the Commonwealth*. London: Macmillan and Co. Ltd, 1916.

———. *Papers Relating to the Application of the Principle of Dyarchy to the Government of India to Which are Appended the Report of the Joint Select Committee and the Government of India Act, 1919*. Oxford: Clarendon Press, 1920.

Curzon, George Nathaniel. *British Government in India*. London, New York: Cassell and Company, 1925.

Desika Char, S. V., (ed.), *Readings in the Constitutional History of India, 1757–1947*. Delhi: Oxford University Press, 1983.

Dickinson, John. *India: its Government under a Bureaucracy*. London: Saunders and Stanford, 1853.

Duncan, J. *Regulations for the Administration of Justice in Courts of Dewannee Adaulat passed in Council, the 5th July, 1783*. Calcutta: At the Honourable Company's Press, 1785.

Dutt, Kalimohun. *Ukil Gyananjan: A Handbook for the Guidance of Native Pleaders*. Calcutta, 1844.

Elphinstone, Monstuart. *The Rise of the British Power in the East*. London: J. Murray, 1887.

Galloway, Archibald. *Observations on the Law and Constitution and Present Government of India, on the Nature of Landed Tenures and Financial Resources, as Recognized by the Moohummudan Law and Moghul Government, with an Inquiry into the Administration of Justice, Revenue, and Police, at Present Existing in Bengal*. London: Parbury, Alen, and Co., 1832.

Gandhi, Indira. *Prime Minister's Broadcast to the Nation on Proclamation of Emergency*. New Delhi: Government of India Division of Audio-Visual Publicity, 1975.

Gandhi, Mohanda Karamchand. 'Practicing Lawyers', in *Young India* of 30th March 1921. *Young India 1919–22*. New York: B.W. Huebsch, 1923.

———. *An Autobiography: Or the Story of My Experiments With Truth*. Ahmedabad: Navajivan Publishing House, 1959.

———. *The Law and the Lawyers*. S.B. Kher (ed.). Ahmedabad: Navajivan Publishing House, 1959.

———. *The Moral and Political Writings of Mahatma Gandhi*, 3 vols. R. Iyer (ed.). Oxford: Clarendon Press, 1986.

——. *The Collected Works of Mahatma Gandhi*. New Delhi: Publications Division, Ministry of Information and Broadcasting, Government of India, 1958–94.

——. *The Mahatma and the Poet: Letters and Debates Between Gandhi and Tagore, 1915–1941*. S. Bhattacharya (ed.). New Delhi: National Book Trust, 1997.

Gauba, K.L. *Famous and Historic Trials*. Lahore: Lion Press, 1946.

Gilchrist, R.N. *Separation of Executive and Judicial Functions: A Study in the Evolution of the Indian Magistracy*. Calcutta: University of Calcutta Press, 1923.

Ghose, Aurobindo. *New Lamps for Old*. Pondicherry: Sri Aurobindo Ashram, 1974.

——. 'Bande Mataram', 21/22 August 1906 in *Sri Aurobindo: Supplement*. Pondicherry: Sri Aurobindo Ashram, 1973.

——. *Sri Aurobindo: Writings in Bengali including editorials from Dharma*. Pondicherry: Sri Aurobindo Ashram, 1970.

Ghosal, J. *Celebrated Trials in India*, 2 vols. Calcutta: Manomohan Press, 1902.

Ghosh, Nagendra Nath. *England's Work in India*. Calcutta: University of Calcutta Press, 1919.

——. *Comparative Administrative Law with Special Reference to the Organization and Legal Position of the Administrative Authorities in British India*. London: Butterworth and Co., 1919.

Ghosh, Rashbehari. *Speeches and Writings Delivered on Various Occasions*. Calcutta: R. Cambray, 1915.

Glieg, G.R. *Memoirs of the Life of the Right Hon. Warren Hastings, first governor-general of India*, 3 vols. London: R. Bentley, 1841.

Grotius, Hugo. *On the Law of War and Peace, Three Books*. Oxford: Clarendon Press, 1925.

Gupta, Bipin Bihari. *Puratan Prasanga*. Calcutta, Bidyabharati, 1966.

Gupta, Partha Sarathi (ed.). *Towards Freedom: Documents on the Movement for Independence in India, 1943–1944*. 3 vols. Delhi : Oxford University Press, 1997.

Hancock, W.K. *Survey of British Commonwealth Affairs*. 2 vols. London: New York: Oxford University Press, 1937–42.

Harington, John Herbert. *Elementary Analysis of the Laws and Regulations Enacted by the Governor General in Council at Fort William in Bengal for the Civil Government of the British Territories Under that Presidency in Six Parts*. Calcutta: Printed at the Honorable Company Press, 1805 and 1809.

Hastings, Warren, *The Defence of Warren Hastings, Esq. (Late Governor General of Bengal) at the Bar of the House of Commons, upon the Matter of the several Charges of High Crimes and Misdemeanors, presented against him in the Year 1786*. London: Printed for John Stockdale, Opposite Burlington House, Piccadilly, 1786.

Hastings, William. *Memoirs relative to the state of India*. London: J. Murray, 1786.

——. *Warren Hastings' Letters to Sir John Macpherson*. H. Dodwell. London: Faber and Gwyer, 1927.

Hegel, G.W.F. *Elements of the Philosophy of Right*. Cambridge: Cambridge University Press, 1991.

Hickey, William. *Memoirs of William Hickey*. London: Hurst and Blackett, Ltd., 1960.

Higgins, W. *Sketches of India treating on subjects connected with the Government*. London: Longman, Hurst, Rees, Orme, Brown and Green, 1824.

Hobbes, Thomas. *Leviathan*. C.B. Macpherson (ed.), Harmondsworth: Penguin Books, 1981.

——. *The Elements of Law, Natural and Politic*. Ferdinand Tonnies (ed.). Cambridge: Cambridge University Press, 1928.

Hoyland, John S. (ed.), *Gopal Krishna Gokhale, his Life and Speeches*, Calcutta: Y.M.C.A. Publishing House, 1947.

Hunter, W.W. *The Imperial Gazetteer of India*. 9 vols. London : Trübner & Co., 1881.

——. *The India of the Queen and Other Essays*. London, New York, Bombay: Longmans, Green and Co., 1903.

Ilbert, C. *Legislative Methods and Forms*. Oxford: Clarendon Press, 1901.

Kant, Immanuel. 'Perpetual Peace, A Philosophical Sketch', in *Political Writings*. Hans Reiss (ed.). Cambridge: Cambridge University Press, 1991.

Kaye, J.W. *The Administration of the East India Company: A History of Indian Progress*. London: R. Bentley, 1853.

Keith, A.B. *A Constitutional History of India 1600–1935*. (Rpt), New York: Barnes and Noble, 1969.

Ker, J.C. *Political Trouble in India 1907–1917*. Calcutta: Superintendent, Government Printing, 1917.

Khan, Panchkouree. *The Revelations of an Orderly. Being an Attempt to Expose the Abuses of Administration by the relation of Every-day Occurences in the Mofussil Courts*. Benares: E.J. Lazarus & Co., 1866.

Liebniz, Gottfried Wilhelm. *Political Writings*. Patrick Riley (ed.). Cambridge: Cambridge University Press, 1972.

Locke, John. *Two Treatises of Government*. Edited with an introduction by Peter Laslett. Cambridge: Cambridge Univeristy Press, 1960.

——. *An Essay Concerning Human Understanding*. Abridged and edited by A.D. Woozley. New York: New American Library, Meridien Books, 1964.

Lovett, Verney. *A History of the Indian Nationalist Movement*. London: John Murray, 1921.

Ludlow, J.M. *Thoughts on the Policy of the Crown towards India*. London: James Ridgway, 1859.

Lyall, John Edwards. *An Introductory Discourse on the Nature and Study of the Laws of India*. Calcutta: P.S. D'Rozario and Co., 1843.

Macaulay, Thomas Babington. *Warren Hastings*. New York: Chautauqua Press, 1886.

———. *Lord Macaulay's Legislative Minutes*. Selected with a historical introduction by C.D. Dharkar. London: Oxford University Press, 1946.

———. *Selected Writings*. Edited by John Clive and Thomas Pinney. Chicago: University of Chicago Press, 1968.

Madison, James, Alexander Hamilton and John Jay. *The Federalist Papers*. Isaac Kramnick (ed.). London, New York: Penguin Books, 1987.

Maine, Henry. *Lectures on the Early History of Institutions*. New York: H. Holt and Co., 1878.

———. *Popular Government*. New York: H. Holt and Company, 1886.

———. *Ancient Law*. London, Toronto: J.M. Dent and Sons, Ltd.; New York: E.P. Dutton and Co., 1917.

Maitland, Frederic William. *The Constitutional History of England: A Course of Lectures*. Cambridge: Cambridge University Press, 1963.

Majumdar, J.K. (ed.). *Indian Speeches and Documents in British Rule, 1821–1918*. Calcutta, London, New York: Longmans, Green and Co. Ltd., 1937.

Malaviya, M.M. *Speeches of Pandit Madan Mohan Malaviya*. Madras: Madras Press, 1910.

Malcolm, John. *The Government of India*. London: J. Murray, 1833.

Mansergh, Nicholas and E.W.R. Lumby (eds). *The Transfer of Power 1942–47*. 12 vols. London: His Majesty's Stationery Office, 1970–83.

Marx, K. and F. Engels. *Collected Works*. London: Lawrence and Wishart, 1975.

Menon, V.P. *The Transfer of Power in India*. Princeton. New Jersey: Princeton University Press, 1957.

Mill, James. *The History of British India, with notes and continuation by Horace Hayman William*. 9 vols. London: J. Madden, 1840–6.

———. *Writings on India by J.S. Mill*. John M. Robson, Martin Moir and Zawahir Moir (ed.). Toronto: University of Toronto Press, 1990.

Millar, John. *An Historical View of the English Government, from the Settlement of the Saxons in Britain to the Revolution in 1688: to which are Subjoined some Dissertations Connected with the History of the Government from the Revolution to the Present Time*. 4 vols. London: J. Mawman, 1803.

Mitra, Peary Chand. *Alaler Gharer Dulal, Tekchand Thakura pranita*. Kalikata: Bangiya-Sahitya-Parisat, 1940.

Montesquieu, Charles de Secondat. *The Spirit of the Laws*. Anne M. Cohler, Basia Carolyn Miller and Harold Samuel Stone (ed.). Cambridge: Cambridge University Press, 1989.

Montriou, W.A. *Decisions of Supreme Court of Judicature on the Plea, Equity, Ecclesiastical, Administrative and Crown Sides from the Date of the Charter 1774–1841, with notes by T.C. Morton*. Calcutta: D'Rozario and Co., 1851.

———. *Institutes of Jurisprudence (a resume of oral lectures delivered to the law classes of Presidency College)*. Calcutta: P.S. D'Rozario and Co., 1866.

Moor, E. *Oriental Fragments*. London: Smith and Elder and Co, 1834.

Moore, Edmund J. *Reports of cases heard and determined by the Judicial Committee and the Lords of His Majesty's most Honourable Privy Council on appeal form the Supreme and Sudder Dewannee courts in the Eat Indies*. London: J.H. Clark, 1838–73.

Morley, W.H. *The Administration of Justice in British India: It's Past History and Present* State. London: Williams and Norgate, 1858.

Mukharji, Bisvesvar. *Indian Lawyers*. 2 vols. Calcutta: S.C. Auddy and Co., 1904.

Naoroji, Dadabahi. *Speeches and Writings*. Madras: Natesan, 1917.

———. *Poverty and Un-British Rule in India*. London: Swan Sonnenschein & Co. Ltd, 1901.

———. 'Extract from the Presidential Address of Dadabhai Naoroji at the twenty-second session of the Indian National Congress, Calcutta, December, 1906'. in *Indian Speeches and Documents on British Rule, 1821–1918*, J.K. Majumdar (ed.), pp. 168–70. Delhi: Kanti Publications, 1987.

Nehru, Jawaharlal. *The Unity of India, Collected Writings 1937–1940*. London: Lindsay Drummond, 1941.

———. *The Discovery of India*. Delhi, New York: Oxford University Press, 1989.

———. *The Essential Writings of Jawaharlal Nehru*, 2 vols. S. Gopal and Uma Iyengar (eds). New Delhi: Oxford University Press, 2003.

Nehru, Motilal. *The Nehru Report: An Anti-Separatist Manifesto*. New Delhi: Michiko and Panjathan, 1928.

Norton, J.B. *The Administration of Justice in Southern India*. Madras: Messrs. Pharoah and Co., Athanaeum Press, 1853.

———. *The Rebellion in India: How to Prevent Another*. London: Richardson Brothers, 1857.

———. *Topics for Indian Statesmen*. London: Richardson Brothers, 1858.

———. *Topics of Jurisprudence or Aids to the Office of the Indian Judge*. Madras: Higgenbotham and Co., 1870.

O'Malley, L.S.S. *Report on the Census of India, Bengal, Bihar and Orissa and Sikkim*. Part 1. Calcutta: Bengal Secretariat, 1913.

——. *History of Bengal, Bihar and Orissa under British Rule*. Calcutta: Bengal Secretariat Book Depot, 1925.

——. *Modern India and the West: a study of the interaction of their civilizations*. London, New York: Oxford University Press, 1941.

——. *Indian Civil Services, 1601–1930*. London: F. Cass, 1965.

Pal, Bipin Chandra. 'Swadeshi and Swaraj', in *The Rise of New Patriotism*. Calcutta: Yugayatri Prakashak Limited, 1954.

Parkes, Joseph. *A History of the Court of Chancery; with Practical Remarks on the Recent Commission, Report, and Evidence, and On the Means of Improving the Administration of Justice in the English Courts of Equity*. London: Longan, Rees, Orme, Brown, and Green, 1828.

Phillips, H.A.D. *Indian Legislation and Legislative Councils*. Calcutta: City Press, 1890.

Pike, Luke Owen. *A Constitutional History of the House of Lords from Original Sources*. London and New York: Macmillan and Co., 1894.

Pufendorf, S. *The Law of Nature and Nations, Eight Books*. Oxford: Clarendon Press, 1934.

Rai, Lala Lajpat. *Young India: An Interpretation and a History of the Nationalist Movement from Within*. New York: Howard Fertig, 1916.

——. *The Political Future of India*. New York: B.W. Huebsch, 1917.

——. *Autobiographical Writings*. Edited by Vijaya Chandra Joshi. Delhi: University Publishers, 1965.

Rankin, George Claus. *Background to Indian Law*. Cambridge: Cambridge University Press, 1946.

Rao, B. Shiva. *The Framing of India's Constitution: Select Documents*. Delhi: Indian Institute of Public Administration, 1965–6.

Rau, B.N. *Constitutional Precedents*. Delhi: Manager of Publications, Government of India Press, 1946, Third Series.

——. *India's Constitution in the Making*. Calcutta: Orient Longman, 1960.

Report of the Joint Committee on Indian Constitutional Reform, 1934, H.C. 5.

Risley, H.H. *The People of India*. London: Thacker, 1908. [Based on *Report on the Census of India, 1901*, authored by H.H. Risley and E.A. Gait. Calcutta: Office of the Superintendent of Government Printing.]

Rousseau, Jean-Jacques. *The Social Contract*. New York: St Martin's Press, 1978.

——. 'On the Social Contract', in *The Basic Political Writings*. Donald A. Cress (ed.). Indianapolis: Hackett Publishing Company, 1987.

Roy, Rammohan. *Selected Works of Raja Rammohan Roy*. New Delhi: Publications Division, Ministry of Information and Broadcasting, Government of Inda, 1977.

Sanyal, R.G. *Reminiscences and Anecdotes of Great Men of India, both Official and Non-Official for the Last Hundred Years*. Calcutta, 1895.

Sapru, Tej Bahadur and others. *Constitutional Proposals of the Sapru Committee*, 2nd edition. Delhi: Padma Publications Ltd, 1946.

Sarkar, S.C. *Notable Indian Trials*. Calcutta: M.C. Sarkar & Sons, 1948.

Sastri, Sibnath. *Ramtanu Lahiri o Tatkalin Bangasamaj*. Calcutta: New Age, 1957.

Sen, J.M. *The Secrets of Success at the Bar*. Serampore: J.M. Sen at Law Press, 1884.

Senal, Dakshinachara. *Mamla Mokaddama: A Pamphlet Condoning the Present Judicial System and Suggesting Some Reforms*. Calcutta, 1870.

Shaw, George Bernard. 'Preface for Politicians', in *John Bull's Other Island and Major Barbara: Also How He Lied to Her Husband*. London: Archibald Constable and Co., 1907.

Sitaramayya, P. *The History of the Indian National Congress, 1885–1935*. Allahabad: The Working Committee of the Congress, 1935.

Smith, Adam. *Lectures on Jurisprudence*. Glasgow: Liberty Fund, 1766; rpt 1982.

Smoult, W.H. and E.B. Ryan, *Rules and orders of the Supreme Court of Judicature at Fort William in Bengal*. 2 vols. Calcutta; Samuel Smith and Co., 1839.

Srinivasa Rao, P. *Legal Maxims illustrated with special reference to laws in force in British India*. Madras: Higginbotham and Co., 1873.

Stephen, James Fitzjames. *Liberty, Equality, Fraternity*. London, Smith, Elder, & Co., 1873.

———. 'Foundations of the Government of India', *Nineteenth Century*, no. LXXX (October 1883), p. 564.

———. *The Story of Nuncomar and the Impeachment of Elijah Impey*, 2 vols. London: Macmillan, 1885.

Stephen, Leslie. *English Thought in the Eighteenth Century*, 2 vols. London: Smith, Elder and Co., 1881.

Stokes, W. *The Anglo Indian Codes*. Oxford: Clarendon Press, 1887–8.

Story, Joseph. *Commentaries on Equity Jurisprudence as Administered in England and America*. Boston: Little Brown and Co., 1886.

Strachey, John. *India, its administration and progress*. London: Macmillan, 1911.

———. *India*. London: Thacker, 1888.

———. *Hastings and the Rohilla War*. Oxford: Clarendon Press, 1892.

Strangman, Thomas. *Indian Courts and Characters*. London: W. Heinemann, 1931.

Subbannacharyar, T. *A Manual of Vakeels' Duties*. Madras, Caleb Foster, 1868.

Temple, Richard. *India in 1880*. London: J. Murray. 1881.

———. *Men and Events of My Time in India*. London: J. Murray, 1882.

Tendulkar, D.G. *Mahatma, Life of Mohandas Karamchand Gandhi*. Bombay: Jhaveri and Tendulkar, 1953.

Thornton, Edward. *India, State and Prospects*. London: Parbury, Allen and Co., 1835.

Tilak, B.G. 'Speech in the Congress Session of 1904', in *Samagra Lokmanya Tilak*. Poona: Kesari Prakashan, 1975.

Vattel, Emmerich de. *The Law of Nations, or, Principles of Law of Nature, Applied to the Conduct and Affairs of Nations and Sovereigns*. Joseph Chitty (ed.). Philadelphia: T. and J.W. Johnson and Co., 1852.

Vitoria, Francisco de. *De Indis et de Iure Belli Relectiones* (1696). Classics of International Law, no. 7. Washington: Carnegie Institution, 1917.

Vivekananda, *The Complete Works of Swami Vivekananda*. Calcutta: Advaita Ashrama, 1955.

Wedderburn, W. *Allan Octavian Hume 'Father of the Indian Nation', 1829–1912*. London: Unwin, 1913.

Woodhouselee, A.F.T. *Considerations on the Present Political State of India*. London: Black, Parry and Co., 1815.

Zaidi, A.M. (ed.), *Speeches and Writings of Dr. Sir Rashbehari Ghose: an exhaustive and comprehensive collection*, Madras: G.A. Natesan, 1929.

SECONDARY SOURCES

Abel-Smith, Brian and Robert Stevens with the assistance of Rosalind Brooke. *Lawyers and the Courts; A Sociological Study of the English Legal System, 1750–1965*. Cambridge, Mass.: Harvard University Press, 1967.

Ackerman, Bruce. *Social Justice and the Liberal State*. New Haven: Yale University Press, 1980.

Adler, Mortimer J. *The Idea of Freedom*. 2 vols. New York: Doubleday and Company, 1961.

Agamben, Georgio. *Homo Sacer: Sovereign Power and Bare Life*. Daniel Heller-Razen (trans). Stanford: Stanford University Press, 1998.

——. *State of Exception*. Kevin Attell (trans). Chicago and London: University of Chicago Press, 2005.

Alam, M. *The Crisis of Empire in Mughal North India: Awadh and the Punjab, 1707–1748*. Delhi, Oxford University Press, 1986.

Albrow, M. *The Global Age*. Cambridge: Polity Press, 1996.

Allen, C.K. *Law in the Making*. London, Oxford, New York: Oxford University Press, 1964.

Amin, Shahid. 'Gandhi as Mahatma', in *Subaltern Studies III: Writings on South Asian History and Society*, R. Guha (ed.). Delhi: Oxford University Press, 1984.

——. 'Approver's Testimony, Judicial Discourse: The case of Chauri Chaura', in *Subaltern Studies VI: Writings of South Asian History and Society*. R. Guha (ed.). Delhi: Oxford University Press, 1987.

——. *Event, Metaphor, Memory: Chauri Chaura, 1922–1992*. Berkeley: University of California Press, 1995.

Anderson, Benedict. *Imagined Communities: Reflections on the Origin and Spread of Nationalism*. London and New York: Verso, 1983.

Appadurai, Arjun. *Modernity at Large: Cultural Dimensions of Globalization*. Minneapolis: University of Minnesota, 1996.

Arendt, Hannah. *On Revolution*. Westport, Connecticut: Greenwood Press, 1982.

Argov, D. *Moderates and Extremists in the Indian National Movement, 1883–1920: With Special Reference to Surendranath Banerjea and Lajpat Rai*. New York: Asia Publishing House, 1967.

Armitage, David. *Ideological Origins of the British Empire*. Cambridge and New York: Cambridge University Press, 2000.

Arneil, Barbara. *John Locke and America: The Defence of English Colonialism*. Oxford: Clarendon Press, 1996.

Austin, Granville. *The Indian Constitution: Cornerstone of a Nation*. Oxford: Clarendon Press, 1966.

Bagal, J.C. *History of the Indian Association, 1876–1951*. Calcutta: Harendra Nath Mazumdar, 1951.

Bailyn, Bernard. *Ideological Origins of the American Revolution*. Cambridge: Belknap Press of Harvard University Press, 1967.

Baker, Christopher John. *The Politics of South India 1920–1937*. Cambridge: Cambridge University Press, 1976.

Baker, J.H. *An Introduction to English Legal History*, 4th edn. New York: Oxford University Press, 2002.

Baker, Keith M. *Inventing the French Revolution: Essays on French Political Culture in the Eighteenth-Century*. Cambridge: Cambridge University Press, 1990.

Ballhatchet, K. *Race, Sex and Class Under the Raj: Imperial Attitudes and Policies And their Critics, 1793–1905*. London: Weidenfield and Nicolson, 1980.

Bandyopadhyay, Sekhar. *Caste, Protest, and Identity in Colonial India: The Namasudras of Bengal, 1872–1947*. Surrey: Curzon, 1997.

Banerjee, A.C. *The Constitutional History of India*. 3 vols. Calcutta: Macmillan Co. of India, 1977–8.

——. *Making of the Indian Constitution*. Calcutta: A. Mukherjee and Co., 1948.

Barker, Ernest. *Political Thought in England 1848–1914*. London: Thornton Butterworth Ltd., 1915.

——. *The Ideas and Ideals of the British Empire*. Cambridge: Cambridge University Press, 1951.

Barnett, Richard B. *North India between Empires: Awadh, the Mughals, and the British, 1720–1801*. Berkeley: University of California Press, 1980.

Basu, Durga Das. *Commentary on the Constitution of India (Being a comparative treatise on the universal principles of Justice and Constitutional Government with special reference to the Organic instrument of India)*, 3rd edn. 2 vols. Calcutta: S.C. Sarkar and Sons, Ltd., 1955.

———. *Introduction to the Constitution of India*, 5th edn, Calcutta: S.C. Sarkar & Sons Ltd, 1971.

———. *On Limited Government and Judicial Review*. Calcutta: S.C. Sarkar & Sons (Private) Ltd, 1972.

Basham, A.L. 'Traditional Influences on the Thought of Mahatma Gandhi', in *Essays on Gandhian Politics: The Rowlatt Satyagraha of 1919*, Ravindra Kumar (ed.). Oxford: Clarendon Press, 1971, pp. 17–42.

Baxi, Upendra. *The Supreme Court and Politics*. Lucknow: Eastern Book Company, 1980.

———. '"The State's Emissary": The Place of Law in Subaltern Studies', in *Subaltern Studies VII: Writings on South Asian Society and History*, Partha Chatterjee and Gyanendra Pandey (eds). Delhi: Oxford University Press, 1992.

———. *Jaal Rajar Kotha: Bordhomaner Pratapchand*. Kolkata: Ananda Publishers, 2002.

Bayly, C.A. *Preventive Detention in India*. Calcutta: Firma Mukhopadhaya, 1962.

———. *Local Roots of Indian Politics: Allahabad 1880–1920*. Oxford: Clarendon Press, 1975.

———. *Rulers, Townsmen and Bazaars: Northern Indian Society in the Age of British Expansion, 1770–1870*. Cambridge: Cambridge University Press, 1983.

———. *Imperial Meridian: The British Empire and the World, 1780–1830*, Studies in Modern History. Singapore: Longman, 1989.

———. *Origins of Nationality in South Asia: Patriotism and Ethical Government in the Making of Modern India*. Delhi: Oxford University Press, 1998.

———. *Empire and Information: Intelligence Gathering and Social Communication in India, 1780–1870*. Cambridge and New York: Cambridge University Press, 1996.

———. 'The Second British Empire', in *The Oxford History of the British Empire, Vol. 5, Historiography*. R.W. Winks (ed.). Oxford: Oxford University Press, 1999.

———. 'Rammohan Roy and the Advent of Constitutional Liberalism in India, 1800–1830', *Modern Intellectual History*, 4 (1), 2007, pp. 25–41.

Bayly, Susan. *The New Cambridge History of India IV. 3. Caste, Society, and Politics in India from the Eighteenth Century to the Modern Age*. Cambridge: Cambridge University Press, 1999.

Benhabib, S. (ed.), *Democracy and Difference: Contesting the Boundaries of the Political*. Princeton, New Jersey: Princeton University Press, 1996.

Benton, Lauren. 'Colonial Law and Cultural Difference: Jurisdictional Politics and the Formation of the Colonial State', *Comparative Studies in Society and History* 41 (3), July 1999, pp. 563–88.

——. *Law and Colonial Cultures: Legal Regimes in World History, 1400–1900*. New York: Cambridge University Press, 2002.

Berlin, Isaiah. *Four Essays on Liberty*. Oxford: Oxford University Press, 1969.

Bhabha, Homi. *Nation and Narration*. London: Routledge, 1990.

Bhadra, Gautam. 'Four Rebels of Eighteen-Fifty-Seven', in *Selected Subaltern Studies*, Ranajit Guha and Gayatri Chakravorty Spivak (eds). New York: Oxford University Press, 1988.

——. *Jaal Rajar Kotha: Bordhomaner Pratapchand*. Kolkata: Ananda Publishers, 2002.

Bhagavan, Manu. *Sovereign Spheres: Princes, Education and Empire in Colonial India*. New Delhi: Oxford University Press, 2003.

Bilgrami, Akeel. 'Gandhi's Integrity: The Philosophy behind the Politics', *Postcolonial Studies*, 5 (1), 2002, pp. 79–93.

Bock, Gisela, Quentin Skinner, and Maurizio Viroli (eds). *Machiavelli and Republicanism*. Cambridge, New York, Port Chester, Melbourne, Sydney: Cambridge University Press, 1990.

Bonnerji, S. *Life of W.C. Bonnerji: First President of the Indian National Congress*. Calcutta: Bhowanipore Press, 1944.

Bourdieu, Pierre. 'The Force of Law: Towards a Sociology of the Judicial Field', *Hastings Law Journal*, vol. 38, July 1987, 814–53.

Bowen, H.V. 'British Conceptions of Global Empire', *The Journal of Imperial and Commonwealth History* XXVI (3), September 1998, pp. 1–27.

Breckenridge, C. and Van Der Veer, P. *Orientalism and the Postcolonial Predicament: Perspectives on South Asia*. Philadelphia: University of Pennsylvania, 1993.

Brimnes, Niels. 'Beyond Colonial Law: Indigenous Litigation and the Contestation of Property in the Mayor's Court in Late Eighteenth Century Madras', *Modern Asian Studies*, 37 (3), 2003, pp. 513–50.

Brockington, J.L. 'Warren Hastings and Orientalism', in *The Impeachment of Warren Hastings: Papers from a Bicentenary Commemoration*, Geoffrey Carnall and Colin Nicholson (ed.). Edinburgh: Edinburgh University Press, 1989, pp. 91–108.

Broomfield, J.H. *Elite Conflict in a Plural Society: Twentieth Century Bengal*. Berkeley: University of California Press, 1968.

Brown, Judith M. *Gandhi: Prisoner of Hope*. New Haven: Yale University Press, 1989.

Brown, Judith M. and Martin Prozesky (eds). *Gandhi and South Africa: Principles and Politics*. New York: St Martin's Press, 1996.

Brundage, Anthony and Richard A. Cosgrove. *The Great Tradition: Constitutional History and National Identity in Britain and the United States, 1870–1960*. Stanford: Stanford University Press, 2007.

Buckland, C.E. *Bengal under the Lieutenant-Governors: Being a narrative of the principal events and public measures during their periods of office from 1854–1898*. 2 vols. New Delhi: Deep Publications, 1976.

Buckle, Stephen. *Natural Law and the Theory of Property: Grotius to Hume*. Oxford: Clarendon Press, New York: Oxford University Press, 1991.

Burke, Kenneth. *The Grammar of Motives*. Berkeley: University of California Press, 1969.

Burton, Antoinette. 'Who needs the nation? Interrogating "British" history', in *Cultures of Empire: Colonizers in Britain and Empire in the Nineteenth and Twentieth Centuries, a Reader*, Catherine Hall (ed.). New York: Routledge, 2000.

Cain, P.J. and A.G. Hopkins. *British Imperialism*, 2 vols. London: Longman, 1993.

Canavan, Francis P. *The Political Reason of Edmund Burke*. Durham: Duke University Press, 1960.

Cashman, R.I. *The Myth of the Lokmanya: Tilak and Mass Politics in Maharashtra*. Berkeley: University of California Press, 1975.

Chakraborty, Bidyut. *Subhas Chandra Bose and Middle Class Radicalism: A Study in Indian Nationalism 1928–1940*. London: London School of Economics and Political Science in Association with I. B. Tauris, 1990.

Chakraborty, Dipesh. 'Postcoloniality and the Artifice of History: Who Speaks for the "Indian' Pasts"', *Representations* 37 (Winter 1992): pp. 1–26.

——. *Provincializing Europe: Postcolonial Thought and Historical Difference*. Princeton: Princeton University Press, 2000.

——. *Habitations of Modernity: Essays in the Wake of Subaltern Studies*. Chicago: University of Chicago Press, 2002.

Chakraborty Dipesh, Rochona Majumdar, and Andrew Sartori (eds). *From the Colonial to the Postcolonial: India and Pakistan in Transition*. New Delhi: Oxford University Press, 2007.

Chandra, Bipan. *The Rise and Growth of Economic Nationalism in India: Economic Policies of Indian National Leadership, 1880–1905*. New Delhi: People's Publishing House, 1966.

——. *Nationalism and Colonialism in Modern India*. New Delhi: Orient Longman, 1979.

——. 'Colonialism, Stages of Colonialism, and the Colonial State', *Journal of Contemporary Asia*, 10 (3), 1980, pp. 272–85.

——. *Indian National Movement: The Long–term Dynamics.* Delhi: Vikas Publishing House Pvt Ltd, 1988.

Chandra Bipan, Aditya Mukherjee, Mridula Mukherjee, K.N. Panikkar, and Sucheta Mahajan. *India's Struggle for Independence, 1857–1947.* New Delhi: Viking, 1988.

Chatterjee, Indrani. *Gender, Slavery and Law in Colonial India.* New York: Oxford University Press, 1999.

Chatterjee, Partha. *Nationalist Thought and the Colonial World: A Derivative Discourse?* London: Zed Books, 1986.

——. *The Nation and Its Fragments: Colonial and Postcolonial Histories.* Princeton: Princeton University Press, 1993.

——. *A Princely Impostor? The Strange and Universal History of the Kumar of Bhawal.* Princeton and Oxford: Princeton University Press, 2002.

Chaturvedi,Vinayak (ed.). *Mapping Subaltern Studies and the Postcolonial.* London: Verso, 2000.

Chaudhuri, S.B. *Civil Rebellions in the Indian Mutinies.* Calcutta: The World Press Private Ltd, 1957.

——. *English Historical Writings on the Indian Mutiny, 1857–1859.* Calcutta: The World Press Private Ltd, 1979.

Chavan, Sheshrao, (ed.). *The Makers of India Constitution: Myth and Reality.* New Delhi: Bharatiya Vidya Bhavan, 2000.

Cohen, Marshall, Thomas Nagel, and Thomas Scanlon. *Marx, Justice and History.* Princeton: Princeton University Press, 1980.

Cohn, Bernard S. 'From Indian Status to British Contract', *The Journal of Economic History.* 21 (4), 1961, pp. 613–28.

——. *An Anthropologist among the Historians and Other Essays.* Delhi, New York: Oxford University Press, 1987.

——. *Colonialism and its Forms of Knowledge.* Princeton: Princeton University Press, 1996.

Collett, N.A. *The Butcher of Amritsar: General Dyer.* London; New York: Palgrave Macmillan, 2005.

Collet, S.D. *Life and Letters of Rammohan Roy.* Calcutta: Colet, 1900.

Conniff, James. 'Burke and India: The Failure of the Theory of Trusteeship', *Political Research Quarterly,* 46 (2), June 1993, pp. 291–309.

Conrad, Dieter. 'Gandhi as Mahatma: Political Semantics in an Age of Cultural Ambiguity', in *Charisma and Canon: Essays on the Religious History of the Indian Subcontinent,* Vasudha Dalmia, Angelika Malinar, and Martin Christof (eds). New York: Oxford University Press, 2003, pp. 223–49.

Cooper, Frederick, and Ann Laura Stoler, (eds). *Tensions of Empire: Colonial Cultures in a Bourgeois World.* Berkeley, Los Angeles, London: University of California Press, 1997.

Copland, Ian. *The Princes of India in the Endgame of Empire, 1911–1947.* Cambridge: Cambridge University Press, 1997.

Corrigan, Philip and Derek Sayer. *The Great Arch: English State Formation as Cultural Revolution*. Oxford: Basil Blackwell, 1985.

Cronin, R.P. *British Policy and Administration in Bengal: Partition and the New Province of Eastern Bengal and Assam 1905–12*. Calcutta: Firma K.L. Mukhopadhyay, 1977.

Dalrymple, William. *The Last Mughal: The Fall of a Dynasty, Delhi 1857*. New York: Vintage, 2008.

Dalton, Dennis. *Indian Idea of Freedom: Thought of Swami Vivekananda, Aurobindo Ghose, Mahatma Gandhi, and Rabindranath Tagore*. New York: Academic Press, 1982.

Daniels, Norman (ed.). *Reading Rawls: Critical Studies on Rawls's 'A Theory of Justice'*. Oxford: Blackwell, 1976.

Darby, Phillip. *Three Faces of Imperialism: British and American Approaches to Asia and Africa 1870–1970*. New Haven: Yale University Press, 1987.

Dasgupta, Uma. *Rise of an Indian Public: Impact of Official Policy, 1870–1880*. Calcutta: Rddhi, 1977.

Datta, V.N. *Jallianawala Bagh*. Punjab: V.K. Arora, Kurukshetra University Books, 1969.

De, Barun (ed.). *Essays in Honour of Professor S. C. Sarkar*. New Delhi: People's Publishing House, 1976.

Deleuze, Gilles and Felix Guattari. *What is Philosophy?* New York: Columbia University Press, 1994.

d'Entreves, Alexander Passerin. *Natural Law: An Introduction to Legal Philosophy*. New Brunswick and London: Transaction Publishers, 2004.

Derrett, J.D.M. 'Justice, Equity and Good Conscience', in *Changing Law in Developing Countries*, J.N.D. Anderson. New York: George Allen and Unwin, Ltd, 1963, pp. 114–53.

———. *Religion, Law and State in India*. London: Faber and Faber, 1968.

———. *History of Indian Law*. Leiden: Brill, 1973.

Desai, A.R. *Social Background of Indian Nationalism*. 3rd edn. Bombay: Popular Book Depot, 1959.

Desika Char, S.V. *Centralized Legislation: A History of the Legislative System of British India from 1834–1861*. Bombay, New York: Asia Publishing House, 1963.

——— (ed.). *Readings in the Constitutional History of India, 1757–1947*. Delhi: Oxford University Press, 1983.

Devji, Faisal Fatehali. 'A Practice of Prejudice: Gandhi's Politics of Friendship', in *Muslims, Dalits, and the Fabrications of History, Subaltern Studies XII*. Shail Mayaram, M.S.S. Pandian, and Ajay Skaria (eds). New Delhi: Permanent Black and Ravi Dayal Publishers, 2005, pp. 78–98.

Dhavan, Rajeev. *Justice on Trial: The Supreme Court and Parliamentary Sovereignty*. Delhi: Sterling Publishers, 1976.

Dicey, A.V. *Introduction to the Study of the Law of the Constitution*. 9th edn. London: Macmillan, 1939.

Dirks, N. 'From Little King to Landlord: Property, Law, and the Gift under the Madras Permanent Settlement.' *Comparative Studies in Society and History*, 28 (2), April 1986, pp. 307–33.

———. *The Hollow Crown: Ethnohistory of an Indian Kingdom*. Cambridge: Cambridge University Press, 1988.

———. *Castes of Mind: Colonialism and the Making of Modern India*. Princeton and Oxford: Princeton University Press, 2001.

———. *The Scandal of Empire: India and the Creation of Imperial Britain*. Cambridge, Massachusetts and London, England: Harvard University Press, 2006.

Dobb, Maurice H. *Studies in the Development of Capitalism*. London: G. Routledge and K Paul, 1946.

Draper, Alfred. *Amritsar: The Massacre that Ended the Raj*. London: Cassell, 1981.

Dreyer, Frederick A. *Burke's Politics: A Study in Whig Orthodoxy*. Waterloo: Wilfred Laurier University Press, 1979.

Duncan, Christopher M. *The Anti-Federalists and Early American Political Thought*. Dekalb, Ill: Northern Illinois University Press, 1995.

du Toit, Brian M. 'The Mahatma Gandhi and South Africa', *Journal of Modern African Studies* 34(4), 1996, 643–60.

Dutt, Rajani Palme. *India Today*. Bombay: People's Publishing House, 1949.

Dutta, V.N. *Jallianwala Bagh*. Kurukshetra, Punjab: Kurukshetra University Books, 1969.

Dworkin, Ronald. *Taking Rights Seriously*. Cambridge: Harvard University Press, 1978.

———. *Law's Empire*. Cambridge: Harvard University Press, 1986.

Elster, Jon and Rune Slagstad (eds). *Constitutionalism and Democracy*. Cambridge: Cambridge University Press, 1988.

Engelstein, Laura. 'Combined Underdevelopment: Discipline and the Law in Imperial and Soviet Russia', *The American Historical Review*, 98 (2), April 1993, 338–53.

Erikson, Eric H. *Gandhi's Truth: On the Origins of Militant Non-Violence*. New York: W.W. Norton, 1969.

Ewald, Francois. 'Norms, Discipline, and the Law', *Representations*, 30 (Special Issue), Law and the Order of Culture, Spring 1990, pp. 138–61.

Fanon, Frantz. *Black Skins, White Masks*. Charles Lam Markmann (trans.). New York: Grove Press, 1968.

———. *The Wretched of the Earth*. Constance Farrington (trans). New York: Grove Press, 1968.

Feiling, Keith. *Warren Hastings*. London: Macmillan, 1954.

Fein, Helen. *Imperial Crime and Punishment: The Massacre at Jallianwala Bagh and British Judgement, 1919–1920.* Honolulu: University Press of Hawaii, 1977.

Ferguson, Niall. *How Britain made the Modern World.* London: Penguin, 2003.

Fieldhouse, David. *Economics of Empire, 1830–1914.* Ithaca: Cornell University Press, 1973.

Finnis, John. *Natural law and Natural Rights.* Oxford: Oxford University Press, 1980.

Fisher, Michael. *Indirect Rule in India.* Delhi: Oxford University Press, 1991.

Foucault, Michel. *The Order of Things: An Archeology of the Human Sciences.* New York: Vintage Books, 1970.

———. *The Archaeology of Knowledge and the Discourse on Language.* A.M. Sheridan Smith (trans.), London: Tavistock, 1972.

———. *Discipline and Punish: The Birth of the Prison.* New York: Vintage Books, 1979.

———. *Power/Knowledge: Selected Interviews and Other Writings 1972–1977,* Colin Gordon (ed.), New York: Pantheon Books/Random House, 1980.

Franklin, Julian H. *Jean Bodin and the Rise of Absolutist Theory.* Cambridge: Cambridge University Press, 1973.

Freitag, Sandria B. *Collective Action and Community: Public Arenas and the Emergence of Communalism in North India.* Berkeley: University of California Press, 1989.

Furber, Holden. 'Constitution-Making in India', *Far Eastern Survey,* 18 (8), April 1949, pp. 87–9.

Furneaux, Rupert. *Massacre at Amritsar.* London: George Allen and Unwin, 1963.

Galanter, Marc. *Competing Equalities: Law and the Backward Classes in India.* Delhi: Oxford University Press, 1984.

———. *Law and Society in Modern India.* Delhi: Oxford University Press, 1989.

Gallagher, John and Ronald Robinson, 'The Imperialism of Free Trade', *Economic History Review,* Second Series, VI (1), 1953.

Gallagher, J., G. Johnson and A. Seal (eds). *Locality, Province and Nation: Essays in Indian Politics.* London: Cambridge University Press, 1973.

Galston, William. *Liberal Purposes: Goods, Virtues and Duties in the Liberal State.* Cambridge: Cambridge University Press, 1991.

Ganguli, B.N. *Dadabhai Naoroji and the Drain Theory.* Bombay: Asia Publishing House, 1965.

Getz, Michael J. *Subhas Chandra Bose; A Biography.* Jefferson, N.C.: McFarland and Co., 2002.

Ghose, Sisirkumar. *Rethinking Tagore: Three Lectures.* Mysore: University of Mysore, 1982.

Gibbon, Edward. *The History of the Decline and Fall of the Roman Empire.* 7 vols. Edited with introduction by J.B. Bury. London: Methuen & Co., 1909–26.

Gopal, S. *British Policy in India.* Cambridge: Cambridge University Press, 1965.

Gordon, Leonard A. *Bengal: The Nationalist Movement, 1876–1940.* New York: Columbia University Press, 1974.

———. *Brothers Against the Raj: A Biography of Indian Nationalist Leaders Sarat and Subhas Chandra Bose.* New York: Columbia University Press, 1990.

Green, Jack P. *Understanding the American Revolution: Issues and Actors.* Charlottesville: University Press of Virginia, 1967.

Green, Martin. *The Origins of Nonviolence: Tolstoy and Gandhi in Their Historical Settings.* University Park: Pennsylvania State University Press, 1986.

Gopal, S. *British Policy in India, 1858–1905.* Cambridge: Cambridge University Press, 1965.

———. *Jawaharlal Nehru, A Biography,* 3 vols. Cambridge, Mass.: Harvard University Press, 1975–84.

Goswami, D.C., R.K. Nayak, and Shankar Dayal Singh. *Motilal Nehru: A Great Patriot.* New Delhi: National Forum of Lawyers and Legal Aid, 1976.

Goswami, Manu. *Producing India: From Colonial Economy to National Space.* Chicago: University of Chicago Press, 2004.

Gough, Kathleen, and Hari P. Sharma (eds). *Imperialism and Revolution in South Asia.* New York: Monthly Review Press, 1973.

Greene, Jack P. *Understanding the American Revolution: Issues and Actors.* Charlottesville: University Press of Virginia, 1995.

Green, Martin. *The Origins of Nonviolence: Tolstoy and Gandhi in Their Historical Settings.* University Park: Pennsylvania State University Press, 1986.

Greenough, Paul. *The Death of an Uncrowned King: C.R. Das and and Political Crisis in Twentieth-Century Bengal.* Iowa: Center for International and Comparative Studies, University of Iowa, 1984.

Guha, Amalendu. *Planter Raj to Swaraj: Freedom Struggle and Electoral Politics in Assam, 1826–1947.* New Delhi: Indian Council of Historical Research, 1977.

Guha, R. 'Dominance without Hegemony', in *Subaltern Studies 7: Writings in South Asian History and Society.* R. Guha (ed.). New York: Oxford University Press 1973.

———. *A Rule of Property for Bengal: An Essay on the Idea of Permanent Settlement.* New Delhi: Orient Longman, 1983.

———. *Elementary Aspects of Peasant Insurgency in Colonial India.* Delhi: Oxford University Press, 1983.

Guha, Sumit and Michael Anderson (ed.). *Changing Concepts of Rights and Justice in South Asia*. Delhi: Oxford University Press, 1998.

Gupta, Manmathnath. *History of the Indian Revolutionary Movement*. Bombay and New Delhi: Somaiya Publications Pvt Ltd, 1972.

Gutmann, Amy and Dennis Thompson (eds). *Democracy and Disagreement*. Cambridge, Mass.: Belknap Press, 1996.

Habermas, Jurgen. *The Structural Transformation of the Public Sphere: An Inquiry into a Category of Bourgeois Society*. T. Burger (trans.). Cambridge, Mass.: MIT Press, 1989.

———. *Between Facts and Norms: Contributions to a Discourse Theory of Law and Democracy*. William Rehg (trans). Cambridge, Mass.: MIT Press, 1996.

Habib, Irfan. *Interpreting Indian History*. Shillong: North-Eastern University Publications, 1987.

———. *Essays in Indian History: Towards a Marxist Perception*. New Delhi: Tulika, 1995.

Hadenius, Alex, (ed.). *Democracy's Victory and Crisis*. Cambridge: Cambridge University Press, 2000.

Hale, Matthew. *The History of the Common law of England*. Charles M. Gray (ed.). Chicago: The University of Chicago Press, 1971.

Hancock, W.K. *Survey of British Commonwealth Affairs*, 2 vols. London: Oxford University Press, pp. 1937–42.

Hardiman, David. *Peasant Nationalist of Gujarat: Kheda District 1917–1934*. Delhi: Oxford University Press, 1982.

Hardt, Michael and Negri Antonio, . *Empire*. Cambridge, Mass: Harvard University Press, 2000.

Hart, Herbert Lionel Adolphus. *The Concept of Law*. Oxford: Oxford University Press, 1961.

———. *Essays in Jurisprudence and Philosophy*. Oxford: Clarendon Press, 1983.

Hasan, Zoya, E. Sridharan, and R. Sudarshan (eds). *India's Living Constitution: Ideas, Practices, Controversies*. London: Anthem Press, 2005.

Haskins, George L. *The Growth of English Representative Government*. Philadelphia: University of Pennsylvania Press, 1948.

Hay, Douglas. 'Property, Authority and Criminal Law', in *Alibion's Fatal Tree: Crime and Society in Eighteenth-Century England*, Douglas Hay, Peter Linebaugh, John G. Rule, E.P. Thompson, and Cal Winslow (eds). New York: Pantheon Books, 1975, pp. 17–64.

Heehs, Peter. *Sri Aurobindo, a Brief Biography*. Delhi, New York: Oxford University Press, 1989.

Hegel, Georg Wilhelm Friedrich. *Elements of the Philosophy of Right*. Allen W. Wood (ed.). Cambridge: Cambridge University Press, 1991.

Henningham, Stephen. *Peasant Movements in Colonial India: North Bihar, 1917–1942*. Canberra: Australian National University, 1982.

Hirschman, Edwin. *'White Mutiny': The Ilbert Bill Crisis in India and the Genesis of the Indian National Congress*. Columbia, MO: South Asia Books, 1980.

Hobsbawm, E.J. *Industry and Empire from 1750 to the present day*. Harmondsworth, England: Penguin Books, 1970, rpt 1984.

——. 'America's Imperial Delusion: The US drive for world domination has no historical precedent', *Guardian*, 14 June 2003.

Hobson, A. *Imperialism: A Study*. London: J. Nisbet, 1902.

Holdsworth, William Searle. *A History of English Law*, 17 vols. Boston: Little, Brown and Company, 1922–72.

Holorenshaw, Henry. *The Levellers and the English Revolution*. New York, H. Fertig, 1971.

Hooker, M.B. *Legal Pluralism: An Introduction to Colonial and Neo-Colonial Laws*. Oxford: Clarendon Press, 1975.

Hunt, Alan. 'Foucault's Expulsion of Law: Toward a Retrieval', *Law and Social Inquiry*, 17 (1), Winter 1992, pp. 1–38.

Hussain, Nasser. *The Jurisprudence of Emergency: Colonialism and the Rule of Law*. Ann Arbor: University of Michigan Press, 2003.

Hutchins, Francis G. *India's Revolution: Gandhi and the Quit India Movement*. Cambridge: Harvard University Press, 1973.

——. *The Illusion of Permanence: British Imperialism in India*. Princeton: Princeton University Press, 1984.

Huttenback, Robert A. *Gandhi in South Africa: British Imperialism and the Indian Question, 1860–1914*. Ithaca, N.Y.: Cornell University Press, 1971.

Ignatieff, Michael. 'The Burden', *New York Times Magazine*, 5 January 2003.

Inden, R. *Imagining India*. Cambridge: Basil Blackwell, 1990.

Irschick, Eugene. *Politics and Social Conflict in South India: The Non-Brahman Movement and Tamil Separatism, 1916–1929*. Berkeley and Los Angeles: University of California Press, 1969.

——. *Dialogue and History: Constructing South India, 1795–1895*. Berkeley: University of California Press, 1994.

Jaffrelot, Christophe. *Dr Ambedkar and Untouchability: Analysing and Fighting Caste*. London: C. Hurst & Co., 2005.

Jain, M.P. *Outlines of Indian Legal History*. Bombay: N.M. Tripathi Private Ltd, 1972.

Jalal, A. *The Sole Spokesperson: Jinnah, the Muslim League and the Demand for Pakistan*. Cambridge: Cambridge University Press, 1985.

Janes, Regina. 'At Home Abroad: Edmund Burke in India', *Bulletin of Research in the Humanities*, vol. 82, 1979, pp. 160–74.

Jeffrey, Robin (ed.). *People, Princes, and Paramount Power*. Delhi: Oxford University Press, 1978.

Jennings, Sir Ivor. 'The Constitution of India', in *The Commonwealth in Asia*. Oxford: Clarendon Press, 1951.

———. *Some Characteristics of the Indian Constitution, being lectures given in the University of Madras during March 1952 under the Sir Alladi Krishnaswami Aiyer Shashtiabdapoorthi Endowment*. London: Geoffrey Cumberlege, Oxford University Press, 1953.

Johnson, Gordon. *Provincial Politics and Indian Nationalism: Bombay and the Indian National Congress 1880 to 1915*. Cambridge: Cambridge University Press, 1973. Rama Jois, M. *Legal and Constitutional History of India*. New Delhi: Universal Law Publishing, 2004.

Joshi, V.C. (ed.). *Rammohan Roy and the Process of Modernization in India*. Delhi: Vikas Publishing House, 1975.

Kairys, D. *The Politics of Law*. New York: Pantheon, 1990.

Kaminsky, Arnold P. *The India Office 1880–1910*. London: Greenwood Publishing House, 1986.

Kant, Immanuel. *Metaphysical Elements of Justice*. New York: Macmillan, 1965.

———. *Lectures on Ethics*. London: Metheun and Co. Ltd, 1930.

Kaviraj, Sudipto. *The Unhappy Consciousness: Bankimchandra Chattopadhyay and the Formation of Nationalist Discourse in India*. Delhi: Oxford University Press, 1995.

———. 'Modernity and Politics in India', *Daedalus*, 129 (1), Summer 2000, pp. 137–62.

———. 'Ideas of Freedom in Modern India.' in Robert H. Taylor (ed.), *The Idea of Freedom in Asia and Africa*. Stanford: Stanford University Press, 2002.

Keay, John. *The Honourable Company: A History of the English East India Company*. New York: Macmillan Publishing House, 1991.

Keer, Dhananjay. *Dr Ambedkar, Life and Mission*, 2nd edn. Bombay, Popular Prakashan, 1962.

Kelly, Alfred H. and Winfred A. Harbison. *The American Constitution: Its Origins and Development*. New York: W.W. Norton and Company, 1976.

Kelman, M. *A Guide to Critical Legal Studies*. Cambridge: Harvard University Press, 1987.

Kennedy, D. 'Toward an Historical Understanding of Legal Consciousness: The Case of Classical Legal Thought in America, 1850–1940', *Research in Law and Sociology*, vol. 3, 1980, pp. 3–24.

Khilnani, Sunil. *The Idea of India*. New York: Farrar, Straus and Giroux, 1997.

Kiernan, V.G. *Marxism and Imperialism: Studies*. London: Edward Arnold, 1974.

Kley, Dale Van (ed.). *The French Idea of Freedom: The Old Regime and the Declaration of Rights of 1789*. Stanford: Stanford University Press, 1994.

Kohli, A. *Democracy and Discontent: India's Growing Crisis of Governability*. Cambridge: Cambridge University Press, 1990.

———. 'On Sources of Social and Political Conflicts in Follower Democracies', in *Democracy's Victory and Crisis*. Alex Hadenius (ed.). Cambridge: Cambridge University Press, 1997, pp. 71–80.

———. (ed.). *The Success of India's Democracy*. Cambridge: Cambridge University Press, 2001.

Konig, David Thomas (ed.), *Devising Liberty: Preserving and Creating Freedom in the New American Republic*. Stanford: Stanford University Press, 1995.

Kopf, David. *British Orientalism and the Bengal Renaissance*. Berkeley: University of California Press, 1972.

Kolsky, Elizabeth. 'Codification and the Rule of Colonial Difference: Criminal Procedure in British India', *Law and History Review*, 23 (3), September 2005.

Kostal, R.W. *A Jurisprudence of Power: Victorian Empire and the Rule of Law*. New York: Oxford University Press, 2005.

Krieger, Leonard. *The German Idea of Freedom: History of a Political Tradition*. Chicago: University of Chicago Press, 1962.

Krieger, L. *The Politics of Discretion: Pufendorf and the Acceptance of Natural Law*. Chicago: University of Chicago Press, 1965.

Krishna, Gopal. 'The Development of the Indian National Congress as a Mass Organization, 1918–1923', *Journal of Asian Studies*, vol. 25, 1965, pp. 413–30.

Kulke, Hermann and Dietmar Rothermund. *A History of India*. Calcutta: Rupa and Co., 1993.

Kumar, Ravindra (ed.). *Essays on Gandhian Politics: The Rowlatt Satyagraha of 1919*. Oxford: Clarendon Press, 1971.

Kymlicka, Will. *Multicultural Citizenship, A Liberal Theory of Minority Rights*. Oxford: Oxford University Press, 1995.

Laski, Harold. *Political Thought in England from Locke to Bentham*. New York: Henry Holt and Company; London: William and Norgate, 1920.

Lavrin, Janko. 'Tolstoy and Gandhi', *Russian Review,* vol. 19, 1960, 132–9.

Lawson, Philip. *The East India Company: A History*. London: Longman, 1993.

Lee-Warner, William. *The Life of the Marquis of Dalhousie*. London, New York: Macmillan, 1920.

Lenin, V.I. *Imperialism, the Highest Stage of Capitalism: A Popular Outline*. New York: International Publishers, 1933.

Lieberman, David. *The Province of Legislation Determined: Legal Theory in Eighteenth-Century Britain.* Cambridge, New Rochelle, Melbourne, Sydney, 1989.

Lieven, Donald. *Empire: The Russian and Its Rivals.* London: John Murray, 2000.

Low, D.A. *Eclipse of Empire.* Cambridge: Cambridge University Press, 1991.

——— (ed.). *Soundings in Modern South Asian History.* Berkeley, University of California Press, 1968.

Luard, E. *The Globalization of Politics.* London: Macmillan, 1990.

Lucas, John. *On Justice.* Oxford: Clarendon Press, 1989.

Macaulay, Thomas Babington. *Warren Hastings.* New York: Chautauqua Press, 1886.

Maccunn, John. *The Political Philosophy of Burke.* London: Edward Arnold, 1913.

Macpherson, C.B. *Burke.* New York: Hill and Wang, 1980.

Majeed, Javed. *Ungoverned Imaginings: James Mill's The History of British India and Orientalism.* Oxford, England: Clarendon Press; New York : Oxford University Press, 1992.

Majumdar, Bimanbehari. *Indian Political Associations and Reform of Legislature 1818–1917.* Calcutta: Firma K.L. Mukhopadhyay, 1965.

———. *Militant Nationalism in India and its Socio-Religious Background, 1897–1917.* Calcutta: General Printers and Publishers, 1966.

———. *History of Indian Social and Political Ideas from Rammohan to Dayananda.* Calcutta: Bookland, 1967.

Majumdar, Bimanbehari and Bhakta Prasad Majumdar. *Congress and Congressmen in the pre-Gandhian era, 1885–1917.* Calcutta: Firma K. L. Mukhopadhyay, 1967.

Maine, Henry. *Ancient Law.* London: Dent Dutton, 1954.

Mamdani, Mahmood. *Citizen and Subject: Contemporary Africa and the Legacy of Colonialism.* Princeton: Princeton University Press, 1996.

———. *When Victims Become Killers: Colonialism, Nativism, and the Genocide in Rwanda.* Princeton and Oxford: Princeton University Press, 2001.

———. 'Beyond Settler and Native as Political Identities: Overcoming the Political Legacy of Colonialism', *Comparative Studies in Society and History*, 43 (4), October 2001, pp. 651–64.

Marshall, Peter J. *The Impeachment of Warren Hastings.* London: Oxford University Press, 1965.

———. *East India Fortunes: The British in Bengal in the Eighteenth Century.* Oxford: Clarendon Press, 1976.

———. *Bengal: The British Bridgehead. Eastern India, 1740–1828. Vol. 2.2 of The New Cambridge History of India.* Cambridge: Cambridge University Press, 1987.

——. 'Imperial Britain', *The Journal of Imperial and Commonwealth History*, XXIII (3), September 1995, pp. 382–3. (ed.). *The Oxford History of the British Empire*. Oxford and New York: Oxford University Press, 1998.

——. 'The Making of an Imperial Icon: The Case of Warren Hastings', *The Journal of Imperial and Commonwealth History*, XXVII (3), September 1999, pp. 1–16.

Martineau, John. *The Life and Correspondence of the Right Hon. Sir Bartle Frere*. London: John Murray, 1895.

Masani, R.P. *Dadabhai Naoroji: the Grand Old Man of India*. London, G. Allen & Unwin, Ltd, 1939.

McCahill, Michael W. *Order and Equipoise: The Peerage and the House of Lords, 1783–1806*. London: Royal Historical Society, 1978.

McIlwain, Charles Howard. *The High Court of Parliament and its Supremacy: An Historical Essay on the Boundaries between Legislation and Adjudication in England*. New Haven: Yale University Press, 1910.

——. *Constitutionalism, Ancient and Modern*. Ithaca: Cornell University Press, 1947.

McLane, John R. *Indian Nationalism and the Early Congress*. Princeton: Princeton University Press, 1977.

——. 'The Drain of Wealth and Indian Nationalism at the turn of the century', in *India and the World Economy, 1850–1950*, Gopalan Balachandran (ed.). Delhi: Oxford University Press, 2003, pp. 70–92.

Mehrotra, S.R. *India and the Commonwealth 1885–1929*. London: George Allen and Unwin Ltd, 1965.

——. *The Emergence of the Indian National Congress*. Delhi: Vikas Publications, 1971.

Mehta, Pratap Bhanu. 'The Inner Conflict of Constitutionalism: Judicial Review and the Basic Structure.' *India's Living Constitution: Ideas, Practices, Controversies*. Zoya Hasan, E. Sridharan, and R. Sudarshan (eds). London: Anthem Press, 2005, pp. 179–206.

Mehta, Uday Singh. *Liberalism and Empire: A Study in Nineteenth Century Liberal Thought*. Chicago and London: The University of Chicago Press, 1999.

——. 'Indian Constitutionalism: The Articulation of a Political Vision', in *From the Colonial to the Postcolonial: India and Pakistan in Transition*. Dipesh Chakrabarty, Rochona Majumdar, and Andrew Sartori (eds). New Delhi: Oxford University Press, 2007, pp. 13–30.

Metcalf, Thomas R. *Aftermath of Revolt: India, 1857–1870*. Princeton: Princeton University Press, 1964.

——. *Ideologies of the Raj*. Cambridge: Cambridge University Press, 1994.

Mill, John Stuart. *Utilitarianism, Liberty and Representative Government*. New York: E.P. Dutton, 1951.

Miller, David. *Social Justice*. Oxford: Clarendon Press, 1978.

Mines, Mattison. 'Courts of Law and Styles of Self in Eighteenth-Century Madras: From Hybrid to Colonial Self', *Modern Asian Studies*, 35 (1), 2001, pp. 33–74.

Misra, B.B. *The Indian Middle Classes; Their Growth in Modern Times.* London, New York: Oxford University Press, 1961.

———. *The Judicial Administration of the East India Company in Bengal 1765–1782*. Delhi: Motilal Banarasidas, 1961.

Mitra, Sisirkumar. *Sri Aurobindo and Indian Freedom*. Madras: Sri Aurobindo Library, 1948.

Moon, Vasant (ed.). *Dr Babasaheb Ambedkar: Writings and Speeches*, 16 vols. Bombay: Government of Maharashtra, 1979–2006.

Moore, R.J. *Sir Charles Wood's Indian Policy: 1853–1866*. Manchester: Manchester University Press, 1966.

———. *Liberalism and Indian Politics 1872–1922*. London: Edward Arnold, 1966.

Morley, John. *Edmund Burke, a Historical Study*. New York: Knopf, 1924.

Mukerjee, Hirendranath. *Indian Renaissance and Raja Rammohun Roy*. Poona: Poona University Press, 1975.

Mukherjee, Haridas, and Uma. *Bipan Chandra Pal and India's Struggle for Swaraj*. Calcutta: Mukhopadhyay, 1958.

———. *Sri Aurobindo and the New Thought in Indian Politics. Being a study in the ideas of Indian nationalism, based on the rare writings of Sri Aurobindo in the daily Bande mataram during the years 1906–1908*. Calcutta, Firma K.L. Mukhopadhyay, 1964.

Mukherjee, Mithi, 'Justice, War and the Imperium: India and Britain in Edmund Burke's Prosecutorial Speeches in the Impeachment Trial of Warren Hastings.' *Law and History Review*, 23 (3), Fall 2005, pp. 589–630.

Mukherjee, Rudrangshu. *Awadh in Revolt, 1857–1858: A Study of Popular Resistance*. Delhi: Oxford University Press, 1984.

Mukherji, Ramkrishna. *The Rise and Fall of the East India Company: A Sociological Appraisal*. New York: Monthly Review Press, 1974.

Mukhopadhyay, Anindita. *Behind the Mask: The Cultural Definition of the Legal Subject in Colonial Bengal (1715–1911)*. New Delhi: Oxford University Press, 2006.

———. 'The Encounter of the Sant and the Dacoit', in Satish Saberwal and Supriya Varma (eds). *Traditions in Motion: Religion and Society in History*. New Delhi: Oxford University Press, 2005.

———. 'Rammohun Roy and the Conceptual History of Governance and Law', in *Proceedings of the Indian History Congress*, 66th Session, Santiniketan, 2005. Delhi: Indian History Congress, 2006–7.

Nagaraj, D.R. *The Flaming Feet: A Study of the Dalit Movement*. Bangalore: South Forum Press, 1993.

Nagel, Thomas. *Equality and Partiality*. Oxford: Oxford University Press, 1991.

Nanda, B.R. *Gokhale: The Indian Moderates and the British Raj*. Delhi: Oxford University Press, 1977.

——. *The Moderate Era in Indian politics: Dadabhai Naoroji Memorial Prize Fund Lecture*. Delhi, New York: Oxford University Press, 1983.

——. (ed.). *Socialism in India*. Delhi: Vikas Publications, 1972.

Nandi, A. *The Intimate Enemy: Loss and Recovery of Self Under Colonialism*. Delhi: Oxford University Press, 1983.

——. *Rabindranath Tagore and The Illegitimacy of Nationalism*. Delhi: Oxford University Press, 1994.

Natarajan. J. *History of Indian Journalism*. Delhi: Publications Division, Ministry of Information and Broadcasting, 1955.

Nayar, Pramod K. (ed.). *The Trial of Bahadur Shah Zafar*. New Delhi: Orient Longman, 2007.

Noorani, A.G. *Indian Political Trials 1775–1947*. Delhi: Oxford University Press, 2005.

Nozick, Robert. *Anarchy, State and Utopia*. New York: Basic Books, 1974.

Nussbaum, Martha C. 'Patriotism and Cosmopolitanism', in *For Love of Country: Debating the Limits of Patriotism, Martha C. Nussbaum with Respondents* Joshua Cohen (ed.). Boston: Beacon Press, 1996, pp. 3–17.

O'Brien, Conor Cruise. *The Great Melody: A Thematic Biography and Commented Anthology of Edmund Burke* Chicago: University of Chicago Press, 1992.

O'Hanlon, R. 'Recovering the Subject: Subaltern Studies and Histories of Resistance in Colonial South Asia', *Modern Asian Studies*. 1988, pp. 189–224.

O'Hanlon, R. and David Washbrook. 'After Orientalism: Culture, Criticism, and Politics in the Third World', *Comparative Studies in Society and History*, 34 (1), 1992, pp. 141–67.

Ohmae, K. *The End of the Nation State*. New York: Free Press, 1995.

Oldenburg, Veena Talwar. *The Making of Colonial Lucknow, 1856–1877*. Princeton: Princeton University Press, 1984.

——. *Dowry Murder: The Imperial Origins of a Cultural Crime*. Oxford: New York: Oxford University Press, 2002.

Omvedt, Gail. *Dalits and the Democratic Revolution: Dr Ambedkar and the Dalit Movement in Colonial India*. New Delhi; Newbury Park: Sage Publications, 1993.

——. *Ambedkar: Towards an Enlightened India*. New Delhi; New York: Penguin, 2004.

Onuf, Peter S. (ed.). *Maryland and the Empire, 1773: The Antilon-First Citizen Letters*. Baltimore: Johns Hopkins University Press, 1974.

Owen, H.F. 'Towards Nation-Wide Agitation and Organization: The Home Rule Leagues, 1915–1918', *Soundings in Modern South Asian History*, D.A. Low (ed.). London: Weidenfeld & Nicolson, 1968, pp. 159–95.

Pagden, Anthony. *Lords of All the World: Ideologies of Empire in Spain, Britain and France, c. 1500–c.1800*. New Haven: Yale University Press, 1995.

Pandey, B.N. *Introduction of English Law into India: The Career of Elijah Impey in Bengal, 1774–1783*. London: Asia Publishing House, 1967.

Pandey, Gyanendra. *The Ascendency of the Congress in Uttar Pradesh 1936–34: A Study in Imperfect Mobilization*. Delhi; New York: Oxford University Press, 1978.

Pantham, Thomas. 'Thinking with Mahatma Gandhi: Beyond Liberal Democracy', *Political Theory*, 11 (2), 1983, pp. 165–88.

Parekh, Bhikhu. *Colonialism, Tradition, and Reform: An Analysis of Gandhi's Political Discourse*. New Delhi: Sage Publications, 1989.

———. 'Decolonizing Liberalism', in *The End of 'Isms': Reflections on the Fate of Ideological Politics after Communism's Collapse*, A. Shtromas (ed.). Oxford: Cambridge, MA: Blackwell, 1994, pp. 85–103.

Parel, Anthony J. (ed.). *Gandhi, Freedom, and Self-Rule*. Lanham, Md.: Lexington Books, 2000.

Pelinka, Anton. *Democracy Indian Style: Subhas Chandra Bose and the Creation of India's Political Culture*. New Brunswick, N.J.: Transaction Publishers, 2003.

Philips, Cyril Henry. *The East India Company, 1784–1834*. Manchester: Manchester University Press, 1961.

Pocock, John Greville Agard. *The Ancient Constitution and the Feudal Law: A Study of English Thought in the Seventeenth Century*. Cambridge: Cambridge University Press, 1987.

———. 'Political thought in the English-speaking Atlantic, 1760–1790: The Imperial Crisis', in *The Varieties of British Political Thought, 1500–1800*, J.G.A. Pocock, (ed.). Cambridge and New York: Cambridge University Press, 1993.

Pollock, F. and F.M. Maitland. *History of English Law Before the Time of Edward I*. Cambridge: Cambridge University Press, 1911.

Pollock, Sheldon. *The Language of the Gods in the World of Men: Sanskrit, Culture, and Power in Premodern India*. Berkeley; Los Angeles; London: University of California Press, 2006.

Prakash, G. 'Writing Post-Orientalist Histories of the Third World: Perspectives from Indian Historiography', *Comparative Studies in Society and History*, 32(2), April 1990, pp. 383–408.

———. 'Can the "Subaltern" Ride: A Reply to O'Hanlon and Washbrook', *Comparative Studies in Society and History*, 34 (1), January 1992, pp. 168–84.

———. 'Subaltern Studies as Postcolonial Criticism', *American Historical Review*. 99 (5), December 1994, pp. 1475–90.

———. *After Colonialism: Imperial Histories and Postcolonial Displacements*. Princeton: Princeton University Press, 1994.

Prasad, Bimla and Sangita Mallik (eds). *Ideas and Men Behind the Indian Constitution: Selections from the Indian Constituent Assembly Debates, 1946–49*. Delhi: Konark Publishers, 2001.

Prashad, Ganesh. 'Whiggism in India', *Political Science Quarterly*. 81 (3), September 1966, pp. 412–31.

Prashad, Vijay. *Untouchable Freedom: A Social History of the Dalit Community*. New Delhi: Oxford University Press, 2000.

Price, Pamela G. 'The "Popularity" of the Imperial Courts of Law: Three Views of the Anglo-Indian Legal Encounter', in *European Expansion and Law: The Encounter of European and Indigenous Law in 19th-and 20th -Century Africa and Asia*, W. J. Mommsen and J.A. de Moor (eds). Oxford: Berg, 1992, pp. 179–200.

Pylee, M.V. *Constitutional History of India, 1600–1950*. Bombay: Asia, 1967.

Raab, Felix. *The English Face of Machiavelli: A Changing Interpretation, 1500–1700*. London: Routledge and Kegan Paul; Toronto: University of Toronto Press, 1964.

Raghuramaraju, A. (ed.). *Debating Gandhi: A Reader*. New Delhi: Oxford University Press, 2006.

Rama, M. Jois. *Legal and Constitutional History of India*. New Delhi: Universal Law Publishing, 2004.

Ramusack, Barbara. *The Princes of India in the Twilight of Empire*. Columbus: Ohio State University Press, 1978.

Rankin, George C. *Background to Indian Law*. Cambridge: Cambridge University Press, 1946.

Rao, B. Shiva. *The Framing of India's Constitution: A Study*. Delhi: Indian Institute of Public Administration, 1968.

Rau, B.N. *India's Constitution in the Making*. Calcutta: Orient Longmans, 1960.

Rawls, John. *A Theory of Justice*. Cambridge, Mass.: Harvard University Press, 1971.

Ray, Rajat Kanta. *Social Conflict and Political Unrest in Bengal, 1875–1927*. Delhi: Oxford University Press, 1984.

Raychaudhuri, Tapan. *Europe Reconsidered: Perceptions of the West in Nineteenth Century Bengal*. Delhi: Oxford University Press, 1988.

Raz, Joseph. *Ethics in the Public Domain: Essays in the Morality of Law and Politics*. Oxford: Clarendon Press, 1994.

Reid, John Phillip. *The Concept of Representation in the Age of the American Revolution*. Chicago and London: The University of Chicago Press, 1989.

Riley, Patrick. *Leibniz' Universal Jurisprudence: Justice as the Charity of the Wise*. Cambridge, Massachusetts: Harvard University Press, 1996.

Robertson, Bruce. *Raja Rammohan Roy: The Father of Modern India*. Delhi: Oxford University Press, 1995.

Rosenfeld, Michael (ed.). *Constitutionalism, Identity, Difference and Legitimacy: Theoretical Perspectives*. Durham and London: Duke University Press, 1994.

Rudolph, Lloyd I. and Susanne H. Rudolph. *Gandhi, the Traditional Roots of Charisma*. Chicago: University of Chicago Press, 1983.

——. *Postmodern Gandhi and Other Essays: Gandhi in the World and at Home*. Chicago: University of Chicago Press, 2006.

Rudolph, Susan Hoeber. 'The New Courage: An Essay on Gandhi's Psychology', *World Politics*, 16 (1), October 1963, pp. 98–117.

Rukmani, T.S. 'Tagore and Gandhi.' in *Indian Critiques of Gandhi*. Harold Coward (ed.). Albany: State University of New York Press, 2003, pp. 107–28.

Saberwal, Satish. 'Introduction: Civilization, Constitution, Democracy', in *India's Living Constitution: Ideas, Practices, Controversies*. Zoya Hasan, E. Sridharan, and R. Sudarshan (eds). London: Anthem Press, 2005, pp. 1–30.

Saberwal, Satish and Varma, Supriya (eds). *Traditions in Motion: Religion and Society in History*. New Delhi: Oxford University Press, 2005.

Said, E. *Orientalism*. New York: Vintage Books, 1978.

Sarkar, Sumit. *Swadeshi Movement in Bengal 1903–1908*. New Delhi: People's Publishing House, 1973.

——. *Modern India, 1885–1947*. New Delhi: Macmillan, 1983.

——. *'Popular' Movements and 'Middle' Class Leadership in Late Colonial India*. Calcutta: Bagchi, 1983.

——. 'The Decline of the Subaltern in Subaltern Studies', in *Writing Social History*. Delhi: Oxford University Press, 1997.

——. 'Orientalism Revisited: Saidian Frameworks in the Writing of Modern Indian History', *Oxford Literary Review*, 16 (1–2), 1994, pp. 205–24.

——. *Writing Social History*. Delhi: Oxford University Press, 1997.

Sandel, Michael. *Liberalism and the Limits of Justice*. Cambridge: Cambridge University Press, 1982.

Sangari, K. and S. Vaid. *Recasting Women: Essays in Colonial History*. New Delhi: Kali for Women, 1989.

Sassen, Saskia. *Losing Control? Sovereignty in an Age of Globalization*. New York: Columbia University Press, 1996.

Sathe, S.P. *Judicial Activism in India: Transgressing Borders and Enforcing Limits*. New Delhi: Oxford University Press, 2002.

Savarkar, V.D. *India's First War of Independence*. Bombay: Phoenix Publications, 1947.

Schmitt, Carl. *The Crisis of Parliamentary Democracy.* Ellen Kennedy (trans.). Cambridge, Massachusetts: The MIT Press, 1985.

———. *Political Theology: Four Chapters on the Concept of Sovereignty.* George Schwab (trans.). Cambridge, Massachusetts: MIT Press, 1985.

———. *The Concept of the Political.* Chicago: University of Chicago Press, 1996.

———. *The Leviathan in the State Theory of Thomas Hobbes: Meaning and Failure of a Political Symbol.* Westport, Conn.: Greenwood Press, 1996.

Schmitthenner, Samuel. 'The Development of the Legal Profession in India', presented at the Conference on the Comparative Study of the Legal Profession with Special Reference to India, August, 1967.

Scott, David. 'Colonial Governmentality', *Social Text*, 43, Autumn 1995, pp. 191–220.

Seal, Anil. *The Emergence of Indian Nationalism: Competition and Collaboration in the Later Nineteenth Century.* Cambridge: Cambridge University Press 1971.

Seely, J.R. *Expansion of England.* Chicago: University of Chicago Press, 1971.

Seervai, H.M. *The Position of the Judiciary Under the Constitution of India.* Bombay: University of Bombay Press, 1970.

Sen, Amartya. 'Justice: Means vs. Freedom', *Philosophy and Public Affairs*, vol. 19, 1990, pp. 111–21.

Sen, D.N. *From Raj to Swaraj.* Calcutta: Vidyodara Library, 1954.

Sen, Neil. 'Warren Hastings and British Sovereign Authority in Bengal, 1774–80', *The Journal of Imperial and Commonwealth History*, XXV (1), January 1997, pp. 68–70.

Sen, Sudipta. *Distant Sovereignty: National Imperialism and the Origins of British India.* New York and London: Routledge, 2002.

Setalvad, M.C. *The Rise of the Common Law.* London: Steven, 1960.

Seth, Sanjay. 'Rewriting Histories of Nationalism: The Politics of "Moderate Nationalism" in India, 1870–1905', *American Historical Review*, vol. 104, February 1999, pp. 95–116.

Shamir, Ronen. *Colonies of Law: Colonialism, Zionism and Law in Early Mandate Palestine.* Cambridge Studies in Law and Society. Cambridge: Cambridge University Press, 2000.

Shannon, Timothy J. *Indians and Colonists at the Crossroads of Empire: The Albany Congress of 1754.* Ithaca and London: Cornell University Press, 2002.

Sharan, Parmatma. *The Imperial Legislative Council of India.* Delhi: S. Chand and Co., 1961.

Siddiqi, Majid. *Agrarian Unrest in North India-United Provinces 1918–1922.* New Delhi: Vikas, 1978.

Singha, Radhika. *A Despotism of Law: Crime and Justice in Early Colonial India.* New Delhi: Oxford University Press, 1998.

Sinha, Chittaranjan. *Indian Civil Judiciary in Making 1800–1833.* New Delhi: Munshi Manoharlal, 1971.

Sinha, Mrinalini. *Colonial Masculinity: The 'Manly Englishman' and the 'Effeminate Bengali' in the Late Nineteenth Century India.* New York: Manchester University Press, 1995.

——. *Specters of Mother India: The Global Restructuring of an Empire,* Durham: Duke University Press, 2006.

Sisson, Richard and Stanley Wolpert, (eds). *Congress and Indian Nationalism: The Pre-Independence Phase.* Berkeley: University of California Press, 1988.

Sitaramayya, B. Pattabhi. *History of the Indian National Congress.* 2 vols. Delhi: S. Chand, 1969.

Skaria, Ajay. 'Gandhi's Politics: Liberalism and the Question of the Ashram', *South Atlantic Quarterly,* 101 (4), 2002, pp. 955–86.

——. *Hybrid Histories: Forests, Frontiers, and Wildness in Western India.* Delhi; New York: Oxford University Press, 1999.

Skinner, Quentin. *The Foundations of Modern Political Thought.* 2 vols. Cambridge; New York: Cambridge University Press, 1978.

——. *Machiavelli.* New York: Hill and Wang, 1981.

Skuy, David. 'Macaulay and the Indian Penal Code of 1862: The Myth of the Inherent Superiority and Modernity of the English Legal System Compared to India's Legal System in the Nineteenth Century', *Modern Asian Studies,* 32 (3), July 1998, pp. 513–57.

Spivak, Gayatri Chakrabarty. *A Critique of Postcolonial Reason: Toward a History of the Vanishing Present.* Cambridge: Harvard University Press, 1999.

Stanlis, Peter J. 'Edmund Burke and the Law of Nations', *The American Journal of International Law,* 47 (3), July 1953, pp. 397–413.

——. *Edmund Burke and the Natural Law.* Ann Arbor: The University of Michigan Press, 1958.

Canavan, Francis P. *The Political Reason of Edmund Burke.* Durham: Duke University Press, 1960.

Stein, Peter. *Legal Evolution: The Story of an Idea.* Cambridge: Cambridge University Press, 1980.

Stokes, Eric. *The English Utilitarians and India.* Oxford: The Clarendon Press, 1959.

——. *The Peasant Armed: The Indian Revolt of 1857.* C.A. Bayly (ed.). Oxford: Oxford University Press, 1986.

Storing, Herbert J. *What the Anti-Federalists Were For.* Chicago: University of Chicago Press, 1981.

Strauss, Leo. *Natural Right and History.* Chicago: University of Chicago Press, 1953.

Suhrud, Tridib. 'Emptied of all but love: Gandhiji's first public fast', in *Rethinking Gandhi and Nonviolent Relationality: Global Perspectives*. Debjani Ganguly and John Docker (eds). London and New York: Routledge, 2007, pp. 66–79.

Suleri, Sara. *The Rhetoric of English India*. Chicago: University of Chicago Press, 1992.

Sunstein, Cass. R. *Free Markets and Social Justice*. New York: Oxford University Press, 1997.

Suntharalingam, R. *Indian Nationalism: A Historical Analysis*. New Delhi: Vikas Publishing House, 1983.

Sutherland, Lucy S. *The East India Company in Eighteenth-Century Politics*. Oxford: Clarendon Press, 1952.

Swan, Maureen. *Gandhi: The South African Experience*. Johannesburg: Ravan Press, 1985.

Swinfen, David B. *Imperial Appeal: The Debate on the Appeal to the Privy Council, 1833–1986*. Manchester: Manchester University Press, 1987.

Tendulkar, D.G. *Mahatma, Life of Mohandas Karamchand Gandhi*. 8 vols. Bombay: Jhaveri and Tendulkar, 1953.

Thompson, E.P. *The Making of the English Working Class*. New York: Pantheon, 1964.

———. *Whigs and Hunters: The Origin of the Black Act*. London: Allen Lane, 1975.

Travers, Robert. *Ideology and Empire in Eighteenth-Century India: The British in Bengal*. Cambridge: Cambridge University Press, 2007.

Tripathi, Amalesh. *The Extremist Challenge: India between 1890 and 1910*. Bombay: Orient Longman, 1967.

Tuck, Richard. *The Rights of War and Peace: Political Thought and the International Order from Grotius to Kant*. Oxford: Oxford University Press, 1999.

Tully, James. *An Approach to Political Philosophy: Locke in Contexts*. Cambridge: Cambridge University Press, 1993.

Turberville, A.S. *The House of Lords in the XVIIIth Century*. Westport, Connecticut: Greenwood Press Publishers, 1970.

Unger, R.M. *The Critical Legal Studies Movement*. Cambridge: Harvard University Press, 1986.

Vaughan, Charles E. *Studies in the History of Political Philosophy Before and After Rousseau*. New York: Longmans, Green and Co., 1925.

Washbrook, D.A. *The Emergence of Provincial Politics, The Madras Presidency 1870–1920*. Cambridge: Cambridge University Press, 1976.

———. 'Law, State, and Agrarian Society in Colonial India', *Modern Asian Studies*. 15 (3), 1981, pp. 649–721.

Washbrook, David, and Rosalind O'Hanlon. 'After Orientalism: Culture, Criticism and Politics in the Third World', *Comparative Studies in Society and History*, 34 (1), January 1992, pp. 141–67.

Weitzman, Sophia. *Warren Hastings and Philip Francis*. Manchester: Manchester University Press, 1929.

Weston, C.C. *English Constitutional Theory and the House of Lords, 1556–1832*. New York: Columbia University Press, 1965.

Wheelan, Frederick G. *Edmund Burke and India: Political Morality and Empire*. Pittsburg: University of Pittsburgh Press, 1996.

Williams, Bernard. *Ethics and the Limits of Philosophy*. Cambridge, Mass.: Harvard University Press, 1997.

Walzer, Michael. *Spheres of Justice: A Defense of Pluralism and Equality*. New York: Basic Books, 1983.

Wheare, K.C. *The Constitutional Structure of the Commonwealth*. Oxford: Clarendon Press, 1960.

Wolpert, Stanley A. *Nehru: A Tryst with Destiny*. New York: Oxford University Press, 1996.

———. *Tilak and Gokhale: Revolution and Reform in the Making of modern India*. Berkeley, University of California Press, 1962.

———. *Morley and India, 1906–1910*. Berkeley, University of California Press, 1967.

———. *Shameful Flight: The Last Years of the British Empire in India*. New York: Oxford University Press, 2006.

Yang, Anand A. (ed.). *Crime and Criminality in British India*. Tucson, Arizona: Published for the Association for Asian Studies by the University of Arizona Press, 1985.

———. *The Limited Raj: Agrarian Relations in Colonial India, Saran District, 1793–1920*. Berkeley: University of California Press, 1989.

Yardley, D.C.M. *Introduction to British Constitutional Law*. London: Butterworths, 1978.

Young, Iris. *Justice and the Politics of Difference*. Princeton: Princeton University Press, 1991.

Young, Robert. *White Mythologies: Writing History and the West*. London and New York: Routledge, 1990.

Zelliot, Eleanor. 'Congress and Untouchables: 1917–1950', in *Congress and Indian Nationalism: The Pre-Independence Phase*, Richard Sisson and Stanley Wolpert (eds). Berkeley: University of California Press, 1988, pp. 182–98.

NEWSPAPERS AND SERIALS (1774–1950)

Amrita Bazaar Patrika
Bengalee
Bengal Hurkaru
Bengal Spectator
Calcutta Gazette

Calcutta Monthly Journal
Calcutta Review
Friend of India
Hindoo Patriot
Indian Jurist
The Statesman

INDEX

Cabinet Mission Plan, 1946 203,
   204
Calcutta, riots in 179
Cambridge School of
   historiography xxixn, xxxivn,
   110, 111
Canning, Charles John Viscount
   77n, 78, 79, 89
caste, xiv, 93, 99, 100, 101, 102,
   103, 152, 199, 204, 205, 206,
   210, 214, 225
   politicization of 99, 100, 103
   and social identity 100
categorical sovereignty 181, 185,
   199
   see also sovereignty
Catholic Emancipation Law,
   England 122
Census xxxiiin, 103
   of 1872 100, 101
   of 1891 and 1901 98, 100, 101
   of 1961 211
   commissioner 100, 101
   see also Risley
Champaran 165
Chancellor 87
Chancery courts 86, 87, 88
   see also courts of chancery
Chand, Lalla Hukum 123
Chandra, Bipan xxivn, xxixn, 112,
   142, 145
charity 85n, 86, 87, 90, 106, 126,
   127, 128
Charter Act of 1833 63, 64, 65
   of 1853 63, 65, 67, 69
Chatham 130
Chatterjee, Bankim Chandra xxix,
   159, 160, 161, 173
Chatterjee, Partha x, xivn, xxxn,
   xxxiin, 172
Churchill, Winston 207, 208
Citizenship of the Empire 132
Civil Disobedience Movement,
   1930 166

civilizing mission 75
Clavering, John 51, 52
Cohn, Bernard S. ix, xvin, xviin,
   xixn, xxxiin, xxxiiin, 16n, 78n
Coke 31, 32, 87
Colonial Conference, of 1907 133
colonial, discourse of ix, xivn, xvii,
   xxxiiin, 19, 27, 74, 94, 95, 152
colonial executive 48, 96, 98,
   114n, 117, 123
colonial sovereignty, discourse of
   3, 14, 41
   see also colonial, discourse of
colonization, constitutional
   implications of 11
common law xviiin, xx, 8, 12, 16,
   19, 23, 24, 25, 31, 32, 35, 43,
   85, 86, 87, 88, 129, 190, 191
Commonwealth idea 133, 134, 135
communal representation, in
   legislative council 204
Congress xiv, xxvi, xxxvi, xxxviii,
   75, 76, 84, 104, 109–10, 123,
   141, 220, 222, 223, 225
   anticolonial movement of xv,
   xxiii, xxivn, xxv, 90, 113
   and Constitution-making 202,
   203
   discourse of freedom xxiv, xxv,
   132
   electoral defeat of 224
   home rule goal of xxvi, 102,
   103, 132–3
   on justice 125, 128, 136, 139n
   Karachi Resolution of 1931
   199
   M.K. Gandhi and xxx
   mobilization against British
   Empire 103
   political discourse of 106, 122,
   132
   in Provincial Legislature 205
   Report of 1887 115
   on Revolt of 1857 126